AI STARTUP STRATEGY

A BLUEPRINT TO BUILDING SUCCESSFUL ARTIFICIAL INTELLIGENCE PRODUCTS FROM INCEPTION TO EXIT

Adhiguna Mahendra

Apress®

AI Startup Strategy: A Blueprint to Building Successful Artificial Intelligence Products from Inception to Exit

Adhiguna Mahendra
Nodeflux, Jakarta, Indonesia

ISBN-13 (pbk): 978-1-4842-9501-4   ISBN-13 (electronic): 978-1-4842-9502-1
https://doi.org/10.1007/978-1-4842-9502-1

Managing Director, Apress Media LLC: Welmoed Spahr
Acquisitions Editor: Shiva Ramachandran
Development Editor: James Markham
Coordinating Editor: Jessica Vakili

Distributed to the book trade worldwide by Springer Science+Business Media New York, 1 New York Plaza, New York, NY 10004. Phone 1-800-SPRINGER, fax (201) 348-4505, e-mail orders-ny@springer-sbm.com, or visit www.springeronline.com. Apress Media, LLC is a California LLC and the sole member (owner) is Springer Science + Business Media Finance Inc (SSBM Finance Inc). SSBM Finance Inc is a **Delaware** corporation.

For information on translations, please e-mail booktranslations@springernature.com; for reprint, paperback, or audio rights, please e-mail bookpermissions@springernature.com.

Apress titles may be purchased in bulk for academic, corporate, or promotional use. eBook versions and licenses are also available for most titles. For more information, reference our Print and eBook Bulk Sales web page at http://www.apress.com/bulk-sales.

Paper in this product is recyclable

To my parents, whose unwavering support has been the bedrock of my journey, I dedicate this work to you.

To my wife, Anissa, your love, patience, and understanding have been my steadfast companions, making this journey possible.

To my children, Farrel, Rafale, and Xavier, your boundless energy and joy illuminate my life and fuel my endeavors. This is for you.

And to my colleagues at Nodeflux, who've shared the triumphs and transformative power of our work in the toil, this book is a testament to our collective passion and persistence.

Contents

About the Author

Adhiguna Mahendra, with his extensive academic and industry experience, brings a wealth of knowledge to this book. He obtained his MS degree in Computer Vision and Robotics from the University of Heriot-Watt, UK, in 2008 and his PhD in Machine Learning and Computer Vision from the Universite de Dijon, France, in 2012.

Currently, he serves as Chief of AI, Business, and Products at Nodeflux, Indonesia's leading AI vision company. At Nodeflux, he has spearheaded the development and commercialization of AI products, overseeing everything from product design and algorithm development to operationalization through MLOps.

His 20+ years of experience span across global and national companies, developing intelligent systems across various sectors. Alongside, he serves as a lecturer at Swiss German University and Central Queensland University, honored with the Best Lecturer Award in 2018. Adhiguna is also the founder of the AI Business Institute, an online platform offering courses in deep learning and AI product management. Adhiguna is also a key contributor to AI policy-making in Indonesia and serves as an AI trainer and technology advisor.

Adhiguna has a robust academic footprint with publications in esteemed platforms like SPIE, ICME, ICoDSE, and IEEE. He also balances his work with his love for Muay Thai, jazz piano, and soccer, which he enjoys with his three boys. In this book, he shares valuable insights on building AI startups, drawing from his extensive experience and knowledge.

www.linkedin.com/in/adhigunamahendra/

https://twitter.com/Adhiguna_AIaaS

www.aistartupstrategy.com

www.aibusinessinstitute.com

The Praise for
AI Startup Strategy

This book helps to understand the concept using simple and thorough method for those who explore on how AI can improve his business processes or how AI-based startup positioned Coming from his academic, professional background and his researches, the book covers examples from different industries, such as logistics, manufacturing to marketing, and using those real cases to identify room for improvements.

—Alexander Sufjan

Founder, Logicnesia

Whether you dream of becoming a product manager or excelling in business development in the AI startup space, "AI Startup Strategy" equips you with the tools and knowledge needed to succeed. Don't miss out on this invaluable resource from one of Indonesia's leading voices in artificial intelligence. Whether you dream of becoming a product manager or excelling in business development in the AI startup space, "AI Startup Strategy" equips you with the tools and knowledge needed to succeed. Don't miss out on this invaluable resource from one of Indonesia's leading voices in artificial intelligence.

—Williem Pao Ph.D

Founder, Verihubs, YCS21

While we're all trying to wrap our heads around the potential of AI for our businesses, Adhiguna wrote the guidebook for creating new AI-powered innovations. Thorough, actionable, and instantly relevant; make sure you read AI Startup Strategy before your competitors can get to it.

—Étienne Garbugli

Author of Lean B2B & Solving Product

Key headwinds for humanity that may be remedied with the help of AI include issues of climate change, financial exclusion, and lack of democratization or equalization of opportunities. While it is obvious how economically value accretive AI will be to the various business verticals, one must also be cognizant of AI's potential pitfalls. AI can be construed as a process of hallucinations that must be shepherded in a multi disciplinary manner as to involve as many non-technologists as possible. This is to prevent the journey forward from becoming dystopian.

"AI Startup Strategy" is a key tool for all stakeholders concerned, particularly in the developing economies.

—Gita Wirjawan

Chairman, Ancora Group, Indonesia's former minister of trade, Visiting Scholar, Stanford University

AI is rocking the world of tech and everyone is suddenly interested and excited in relation to its potential impact on business, but what is AI and how can we really harness it to bring about amazing innovation?

Adhiguna Mahendra is no stranger to me and has advised my company on areas of product development around AI as well as been a partner on joint ventures. In this book he brings together his nearly 20 years of experience operating in an area that for most is just new. In over 400 pages he looks at multiple case studies and produces one of the most comprehensive books on this vital subject, available in the market today.

The book is a must read for aspiring AI professionals through to technology leaders. By looking at real case studies Mr. Mahendra cuts out a lot of the jargon and gets to the nuts and bolts of a subject which is likely to be one of the most important technology advancements of the coming decade.

—Martyn Terpilowski

Founder and Investor, Bhumi Varta Technology

The book is a thoughtful, engaging and game-changing read for any entrepreneur, technology leader, decision-maker, product manager/business strategist, developer/AI enthusiast, investor/venture capitalist, researcher or student. I appreciate the opportunity to collaborate with Dr. Mahendra at this level and his consideration of me in an association. Personally for me, as I continue my career in venture capital and entrepreneurship, the book will serve as a desktop resource for the basis of my critical thinking and decision-making. With so much fairy tale and melodramatic hype surrounding AI at this time, this is a must—read that brings some reality into the reader's perspective from a builder's insight to a consumer's insight. The book unwaveringly pulls no punches and gives its readers the proper thinking about what AI means for society and how we can safely and successfully implement and consume it.

—Paul Claxton

Managing General Partner, Q1 Velocity Venture Capital

AI Startup Strategy" is a must-read for anyone navigating the AI startup land-scape. It's a true "Handbook for the AI Entrepreneur", providing a unique framework that bridges the gap between the allure of the science for tech-nologists and the practical, revenue-boosting solutions sought by clients. This book has prompted me to reflect on my work experiences and consider implementing new processes. It's not just insightful, but also thought-provok-ing, offering a structured approach to tackle the intriguing dilemma of aligning interests in the AI field. This book is an invaluable guide for those looking to harness the potential of AI in business.I wanted to express my appreciation for the insights your book has provided and the impact it has had on my per-spective towards AI in business.

—Federico Moreno

CEO&Co-Founder, Optima

Introduction

In the Fourth Industrial Revolution realm, where artificial intelligence (AI) is the bedrock of technological innovation, we are on the precipice of a new age – the age of artificial general intelligence (AGI). In this fascinating epoch, the rise of transformer-based large language models (LLMs) such as OpenAI's GPT-4 marks a profound shift in the AI landscape. These models, which form the backbone of advanced language understanding and generation, are being seen as a precursor to the dawn of AGI, a time when machines will possess the capacity to perform any intellectual task that a human can.

As we move deeper into the AI era, it becomes increasingly apparent that all technology companies must transition toward becoming AI companies to remain competitive and relevant. However, the democratization of AI – largely due to the proliferation of open source platforms and the vast number of AI research publications – means that every organization, regardless of size, now has equal access to this transformative technology. In this landscape, even tech behemoths like Google can no longer rely on the exclusivity of AI technology as a competitive moat.

This new reality brings us to a critical realization: the key differentiator among AI companies will no longer be merely technological superiority or groundbreaking AI algorithms. Instead, it will be a deeper understanding of the customer's context – their pain points, buying processes, stakeholders, business processes, and value chains. Coupled with a solid technology architecture and operationalization strategy to solve these problems, this understanding will be the driving force behind successful AI startups.

This book is designed to guide you through the intricate journey of building an AI startup, from inception to exit. It is not a technical manual on how to code AI algorithms; plenty of such resources already exist. Instead, this book offers insights into the human and business aspects of running an AI startup. It will help you comprehend and navigate the complex business environment, understand your customers on a deeper level, and use this understanding to drive your AI solutions.

The following chapters will delve into the fundamentals of understanding an AI startup, validating your AI product idea, and building a robust strategy roadmap. We will explore various business models best suited for your venture and delve into designing user and developer experiences that resonate with your target audience. We will also discuss building a robust platform, mastering the operationalization of AI, and assembling a team that shares your vision and can bring it to fruition. Finally, we will outline strategies for market penetration and discuss potential exit strategies.

The world of AI startups is dynamic and filled with opportunities. You can navigate this landscape successfully with a deep understanding of your customers and a clear vision. This book is your guide on this exciting journey. Let's begin.

This Book Is for You If…

- **You're an entrepreneur** who is passionate about leveraging AI technology to solve pressing business problems and build a successful startup.

- **You're a technology leader or a decision-maker** seeking to integrate AI into your existing business framework and pivot your company toward an AI-first approach.

- **You're a product manager or a business strategist** looking to understand how AI can be used to enhance product offerings, improve user experience, and create a competitive edge in the market.

- **You're a developer or an AI enthusiast** curious about the business aspects of AI technology, keen to understand how to translate technical expertise into a successful AI startup.

- **You're an investor or venture capitalist** seeking insights into the dynamic world of AI startups to make informed investment decisions.

- **You're a student or a researcher** aspiring to step into the entrepreneurial world, aiming to use your knowledge and skills in AI to make a tangible impact in the industry.

This book is for anyone excited about the prospect of blending AI technology with business acumen to create innovative solutions that address real-world problems. If you see AI as more than algorithms and code and believe in its potential to transform business landscapes, this book will be an invaluable guide.

Fundamental of AI Startups

Artificial intelligence is a machine that can reproduce human cognitive capabilities and perform better than humans in scale, speed, endurance, and accuracy. Such capabilities include vision, speech recognition, natural language processing (NLP), learning, planning, and strategy. They are made possible by the availability of large amounts of data, growing computing power, and improved learning algorithms.

Artificial intelligence (AI) is the backbone of many daily software applications and services. The technology behind these programs – machine learning (ML), neural networks, decision optimization (DO), etc. – has been around for decades, but it's only recently that it has started to be applied in such vast numbers to products with AI at their core.

In a world where AI is rapidly being adopted in every single industry, it's predicted that by 2030 this will have contributed about $15.7 trillion and boosted local economies by around 26%.[1]

As the book is being written, generative AI, led by platforms like ChatGPT and Midjourney, has swept the world, revolutionizing interactions, content creation, and problem-solving. These large language models (LLMs) have

---

[1] PwC's Global Artificial Intelligence Study: Sizing the prize

© Adhiguna Mahendra 2023
A. Mahendra, *AI Startup Strategy*, https://doi.org/10.1007/978-1-4842-9502-1_1

revolutionized the way we interact, create content, and solve problems across various domains. LLMs are a subset of generative AI, which uses deep learning techniques to generate human-like text based on a given input or context. Transforming industries like marketing, entertainment, and education enables personalized content, automates tasks, and enhances creativity. This technology fosters efficiency and innovation and redefines human-machine boundaries, reshaping life, work, information search, and communication in the digital era. If you are reading this book, you are probably ready to be part of this revolution. Maybe you are already a product manager interested in building an AI into your product, or perhaps you are a data scientist who aspires to build an AI startup.

You may also be an experienced Software as a Service (SaaS) entrepreneur willing to join the AI bandwagon. You wonder how an AI startup with fewer than 30 employees can scale its solutions globally and exits for multimillion or even multibillion dollars.

In this chapter, you will learn about the fundamental concepts of AI startups. We will explain the foundation of AI technologies, the AI startup landscape, and AI product management and wrap it up with the patterns of successful AI startups.

Historical Perspective: The Fourth Revolution

Over the last three decades, we've seen new platforms emerge that have created tremendous opportunities for startups: the PC platform in the 1970s, 1980s, and 1990s, followed by the Web Revolution two decades ago.

Then mobile came around as the broadest computing device enabling people to do more than one thing at once – like checking email alongside reading news articles on their phone while listening to podcasts while answering messages. Yahoo, Google, and Amazon followed and rode the Internet and the World Wide Web Revolution.

In 2007, Apple released the iPhone, which defined the birth of the new era, the mobile wave. Facebook rode the wave, followed by some new companies that emerged and disrupted market leaders that did not innovate and adapt. Amazon disrupted Barnes & Noble before becoming the largest ecommerce platform, and Netflix disrupted Blockbuster before eventually also disrupting cable companies.

In the business software landscape, with the Web and Mobile Revolution enabling the SaaS proliferation, many cloud-based SaaS startups are born in multiple industries serving multiple value chains. The SaaS constituted business digitization and replaced Excel and papers with web-based applications. Enterprises are adopting SaaS at a rapid pace.

Then, the Fourth Revolution is coming.

In the 2010s, the advent of cheap GPU-based computing and cloud technology, which leveraged Internet-based compute, storage, and network, enabled new methods of scaling a deep neural network fed by a massive amount of data. This marks the new era of big data and AI/ML.

Artificial intelligence and machine learning (AI/ML) enabled by big data technology have become game-changing technologies that are set to disrupt a wide range of markets due to their capability to imitate some cognitive aspects of humans to accomplish some tasks.

Artificial intelligence and machine learning (ML) are used interchangeably, but artificial intelligence is an umbrella for the replication of human intelligence in the form of software with machine learning as a subset. Machine learning is defined as a modern software development technique and a type of artificial intelligence (AI) that enables computers to solve problems by using examples of real-world data.

Around 2013, open source deep learning frameworks like Chainer, Theano, and Caffe were released, followed by TensorFlow by Google in 2015 and PyTorch by Facebook in 2016. These frameworks are an important factor in AI democratization, enabling startups to infuse some kind of intelligence into their products and transform themselves into AI startups.

With cloud technology adopted by enterprises, software giants like Amazon, Google, and Microsoft Azure started to look at data as the fundamental proposition and position themselves as big data and analytics providers.

In 2014, Amazon started to push Elastic MapReduce (EMR), while Google pushed BigQuery as a data warehouse on the Web. Microsoft took a different route by partnering with Hortonworks, a Hadoop-based big data startup, to release Azure HDInsight, a managed Apache Hadoop service in the cloud. They also launched Azure Data Lake Storage and Analytics.

Riding the AI/ML hype, they also released low-code machine learning services such as Amazon Web Services (AWS) Machine Learning in 2015, Google Cloud Machine Learning in 2016, and Microsoft Azure Machine Learning in 2018 to make it easy for a nonspecialist to design, implement, and deploy a machine learning model in the cloud.

The tools and platforms mentioned are responsible for the birth of a new generation of startups, AI-powered or AI startups for short. Some entrepreneurs find creative ways to use these tools in their business models and products.

The rise in interest in artificial intelligence and machine learning over 2012–2014 has led to a dramatic increase in funding for these technologies. The venture, corporate, and seed investors started heavily funding AI startups in 2013 onward.

In 2022, a groundbreaking revolution emerged within the realm of artificial intelligence. The birth of ChatGPT, powered by advanced transformer technology, marked a turning point in the capabilities of AI. This state-of-the-art innovation facilitated a paradigm shift in natural language processing, fostering more nuanced, context-aware, and sophisticated interactions between humans and machines. As a result, ChatGPT has contributed significantly to enriching AI applications across various industries and domains, setting a new benchmark for the future of intelligent systems. The emergence of ChatGPT has ushered in a new era in the quest for artificial general intelligence (AGI). As AI systems progress, the pursuit of AGI – where machines exhibit human-like intellectual capabilities – becomes more feasible. Innovations like ChatGPT equip researchers to tackle AGI development challenges, signifying a notable milestone in AI research.

In just a few short years, artificial intelligence has gone from being something that was seen as far-fetched and unrealistic to becoming one of the biggest trends, if not *the* biggest, in today's world. Every day we read headlines about new advancements within this field, which brings it closer to reality than ever before. Whether you believe AI will happen sooner rather than later seems irrelevant because here we are at least taking steps toward its fruition! The United States alone invests $9 billion in funding for AI startups each year.

Artificial intelligence (AI) will remain a major trend in the coming years. According to Forbes, AI will contribute $15.7 trillion to global GDP by 2030.[2] The fundamental premise is that every company now strives to be an AI-first company, not just a data-driven one.

Historically and still widely practiced in many companies, the data always means transactional data stored in a relational database, which translates into a few dashboards for fundamental analysis of what happened to the business recently.

But to become AI-first, the data and artificial intelligence must be integrated into a set of business processes for analytical and operational purposes. This lays the groundwork for transforming into a smart, automated, and self-governing digital enterprise – where business metrics undergo real-time analysis, sales leads are processed automatically, inventory forecasting and ordering are automated, staff and vehicle scheduling is streamlined, AIOps monitors IT systems round-the-clock, customer churn is anticipated, and ad placements are optimized automatically. This disruptive AI-first movement has been enabled by close integration between data technology (i.e., big data infrastructure, streaming data architecture) on one side and AI (especially machine learning and deep learning) on the other.

[2] www.forbes.com/sites/greatspeculations/2019/02/25/ai-will-add-15-trillion-to-the-world-economy-by-2030/?sh=4be73fba1852

AI Startups vs. AI-First Companies

Let's go back to the definition of AI startups and how it differs from another hype terminology, AI-first companies.[3] An AI startup is defined as a technology company that leverages AI and data as a core differentiating factor to solidify its position and maintain an edge over competitors. Examples of AI startups are AI-first SaaS and AIaaS (AI as a Service). We will learn more about this in the next chapter.

AI startups should be differentiated from an AI-first company in different verticals that leverage valuable data from day one, use that data to train predictive models, and then use those predictions to automate and scale their work.

The main difference is that AI startups have the following:

1. The ultimate dependence on AI algorithms such as deep learning, reinforcement learning, evolutionary algorithm and Large Language Model (LLM) as their main products as well as their core technology.

2. AI infrastructure and tools, such as hardware, end-to-end data, and an analytics platform or machine learning optimization tool, to accelerate and/or augment the implementation of AI-based solutions

While AI-first companies use AI to leverage their main products and services, which can be anything from movie streaming and insurance to education platforms, AI-first companies usually do not develop their own AI platform. They just use ready-made AI platforms and tools and customize them to match their needs.

So AI startups sell AI as their primary commodities (sell side), and AI-first companies use AI to empower their value propositions (buy side).

An AI startup cannot function without AI. In contrast, an AI-first company is doing very well because of AI. AI-first companies can be traditional/tech companies selling products or services to consumers and businesses.

Understanding Enterprise AI

Successful AI startups understand the nature of AI technology and how to package to a customer and sell it. They understand that AI is an enabling technology – just like the World Wide Web or microprocessor.

---

[3] www.theaifirstcompany.com/

It is a revolutionary innovation that can be used to drive change to our fundamental assumptions, our behavior, the way we work, and even our culture. An interesting way of examining this definition would be discussing how the World Wide Web has changed some of the assumptions underlying software development and its distribution.

The Web has dramatically reduced the costs and delays associated with developing and distributing applications. The Web has enabled technology and business models of software such as ecommerce, social media, and SaaS, to name a few.

Another example is how microprocessor technology changed the fundamental assumptions of hardware design. The microprocessor, for example, changed the size, reliability, cost, and performance assumptions underlying hardware design. As a result, new applications and design approaches for hardware systems became feasible. The microprocessor enabled PC revolutions and later a mobile revolution.

On a smaller scale, a SQL database is also an enabling technology that allows structured data to be stored and queried in a tabular format.

This gave rise to enterprise resource planning (ERP), CRM (customer relationship management), and other software industries to grow worth billions of dollars today – just one example of how innovations like this change our world.

Similarly, artificial intelligence as enabling technology has enabled many use cases, such as automotive navigation systems that help self-driving cars navigate busy streets. AI is also used in nearly every industry, from detecting manufacturing defects, recognizing transaction fraud and stock trading, and reviewing the clauses in your legal documents. AI is an enabling technology set to revolutionize many industries, and as such, it will significantly impact how we do business.

Businesses are often at the forefront of adopting new technologies like this one; they're looking for ways to become more efficient and succeed while reducing costs or increasing revenue margins through automation where possible – this is possible because of AI.

This is the reason the majority of AI startups are focused on solving enterprise problems. So most of the AI startups are selling to businesses (B2B), government (B2G), or application developers (B2D). Therefore, enterprise AI is an application of AI to solve specific high-value large-scale business problems. The AI can be infused into the organization's business process in the value chain to give some kind of intelligence that will produce meaningful value.

The main function of enterprise AI is to improve and scale the quality and quantity of business decisions. A good business decision and actions will create business value. Forward-thinking enterprises are leveraging the power of AI to drive digital transformation. This is accomplished by combining sophisticated machine learning techniques with other forms of artificial intelligence, like classical rule-based systems or decision optimization, for an all-inclusive approach that results in increased revenue, reduced cost, and risk reduction throughout the enterprise value chain.

Enterprise AI is the core enabler of digital transformation. In the coming years, nearly every enterprise software application will be AI-enabled. Just as organizations today would not be able to conduct business without a CRM or ERP system, organizations will not be able to operate and compete without enterprise AI capabilities effectively. The AI capabilities for enterprises are also enabled by elastic cloud computing, big data, and the Internet of Things (IoT).

Large organizations often require dozens to hundreds of enterprise AI solutions to address various use cases across their value chains. However, developing and deploying custom enterprise AI solutions at scale presents significant challenges, being time-consuming, costly, and often impractical. The vast amounts of data required, coupled with the specialized skills and expertise needed to create such systems, are beyond the reach of most organizations. For instance, obtaining a million facial images and hiring computer vision PhDs and seasoned security experts solely to develop facial recognition technology to authorize building access is not feasible. Instead, purchasing readily available off-the-shelf facial recognition solutions is a more practical approach for such organizations.

Similarly, there is little rationale for developing proprietary inventory optimization applications when sophisticated inventory analytics and optimization platforms already exist. These platforms are crafted by highly skilled PhDs who have developed patented algorithms for exceptional performance and efficiency.

This is where AI startups play a pivotal role. By offering specialized AI solutions, they cater to the diverse needs of various industries and organizations. By leveraging the expertise of AI startups, businesses can access cutting-edge technologies without the substantial investment required to develop in-house solutions, thus streamlining operations and fostering innovation.

The central premise of this book explores the strategies through which a startup can effectively capitalize on enterprise AI as a product offering. By examining methods to scale such solutions and, when the opportunity arises, successfully sell the startup for substantial returns, this book aims to provide a comprehensive guide for entrepreneurs seeking to create a significant impact in the AI market, potentially generating millions or even billions in revenue.

Fundamental of AI Technologies

This work provides an overview of artificial intelligence, a collection of powerful algorithms employed by successful AI startups such as Waymo, Pony. ai, CrowdStrike, and Uptake Technologies. These organizations leverage AI to perform intelligent tasks, such as autonomous driving, preemptive cyberattack detection, and engine failure prediction. We delve into the fundamentals of artificial intelligence, acknowledging that AI extends beyond merely machine learning or deep learning. Since the 1940s, AI has evolved into a multidisciplinary science comprising various mathematical methods and algorithms.

For AI product developers, choosing the most appropriate algorithms from the extensive range of AI techniques poses a distinct challenge. AI is defined as the science and engineering of creating software and computer systems capable of performing cognitive functions typically associated with human minds, such as perception, reasoning, learning, planning, environmental interaction, problem-solving, and creativity.

This definition aligns with the perspectives of eminent AI scientists Russell and Norvig, who conceptualize AI as a software or application embodied within an intelligent agent. According to Russell and Norvig, AI encompasses the study of agents that perceive their environment and act based on those perceptions. Intelligent agents have been developed across various fields, including robotics for factory automation and autonomous vehicles, as well as in government agencies like NASA.

Going further in the business applications, the software as an intelligent agent employing these AI functions will likely obtain advantages and proficiencies in many areas, such as algorithmic marketing, algorithmic trading, automated manufacturing, autonomous vehicle operations, etc.

Most of these cognitive functions of an AI agent can be performed using the following exhaustive AI techniques:

- *Searching*: In artificial intelligence, search techniques are universal problem-solving methods to solve a specific problem and provide the best result. Many search methods include uniformed search, heuristic search, and heuristics function. Examples of applications are information retrieval domains such as Search Engine as a Service (i.e., Algolia, Meilisearch) and route optimization engines (i.e., Routific, Routyn, OptimoRoute, Optergon, etc.).

- *Knowledge representation and reasoning (KRR)*: The knowledge representation and reasoning process is the mental act of deriving logical conclusions and making predictions from available data, usually in language. In artificial intelligence, the reasonings are essential because they allow for thought just like humans do – which helps create more complex computer behaviors when given various tasks at once. Several reasoning techniques include Propositional Logic, First-Order Logic, Knowledge Graph, and Fuzzy Systems. Reasoning and NLP (natural language processing) are also usually combined. The example applications are conversational design (Skelter Labs), fault diagnosis (Iconics), and medical diagnosis (Infermedica).

- *Planning*: Planning tasks involve finding the best course for an artificial system, given its declarative descriptions. Another popular term for AI planning is decision optimization.

  A planner has some initial state, which transforms into the desired goal by applying actions in its environment. Some of the planning techniques are Constraint Programming, Markov Decision Process, and Goal Stack Planning, among others. The application examples are automated production planning (i.e., Productoo, MRPeasy), supply chain optimization (i.e., RiverLogic, anyLogistix), vessel planning (Innovez One), and automated rostering/scheduling problems (Deputy, EZShift).

- *Learning*: As one of the most fundamental and the most popular techniques of AI, learning is a process that improves the knowledge of an AI program by making observations about its environment. From a mathematical standpoint, AI learning processes focus on processing a collection of input-output pairs for a specific function and predicting the outputs for new inputs. Most of the basic artificial intelligence(AI) literature identifies two main groups of learning models: supervised and unsupervised. The techniques used in learning are machine learning, such as Support Vector Machine, Decision Tree, Bayesian network, and neural network with subsets such as deep learning and reinforcement learning. Applications of AI learning, for example, are predictive B2B marketing (i.e., 6sense, Demandbase), predictive maintenance (Uptake, Aveva), fraud analytics (i.e., Shift Technology, Friss), and cybersecurity detection (CrowdStrike, SentinelOne).

- *Perception*: Perception in artificial intelligence is the technique of interpreting visuals, sounds, smells, and touch captured from the real world. Perception helps the software to sense, think, and react like humans. These algorithms have several applications, such as computer vision, which mimics how people see, and audio/speech recognition, which mimics how people hear. The perception algorithms are also applying learning algorithms like deep learning quite heavily. Some computer vision companies focus on video analytics (Viisights.com, Nodeflux.io) or medical imaging (Aidoc.com, Viz.ai). Speech recognition startups focus on speech engines (Vocitec.com, Deepgram.com) or conversation analysis (Prosa.ai, Invoca).

    Artificial intelligence products and applications can be divided into two categories: narrow AI, which can outperform humans in certain tasks, and artificial general intelligence (AGI or strong AI), which are theoretical systems that could do well at any given job.

Although the development of artificial general intelligence (AGI) has not yet been realized, numerous startups continue to make strides by creating AI products that incorporate advanced concepts such as lifelong (gradual) learning, open-mindedness, generalization/extrapolation of meta-learned algorithms, and generative AI.

Additionally, efforts to reverse engineer the neocortex, the most substantial part of the human brain associated with intelligence, have gained traction. Prominent AGI startups such as OpenAI, DeepMind, GoodAI, and Numenta are at the forefront of these innovations, pushing the boundaries of AI research and development. As AI technology, including generative AI, continues to evolve, the contributions of these startups are vital in advancing the field and bringing us closer to achieving AGI.

Large Language Models (LLMs) and AGI

The field of AI has seen tremendous advancements in recent years, with the advent of large language models (LLMs) like OpenAI's GPT-4, considered to be the first steps toward artificial general intelligence (AGI).[4] These LLMs, based on transformer technology, exhibit a broad understanding of language and can generate human-like text, making them highly versatile and applicable to an array of scenarios.

---

[4] https://arxiv.org/abs/2303.12712

However, the majority of AI startups focus on the enterprise sector,[5] and there are compelling reasons for this. Enterprises today are increasingly digitized and generate a wealth of data that can be leveraged for valuable insights, process automation, and decision-making. Enterprises also have the resources and motivation to invest in AI technology that can enhance their productivity, competitiveness, and profitability.

While AGI-like LLMs promise a great deal of potential, they do have significant limitations when applied to the enterprise context. One major concern is their unpredictability.[6] Enterprises need AI systems that provide reliable, predictable, and repeatable results. LLMs, in their current form, can sometimes produce outputs that are unexpected or hard to understand, which can be problematic in a business environment where accuracy and precision are paramount.

In contrast, traditional AI algorithms, often referred to as artificial narrow intelligence (ANI), excel in this regard. These algorithms are designed for specific tasks and can be fine-tuned for predictability and precision. Their outputs are more easily controlled, and they can offer a high level of performance in their specific domains. This is why ANI continues to have significant potential and relevance for enterprise-focused AI startups. ANI systems can be custom-built to solve particular business problems, providing consistent and reliable results.

Looking ahead, AGI technology will undoubtedly find applications within the enterprise sector. Potential use cases could range from advanced data analytics, where the AGI could understand and predict complex patterns, to customer service, where it could understand and respond to a wide array of customer queries. AGI could also be used in strategic decision-making, simulating potential business scenarios and outcomes.

However, these applications will need to overcome the challenges of unpredictability and control. They will need to balance the vast capabilities of AGI with the precision, reliability, and explainability required in a business context. Until then, traditional ANI algorithms will continue to play a crucial role in enterprise AI applications. They offer an effective, reliable, and often more transparent way to leverage AI technology, making them an attractive option for AI startups targeting the enterprise sector.

---

[5] www.seedtable.com/startups-ai
[6] www.moveworks.com/insights/chatgpt-is-shaking-up-the-status-quo-part-one

Enterprise AI, Analytics, and Automated Decision

There is a similarity in the goal of most AI startups: they are *enabling* enterprise AI. Enterprise AI is the application of AI to speed up or automate decisions and actions to enable digital transformation, enhancing the organization's value.

Enterprise AI is intersected with AI and analytics (Figure 1-1). The intersection of the three uses a technique such as machine learning (ML). The enterprise AI and analytics intersection uses decision optimization (DO) and business rule management system (BRMS) techniques.

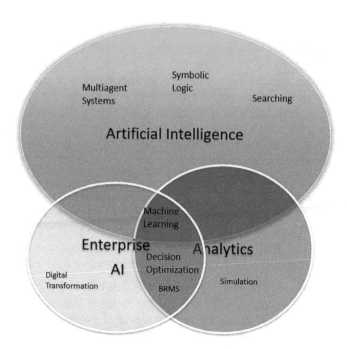

Figure 1-1. Enterprise AI, AI, and analytics Venn diagram

Analytics is gaining knowledge and understanding from data that borrows methods from applied mathematics, statistics, and machine learning. Analytics can be broken down into three different stages described as follows and shown in Figure 1-2.

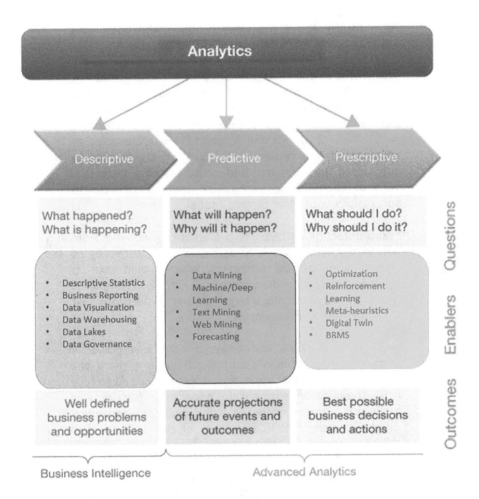

Figure 1-2. From descriptive to prescriptive analytics

- Descriptive analytics tells what happened in the past. We use a method like descriptive statistics and tools such as data warehouses.

- Predictive analytics predicts what is most likely to happen in the future. We use methods like machine learning, Bayesian networks, and deep learning to perform prediction and forecasting.

- Prescriptive analytics recommends actionable decisions we can take to optimize outcomes. The methods used are classical operations research such as linear programming and integer programming, metaheuristics, and, recently, reinforcement learning.

As it usually solves the same problem, this book uses analytics terms interchangeably with enterprise AI.

The goal is to automate the decision in the organization. Automation and the automation of decisions can lead to immense efficiency, speed, or even new business models that were not possible before. For example, streaming companies like Netflix and Amazon Prime are enabled by recommendation systems. Uber and Lyft are enabled by automated fleet dispatch and route planning systems – without them these companies couldn't operate as successfully with their current model.

Fraud detection software also dramatically benefits from automating vital tasks such as credit card processing to save time on manual processes, which would take up valuable employee hours instead. Every day, companies and organizations make a large number of decisions that have concrete consequences.

Artificial intelligence and analytics can be a powerful complement to human decision-making, but there are times when it is most appropriate. We can use AI to fully make the decision, augment the decision, or just serve as a decision support system (a 1980s concept), depending on the complexity and frequency of the decision. The difference is as follows:

- *Decision automation:* The AI fully makes the decision using prescriptive or predictive analytics. An example is a fraud detection use case. AI systems swiftly analyze vast quantities of financial transactions to pinpoint potential fraud. The AI automatically flags or blocks suspicious activities by making real-time decisions using pre-established rules and patterns, effectively safeguarding banks and their customers from fraudulent transactions.

- *Decision augmentation:* The AI recommends a decision to humans using prescriptive or predictive analytics. This kind of AI benefits from the collaboration between human knowledge/wisdom and the capability of AI to analyze a high volume of data at high speed. An example is in AI-assisted medical diagnosis. Algorithms examine medical images like X-rays or MRIs to identify disease indicators or abnormalities. The AI then offers recommendations to healthcare professionals, who leverage their expertise for the final diagnosis. This synergy between AI and human knowledge enables precise and prompt detection of medical conditions, enhancing patient care and outcomes.

- *Decision support*: The AI practically only supports human decision-making enabled by data-driven insights provided by descriptive analytics. An example is in supply chain optimization. AI systems evaluate historical data and market trends to deliver insights on supply and demand patterns. Using descriptive analytics, the AI presents this information to supply chain managers, who leverage their expertise to make informed decisions on inventory, production, and distribution.

When to Deploy AI in Decision-Making

Whether AI can automate, augment, or just support the decision depends on two variables:

1. *The frequency of the decision-making*: How often an organization should decide for a timeframe: one-off to a routine decision.

2. *The complexity of the decision*: The predictability and interdependencies of entities in an organization or system. Decision complexity based on the Cynefin framework (see Figure 1-3) consists of

    - *Simple decision*: Decision in routine, stable, and predictable situations; has a clear cause and effect.

    - *Complicated decision*: Decision in a situation that needs expertise or deeper analysis to identify cause and effect. It uses long-learned expertise with some known problem-solving frameworks.

    - *Complex decision*: Decision in a situation that involves multiple relationships, entities, and interdependencies. To make such a complex decision, one requires a 30,000-foot view analysis.

- *Chaotic decision*: Decision to be made in a situation where the causes and effects seem random and difficult to map, with unclear interdependencies. Decision-making in this situation is mostly using experimentation or "gut feeling."

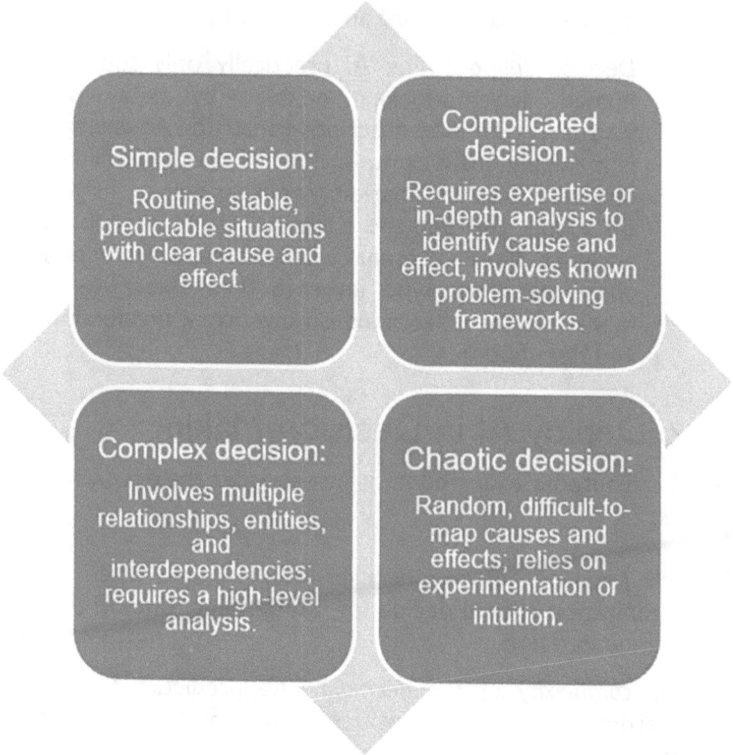

Simple decision:

Routine, stable, predictable situations with clear cause and effect.

Complicated decision:

Requires expertise or in-depth analysis to identify cause and effect; involves known problem-solving frameworks.

Complex decision:

Involves multiple relationships, entities, and interdependencies; requires a high-level analysis.

Chaotic decision:

Random, difficult-to-map causes and effects; relies on experimentation or intuition.

Figure 1-3. Cynefin framework

A company generally makes three types of decisions:

1. **Strategic decision**

   The board of directors is elected by a company's shareholders and appointed for specific terms to ensure stability during their tenure on the board. These individuals make strategic decisions that have a long-term or material impact on the business, such as

   - Deciding where and when investments should be made (e.g., building new plants, more products, and services)

- Defining strategies that help the company grow revenue overtime

  - How can I increase company valuation?

  - Adoption of employee benefit plans.

  - Merger and acquisition strategy.

Strategic decisions are vital for a company's long-term success. A board of directors has fiduciary duties, so it generally must act in the best interests of its shareholders with care not only now but also in perpetuity. The nature of the strategic decisions is usually one-off, complex, and chaotic; it needs a long contemplation and lots of support, data, and intuition. Automating strategic decisions is quite challenging. Therefore, AI products for strategic decisions usually help human decision-making or as decision support.

2. **Tactical decisions**

The senior managers make tactical decisions for the company. These are more detailed implementations of directors' general strategy, usually with an impact on how things will look in six months to one year, such as the following:

- Define optimal advertising channels.

- Allocate purchases within a previously approved budget.

- Define work assignments allocated to particular groups and people.

- Plan a delivery route for the next two weeks.

Most tactical decisions and plans are more detailed and certain than strategic decisions and plans. The tactical decisions are by nature more regular in frequency with the spectrum of complicated to rather complex. The most tactical decision can be semi-automatically assisted by AI (augmented decision).

3. **Operational decisions**

The specialists and operators make daily operational decisions for the company. These are short-term, day-to-day matters that have an immediate impact on a business, such as

- Allocating tasks to staff
- Data entry of purchase order
- Dispatching fleets of trucks
- Allocating which ad to show to the viewer
- Allocating machines in floor production
- Executing stock trading buy and sell
- Matching face with ID

Operational decisions have a high degree of certainty and can be made quickly. These types of operational actions do not usually carry long-term impacts and are located in the simple to complicated spectrum, but they help with implementation within strategic or tactical decisions. The operational decisions are higher in frequency (routine). Hence, it is sensible to make it more automatic, given the data and constraints.

Humans do not optimally make these kinds of decisions because the frequency of these decisions is very large and the input parameters for these decisions are also complex.

AI products are targeted to augment/automate some tactical and operational decisions and support strategic decisions in the organizations (see Table 1-1).

Table 1-1. The Strategic, Tactical, and Operational Decisions

Decision Level	User	Task	Degrees	Impact	Complexity
Strategic	C-levels	Capital allocation, merger and acquisition	Supporting decision	Long term	Complex-chaotic
Tactical	Managers	Allocating resource, planning ad channels	Augmenting decision	Mid-term	Complicated-complex
Operational	Staff	Dispatching fleets, allocating staff	Automating decision	Short term	Simple-complicated

Even operational tasks like car driving cannot be 100% automated without human assistance. AI is shining in automating and augmenting tactical and operational decisions, while for the time being, it is more as decision support for strategic decisions.

By the time this book was written, even the advancement of language models like ChatGPT (powered by Large Language Models), most AI products were not feasible technologically to completely replace humans, especially when complex cognition still is required (i.e., strategy development and management).

Automated Decision and the SETDA Loop

Any business makes money when they perform the right business action. As you can see from the previous section, this is the role of an AI. AI can help us support, augment, or automate our decisions, eventually directing us in which action to take. To understand how AI can be applied to help us with decisions and business actions, we need to understand AI at a high level. Just like humans, any intelligent agent based on AI follows the OODA loop model for decision-making.

OODA is an acronym for "Observe, Orient, Decide, and Act." It's a model originally developed by American military strategist Colonel John Boyd for combat but has since been applied to business and general strategy fields.

The OODA framework defines the best practice for decision-makers to collect and filter data and identify and neutralize threats before becoming critical. Organizations use the OODA loop in business settings to benchmark their ability to predict, react, and continuously improve their decision cycles to obtain optimal outcomes.

The OODA applies to an artificial intelligence–powered product that helps businesses make a decision and perform business activities.

"Observe" can be understood as the acquisition of data. The product's intelligent algorithm then "Orient" by making sense of the unstructured and disorganized data observations. The algorithmic product then allows our AI product to automatically "Decide" and "Act" or augment human engagement in these two phases.

Unlike the military purpose, OODA loops for AI products are driven by business outcomes: fraud risk reduction, customer conversion, employee overtime reduction, supply chain cost reduction, and so on.

We extend the OODA loops into a proprietary decision framework for AI products called SETDA: Sense, Explain, Think, Decide, and Act (see Figure 1-4).

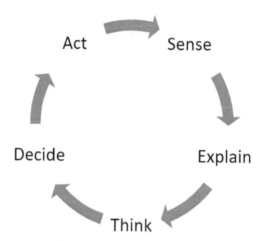

Figure 1-4. SETDA loops

Sense is similar to Observe. Explain and Think are similar to Orient. Decide and Act are the same between OODA and SETDA. We categorize AI products by their capability to operate in one phase (or two phases) within SETDA loops:

- *Sense:* The phase of acquiring and transforming unstructured/structured data into information, knowledge, or wisdom
- *Explain:* The phase of summarizing, describing, managing, and visualizing data
- *Think:* The phase of learning, predicting, reasoning, and correlating from data
- *Decide:* The phase of planning, optimizing, and recommending some actions
- *Act:* The phase of performing some action, like choosing, moving, creating, driving, etc.

Any AI product usually operates within one or two phases on the SETDA loop. For example, computer vision (i.e., Nodeflux, Valossa) and speech recognition (i.e., Deepgram, Jasper) startups operate within the *Sense* phase.

Startups operating in business intelligence and visual analytics, such as Geckoboard and Databoards, primarily focus on the *Explain* phase. They utilize AI techniques like data mining and machine learning to analyze and visualize data.

In contrast, predictive analytics startups operate within the *Think* phase, employing AI techniques such as machine learning and deep learning to make predictions, as seen in credit scoring (e.g., Zest AI) and predictive maintenance (e.g., Aveva).

Prescriptive analytics startups concentrate on the *Decide* phase, typically using machine learning and decision optimization techniques to optimize processes, such as supply chain optimization (e.g., Daitum) and demand forecast/inventory optimization (e.g., Antuit).

Lastly, autonomous robots and autonomous vehicle startups like Nuro and Embark operate within the *Act* phase. AI startups that generate new content or products, such as creating new songs (e.g., Starmony), new materials (e.g., Kebotix), or new organic molecules (e.g., Molecule One), can also be categorized within the *Act* phase (see Figure 1-5).

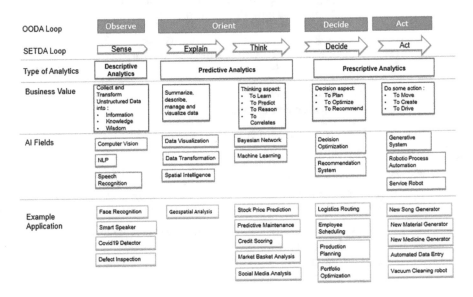

Figure 1-5. OODA loop and applications

Conclusion

As AI has been immersed into our life as part of the Fourth-Wave Revolution, AI startups play an important role in the revolution as they will be the enabler of AI-first companies.

The role of AI in the enterprise is mainly to help businesses automate or augment the decision-making process. In the next chapter, we will explore the AI startup landscape and the fundamental of AI product management.

As we move forward delving into the AI startup landscape and examining the fundamentals of AI product management, we will gain a deeper understanding of the impact and potential of AI in shaping the future of businesses and our everyday lives.

Key Takeaways

- Companies can use AI to make the decision fully (decision automation), augment the decision-making (decision augmentation), or just support the decision (decision support).

- AI can help in strategic, tactical, and operational decision-making in the company.

- Cloud and big data technologies are the enablers of AI and the Machine Learning Revolution.

- Deep learning started to be democratized with the release of open source deep learning frameworks such as TensorFlow and PyTorch.

- Every company is now striving to be an AI-first company, not only a data-driven company.

- An AI-first company means that the data and AI are integrated into the core business process.

- Artificial intelligence is an enabling technology for the enterprise, just like the World Wide Web is an enabling technology for the growth of the Internet-based business.

- The difference between an AI startup (AI-first SaaS and AIaaS) and an AI-first company is that an AI startup sells AI as a product (sell side) and uses AI to empower and scale its operational capabilities.

- AI is not only machine learning. Other AI techniques like searching, knowledge representation/reasoning, and planning are made to replicate human cognitive systems.

- Enterprise AI is the application of AI to speed up or automate decisions and actions to enable digital transformation, enhancing the organization's value.

- Analytics is used interchangeably with enterprise AI and broken down into descriptive, predictive, and prescriptive.

- AI products operate in one phase (or two phases) within SETDA (Sense-Explain-Think-Decide-Action) loops.

AI Startup Landscape

In the previous chapter, we built a conceptual understanding of the fundamental of AI techniques and their applications, the foundation of AI startups, and how AI helps enterprises become AI-first companies.

In this chapter, we will dive deeper into the fascinating landscape of AI startups, exploring the vast array of business models and monetization strategies that are used to turn cutting-edge AI technology into profitable and sustainable business ventures. We'll begin by taking a closer look at the specific problems that AI startups seek to solve and examining how these solutions fit within the broader context of the enterprise. From there, we'll delve into the critical role played by AI product managers (APMs) in driving innovation and success within these startups.

We'll also explore some of the most common AI business models, including those focused on developing AI-powered products or providing AI-powered services. By understanding these business models and how to exploit the unique value proposition (UVP) of AI within the company value chain, entrepreneurs and product managers can unlock new opportunities for growth and success.

Finally, we'll look at the intriguing AI startup valuation and acquisition world. Building a successful AI startup is a challenging and often unpredictable

© Adhiguna Mahendra 2023
A. Mahendra, *AI Startup Strategy*, https://doi.org/10.1007/978-1-4842-9502-1_2

endeavor. Still, those who can achieve it can reap tremendous rewards through lucrative buyouts and acquisitions. We'll explore the various factors that can impact an AI startup's value and examine successful AI entrepreneurs' strategies to maximize their chances of securing a profitable exit.

What Problems Do AI Startups Solve?

Developing AI solutions in-house is costly and time-consuming. Developing AI solutions requires significant investment in infrastructure, data collection, data annotation, subject matter experts (SMEs), and AI experts. Acquiring the necessary knowledge and experience to develop AI solutions effectively can take time and effort. Many companies may underestimate the costs associated with these factors.

An AI startup does precisely this. AI startups build and provide off-the-shelf AI solutions that customers can easily consume and integrate without an AI expert, eventually providing instant business value for them, all without requiring the services of an entire IT team to manage the necessary infrastructure, updating, validating, and deploying the AI model continuously. To deliver this, AI startups need to understand how to frame the problems and needs of their target customers and then build standardized AI solutions that will perform immediately in the most common scenarios.

The AI product properly done could provide incredible business benefits for customers. But AI startups should do a deep analysis of how their AI product can be customized and complemented with services to solve a variety of problems of their customers because, fundamentally, there is no one-size-fits-all solution for AI products.

The Role of an AI Product Manager

A product manager is a multidisciplinary individual who identifies:

- What product to build
- When to build it
- Why it needs to be built

The product manager must understand their customers' needs, pain, gain, and goals and what excites them and then prioritize what needs to be done.

The role of a product manager is relatively recent, around 25 years. There is even a new product manager, an AI product manager (APM; see Figure 2-1). The AI product manager is focused on managing products that utilize AI algorithms as their core value proposition, not only for complementing or optimizing the product. As a central figure in any AI startup, an AI product manager is focused on managing products that utilize AI algorithms. The AI product manager will lead the vision, considering the data availability, measuring the AI algorithm feasibility to solve real business problems, facilitating the collaborations between AI scientists and engineers, listening to the customer, and driving adoption and growth measured by business metrics.

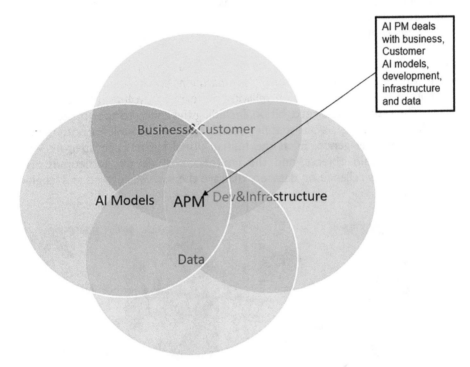

Figure 2-1. The AI product manager's role encompasses AI, business, data, and development

In an AI startup where AI is the core product, it is mandatory for a product manager to deeply understand how AI works, along with the base platform's architectural design and its limitation.

The field of AI, especially machine learning–related algorithms, is probabilistic and non-deterministic by nature. The main problem with AI is edge cases and unexplainable mistakes, although now a new trend is coming, the XAI (*explainable AI*).

Even a very comprehensive stress test doesn't guarantee that the AI systems will perform satisfactorily 100% all the time.

Due to edge cases that will certainly happen, AI product managers must regularly discuss revising the foundational design of the AI algorithms and the platform architecture, such as deep learning model architecture. Therefore, the AI product manager must be extremely technical because they will communicate intensively with AI engineers, data scientists, developers, and testers for highly complex problems.

The following is the reason for the complexity of AI product development:

The goal of the AI solution is to replicate human cognitive systems by giving an output (prediction, recognition, or insights) given an input (image, video, text, speech), so head-to-head comparison with human perception (which itself is different from human to human) is somehow an intuitive thing to do, but it is wrong. It is not uncommon to hear a complaint from AI product users such as "How can the AI not [recognize/understand] the [object/speech/text]? It is extremely clear for ME." Comparing human-made AI systems with the human brain resulting from millions of years of evolution is certainly a fallacy. The task of visual recognition, including the ability to spot objects such as wolves (Figure 2-2), is one that has been historically difficult for both human and artificial intelligence. Even the human visual system can struggle with identifying certain objects, and the limitations of AI are sometimes also attributed to its reliance on datasets that are themselves curated and labeled by humans.

Figure 2-2. Which dog is a husky, Alaskan malamute, and wolf? Even trained eyes have difficulties spotting them with 100% accuracy

- AI product development is not only about developing robust algorithms and platforms but also developing robust end-to-end processes of data acquisition, annotation, model development, and deployment with failover mechanisms and feedback loops.

- Since an AI product is usually located in one abstraction layer and integrated with other software-based products, an AI product is mainly consumed and/or integrated by a technical person such as a developer. Therefore, understanding DX (*developer experience*), including the REST API and microservices, SOA (service-oriented architecture), SDK (Software Development Kit) design, and SQL/RDBMS concept, is essential for the AI product manager who will design the AI product and documentation.

- Due to AI's nature, which involves the acquisition and processing of unstructured and structured data, AI product development involves quite complex architectural design. The foundation of architectural software design is necessary for AI product managers.

- Understand how the metrics of AI performance (i.e., *ROC, AUC, precision, and recall*) will relate to business performance. This would need a thorough understanding of statistical and business analysis.

- Understand how the metrics of business performance (i.e., cost saving, profit) will correlate with the overall improvement of the business process and the financial improvement (i.e., *ROI, payback period*).

Therefore, an AI product manager must deeply understand:

- How AI and the human cognitive systems work
- AI process design and operationalization
- How developers think (developer experience-DX)
- Architectural design and software development of a data-intensive platform
- Statistical analysis
- Business analysis

AI Startup Business Model

A business model is defined as a plan for how the business identifies the sources of revenue and target market, which will affect the operations, product architecture, and organization design.

AI startups have a unique business model different from SaaS (Software as a Service). The main difference between AI startups and SaaS startup is that AI startups always need data, huge computing power, and complex algorithms. An AI company is innately more difficult to understand for customers than SaaS company and solves different problems. SaaS digitizes manual processes performed by humans, and AI automates decisions or generates insights from a huge amount of data previously generated by humans and information systems. The implication is that AI technology must be sold, monetized, and operated differently.

There are two major landscapes of AI companies:

1. *Horizontal AI startups (AI as a Service)*: This type of AI company helps developers and data scientists develop and deploy AI for their products. These AI companies can be categorized by their products:

   a. *AI platform*: An end-to-end computational platform from data acquisition and annotation to ML model training and deployment. The end-to-end computational platform examples are AWS Sagemaker, IBM Watson, DataRobot, Azure Machine Learning, and Google Cloud AI Platform.

   b. *AI tool*: The tools to develop AI models, for example, a tool for machine learning model monitoring, data annotation, XAI, etc. Examples of AI tools are Dataiku (MLOps and DataOps platform), Scale.ai (data platform), Iguazio (MLOps platform), Neptune AI (ML experiment management), Fiddler AI (machine learning monitoring), Super AI (automatic data annotation), and Modzy (ModelOps and MLOps platform).

   c. *AI engine*: AI models such as machine learning, deep learning, or decision optimization that are packaged as a service and can be accessed through REST API or SDK. The examples are Deepgram (Speech Recognition as a Service), Trueface (Face Recognition as a Service), Routific (Route Optimization as a Service), and OpenALPR (License Plate Recognition as a Service).

   Therefore, the users of horizontal AI startups are generally data scientists or developers in tech companies or different industry verticals. The business model they use is generally based on subscriptions.

2. *Vertical AI startups*: These AI companies develop AI solutions for specific use cases. They sell to the business end user in a particular industry (B2B) or end user (B2C). Vertical AI can be categorized further:

   a. *AI-powered SaaS*: This is a traditional B2B SaaS empowered with AI to complement their core solutions (i.e., for sales forecasting or optimization of sales visits). The examples are HubSpot (CRM SaaS powered by AI) and Xero (accounting SaaS powered by AI).

   b. *AI-first SaaS*: A type of B2B SaaS that could not function without AI at its core. The examples are Affectiva (AI SaaS to understand human emotion), Avoma (AI-based meeting assistant), Jumio (AI-based biometrics verification), and Locus (AI-based logistics planning and optimization).

c. *Consumer AI*: An AI-powered product for consumers. Examples are mobile applications such as FaceApp (face transformation app), iRobot (consumer robot), Jarvis (AI-based copywriting software), and Deep Sentinel (AI-based security cameras).

Each type of AI startup also has a monetization model. The typical monetization models of AI startups (Figure 2-3) are:

1. *Customization + license (high-touch deployment)*: In this model, the customers are paying for AI model customization, integration, and deployment. After that, they can pay for the licensing fee for AI model usage and maintenance. This AI solution can be deployed on the customer's premises. Because of the intensive customization, integration, and deployment, the drawback is the sales cycle is long, but the benefit is the AI company can charge a larger amount of money, and usually, once the customer has the AI systems all set up, it is more likely for the customer to keep using the services.

2. *Subscription/pay per use (low-touch deployment)*: This is based on the SaaS business model, where the AI company will charge the customer a monthly or yearly fee or charge per usage of the AI applications. The AI as a Service can be integrated with customers' systems and consumed using a REST API or SDK mechanism. The AI solution accesses data flowing through the systems and processes the data on the cloud or the device, fueling business insights and decision improvement/automation. The benefit of this monetization model is it is fast to deploy, so the sales cycle is quick. However, this is also a very fragile model. If the AI solution does not fulfill the expectation of the customer, it can cause the customer to churn. AI as a Service must provide a robust generalized AI service that gives customers good ROI (return on investment).

3. *Unit based*: This is a monetization model of a startup that creates AI as a part of the product like security cameras, consumer robots, or autonomous cars. They sell by unit sold.

The preceding monetization models can be combined to attain the optimal revenue for the AI startup.

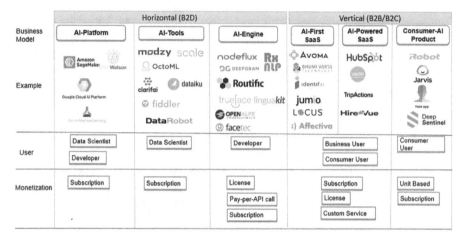

Figure 2-3. AI startup business models

The Business Value Within the Value Chain

One of the reasons AI is important to enterprise business is the possibility of scaling up the value chain by automating decision-making processes (see Figure 2-4). Scaling up the value chain allows companies to grow and gain various benefits, from increasing operational effectiveness to enabling new revenue streams. The following diagram shows four main areas to scale the value chain using AI and their example. The SETDA decision-making framework must be applied to some (or every) activity in the value chain, resulting in business value improvement, which the return on investment and payback period (PBP) can justify.

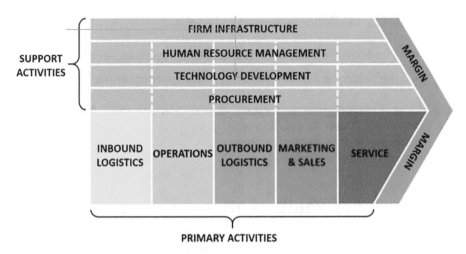

Figure 2-4. AI for business value – scaling the value chain

The SETDA loop implemented in value chain activities can potentially improve one or more of the following business values:

- *Optimizing operational efficiency*: AI can be used to maximize the efficiency of operations and improve production throughput, resulting in reduced operating costs. Examples of applications are production scheduling, predictive maintenance, intelligent supply chain and inventory optimization, automated defect inspection, automated logistic routing, and data center energy optimization.

- *Managing risk*: We can build an AI solution to analyze a stream of real-time data or a massive amount of stored data and then forecast the risk or even detect anomalies indicating a system breach. Example applications are fraud transaction detection, credit and insurance risk assessment and management, document assessment, cyberattack prevention, and IT audit.

- *Increasing revenue*: The AI can be used for applications that help increase revenue and profits, such as churn prevention, dynamic pricing, recommendation systems, CRM, ads targeting, and credit scoring.

- *Improving customer experience*: AI can help with tasks related to customer handling and improving customer satisfaction, such as a customer service chatbot and meeting scheduler.

So basically, the AI solution only has two benefits:

- *Hard/tangible benefits*: Reducing cost or improving revenue
- *Soft/intangible benefits*: Reducing risk, improving satisfaction

AI product managers must understand how to position their AI solutions in the value chain. Their AI solution must provide optimal business value for their customer in that particular value chain. The next chapter will discuss how to analyze AI in the value chain.

The Business Value of an AI Product

Despite the hype surrounding AI technology, selling AI products to companies can be challenging. The ultimate goal of any business is to optimize value, whether through cost savings or revenue enhancement. As such, it is crucial to quantify the value of AI products and initiatives. However, this process is often more of an art than a science, requiring a nuanced understanding of the specific business needs and context.

Effectively measuring the KPI and value of AI products is a universal challenge for all AI startups. But this is the first thing that the AI startups must do, even before developing any AI product. They need to make sure that their AI product

1. *Gets the job done*: Proven to help the customer achieve the concrete result by the decision automation and prediction of the AI, for example, predicting creditworthiness accurately, scheduling staff and equipment efficiently, and forecasting churning customers accurately

2. Has a tangible AI value that is sensible and quantifiable for the customers, which in return will lead to proper pricing

3. Can contribute to additional intangible benefits, such as risk reduction, faster decisions, happier employees, etc.

So basically, the value of AI is the perception of [(tangible value + intangible value) x % of the job that gets done].

What is a tangible AI value? If we look into the customer perspective, especially in the B2B landscape, the final decision-maker of any technology solution is the finance guy, that is, CFO, finance manager, and financial controllers. These guys only need to know two things:

"Is it worth it?" and *"How long until I recover my investment?"*

There are only two widely used financial metrics to answer those questions: ROI (return on investment) and PBP (payback period).

ROI is a return from an investment in a certain period (time horizon).

PBP is the time needed until we recover our investment.

The general guidelines for measuring the value of AI products are as follows:

- Focus on measuring tangible benefits first, which are ROI and PBP. Determine the ROI, which is the investment (all costs included) vs. gains for a period of time:

$$ROI = \frac{Gains - Investment}{Investment} \times 100\%$$

- Gains = Cost saving or revenue generated

- Investment = Data Operation Cost + Integration Cost + Subscription Cost

The gains must be exhaustively listed, including the cost of human reduction and the value from the prediction, optimization, or automation itself.

Then, determine the PBP, which is

$$PBP = \frac{Investment}{Gains}.$$

- List intangible benefits, such as fewer risks, reduced turnovers, happier employees, happier customers, fewer errors, faster decisions, reduced cognitive loads, etc.

- Factor the benefits of building an AI-ready culture.

CASE STUDY: CALCULATE BUSINESS VALUE

Automatic dispatch and route optimization based on AI, that is, Onfleet (www.onfleet.com), Optitrax (www.optitrax.co), or Locus (www.locus.sh), are SaaS helping logistic companies optimize fleet route and dispatch orders to their couriers. To make a solid business case that justifies business values, they must consider quantified potential gains such as

- *The reduction of human dispatchers:* The AI system allows the number of human dispatchers to be reduced. Therefore, the monthly compensation of human dispatchers can be reduced.

- *The reduced cost of fuel:* The more optimized route resulted in reduced fuel costs for all fleets.

- *The reduced cost of couriers' overtime:* The more optimized route resulted in reduced overtime for all couriers.

  So the total annual gains = (salary of human dispatcher replaced + fuel cost reduction + reduction of couriers' overtime per month) x 12.

We also need to calculate the total investment, which is

- *Cost of data operation development:* A new AI system will always need a data operation (DataOps), an automated way of acquiring data and improving data quality for analytics purposes.

- *Cost of system integration:* Any AI system must be integrated with current infrastructures, and the cost is inevitable.

- *Model training and evaluation cost:* Any sufficiently complex AI system, like a route optimization system, needs continuous model training to perform its best.

- *Subscription cost:* The monthly subscription cost.

Let's estimate the cost savings and break it down (Table 2-1).

Table 2-1. Cost Saving Estimate

Gain from Cost Saving (Monthly)	Amount ($)
Human dispatcher compensation (1 person x $2,500/month)	2,500
Fuel cost	3,000
Courier overtime	2,000
Total	7,500

Now we estimate the investment needed for one year (Table 2-2).

Table 2-2. Investment Needed for One Year

Investment (Yearly)	Amount ($)
DataOps development cost	5,000
Training cost	5,000
Integration cost	6,000
Subscription cost ($4,000 monthly x 12 = $48,000)	48,000
Total	64,000

From the preceding table, we can do a back-of-the-envelope yearly ROI estimation using route optimization and a dispatch system:

$$One\ Year\ ROI = \frac{One\ Year\ Gains - One\ Year\ Investment}{One\ Year\ Investment} \times 100\%$$

$$One\ Year\ ROI = \frac{\left(\$7,500 \times 12\right) - \$64,000}{\$64,000} \times 100\%$$

$$One\ Year\ ROI = \frac{\left(\$90,000\right) - \$64,000}{\$64,000} \times 100\% = 41\%$$

So one year ROI is 41%, which is a fantastic number.

How about the payback period (PBP)? Let's calculate:

$$PBP = \frac{Total\ Investment}{One\ Month\ Gains}$$

$$PBP = \frac{DataOps\ Cost + Training\ Cost + Integration\ Cost}{Monthly\ Cost\ Saving - Monthly\ Subscription}$$

$$PBP = \frac{\$5,000 + \$5,000 + \$6,000}{\$7,500 - \$4,000} = \frac{\$16,000}{\$3,500} = 4.5\ months$$

The payback period is only 4.5 months to recoup the initial investment, which is fantastic. So the *one year* ROI of 41% and payback period of 4.5 months are like music to the customer's ears.

This is an example of how an AI company should justify its tangible value. Financial justification like this, however rudimentary, would be a determining factor for an AI company from the business and investment standpoint. After the tangible metrics have been defined and presented to the customer, then intangible metrics or more abstract metrics such as extended vehicle's *Remaining Useful Life* (RUL), improved courier's mental health, increased customer's satisfaction, and fleet manager's reduced cognitive loads can be pitched to the customer.

Understanding the Valuation of AI Startups

The AI startup can be categorized as a deep tech company in the early days. *Deep tech* is coined in certain cutting-edge sectors such as bio robotics, quantum computing, genetic engineering, blockchain, advanced material, and space exploration.

Deep tech companies are usually started by very technical or scientific people and circle around innovative technology. Often, practicality and business applications are not the main concern of the founders.

There are generally three company valuation approaches:

- *Market approach*: Determining the company's value based on the selling price of similar assets

- *Income approach*: Determining the company's value based on the future projection of revenue by taking into account the past and current revenues

- *Asset approach*: Determining the company's value by total business assets (tangible and intangible) and then subtracting its liabilities

The asset approach is the most suitable to be applied to the valuation of deep tech companies, including AI companies that are pre-revenue with minimal or negative cash flows and cannot generate a clear return on investment in the foreseeable future. Therefore, the fair market value of the IP (*intellectual property*; patents), how the future holds for the technology (use cases, monetization model), data, and the founders' credibility will form the basis of the valuation. But overtime, AI solutions are starting to be democratized and adopted by different industry verticals. AI has also become part of any hardware or software product, from smart speakers to SaaS. Therefore, the valuation increasingly resembles the SaaS valuation, which is heavily toward the income approach. Hence, scalability becomes an important part here.

To have a reasonable valuation, an AI startup must provide significant business value for an industry with a fair market size. They must also have robust technology and data moats as well as scalability (see Figure 2-5).

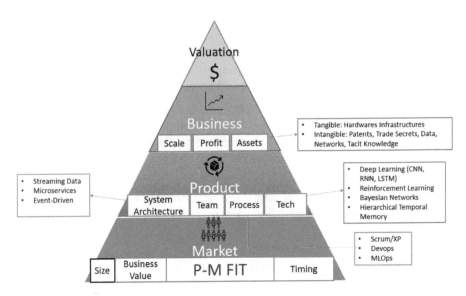

Figure 2-5. The valuation pyramid of AI startups

AI Startup Acquisitions

AI companies prefer one particular exit plan, which is getting acquired. The prevalence of AI startup acquisitions has doubled since 2016 and increased by an average of 46% in the following years. Tech giants like Facebook, Apple, Amazon, Netflix, Intel, Google, and Uber dominate startup acquisitions.

Non-tech Fortune 500 companies are also aggressively acquiring AI startups. Examples are McDonald's (acquires speech recognition Apprente and AI-based personalization platform Dynamic Yield), General Electric (acquires industrial AI startup Wise and Bit Stew), General Dynamics (acquires autonomous driving startup Cruise Automation and Momenta), Hewlett-Packard (acquires distributed machine learning startup Determined AI), and Walmart (acquires natural language processing startup Aspectiva).

Companies acquire other companies to build on the strengths and weaknesses of the acquiring company. This method is also known as business acquisition or business takeover. Through this process, one company takes control of the interest and management of a targeted company.

Before deciding to acquire other companies, a company's management team needs to analyze the strategic match between the acquirer and acquired companies.

There are many reasons tech companies acquire AI companies:

1. *Long-term bet*: To accelerate the growth of the overall business. Examples are Google (acquires DeepMind), Amazon (acquires Zoox), and Microsoft (acquires Lobe).

2. *Strengthening the core AI platform*: Enhancing existing AI capability. Examples are Tesla (acquires DeepScale), ServiceNow (acquires Element AI and Loom Systems), Skyfii (acquires CrowdVision), and SAP (acquires Qualtrics).

3. *Acquiring talents*: Recruiting the best AI team with proven products and capability to acquire tacit and technical knowledge.

4. *Acquiring credentials*: Obtain credentials such as ISO, standard, permit, certification, and license.

5. *Acquiring the base market*: Get access to the network of customers.

6. *Acquiring IP (intellectual property)*: Acquiring intangible intellectual assets such as patents, publications, trademarks, and copyrights, which will increase overall company valuation.

From the preceding six reasons, an AI startup can focus on making itself an interesting acquisition target.

Challenges of Building AI Startups

With the democratization of AI platforms, tools, and libraries, many startup founders think that building AI startups such as AIaaS, MLaaS, and AI-powered SaaS is similar to building traditional SaaS. But building an intelligent product that will improve overtime with more data is more challenging than building a non-intelligent SaaS.

My experience building AI products has challenges as follows:

1. AI is largely dealing with human perception. A good output is often very abstract and not easily defined. For example, automatic quality inspection problems will largely depend on the preference and experience of the human inspector, and the performance of the age detection system will largely depend on how the person visually looks at the image vs. the real age. Figure 2-6 is an example of a photograph of an actress that could

deceive individuals regarding her age. Due to this nature, customer onboarding will always involve a lot of handholding and education. Managing the expectation of the customer is the challenge of any AI startup.

Figure 2-6. Southeast Korean actress Jang Na-ra can spoof any AI-based age predictor (photo: kdramastars)

2. The quality of the data is everything. And it is not cheap. Data operations, an end-to-end data collection cycle, ETL (Extract, Transfer, and Load), annotation, and data quality evaluation are time-consuming and costly. The main premise is that we will never have full control over user-generated data, even with all the training sessions, disclaimers, and guidelines. So though maintaining data quality is a shared responsibility between AI companies and their customers, it is more of the AI company's concern than the customer's.

3. Another challenge with AI is edge cases or long-tail problems, where the AI will inevitably encounter scenarios in which the systems do not perform as required or as expected. We have methods to deal with this situation called active learning. But this will always involve humans doing manual model evaluation and annotation or human in the loop (HITL).

4. Due to data drift, where data that feeds the AI models tends to change over time, AI will always need continual training and redeployment. This can cost a thousand dollars or more for compute and storage infrastructure resources and tools (i.e., for model drift monitoring, XAI (explainable AI), etc.).

5. The complexity of AI development requires a technical team with very strong scientific and software engineering capabilities. We need to hire a person with higher education in AI-related areas (i.e., a master or PhD in computer vision, machine learning, or natural language processing). This will have a consequence of high personnel costs for acquiring and retaining talents.

The Key to Building Successful AI Startups

My definition of a successful AI startup is a startup with a good margin profit, leading to a high valuation and finally being acquired with a fair number. From the previous section, we learned that to be a successful AI startup, the AI company must solve the challenges of cost and scalability. Therefore, there are seven things to do:

1. *Selecting a use case*: Start by choosing the right use case with a significant number of customers that would pay you, and you can solve their problem with the same model.

2. *Solve one problem better than anyone*: Build an AI algorithm that solves that *one* problem perfectly, along with all the edge cases. After you solve this problem, you can explore other problems with other AI models.

3. *Add values without overhauling workflows*: The AI solutions must be easy to install and frictionless. Don't try to replace existing customers' systems, but look to layer the top.

4. *Make the AI systems as self-serve as possible*: The customer must have the capability to change the rules, parameters, dashboard, and even data operations themselves.

5. *Automate everything*: Internally automate the training and data pipeline as much as possible to increase operational efficiency and reduce manual work. Build internal tools that will automate things.

6. *Easy and scalable deployment*: The AI must be easy to deploy and scale across platforms and environments such as local (on-premise) and cloud and different hardware (Android, Intel, etc.).

7. *Reduce data acquisition and user input uncertainty*: Bad data acquisition is the Achilles heel of any AI system, especially machine learning. Therefore, we must have a mechanism to limit the variance and unpredictability of user inputs and condition them so that they will be suitable for our model inference. For example, an AI company building biometrics eKYC (electronic know-your-customer) and face spoof detection for smartphones must always create mobile SDKs to limit users' bad and unacceptable inputs (see Figure 2-7).

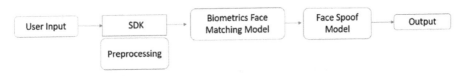

Figure 2-7. Example of a biometrics eKYC machine learning system pipeline

We cannot limit how the users take their facial images. We also cannot control the smartphone and the feature used (i.e., using filters). Therefore, we must create SDKs to be used to create a mobile app that will help us perform the necessary pre-processing tasks (i.e., image enhancement, image alignment) before feeding the image into the machine learning model. The SDK reduces the variety and uncertainties of the user inputs.

The Successful AI Startup Patterns

The journey of an AI startup ideally starts when a subject matter expert (SME), someone with years of experience and network in a particular industry, meets an AI wizard with academic credentials who has years of experience developing AI systems in a similar industry. They have an itch to more intelligently solve a particular problem in their industry domain and scale that solution. Figure 2-8 shows a proven framework from an idea to a successful exit for an AI startup.

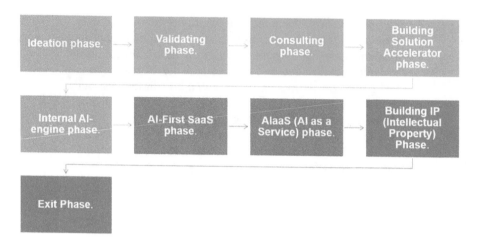

Figure 2-8. The successful AI startup pattern

1. *Ideation phase*: The SME meets the AI wizard. They develop some ideas that will disrupt how people work in a particular industry and domain.

2. *Validating phase*: They validate the market by analyzing the industry deeply, measuring the business and technical feasibility, and finding early adopters to test their idea who would pay for their AI MVP (Minimal Viable Product).

3. *Consulting phase*: They build an AI consulting service together than working on numerous AI projects in a particular domain industry to prove that they can solve problems more efficiently with AI. They will also collect more data and deal with more edge cases from different clients.

4. *Building a solution accelerator phase*: Building a solution accelerator is a useful strategy for AI startups as it can help accelerate the development process and reduce the time to market their products. By pre-building reusable components, frameworks, and modules, startups can focus on developing custom features and fine-tuning their algorithms to meet specific customer needs. This approach can reduce development time and costs and improve scalability and flexibility in deploying the solution to a wider customer base. Additionally, having a well-designed and documented solution accelerator can enhance the startup's credibility and attract potential investors and customers who are looking for proven and scalable AI solutions.

5. *Internal AI engine phase*: The AI solution framework is more refined as more data is collected and more edge cases are handled. The next step is to automate the whole process by building an AI engine to be used internally. The AI engine is comprised of several modules, such as the machine learning/decision optimization module, web/mobile interface, and data handling module.

6. *AI-first SaaS phase*: Time to target a bigger market. They can scale the AI solution by building a more generic and productized version for the larger customer base by building AI-first SaaS. AI-first SaaS is a full-stack application with AI as its core, which can be sold directly to the customers with no handholding process like consulting services.

7. *AIaaS (AI as a Service) phase*: The experience building an internal AI engine and AI-first SaaS is useful for building another type of AI startup, AI as a Service (AIaaS), by productizing and selling your AI engine to developers and other SaaS companies.

8. *Building an IP (intellectual property) phase*: To maximize the value of a platform and its associated algorithms, it is recommended that they be transformed into intellectual property (IP), such as patents and publications. This transformation enhances the platform's valuation and makes it more attractive to potential buyers. Through IP protection, a platform and its algorithms can be safeguarded from unauthorized use, and their value can be maintained over time. Furthermore, publishing research on the platform and its algorithms can increase their visibility and establish them as leaders in their respective fields, ultimately increasing their marketability. Thus, transforming a platform and its associated algorithms into IP is a prudent business strategy for any company seeking to increase its valuation and attract potential buyers.

9. *Exit phase*: When the AI startup has a good user base, data, technology moats, and solid propositions, it is time for the founders to think about an exit strategy. The AI technology landscape is changing very fast; wrong timing for exit may cause disappointment. The typical path for an AI startup is M&A, merging with a company, or selling the whole company and products to a bigger company that sees the strategic fit in the acquisition.

The rule in the AI startup game is to enter quickly and exit fast, as the AI tech landscape changes rapidly. The AI technique working well today may not work well tomorrow. An AI startup must know when to exit at the right moment. AI is an enabling technology. Hence, it is natural that the acquisition by bigger tech companies is the most common exit strategy.

Conclusion

This chapter explains how AI startups solve a substantial problem for their enterprise customers. They are building AI products to be consumed by enterprises. This can significantly save time and cost.

To provide value for their enterprise customers, AI startups must understand the core and supporting activities in the value chain of their target industries and show the tangible benefits of using AI to augment or automate the decision-making process. Therefore, an AI product manager must know about AI and statistics, as well as product management, software development, and business analysis.

Building an AI startup is different from building a traditional SaaS startup. Due to the relatively short-lived nature of AI as a commodity, the goal of any AI startup should be to have the optimal valuation and exit at the right time. AI startup founders must find the recipe for success by providing good business value for customers, building strong AI algorithms and data moats, and scaling up quickly. In the next chapter, we will learn how to validate an AI startup idea's market and technology feasibility.

Key Takeaways

- AI startups provide off-the-shelf AI solutions to easily use and integrate with business users' systems and processes.

- The product manager, as a central figure in AI startups, must deeply understand how AI works along with customer decision problems.

- The product managers must also understand the challenges in data-intensive system architecture and understand developer experience (DX) and AI product management operationalization.

- AI startups have two major business models: horizontal and vertical. Horizontal AI startups sell AI platforms and tools to developers and data scientists, and vertical AI startups sell AI solutions for specific use cases to business users and end consumers.

- AI startups have three major monetization models: licensing, subscription, and unit based.

- The business value from AI in the enterprise value chain can be divided into the

  - *Tangible benefit*: Reducing operational cost, increasing revenue

  - *Intangible benefit*: Managing risk and improving customer experience

- The valuation of an AI startup is based on several factors: business value for customers, algorithm and data moats, market size, and scale.

- AI startups are acquired for their technology, talents, customers, credentials, and patents.

- There are challenges in building AI products. The most prominent is dealing with the quality of data and long-tail problems.

- The key to building a successful AI startup is selecting generic and automated use cases and minimizing user input uncertainty.

- Successful AI startups usually have experienced industry and AI experts. They started with customized AI solutions and then productized as SaaS or AIaaS as they saw the scaling opportunity.

Product-Market Validation for AI-First SaaS

Successful AI startups need to understand the nature of AI technology and how it is bought and used. AI is an enabling technology – a set of tools and technologies that can be applied to solve numerous use cases. Therefore, AI will enable many use cases for enterprises – AI can solve substantial inefficiencies in the corporates and even create a whole new business. Netflix, Amazon, and Uber are examples of companies where AI enables business models.

Due to this enabling nature, an AI product is targeted mainly at enterprise or technical users (at least until OpenAI releases ChatGPT). AI companies whose core product is AI are generally in B2B space (selling to business users) or B2D space (selling to developers). However, picking the most suitable domain, use cases, and industry where AI will contribute to the optimal business value is not trivial. Most AI products fail because AI companies are not doing proper product-market (P-M) validation.

© Adhiguna Mahendra 2023
A. Mahendra, *AI Startup Strategy*, https://doi.org/10.1007/978-1-4842-9502-1_3

This chapter will focus on properly validating AI products for enterprises (B2B). We will first introduce you to the difference between traditional SaaS, AI-first SaaS, AI-powered SaaS, and AI as a Service (AIaaS).

AI-first product validation is the most important step for the success of an AI startup. We have been building a very comprehensive framework on that.

To validate your AI-first SaaS solution, we will guide you through a step-by-step approach: define the ideal founder characteristics, determine the target industry, recruit early adopters, create an AI Minimal Viable Product, and close the deal with a service contract.

This approach is critical to the success of your AI startup. It allows you to test your solution with early adopters and refine it based on their feedback. Following this approach increases your chances of success in the market validation process. However, it requires effort and dedication. With the right team, industry focus, and approach, your AI-first SaaS solution can achieve success in the market.

SaaS and Its Evolution

In this section, the fundamental concept of AI-first SaaS will be explained. AI-first SaaS is the B2B business model of an AI startup, and it is a common model and, usually, the second stage of an AI startup after the AI service model has been validated. But before we explain about AI-first SaaS, we will walk through the concept of SaaS and the difference between AI-first SaaS, AI-powered SaaS, and AIaaS.

What Is SaaS

SaaS is short for *Software as a Service*. It is a model of software delivery based on a subscription-based software model. Enterprises embrace the new technology to minimize the high aggregate cost of buying traditional software licenses. Not only do businesses have this problem, but they also pay hefty annual maintenance fees every time an upgrade or update is in market; it can be quite costly. SaaS businesses differ from traditional software companies because they don't require an end user license. Instead, the company's servers host all the customer data and offer them access at any time without additional cost or hassle – it just requires logging into their account, which can be done on demand through either the Web or even mobile phone. Examples of SaaS are CRM applications such as Salesforce and HubSpot, as well as Zendesk for customer service ticketing systems.

Most SaaS is targeted at enterprise customers. But there is also another minority of SaaS targeted exclusively to consumers (B2C or business to consumer), such as Netflix and Spotify. A trending category of SaaS also serves both the business and consumer markets, such as Shopify and Canva.

From SaaS to AI-Powered SaaS to AI-First SaaS

Historically, SaaS emerged from the rise of cloud computing. The idea that web-based software installed on a third-party remote server reduced the necessary maintenance and could be accessed from anywhere was exciting for small and medium businesses. In its infancy, the SaaS model was thought to be only for startups and small businesses because it was too slow and unstable. But over the next several years, improvements to the Internet infrastructure, database, and web application technology stacks speed up the adoption of SaaS.

SaaS is also evolved. We can observe that fundamentally four different innovation trends have shaped the SaaS industry over the past 15 years, as described in Figure 3-1.

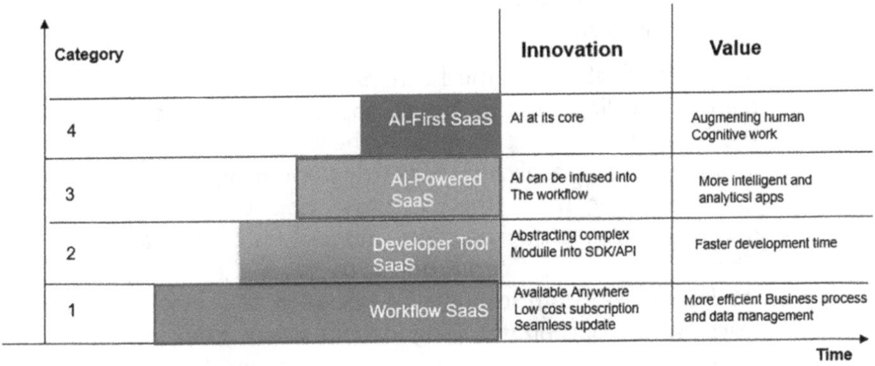

Category		Innovation	Value
4	AI-First SaaS	AI at its core	Augmenting human Cognitive work
3	AI-Powered SaaS	AI can be infused into The workflow	More intelligent and analyticsl apps
2	Developer Tool SaaS	Abstracting complex Moduile into SDK/API	Faster development time
1	Workflow SaaS	Available Anywhere Low cost subscription Seamless update	More efficient Business process and data management

Time

Figure 3-1. The categories of SaaS

At the high level, here is how we categorize it:

- *Workflow SaaS:* Initially, SaaS companies built a web application consisting of the workflow with a database and basic CRUD (Create-Read-Update-Delete) operation to help their users simplify their business process. This type of workflow SaaS helps the users with different standardized business processes such as

  - *Customer relationship management:* Salesforce, HubSpot, Pipedrive
  - *Project and task management:* Asana, Basecamp, ClickUp
  - *Accounting:* QuickBooks, Xero, NetSuite
  - *Customer support and ticketing:* Freshdesk, Zendesk, ServiceNow

This type of SaaS is disrupting the software industry by providing low-cost, available-from-anywhere web-based applications, which can be integrated into the business process of users.

- *Developer tool SaaS:* In the second category, some SaaS companies started building picks and shovels of SaaS applications, making software development much more efficient by abstracting underlying complexity into APIs (Application Programming Interfaces) or SDKs. Twilio, QuickBlox, SendGrid, and Nexmo are developer tool SaaS popular with developers and make the development work more efficient. This type of SaaS disrupts the way a developer works by simplifying the complex development part into components that can be easily integrated into their applications.

- *AI-powered SaaS:* In the third category, the workflow SaaS company realizes that their web application is collecting the data into their database. Still, there is no mechanism for automatically analyzing, optimizing or mining the data. On the other hand, the customer also demands to perform forecasting, prediction, and analysis of the data. This leads the SaaS companies to infuse a kind of intelligent algorithm into their SaaS, such as a machine learning or optimization algorithm, hence the term *AI-powered SaaS*. Almost all leading workflow SaaS are adopting AI now as part of the SaaS evolution. An example of AI-powered SaaS is Salesforce Einstein, which is a set of AI technologies that make the customer success platform smarter. Zendesk is also proudly called an AI-powered SaaS by adopting AI for ticketing using text analysis, that is, sentiment analysis to classify tickets. Zendesk also has a chatbot to solve simple requests from customers. Salesforce and Zendesk are also known for their appetite for AI startup acquisitions. Salesforce is acquiring AI startups MetaMind, Datorama, and Bonobo, while Zendesk acquired AI startups Cleverly and Momentive to expand the AI capabilities of their SaaS platform.

- *AI-first SaaS:* The fourth category is SaaS companies that use AI algorithms, such as deep learning, reinforcement learning, computer vision, mathematical optimization, and machine learning, *at their core* to scale some intelligence to their customers.

AI at its core means that AI capabilities have always been an unseparated part of the architectural design of the product since day one. AI is not something added or infused to the product, but it is the essence of the product. AI-first SaaS has one main goal: *augmenting human intelligence*. This means that AI-first SaaS will be able to make their users able *to stop* doing some cognitive tasks. Without *AI at its core*, AI-first SaaS doesn't have any value proposition. Examples of AI-first companies are

- *Narrative Science*: Their product enables users to *tell a story* from the data, such as sales and expenditure data. This means that their users will *stop writing reports* and let the AI write the report for them.

- *Advance AI*: Their onboarding automation product enables their users to verify the identity of their customers just by their selfie faces and ID pictures. The proposition is that the users will *stop doing manual ID verification* by live interviewing with their customers. Instead, the customer ID can be verified by only taking a selfie because Advance AI utilizes deep learning–based biometrics matching.

- *Locus.sh*: Their product enables their users to automate the logistics routing and dispatching jobs. The proposition is that their users will stop doing manual logistics routing using Excel and whiteboards and stop doing manual dispatching with the phone.

The main difference between AI-powered and AI-first SaaS is that AI-powered SaaS still functions very well even without AI because it is a workflow SaaS on steroids. In contrast, AI-first SaaS cannot function without AI because AI is the core product.

The following is the multitude of benefits of adopting AI-first SaaS for companies:

- *Reduced time and cost*: Building AI is timely and costly. Companies must hire expensive AI experts to build, test, and implement AI systems from scratch. The infrastructure cost for AI development and operationalization is also staggering.

- *Ease of use*: Packaging the AI algorithms as a product with a user interface allows the customers (business users and end users) to use the AI solution easily without requiring expertise.

- *Scalability*: As the AI-first SaaS is usually charged by subscription (pay per use), customers can first experiment with whether AI solves their problems. The uncertainties can be alleviated by starting small and scaling later as the value is proven or the company requirements change.

- *Flexibility*: Flexibility in AI-first SaaS allows the product to adapt to changing needs, relying on machine learning to continuously improve capabilities. It can be achieved through customizability, scalability, and integration with other systems, ensuring the product remains useful and relevant as user needs evolve.

- *A step toward an AI-first company*: As the company starts to get the taste of using AI to support their daily business operations, they are starting to experience the efficiency and benefits and adopt an AI-first and data-driven mindset. This mindset is important for the transformation of the company toward an AI-first company.

AI as a Service (AIaaS)

There is also another category of product that uses AI at its core called AI as a Service (AIaaS). AIaaS is productizing only the AI modules and selling them as a service to be consumed by *developers* as SDK or API. We can think of AIaaS as developer tool SaaS's more intelligent evolution. The main difference between AIaaS and AI-first SaaS is the target user. AIaaS targets developers and data scientists because it is an AI engine, while AI-first SaaS is an AI engine + user interface – it targets business users like other B2B SaaS (see Figure 3-2).

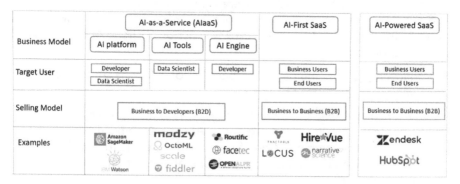

Figure 3-2. The comparison between AIaaS, AI-first SaaS, and AI-powered SaaS

As we have described in a previous chapter, AIaaS is divided into three categories: AI platform, which provides end-to-end AI development and deployment solutions, such as Amazon Sagemaker and IBM Watson; AI tools, which offer features such as data annotation, model monitoring, and machine learning performance optimization, such as Fiddler, OctoML, and Scale AI; and AI engine, which provides pre-built AI models or environments as a service through APIs or SDKs, such as FaceTec for face biometrics, Routific for delivery routing optimization, and OpenALPR for license plate and vehicle recognition.

The benefits of AIaaS for their users are

- *Reduced time and cost*: Using AIaaS, developers and data scientists can save time and cost in building their platforms and AI models. Gluing open source AI solutions together is painstakingly difficult and time-consuming. An AI team can use a ready-made full-stack platform provided by an AIaaS platform provider. Sometimes, technical teams undermine the effort (time, cost, and cognitive load) needed to build acceptable AI solutions. Building a production-ready AI solution is not an easy thing and often not pennyworth, especially if it is not part of the company's core business.

- *Ease of use*: AIaaS provides ready-made AI models from computer vision to recommender systems, which developers can easily consume without the machine learning experience and massive data needed.

- *Scalability*: The developers and data scientists can do trials on available commercial AIaaS to see if their AI solution suits them compared with in-house development. If it is more practical to use AIaaS, the team can easily scale up the usage.

- *Configurability*: Configurability in AI as a Service allows users to customize AI models and services for specific needs, enabling better accuracy and decision-making. It provides flexibility for experimentation and quick adaptation to changes, ultimately improving business outcomes and driving innovation.

Based on the preceding explanation, what is defined as an AI startup is an AI-first SaaS and AIaaS. Therefore, we will focus on these two business models.

Understanding the Fundamental Principles of SaaS

Whether we are building workflow SaaS, AI-powered SaaS, AI-first SaaS, or AIaaS, we need to understand that there are fundamental principles that cannot be violated in the SaaS business. These principles apply universally in any country and industry where SaaS operates. The principles are as follows:

1. **Target a specific market segment**. Do not target a market segment that is too broad. This applies to all categories of SaaS.

2. **Focus on the target market and one value proposition**. Have a strong value proposition in one particular market. Create a SaaS product with a clear value proposition that solves *one* problem properly for one industry. AI must reduce or remove at least *one* problem that takes up customers' time, money, and cognitive loads, better than anyone on the market. Then from that, we can explore other problems in that market and then other problems in adjacent industries. Too many entrepreneurs are trying to solve problems in too many industries. This is a recipe for SaaS disaster.

3. **Track the competition.** Put special attention on the competitive and substitution landscape. This is especially true for AI-first SaaS and AIaaS startups. But unlike traditional SaaS, where the differentiation can be on the number and variety of features, AI products do not need to have many features. We just need one or two core features that solve a customer problem, that is, reducing their work and cognitive loads. So we track our closest competitors and benchmark our AI solutions in terms of product *smartness*, reliability, and user experience. Aside from competitors, we also need to consider humans as our competitors because we are trying to replicate human cognitive systems. We have to make sure that the AI solutions have an edge compared with humans, that is, cost, precision, consistency, and scale.

4. **Never assume that customers want to change the way they work.** We must understand that customers are motivated to adopt SaaS to solve their problems seamlessly with minimum effort and cost. Therefore, we cannot assume that customers are willing to change their workflow and how they work. Make sure you pick a use case where the workflow is as generic as possible. Otherwise, you have to make sure that customers' workflow can be customized and configured by them without making it too complicated to use.

5. **Hang out with your customers.** We need to understand and love the customers in our target industry. Therefore, we have to enjoy hanging out with them. Especially for AI startup founders, we need to understand the most painful problem of the customers, which takes lots of money, time, and cognitive load.

6. **Recruit early adopters.** Early adopters are crucial as part of SaaS development. For AI startups, early adopters help you frame a correct problem to solve and the solutions and provide real-world datasets and edge cases.

7. **Be a consultant first, but draw the line.** Starting a SaaS journey as a solution consultant is a good idea. We can understand customers' problems and expectations more and start collecting datasets (with some terms and agreement) and use cases. As described in the previous chapter, for AI startups, it is almost mandatory that we start from the consulting stage before we build a productized version of the solution in the form of AI-first SaaS or AIaaS. However, we must be strategic in determining which target market to choose and specific problem to solve, to avoid being trapped in the consulting stage forever. The end goal is to become a scalable and valuable AI startup.

Product-Market-Technology (P-M-T) and Validation Framework

SaaS investment is very attractive for venture capital because SaaS businesses provide predictable, recurring revenue. A monthly CRM or HR SaaS subscription is a repeatable, secure income that can be grown by acquiring more subscriptions, compared with a one-off payment of a perpetual license or one-time project fees. SaaS startups can take up as many subscribers as they want with relatively the same fixed costs. This potentially creates high revenue and business scalability.

However, 92% of SaaS companies failed within three years despite growth and funding.[1]

The number one cause of SaaS failure is non-existent product-market fit. Other reasons are a cash flow problem, more churn than growth, and poor management.[2] For deep technology–driven AI-centric products such as AI-powered SaaS, AI-first SaaS, and AIaaS, there is another dominant reason: unmet customer expectations because of the maturity of AI technology. Therefore, technical feasibility is also important in deep tech–driven products such as AI solutions.

So, in AI-centric products, product-market fit is not enough. We also need to do Product-Market-Technology (P-M-T) fit. Product-Market-Technology validation is often skipped due to time and cost constraints. This often results in very negative consequences.

In this section, we will learn about the concept of Product-Market-Technology (P-M-T) validation.

Product-Market Validation Fundamental

Product-market validation is a method of validating the market to ensure that the product answers a customer's problem. The product-market validation method is about minimizing risk and validating product concepts within its target market. Product-market validation will reduce reliance on intuition, which is unreliable.

Several factors need to be considered when validating product-market fit:

1. *Market size*: The size of the potential market for this product.

2. *Competition*: The number of direct and indirect competitors for the product.

3. *Need*: The need of the customers of the product because it does solve their problem.

4. *Willingness to pay*: The willingness of the customer to put a commercial value on the product and pay for it.

---

[1] https://tomtunguz.com/grow-fast-or-die-slow/
[2] www.lightercapital.com/blog/why-do-most-saas-startups-fail/

5. *Business value*: The business value for the customers resulting from the usage of this product. It consists of three things:

   - *Financial value*: Quantified financial ROI and payback period

   - *Nonfinancial value*: The business value other than financial such as customer satisfaction improvement or risk mitigation

   - *Strategic value*: The potential of the product to influence the long-term strategy goal (three to five years), including the business model, operating model, and digital transformation

The main question to be asked for product-market validation is

"Does this product have a reasonable market size that needs the product and is willing to pay?"

There are fundamentally five steps on how to do product-market validation:

1. Write down the hypothesis about the customer and their problem, target market, and value proposition.

2. Assess the market size and share. Estimate the potential size of the market minus the competition.

3. Assess the investment and technology ecosystem.

4. Conduct interviews with your target customers.

5. Test the product and service to early adopters.

Product-market validation aims to attain a product-market fit (P-M fit). P-M fit is a state where the product is already validated for one particular need of the market.

Product-Technology Validation Fundamental

Product-technology validation is the process of validating the technology needed to realize the product's potential. This is especially important in the deep tech field such as space exploration, quantum computing, advanced material, artificial intelligence, biotech, and cleantech, where the technical uncertainty is still very high, and there are still few proven real-life implementation frameworks that have been successfully and comprehensively written.

To validate the product-technology fit, we need to measure three important factors:

1. *Technical feasibility*: The process of proving that state-of-the-art algorithms, engineering methods, and infrastructure (i.e., compute, storage, network bandwidth) are technically viable within some operational conditions.

2. *Data feasibility*: The viability of the data and its acquisition process to make the product work by considering volume, characteristics, bias, privacy, and imbalance of data.

3. *Total Cost of Ownership (TCO)*: The development, implementation, and maintenance costs to make the product work at a reasonable price.

The main question to be asked for product-technology validation is

"Is the current state of technology and data needed for this product to work feasible at a reasonable cost?"

There are four steps on how to do product-technology validation:

1. Write down the problem the product solves.

2. Assess the viability of the state-of-the-art algorithms to solve the problem mentioned in no. 1.

3. Assess whether we can acquire the data needed to solve the problem in a reasonable time.

4. Assess the total cost needed to develop and maintain the technology and its support systems.

In AI-first SaaS and AIaaS, product-technology validation is crucial to ensure that the current state of technologies can solve the technical challenges expected for the product to be successful.

Product-Market-Technology Validation

Finally, for a deep tech product to be viable, we need to assess both the market and technology feasibility. The Product-Market-Technology fit is crucial in the tech-driven product because the product and technology often come first before the market is ready (see Figure 3-3). On the other hand, when the market is ready, the technology and its supporting ecosystem may not be mature yet. Therefore, a Product-Market-Technology fit is expected in deep techs, such as AI-centric products.

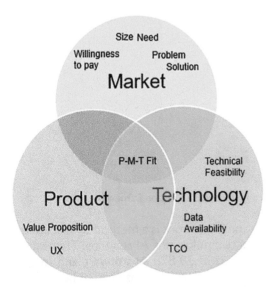

Figure 3-3. Product-Market-Technology fit for deep tech products like AI-first SaaS and AIaaS

The framework for validating AI-first products based on the Product-Market-Technology validation principle will be explained in the next section.

Five-Step AI-First SaaS Validation Framework

In this section, we will learn how to perform Product-Market-Technology (P-M-T) validation of AI-first SaaS. The general steps of the framework are as follows:

1. Selecting the use case and industry

2. Brainstorming ideas

3. Measuring the feasibility

4. Recruiting early adopters

5. Validating Product-Market-Technology fit

After performing the five-step framework, we can build an AI-first SaaS startup.

The whole framework is depicted in the graph in Figure 3-4.

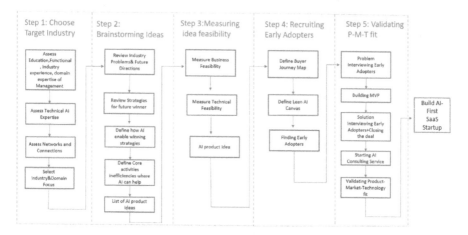

Figure 3-4. Five-step AI-first SaaS validation framework

The five-step validation framework is a method to validate the fit between the product, market, and technology for AI startups. This framework is based on my experience building over 20 B2B AI software and analyzing more than 30 successful AI startups. While not all steps need to be performed by AI startup founders, most will do some of the steps in the framework, eventually becoming patterns and best practices. By following this framework, AI startups can increase their chances of success by ensuring that their product fits the market and technology requirements.

Step 1: Choosing a Target Industry

The typical story of an AI startup is like this:

The founder of the AI startup is a subject matter expert (SME) in a particular industry with years of experience and insights into domain knowledge. They have an idea of automating inefficient, repeatable, and important tasks by transferring their knowledge and best practices gathered over decades into some form of artificial intelligence.

The SME can be specialist doctors, logistic experts, nutritionists, former general managers of hotel chains, former police officers, etc.

This SME then finds a co-founder with AI expertise, someone very technical with years, even decades, of experience building data analytics–, machine learning–, or operations research–based products. This AI expert often holds an academic credential such as MS or PhD in applied math, computer science, machine learning, artificial intelligence, or data science.

After a brief encounter, the SME and AI expert have an idea to productize the knowledge of the SME into a scalable smart product to automate one particular process in the industry.

In short: They want to build an AI-first SaaS.

The story after this can be different:

- Some AI startups will have good market traction and successfully go through an IPO process.

- Some AI startups don't even have a customer, but the technology is so good and acquired by a bigger tech company with a good valuation.

- Some AI startups will have very good market traction and technology and be acquired with staggering valuations by tech giants.

- Some AI startups will fail to make it to market (this is actually the majority,[3] but no one wants to talk about it, and no media wants to share it, so we rarely hear about it).

Whatever story will happen to your startup, it is important to remember that the first step to being successful in building an AI startup is that you need to **know yourself** (including your co-founder) and **choose the relevant target industry and domain with regard to your own experience, domain knowledge, and credentials**. Don't waste your (and anybody else's) time building an AI solution in an area where you are not the subject matter expert. AI is already complex enough to pull.

The starting point is to have an understanding of the strength of the SME and AI expert founders. They need to have

- *Functional expertise*: An experience in particular functions or positions, ideally at the managerial level.

- *Education*: A formal training in particular specializations. Ideally, an SME founder holds a bachelor's degree in the relevant field of study. The AI expert must have relevant technical education related to AI with published works and/or patents.

---

[3] www.forbes.com/sites/danielpitchford/2019/11/22/beating-the-statistics-what-are-the-markers-of-a-successful-ai-startup/?sh=5ae94edb7a2b

- *Industry experience:* An experience in a particular industry, ideally more than five years.

- *Domain knowledge:* Deep knowledge about a particular field in their industry.

- *Networks:* A connection with people relevant to the target market, AI talents, and investment. The founders of AI startups need to have very strong networks in their target market. Due to the complexity of AI, where the talents are rare and expensive, it also helps that they have a network of technical talents.

- *Domicile:* Select the first place to start the AI venture where the target markets are abundant to test the solution and then go global.

The detailed steps:

1. Tabulate the founders' education, functional expertise, industry experience, domain knowledge, and networks.

2. Mark the commonalities of industry and domain between SME and technical experts.

3. The commonalities of industry and domain could indicate that it is an ideal place. Pick an industry and domain focus.

CASE STUDY: CHOOSE THE TARGET INDUSTRY

This is the fictional case study of AI startup entrepreneurs Sarah and Carlos, how they understand themselves and their strengths and weaknesses, and how they choose their target industry.

Sarah, a British national, has extensive experience in the hospitality industry, with an education in hospitality management and a general MBA. She has over 25 years of experience working in top hotels and resorts worldwide, starting as a hotel staff member and climbing up the ladder with the last position as a hotel general manager in one of the leading hotel chains in London. After a career spanning the Asia Pacific and Europe, she returned to the United Kingdom and has lived in London for the last five years. She knows many hotel owners in the United Kingdom.

She knows the hotel business and the operation ins and outs. She witnessed the inefficiencies and problems in this industry and thinks there is a more efficient and automated way of handling it.

She knew that AI could disrupt and change the landscape of the hotel industry, and she wanted to be part of it. She wants to build an AI startup that makes a little dent in the industry but cannot do it alone. She would need a co-founder with technical know-how, especially in AI and data-related fields.

Sarah met Carlos, a Brazilian data scientist working as a data scientist in an airline in London. Carlos holds a PhD in computer science with a thesis in data analytics for supply chain management from a university in Germany. Carlos has been working in the aviation, retail, and hotel sectors building data analytics systems.

After a brief discussion, they knew that they could make something together. Their expertise, experiences, and networks are tabulated in the following (Figure 3-5).

	SME Founder	Technical AI Founder
Functional Expertise	Customer Service Manager, Logistic Managers, Hotel General Manager, Hotel CEO	Data Scientist, Lead Data Scientist
Education	BS Hotel Management (Switzerland), MBA (UK)	PhD Data Analytics Supply Chain Management (SCM) from university in Germany
Industry Experience	Hotel, F&B	Airline, Retail, Hotel
Domain Knowledge	Hospitality management, Customer Service	Call Center, ITSM, SCM
Networks-Customer	Hotels, F&B in France	Airline, Retail industries in Germany and France
Networks-AI related	Brother is AI lead @ Microsoft Research	Universities in Germany with strong Data Science program, Mentor in Data Science communities
Networks-Strategic M&A	Friends are FAANG regional executives and M&A firms	Wife is analyst @ VC firm
Domicile	London, United Kingdom	London, United Kingdom

Figure 3-5. Tabulated list of founder expertise, experience, and network

From the preceding figure, we can infer that Sarah has adequate quality to be the subject matter expert in the industry, as she has hands-on functional expertise and domain knowledge related to customer service, logistics, and general management in the hotel industry. She also has a good network in hospitality and investment and a brother working at Microsoft Research.

Carlos has the quality of an AI expert. He has developed data analytics systems for the airline, retail, and hotel sectors.

His domain knowledge encompasses call centers, ITSM (IT service management), and supply chain management. He doesn't have a strong network in the hospitality industry, but he has a solid network related to AI.

The commonalities (shaded in yellow) between Sarah and Carlos are both experienced in hospitalities, specifically the customer service domain. This is a potential industry and domain for them to explore. And the United Kingdom seems like the perfect place to start because it is the country with the number one hotel establishments in the world.[4]

Step 2: Brainstorming Ideas

After you select the industry and domain focus, it is time to brainstorm ideas for AI solutions (Figure 3-6).

Figure 3-6. Brainstorming ideas for AI solutions

The detailed steps:

1. Collect and study industry analysis and reports about the future of that specific industry.

2. Talk to people in the industry.

3. Learn about the future direction of the industry.

4. List down the future winning strategies of the industry.

5. Define the inefficiencies in the core activities of the industry that will become an obstacle.

6. Define how AI enables the winning strategy factors by removing the obstacles and impacting revenue, cost, legal risk, and customer satisfaction.

7. The output is the list of ideas with the highest possible impacts.

---

[4]www.nationmaster.com/nmx/ranking/number-of-hotels-establishments

CASE STUDY: BRAINSTORMING IDEAS

After a brief encounter, Sarah and Carlos decided to collect the industry analysis of the hospitality industry, including the current and future of the industry. They also managed to talk with their acquaintances in the industry.

Due to the pandemic and the proliferation of platforms such as Airbnb, they conclude that the hospitality industry in the future will be shaped around five important things:

1. *Health and safety:* Following the COVID pandemic, future consumers expect the hotel to provide them with better service related to safety, hygiene, and health procedures to get their trust and confidence.

2. *Wellness:* Consumers are traveling to get new experiences. They expect better wellness facilities such as a gym, organic foods, self-care, medical facilities, etc.

3. *Personalization and privacy:* Consumers expect a unique experience from the moment they book the hotel until they leave, without feeling that their privacy is violated.

4. *Seamless and quick service:* The future consumers are digital natives. They expect the whole experience to be easy and fast. Automation is the key to this. Moreover, automation can potentially improve operational efficiency while reducing costs.

5. *Cost-effectiveness:* The hotel consumer of the future expects better value for money.

The health, safety, and wellness aspects are the main proposition of hotels compared with options such as Airbnb.

The five aspects mentioned here serve as the basis for future winning strategies for the hospitality industry to win over the customer of the future, which can be summarized as the following four factors:

1. **Personalizing** the experience of the consumers

2. Enhancing **trust** by embracing better safety and health procedures

3. Improving the **speed** of the services

4. Giving more sensible **value for money**

So there are four factors of the future winning strategies of the hospitality industry: personalization, trust, speed, and value for money.

Next, Sarah and Carlos analyze the value chain of the hospitality industry, which is their target market. These are what they do:

1. Map the core activities and sub-activities in the value chain and winning strategies.

2. Describe the inefficiencies in each activity and how they will hinder the winning strategies.

3. Ideate the AI opportunities – how AI helps overcome inefficiencies – along with the activities.

4. Measure how the AI opportunity will impact the potential **revenue** improvement, **cost** reduction, **legal risk** mitigation, and improvement of **customer satisfaction**. We note the impacts by color (see Figure 3-7):

    a. *Cyan*: No impact

    b. *Yellow*: Medium impact

    c. *Green*: Significant impact

Core Activities	Inbound Logistics	Operations	Outbound Logistics	Marketing	Sales	Services
Sub-Activities	• Food&drink material supplies • Interior & exterior supplies • Room supplies	• Premises and Facilities maintenance • Staffing • Cooking	• Meal delivery • Room supplies delivery • Room service delivery	• Advertisement • Digital Marketing	• Public Communication • Networking • Booking	• Reception Service • Hall Service • Room Service • Customer complaints
Winning Strategies	• Speed • Value for money	• Speed • Value for money	• Speed	• Personalization	• Personalization • Speed • Value for money	• Value for money • Speed • Personalization • Trust
Inefficiencies as the obstacles for winning strategies	• Overstocking • Understocking	• Understaffing • Overstaffing	• Unsatisfying room condition • Incomplete supplies • Room cleaning taking too long time	• Ineffective campaign • Huge campaign cost vs ROI	• Low occupancy rate • Pricing is not satisfactory for customer	• 24/7 Receptionist and Security guard cost • Unanswered complaints • Slow response • Room availability
AI Opportunity	• Demand Forecasting • Automated Inventory purchase based on demand.	• Automated staff scheduling based on demand	• Automated Room supplies allocation.	• Automated marketing channel campaign based on season	• Hyper dynamic pricing based on actual events and trends • Upsell offerings based on past transactions	• Automated Concierge: Self-Check-In/Out, Loyalty and Surveillance
Revenue Impact						
Cost Impact						
Legal Risk Impact						

Figure 3-7. Value chain analysis of the hospitality industry

5. Focus on the AI solution ideas that potentially align with the winning strategy factors and have the highest impact on revenue, cost, legal risk, and customer satisfaction.

Based on the preceding five steps, the winning strategy factors and revenue, cost, risk, and customer satisfaction impact are analyzed (Figure 3-7). Sarah and Carlos conclude that there are two possible AI opportunities in hospitality customer services and sales:

a. *AI concierge SaaS*: Using face recognition and conversational artificial intelligence (chatbot) to check guests in/out, offer personalization and loyalty programs (upselling), order room service, and answer questions 24/7. This solution can also be connected with security and CCTV systems for 24/7 surveillance. This solution potentially impacts several strategic factors, such as personalization, service speed, and trust. This solution can also potentially impact revenue (by upselling and loyalty programs), save cost (by reducing the number of front offices and security guards), reduce risk (of theft and intruders), and increase customer satisfaction.

b. *AI hyperdynamic pricing and promotion SaaS*: Using AI to search social media automatically, news, and past customer data to predict travel trends and behavior of customers to display adaptive rates and promotions that maximize earning potential. The AI system can adjust prices and promotions to reflect the changes in demand. This solution can potentially impact strategic factors such as personalization and value for money for the customer. For the hospitality industry, this solution can potentially improve revenue. This is depicted in Figure 3-8.

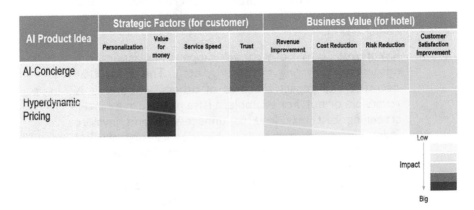

Figure 3-8. AI product ideas and their impact to strategic factors and business values

Step 3: Measuring Idea Feasibility

After we gathered the ideas from step 2, we will score them in a table and rank them. We will score them based on two important factors: business feasibility and technical feasibility. Our AI product idea feasibility uses four unique scores, each of which can be applied to any AI product idea. While the scoring criteria occasionally vary from startup to startup, the following scoring "rules of thumb" (all listed on a 1–4 scale) should serve as useful defaults for developing relative ratings for AI products.

In *business feasibility*, we must evaluate and score the ideas based on the following components:

- *Market size*: The potential market of our product
- *Usage frequency*: The frequency with which users interact with a given product or service
- *Market need*: The need for the product for the market along with their willingness to pay
- *Use case scalability*: Ease of applying the AI solution to different customers with minimum adjustment to AI models and business workflows
- *Competitiveness*: The number of competitors and the substitution in the industry

In *technology feasibility*, we must evaluate and score the ideas based on the following components:

- *The expected level of autonomy*: The level of an AI solution refers to its ability to automate different aspects of a task, such as providing insights, making decisions, or taking action.
- *Risk of error*: The risk of error may happen (misclassification, misdetection, wrong forecasting, etc.). The error that occurred will impact the lives of others, whether it is reversible or not. For example, a false positive in a cancer screening test may lead to unnecessary and invasive follow-up procedures such as biopsies, causing physical discomfort and anxiety for the patient. On the other hand, a false negative in the same test may result in cancer going undetected, leading to delayed treatment and potentially worse outcomes for the patient.

- *Infrastructure*: The complexity of infrastructure is needed. We need to evaluate whether the AI model inference needs to be real time and whether the AI model tends to drift.

- *Algorithmic complexity*: The complexity of an AI algorithm is influenced by the dynamics of the environment it operates in. In highly dynamic environments, like those encountered by self-driving cars, the algorithm is more likely to face long-tail and adversarial problems. Complex algorithms are susceptible to encountering edge cases, which necessitate the implementation of a human in the loop (HITL) mechanism to ensure accuracy and reliability. This approach involves human oversight and intervention in the decision-making process when required, providing an additional layer of safety and control.

- *Data feasibility*: The feasibility of how data will be acquired and annotated consists of the following:

  - *Data generation frequency*: The frequency of data generation refers to how often new data is produced in a balanced manner across different categories. In certain use cases, obtaining new data for a specific class can be challenging, making it important to carefully manage the data collection process to ensure a well-rounded dataset.

  - *Annotation skillset*: The skillset of the annotators. Some annotations can be performed by everyone (including the user themselves); in other cases, they must be annotated by specialists/experts.

After we score and rank them, we select the idea with the highest score.

The output of this step is the AI product idea.

In practice, the feasibility scoring might look something like the simple chart in the following (Figure 3-9).

Feasibility	No	Component	Idea 1	Idea 2	Idea 3
Business Feasibility	1	Market Size	2	3	2
	2	Usage Frequency	2	3	2
	3	Market Need	3	4	1
	4	Use Case Scalability	4	2	2
	5	Competitiveness	2	1	3
Technical Feasibility	6	Expected Level of Autonomy	1	4	1
	7	Risk of Error	2	4	1
	8	Infra complexity	3	4	1
	9	Algorithmic complexity (Minimum Algorithmic Performance)	4	4	1
	10	Data Feasibility	4	4	1
		Total	27	33	15

Figure 3-9. Idea feasibility scoring chart

We can assign weights to each component based on our goals and preferences. We can use multicriteria decision analysis methodologies, such as the Analytical Hierarchical Process (AHP) or Analytic Network Process (ANP), to determine each component's feasibility's relative importance or weight. However, this book assumes that all components have equal relative importance for simplicity.

The detailed framework of how to score the feasibility of each idea by business and technology aspects is explained in the following.

Business Feasibility: Market Size

The first feasibility to measure is the market size of the product. We need to ask these questions:

- *What is the total market value for this AI product?*
- *Can we sell this AI product to the local, regional, national, or global market? If yes, when?*

We differentiate the market coverage to sell the AI product as follows:

- *Local market:* Particular city where the founders operate
- *Regional market:* Larger geographical areas such as districts, provinces, and states
- *National market:* A country level
- *Global market:* International level

Measuring the market size using TAM, SAM, and SOM models is important. TAM, SAM, and SOM are acronyms representing different market subsets:

1. *TAM* – Total Addressable Market/Total Available Market: The total market demand for a product and/or services. TAM takes into account global and country-level market coverage.

2. *SAM* – Serviceable Addressable Market or Served Available Market: The segment of TAM within the company's geographical reach. SAM takes into account regional and national market coverage.

3. *SOM* – Serviceable Obtainable Market or Share of Market: This is the portion of SAM that can be realistically captured after considering other factors, such as

   - Competitor market share

   - Technology infrastructure readiness such as Internet coverage

Steps to calculate TAM-SAM-SOM:

1. Identify the target market of your product.

2. Calculating TAM (Total Available Market):

   - Get primary research (survey, questionnaire, etc.) and/or secondary research (statistics from Statista, industry analysis, news).

   - Estimate the available customers in the whole country at least.

3. Calculating SAM (Serviceable Available Market):

   - Based on TAM, estimate the number of customers that are possible to reach. This can be on the local and regional levels.

4. Calculating SOM (Serviceable Obtainable Market):

   - Based on SAM, minus the share market of the competitors and other factors (i.e., Internet availability and others), estimate the number of customers that are possible to reach.

SOM is the most realistic number. Therefore, we must score the relative market size based on SOM on the following scale:

- *1*: SOM < $10M
- 2: SOM > $10M and < $60M
- 3: SOM > $60M and < $100M
- 4: SOM > $100M

For B2B AI-first SaaS, unless you live in a highly populated country like the United States, China, Indonesia, or India, it is important to ensure that the product can be marketed on a regional to global scale to get a good market size (above 100 million SOM).

Business Feasibility: Usage Frequency

For AI-first SaaS, it is also important to estimate the usage frequency of the product. The frequency users interact with the product tends to correlate with good business potential. Something that becomes a part of regular practice with a large swath of corporates has an opportunity to build a big business. The usage score can be estimated as follows:

- *1* – One-time/scarce usage: An AI used only once every couple of years. An example is the AI solution to forecast the total recoverable oil reserve volumes, used only before an oil exploration project that happens once every several years.

- 2 – Low-frequency usage: An AI solution used every few months. An example is an AI solution recommending the best place to open a new shop, which only happens once every several months.

- 3 – Medium-frequency usage: An AI solution used every couple of weeks. An example is AI for evaluating tender documents, which is only used every few weeks when there is a new tender.

- 4 – High-frequency usage: An AI solution is used several times daily. A biometrics-based eKYC solution for identity verification is an example of an AI solution used several times per day.

Business Feasibility: Market Need

Market need is a very important aspect of any product development.

These are questions we need to ask ourselves related to market needs:

- *Is this AI solution solving a customer problem by supporting, augmenting, or automating some of their tasks?*
- *How big is the problem for customers?*
- *Would they pay for this?*
- *Would they pre-order even before this product is available?*

For any AI product idea, score market needs on the following scale:

- *1*: Lowest evidence of market need (i.e., less than 10% of respondents liked the idea, let alone paying for it)
- *2*: Lower-middle evidence of market need (i.e., more than 50% of respondents said the idea is valid and worth paying for)
- *3*: Upper-middle evidence of market need (i.e., more than 80% of respondents said the idea is valid and worth paying for)
- *4*: Highest evidence of market need (i.e., more than 95% of respondents said the idea is valid and worth paying for)

Note that the 1–4 score is relative to the evidence of market need. This means that you will likely need to calibrate the market need of three to five AI product ideas before having a sense of what a "4" is and what a "1" is.

The relative market need can be estimated from several efforts:

- *Survey*: Questionnaire or questions directed toward a specific audience about the AI product idea. Services like Proved and MetaSurvey can help with a questionnaire and market validation.
- *Informal interview*: Interviewing several people in the industry over coffee or casual meetings/phone calls.
- *Landing and pre-order page test*: The AI product idea definition is written into the brochure and landing page with contact and pre-order form. We can measure the interest level of the potential customer by analyzing the number of visitors willing to share their contacts and

even pre-order the solution. We can use landing page makers like Launchrock and Unbounce to quickly create a landing page and forms and perform A/B testing.

- *Crowdfunding*: A crowdfunding marketplace such as Kickstarter is a platform to raise money to finance a new product or venture. But this platform can also gauge interest in the product and make the community a part of the creation process. We can create a video and sales pitch of the product to attract the attention and interest of the backers who support the product from idea to launch.

Business Feasibility: Use Case Scalability

We must select an AI use case that can be scaled easily, meaning it can be deployed seamlessly to different customers with minimal changes and reconfiguration. The less scalable the use case, the more likely the business model will be into consulting instead of SaaS.

These are questions we need to ask ourselves related to use case scalability:

- *Can this AI solution be deployed to different customers without adjusting the AI models and workflow (configurable)?*

- *Can the customer adjust the AI models and workflow themselves without our involvement by just following documentation (easy to use)?*

- *Do we need an AI expert to customize the AI models and workflow for customers (adaptable)?*

Two aspects affect the AI use case scalability:

1. *Data variation*: The variation of the input data. Retail shelf image recognition is an example of an AI use case with high data variation. Every company must train different data. For example, cosmetics retailers will have a different dataset from liquor retailers. Consequently, we cannot have only one AI model to serve all the customers. We must have different AI models for different customers.

2. *Workflow variation*: The workflow for a specific task, such as route optimization algorithms (vehicle route planning), can vary between companies. These variations are influenced by factors such as vehicle type, the presence of single or multiple depots, and constraints like visitation and goods restrictions. As a result, each company may have a unique workflow tailored to its specific needs and operational requirements.

For any AI product idea, score the use case scalability as in the following:

- *1* – high data variation and high workflow variation: An example use case is AI-based inverse design. AI-based inverse design is an AI optimization method of designing a new solution (materials, drugs, optical systems, etc.) by specifying the desired performance. The object to be designed differs from company to company, and the workflow is also different.

- *2* – high data variation and low workflow variation: The example use case is retail shelf data recognition. The dataset of retail SKU (stock keeping unit) to be trained differs from company to company, with a relatively similar workflow.

- *3* – low data variation and high workflow variation. The example use case is supply chain forecasting and optimization. The dataset used among customers is relatively similar, but every company has different workflows.

- *4* – low data variation and low workflow variation: The example use case is fingerprint recognition. One fingerprint dataset can be used for different customers without too much workflow reconfiguration.

Business Feasibility: Competitiveness

We need to understand the competitive and substitution landscape of our AI solution. We ask the following questions:

- *Are there other companies (AI or not AI) satisfying the same customer need?*

- *Can a human do the tasks performed by AI with less cost?*

For any AI product idea, score the competitiveness on the following scale:

- *1*: Very competitive market regionally (more than 15 direct and indirect competitors, including humans)

- 2: Competitive market (between 10 and 15 direct and indirect competitors, including humans)

- 3: Medium competitive market (between five and ten direct and indirect competitors, including humans)

- 4: Low competitive market (fewer than five direct and indirect competitors, including humans)

Technical Feasibility: Expected Level of Autonomy

The AI use case feasibility depends on the level of autonomy expected.

A fully autonomous AI system means that the AI can fully generate insight, decisions, and actions independently without human intervention.

We need to ask these questions:

- *Is AI augmenting humans or fully replacing humans?*

- *What do we expect AI to do for us autonomously?*

In the previous chapter, we learned that the AI system is ideally based on the OODA (Observe-Orient-Decide-Act) principle, which means we can expect AI to automatically provide us (see Figure 3-10) with

- *Structured data*: AI transforms unstructured data into structured data autonomously. Examples are most computer vision applications such as vehicle counting, people counting, crowd detection, etc.

- *Insights*: An AI system that provides us with prediction and reasoning without our intervention. An example is a prediction of which machine will break down.

- *Decisions*: An AI system that decides for us. For example, an AI system gives us the most optimal production machinery allocation and schedule based on some insights, that is, RUL (Remaining Useful Life) prediction, demand forecast, etc.

- *Actions*: An AI system that acts for us. This AI system is the most complete and can provide insights and decisions. The example use case is the fully autonomous self-driving car.

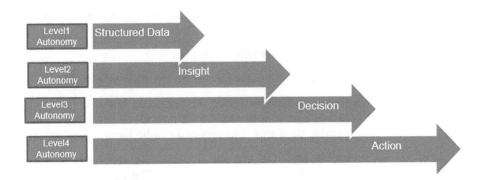

Figure 3-10. Idea Feasibility Scoring Chart

For any AI product idea, score the expected level of autonomy on the following scale:

- *1*: AI is expected to do an action autonomously (level 4 autonomy).

- *2*: AI is expected to decide autonomously (level 3 autonomy).

- *3*: AI is expected to give insights autonomously (level 2 autonomy).

- *4*: AI is expected to provide us with structured data autonomously (level 1 autonomy).

Technical Feasibility: Risk of Error

The risk of error refers to the potential negative outcomes resulting from an AI solution's failure to accurately perform its task, such as making a prediction. The consequences of AI failure can range from minor, insignificant impacts to severe, life-threatening situations, depending on the application and context in which the AI system is used.

You need to ask these questions to assess the risk of error:

- *How big is the impact of the wrong automated or suggested decision resulting from our AI solution?*

- *Is the decision suggested or automated by AI reversible or not?*

A high-impact decision means that if the AI wrongly makes or suggests a decision, there will be financial loss or loss of life.

An irreversible decision means that once the decision is made, there is no return point.

Autonomous car AI is an example of an AI application that automates high-impact and irreversible decisions.

AI is best applied to automate reversible decisions.

For any AI product idea, score the risk of error on the following scale:

- *1* – irreversible and high impact: An example is AI to predict whether a patient has cancer or not. Once the AI makes a mistake, then the consequence can be fatal.

- *2* – irreversible and low impact: An example is AI to predict where and to whom to display ads. The decision to display ads to a particular person is not reversible, but the impact is relatively small.

- *3* – reversible and high impact: An example is AI to recommend which stock to pick. Wrong AI recommendations can potentially result in financial loss, but stock price can change direction anytime; hence, it is reversible.

- *4* – reversible and low impact: An example is AI to check and improve our grammar. It is reversible because humans can still check and edit it. Grammar mistakes also have a relatively low impact.

Technical Feasibility: Algorithmic Complexity

We must pick a use case for an AI solution where the algorithmic complexity is still sensible to be implemented and operationalized efficiently. There are two main challenging AI (especially machine learning) use cases:

- *Adversarial use case*: The use case where a deliberate attack to exploit the machine learning weakness is expected. An example is the face spoof detection system, where the spoofer tries their best to imitate legitimate face patterns to avoid being detected as spoof images.

- *Edge case–prone use case*: The use case where the possibility of an edge case is high. An edge case is a problem or situation that occurs only at an extreme (maximum or minimum) operating condition. Usually, this happens because the machine learning system operates in a dynamic and unpredictable environment. An example is object detection for self-driving AI systems, where the edge case possibilities are high due to the dynamic environment on the road.

The more your AI use case tends to be adversarial and have a high risk of an edge case, the more complex your AI algorithm would be.

You need to ask these questions to assess the algorithm complexity:

- *Will any of the users deliberately trick the AI algorithm?*
- *Is the environment where the AI operates dynamic?*
- *Can we list all possible anomalies of data or behavior of the environment where the AI operates?*

When selecting a use case for AI implementation, choosing one with minimal conflicting interests and infrequent, complex situations is advisable. Conflicting interests refer to situations where multiple objectives or goals are competing against each other, making it challenging to achieve an optimal solution. This involves avoiding adversarial scenarios and edge cases that could make developing a reliable AI model difficult. To evaluate the algorithmic complexity of any AI product idea, consider using a scoring scale, such as the following one:

- *1 – high edge cases and high adversity:* An example is facial spoof detection to detect whether a selfie face is a live human or a spoof. The AI system must handle different spoofing attacks suck as a print attack (face printed on paper), replay attack (face recorded on video), and 3D mask attack. There are also many edge cases as there are almost limitless possibilities of how users will take selfie pictures (Figure 3-11).

Real face   Replay attack   Prints attack   3D Mask attack

Figure 3-11. Examples of spoof face attacks (images courtesy of the International Journal of Internet, Broadcasting, and Communication)

- *2 – high edge cases and low adversity:* An example is AI to detect objects on the road for autonomous driving. The road is very dynamic, and there are many unexpected objects on the road (see Figure 3-12), but it is not a deliberate attack.

Figure 3-12. Edge case example on the road (image courtesy of Cognata ltd)

- *3* – low edge cases and high adversity: An example is AI to predict email spam. The bad guys are deliberately finding a way to mimic legitimate emails. Still, there is no general edge case because the input is only text or numbers with limited length.

- *4* – low edge cases and low adversity: An example is AI for recommendation systems. There are almost no edge cases and adversarial attacks for this use case.

Technical Feasibility: Infrastructure Complexity

Building an AI product is not only about algorithms but also about the infrastructure. AI infrastructure depends on memory, storage, security, and network requirements. Network requirements must be carefully planned, especially for embedded or edge devices. A well-designed infrastructure is crucial for successful AI implementation.

Infrastructure complexity depends on the expected inference speed and AI model consistency.

The expected inference speed refers to the anticipated amount of time it takes for an AI system to generate a prediction or decision. It is differentiated by

- *Batch inference*: The process of generating inference (predictions, recognition) on a batch of observations. The batch jobs are typically generated on some recurring schedule (i.e., hourly, daily, weekly).

- *Real-time/online inference*: The process of generating inference within milliseconds upon request.

Model consistency is the tendency of AI model performance to degrade due to *concept* or *data drift*:

- *Concept drift* is a type of *model drift* where the properties of the dependent variable change. An example is creditworthiness scoring. The *creditworthy person* two decades ago may be different from the *creditworthy person* now. *Concept drift* is prone to dynamic and seasonal use cases such as retail, ecommerce, finance, advertising, and marketing.

- *Data drift* is a type of *model drift* where the properties of the independent variable change. *Data drift* includes changes in the data due to seasonality, a change in sensor sensitivity, etc.

We need to ask these questions to assess the infrastructure complexity of a particular use case:

- *How fast do we expect the AI to return the result to us?*
- *What factors are critical for AI infrastructure (memory, storage, security, and network)?*
- *How fast is the AI model degrades?*

Dealing with model drift and inference speed would be related to the infrastructure architecture. The faster the expected inference speed, the more we must prepare for the infrastructure to deal with a large amount of data in a very short timeframe.

The faster the AI model degrades, the more we must prepare the model reannotation, retraining, and redeployment infrastructure.

For any AI product idea, score the infrastructure complexity on the following scale:

- *1* – real-time inference and low model consistency (high rate of concept and data drift): The example use case is fraud detection, where fraud must be notified and handled in seconds. Fraud detection is also prone to concept drift because the behavior of the fraudster changes quickly over time.

- *2* – batch inference and low model consistency (high rate of concept and data drift): The example use case is sales lead forecasting. The inference can be performed in batches, but the model consistency is low because the behavior of the customers and market change rapidly due to seasonality and dynamic business conditions.

- *3* – real-time inference and high model consistency (low rate of concept and data drift): The example use case is the license plate recognition system for the automated gates. The recognition must be performed in a split second, but the drift is unlikely because the license plate does not change visually overtime.

- *4* – batch inference and high model consistency (low rate of concept and data drift): An example is a store visual merchandising analyzer based on visitor behavior. The inference can be performed in batches, and store visitor behavior (dwelling, trajectory) does not change quickly overtime.

Technical Feasibility: Data Feasibility

Data is the fuel for AI, especially the one based on machine learning systems. Therefore, it is crucial for the feasibility of the AI solution.

For most of the AI use cases based on supervised machine learning, data annotation skillset and data availability are very important aspects that will contribute to the data feasibility.

Data annotation skillset is the data annotation skillset needed to make sure that the AI model has valid and trusted labels. Certain use cases in machine learning may require experts to label the data, such as medical image data that requires specialist doctors to label it accurately. Similarly, plant disease data should be labeled by individuals with expertise in plant pathology, while those with expertise in marine biology should label data on the health of reefs. The involvement of domain experts in the data labeling process is important to ensure that the labeled data is accurate and reflects the nuances of the specific domain. This is particularly critical in medicine and environmental science domains, where mislabeling data can have serious consequences.

In some other use cases, even the user can annotate themselves in an *active learning* mechanism, where the AI system can query the user in case of doubt (Figure 3-13).

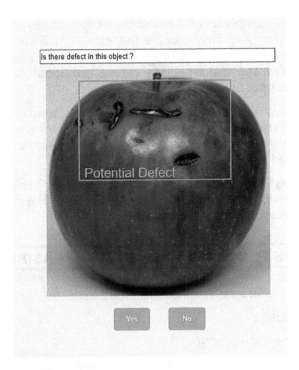

Is there defect in this object ?

Potential Defect

Yes   No

Figure 3-13. Active learning system querying the user to improve

Data availability is how often new data is generated. Depending on the use cases, new data with different classes can be generated every hour, day, week, or even month.

To understand more about data feasibility, we need to ask these questions:

- *Do we need an expert to annotate the new data?*
- *Is the new data coming every hour, day, week, or month?*
- *Do we have abundant data for initial training?*
- *Do we need to create our dataset synthetically?*

For any AI product idea, score the data feasibility on the following scale:

- *1 – low availability of data and needs a specialist to annotate: The example use case is rare cancer detection based on the medical image. We need a specialist doctor to annotate the image, and the new medical data is not easy to get.*

- 2 – low availability of data and the user or any layperson can annotate: The example use case is face spoofing detection. Anyone can easily differentiate between spoofed and real faces, but getting real spoof data is difficult because it is not common.

- 3 – high availability of data and needs a specialist to annotate: The example use case is credit scoring, where the data is abundant but needs to be annotated by a trained credit analyst.

- 4 – high availability of data and the user or any layperson can annotate: An example is vehicle counting. The data is abundant, and anyone can annotate.

CASE STUDY: MEASURING IDEA FEASIBILITY

After Sarah and Carlos selected two ideas for the AI product:

1. AI concierge

2. AI hyperdynamic pricing

it is time to estimate the feasibility. There are two important aspects of feasibility: business and technical feasibility. Estimating business feasibility is relatively trivial, and any entrepreneur or product manager worth their salt can do this without many difficulties, but estimating technical feasibility is quite challenging for a non-technical person. Still, we can use the OODA loop paradigm to simplify the process:

1. Break down the AI product idea into OODA loop phases: Observe-Orient-Decide-Act.

2. In each OODA phase, determine the tasks that will be automated.

3. Describe all the AI models to enable automation in step 2.

4. Analyze the technical feasibility of all AI models in step 3 based on

- Algorithmic complexity

- Data availability

- Infrastructure complexity

- Risk of errors

Let's look at this example. The OODA loop and AI model design for AI concierge are as follows (Figure 3-14).

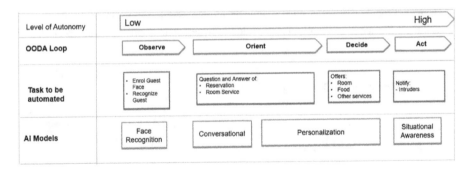

Figure 3-14. AI concierge OODA loop and its AI models

The AI concierge solution will consist of three AI models:

- *Face recognition:* To verify and authenticate the guests based on facial biometric features

- *Conversational:* To have a meaningful conversation about reservation and services with the guest

- *Situational awareness:* To analyze the behavior and recognize unauthorized visitors

And here are the OODA loop and AI model design for AI hyperdynamic pricing (Figure 3-15).

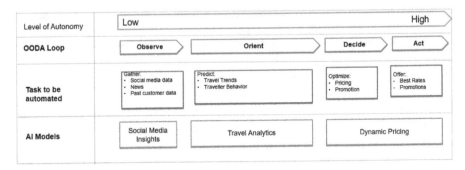

Figure 3-15. AI hyperdynamic pricing OODA loop and its AI model

The AI hyperdynamic pricing solution will consist of three AI models:

- *Social media insights:* To get insights about the latest travel trends and events from social media and news media

- *Travel analytics:* To predict the traveler's behavior

- *Dynamic pricing:* To decide the best rate and promotion to offer to guests

Based on the AI models of each preceding AI idea, Sarah and Carlos estimate the technical feasibility of the AI concierge and AI hyperdynamic pricing solutions. They also estimate the business feasibility.

The following are the feasibility study scores of the two ideas based on the feasibility scoring framework explained (Figure 3-16).

Feasibility	No	Component	AI Concierge	AI Hyperdynamic pricing
Business Feasibility	1	Market Size	2	2
	2	Usage Frequency	1	1
	3	Market Need	3	2
	4	Use Case Scalability	4	4
Technical Feasibility	5	Competitiveness	4	4
	6	Expected Level of Autonomy	1	1
	7	Risk of Error	3	1
	8	Infra complexity	3	1
	9	Algorithmic complexity (Minimum Algorithmic Performance)	1	4
	10	Data Feasibility	2	3
		Total	**24**	**23**

Figure 3-16. Feasibility scores of two AI ideas

As the AI concierge solution has a better feasibility score, Sarah and Carlos choose the AI concierge as the AI product they want to develop.

Step 4: Recruiting Early Adopters

After measuring the feasibility of and scoring the ideas, we get one idea for an AI product. The next step is to find and recruit early adopters willing to buy our AI solution (see Figure 3-17).

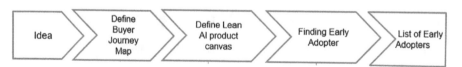

Figure 3-17. Recruiting early adopters

We need to recruit and close the commercial deal with the early adopter for four reasons:

1. To validate the problem and its significance
2. To acquire datasets
3. To validate whether AI can solve the problem or not
4. To validate whether anyone is willing to pay for the AI solution

The steps for recruiting early adopters are as follows:

1. We have identified an inefficiency in one activity in the value chain in a particular industry, and automated decision-making would solve the problem.

2. We then define a buyer journey map to hypothesize how the buyers decide our AI solution is perfect for them.

   The goal is to understand how the product would be bought and decided, along with the buyer type. In this step, do not think about systematizing the buyer journey first. We need to think from the buyer's perspective. The steps are as follows:

   a. Determine three types of buyers:

      i. *The economic buyer (EB)*: This buyer is concerned with ROI. An example is the CFO, the finance manager, because they make financial decisions.

      ii. *The user buyer (UB)*: Concerned with the user experience and day-to-day impact.

      iii. *The technical buyer (TB)*: Concerned with security, interoperability, and robustness. An example is IT managers and developers.

   b. Describe the buying journey from Need-Initial Awareness-Research-Comparison-Selection and Purchase-User Experience.

3. We define the Lean AI product canvas (Figure 3-18) to summarize the main idea of how our AI solution can solve the problem of our customers based on a different persona.

Figure 3-18. Lean AI product canvas template

We can write the following elevator pitch based on this Lean AI product canvas and extend it to the landing page:

For [target customers] on the [value chain] who are dissatisfied with inefficiencies of [the current practice/staff/tool). Our product is a [AI product] that can [automate/ augment] the [thing that is inefficient or cumbersome]. Our product has [benefits/ outcome] for [personas].

Based on the clearer target customers, we can also build a list of early adopters and contact them through emails.

CASE STUDY: RECRUITING EARLY ADOPTERS

Sarah and Carlos decided that *AI concierge SaaS* is an idea that has a good business and technical sensibility.

The next step is that they will define a buyer journey map to help them target potential early adopters.

They define three types of buyers and their motivations (see Table 3-1).

Table 3-1. Buyer Type and Their Motivation

Buyer Type	Persona	Motivation
Economic	• Procurement manager • Service manager • General manager	• ROI of AI concierge
User	• Guest • Service manager • Security	• Intuitive • Quick onboarding • Responsive
Technical	• IT manager • Maintenance manager	• Easy to integrate with web cams and CCTVs • Easy to integrate with the NFC door lock system • Easy to integrate with the hotel reservation system

Based on the economic buyers, they brainstorm the buying journey of the AI concierge solution (Figure 3-19).

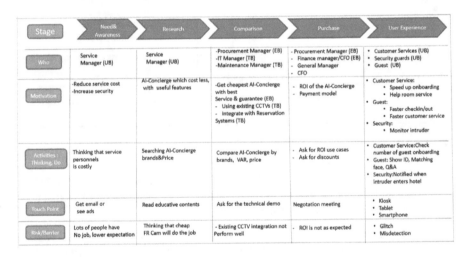

Figure 3-19. Buying journey of AI concierge

After analyzing the buying journey and understanding the motivations of each type of buyer, Sarah and Carlos are now preparing a one-page Lean AI product canvas to summarize the value and persona of the AI product to be developed (AI concierge SaaS; see Figure 3-20).

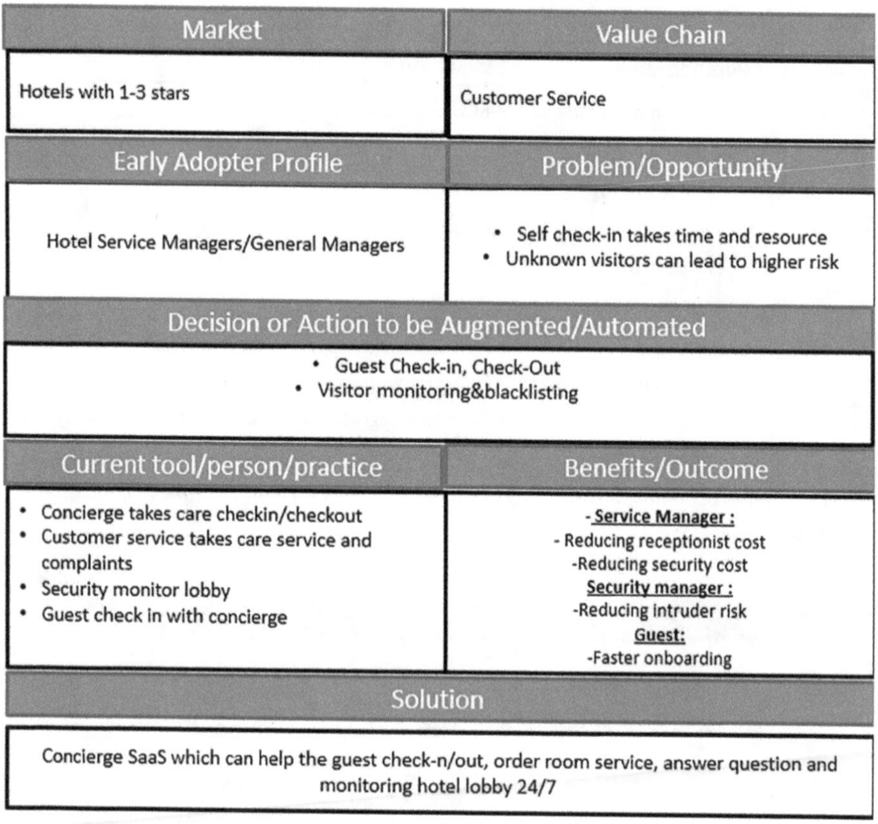

Market	Value Chain
Hotels with 1-3 stars	Customer Service

Early Adopter Profile	Problem/Opportunity
Hotel Service Managers/General Managers	• Self check-in takes time and resource • Unknown visitors can lead to higher risk

Decision or Action to be Augmented/Automated
• Guest Check-in, Check-Out • Visitor monitoring&blacklisting

Current tool/person/practice	Benefits/Outcome
• Concierge takes care checkin/checkout • Customer service takes care service and complaints • Security monitor lobby • Guest check in with concierge	- **Service Manager :** - Reducing receptionist cost -Reducing security cost **Security manager :** -Reducing intruder risk **Guest:** -Faster onboarding

Solution
Concierge SaaS which can help the guest check-n/out, order room service, answer question and monitoring hotel lobby 24/7

Figure 3-20. Lean canvas for AI concierge

The Lean AI canvas is a strategic document that summarizes the problems that the AI solves for a particular persona by automating or augmenting some tasks. Then it describes the product elevator pitch as follows:

For **hotel service managers** on the customer service who are dissatisfied with **inefficiencies of the check-in process** that must be **through concierges**. Our product is an **AI concierge** that **can automate check-in, checkout, room service, and lobby monitoring**. Our product can **reduce costs for guest receptions and security**.

From here, Sarah and Carlos can write a website landing page and start copywriting that tests the AI concierge initial market (Figure 3-21).

Figure 3-21. AI concierge SaaS

The next important step is Sarah, as someone with experience and networks in the hospitality industry, starts cold-calling her ex-colleagues and contacts to offer and sell them the idea.

She must list the potential early adopters and contact them individually to schedule a problem interview.

Step 5: Validating Product-Market-Technology Fit

The founder contacted a list of potential early adopters in the previous step. The next steps are

1. Conducting problem interviews with the early adopters to understand more about their problem.

   The problem interview will consist of several important topics:

   - *Business drivers*: The objects and metrics of the potential users.

   - *Problem*: The current tasks are costly, inefficient, and tedious.

   - *Decision-maker and user*: The decision-maker of the product who will decide on the product purchase and the user who will use the product.

   - *Business process*: The current process consists of multiple tasks that can be automated.

- *Data*: The data required to accomplish the user's specific tasks.

- *Technology landscape*: The technology used in the industry is related to users' tasks.

2. Building an AI Minimum Viable Product to solve the problem. We need to build a product with the Minimum Algorithmic Performancee (MAP) required by early adopters. The objective is to develop an algorithm that can be trained on a broader range of production data without overfitting while simultaneously satisfying the needs of early adopters in terms of performance metrics, such as accuracy, F1 score, precision, and recall. Additionally, the algorithm must be optimal in terms of *compute* and *storage* based on the specific requirements of the task at hand. By meeting these criteria, the algorithm will be better equipped to handle a wider range of data and produce more accurate and reliable results.

3. Conducting solution interviews by showing them how we can solve their problem using our AI solution and then asking them if they would pay for our solution and close the deal. These are the steps to do a solution interview:

   - *Categorize the prospects*: Economic, user, and technical buyers

   - *Verbalize the value*: Reducing cost, improving revenue, improving customer satisfaction, etc.

   - Showing the AI MVP

   - Estimating the timeline for when the product is ready for use

   - Stating the price of customizing the AI solution for the early adopters

   - Closing the deal

4. If we have several paying customers, we can start an *AI consulting service* to get more use cases, data, and best practices and make it into a framework.

5. Validating Product-Market-Technology fit. When we have enough customers and use cases and can solve their problems using state-of-the-art AI algorithms and infrastructure, then we have Product-Market-Technology fit.

6. Build an AI startup. We can productize our AI solution framework into Software as a Service, which can scale to a bigger market (Figure 3-22).

Figure 3-22. Validating Product-Market-Technology fit

CASE STUDY: VALIDATING PRODUCT-MARKET-TECHNOLOGY FIT

After Sarah and Carlos listed the potential early adopters and contacted them, several early adopters were interested in being interviewed by them. The early adopters come from diverse backgrounds related to hotel services, namely, customer service managers, security managers, and general managers.

They interview and prepare the following questions (Figure 3-23).

Topic	Sample questions
Business Drivers	What is your objective and KPI ?
Problem	How do you feel about current situation related with your reception service ? And security in the lobby?
	Do you have specific problem ?
	What is your top three problems? Who are impacted ?
	How much would you willing to pay external contractor to solve the problem?
	How do you currently solve the problem? Competitors?
	If you have a magic wand, how would you solve this problem?
Decision making	Who is involved in decision making?
	What is the process of buying in your company, how long is the process?
Business process	• What is the process of your reception services ? • What is the process of room services? • What is the process of guarding the lobby and hotel perimeters?
Data	• What is data required in verifying guest identity? • What is data required to answer guest's room service queries?
Technology landscape	• What technology do you use for your reception services ? • What technology do you use for your room services ? • What technology do you use for your monitoring lobby entrance ?

Figure 3-23. Questions for early adopters

After understanding the problems better and getting the data required from the early adopters, Carlos builds the AI MVP (Minimum Viable Product) of the AI concierge, which can satisfy the users' needs with minimum algorithmic performance.

Then they invite the early adopters to do solution interviews to see if their MVP is sufficiently valuable for their early adopters.

The most important thing is to ask the early adopters if they are willing to pay for the AI solution. If Sarah and Carlos get several paying early adopters, their AI solution market will be validated.

The next step to expand from this is to create an AI consulting firm that will custom-build AI concierge software for customers.

When they understand the market better and have enough paying customers, they can

productize the consulting service by creating AI-first SaaS.

Conclusion

AI-first SaaS is the next evolution of SaaS. The goal is AI-first SaaS is not only to make workflow efficient but also to augment human intelligence. With the technical complexity involved in AI product development, to increase the possibility of the AI startup being successful, we must analyze the business and technical feasibilities of the AI product thoroughly. Then we must find early adopters willing to work with us to improve the AI solution, providing us with the required data and direction. It is strongly advised that AI startups must start their journey from a service consulting firm to have a rich collection of data and possible edge cases that will be made into a solid solution framework.

Only after productizing our solution framework into software can we scale our AI solution as an AI-first SaaS.

Key Takeaways

- AI-first SaaS can augment human intelligence. This is the main advantage of AI-first SaaS compared with the previous generation of SaaS.

- The main difference between AI-powered SaaS and AI-first SaaS is that the former only infuses intelligence into the workflow, while AI-first SaaS is built with AI at its core. This means AI-first SaaS cannot operate without AI.

- The main benefits of adopting AI-first SaaS for companies are improving efficiency and scalability. But it is also an important step toward becoming an AI-first company.

- AI as a Service (AIaaS) is another category of AI products. The main difference from AI-first SaaS is that AIaaS targets developers and data scientists, while AI-first SaaS targets end users.

- When building a SaaS product, it is crucial to target a specific market with a clear value proposition and to have a good understanding of the competitive landscape. One should not assume that the user will want to change their existing workflow and should seek feedback from users early on, especially from early adopters. Additionally, it is important to be a consultant first and foremost in order to truly understand the needs and pain points of the target market.

- AI is a deep tech product where the technical complexity needs to be validated against the business value. The Product-Market-Technology fit is crucial.

- The Product-Market-Technology fit validation to validate the AI product idea framework consists of five core steps:

  - Selecting the use case and industry

  - Brainstorming ideas

  - Measuring the feasibility

  - Recruiting early adopters

  - Validating Product-Market-Technology fit

Product-Market Validation for AI as a Service (AIaaS)

The previous chapter taught us how to validate AI-first SaaS with the business user as the target market. In this chapter, we will learn more about AI as a Service (AIaaS), which targets the developers' market, and how to validate its market.

Building AIaaS is a natural business expansion from AI-first SaaS. The main idea is to break down the AI models used in our AI-first SaaS, productize them, and sell them separately to developers as APIs or SDKs.

Building AIaaS is easier if we have to build AI-first SaaS first because we would use our AI models and tools daily and become familiar with them — as the saying goes, "eating our own dog food."

© Adhiguna Mahendra 2023
A. Mahendra, *AI Startup Strategy*, https://doi.org/10.1007/978-1-4842-9502-1_4

Aside from AI models, we can also externalize our AI development platform and sell it to data scientists or developers to create and serve their own AI models.

Building and selling AIaaS enables us to have additional revenue and expand our markets.

What Is AIaaS and a Developer-Centric Product

The cloud services such as SaaS, IaaS, and PaaS have been used effectively by enterprises. With as a Service models, we can shift to pay per use by subscription, which reduces spending and speeds up the implementation process. Artificial intelligence models such as machine learning, rule-based systems, and decision optimization can also be sold as a Service, or AIaaS (AI as a Service). AIaaS companies provide a cost-effective solution for businesses willing to use and invest in AI because AI as a Service providers maintain the AI infrastructure and model updates.

AIaaS is one of the business models specifically targeting the technical audience market, such as developers and data scientists, because the person who will implement and use AI solutions is the technical person. AIaaS can be categorized as a developer-centric product, meaning that the whole marketing strategy and experience design, from documentation to dashboard, must primarily satisfy the developer's need.

Definition of AIaaS and B2D

AIaaS is short for Artificial Intelligence as a Service and refers to companies that offer off-the-shelf AI solutions from third-party vendors. Developing and maintaining AI is always costly and timely, and it needs a trained AI specialist with experience in AI operationalization, such as ModelOps and MLOps. Therefore, it is not a feasible option for many startups/companies. Developers can consume and integrate AI as an API, SDK, or development platform.

Due to its nature of augmenting intelligent features of a software product, the main target of AIaaS is developers and data scientists. Marketing to developers is referred to as B2D, or business to developer. The B2D or business-to-developer sector is a category that caters primarily to people who work with code (and data), software/hardware developers and data scientists specifically. In other words, those folks who spend their time writing programs for computers make up the main target audience. The main goal is to give developers more focus on the product they're creating by providing them with ready-to-use tools and systems. So, in short, B2D companies build a product targeted to developers and software development companies (developer-centric products).

Some examples of a developer-centric product are

- *API*: The API (Application Programming Interface) is an easy-to-use, customer-friendly interface that allows the developer to integrate their software with other applications and hardware systems. Examples of APIs are Stripe (payment), QuikBlox (video chat), Elsa (speech recognition), and Wunderground (weather data).

- *SDK*: The Software Development Kit (SDK) is a set of tools and programs used by developers to create applications for specific platforms. These include libraries, documentation, code samples, etc., all in one place. Examples of SDKs are FaceTec (liveness detection) and Identifai (KYC).

- *Software platform*: An end-to-end software tool to create and deploy a particular application. Examples are machine learning development platforms such as Amazon Sagemaker, Google Cloud Machine Learning, Azure Machine Learning, and IBM Watson and game development platforms such as Unity and Unreal.

- *Software tool*: A software tool that helps developers and data scientists in particular areas. Examples are Fiddler AI (machine learning monitoring), OctoML (machine learning deployment), and Stackify (performance monitoring).

- *Software framework*: Templates that provide the foundation for developing software applications. They use shared resources such as libraries and image files as one package and do everything many developers need simultaneously. Examples are Firebase ML Kit (machine learning for mobile), Rasa (conversational AI engine), and PyTorch (deep learning development).

Difference Between B2B and B2D

In the previous chapter, we discussed AI-first SaaS. The main target market is business (B2B model). The B2B model has the following characteristics:

- Selling directly to businesses as end customers.

- The direct buyers are

  - *Economic buyer*: CFO, COO, CEO, finance managers

  - *User buyer*: Operational end users

  - *Technical buyer*: IT managers, CTO, COO, VP Digital

- ROI is almost exclusively a deciding factor, followed by business value for the end users (consumers).

In contrast, the B2D model has the following characteristics (Figure 4-1):

- Selling directly to product developers, who develop applications for businesses or consumers.
- The direct buyers are
  - *Economic buyer:* Product manager, CTO
  - *User buyer:* Developers, data scientists, testers
- Pricing, development time and cost reduction, and improving user engagements are the deciding factors.

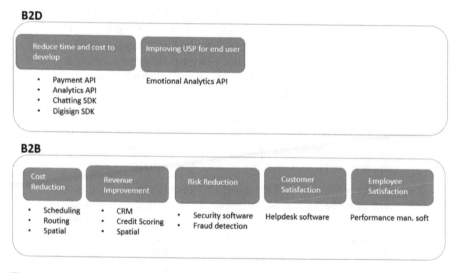

Figure 4-1. Why customers buy for B2D and B2B with examples

So the main differences between B2B and B2D products are as follows:

1. The B2B companies target decision-makers who are usually in the management level such as C-levels, VP, and managers, while the B2D companies target decision-makers who are usually at the technical level, such as developers and data scientists or product managers.

2. For B2B, it is crucial to pitch the ROI and value of the products to end consumers, while for B2D it is more important to pitch the advantage of using the product (build vs. buy) to save development time and cost.

As for the AI products, AI-first SaaS and AI-powered SaaS startups have a B2B model because they directly sell to businesses, while AIaaS startups have a B2D model because they sell to developers (see Figure 4-2).

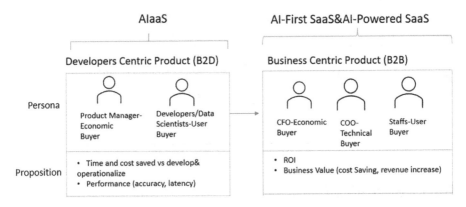

Figure 4-2. The difference between B2D (AIaaS) and B2B (AI-first SaaS/AI-powered SaaS)

Understanding a Developer-Oriented AI Product: API

As we have previously learned, there are several methods of delivering AI as a Service, but API is the most popular way of deploying an AI as a Service product because

1. It is simplest and fastest to be consumed by developers.

2. It is easy to monetize by the AIaaS companies.

   a. *Pay per use*: Pay per API call.

   b. *Freemium API*: Free API for limited use, but pay to use a higher tier or other products like SDKs.

   c. *Subscription*: Consume API with a quota by subscribing per month or year.

3. There are many sales channels to sell API:

   a. *Direct channel*: Sell the API via the website.

   b. Sell the API via a marketplace such as Rapid API, AWS Marketplace, Rakuten, and Prompt API.

These are the examples of AIaaS products with API delivery categorized by different AI methods (see Table 4-1).

Table 4-1. Examples of API-Based AIaaS

AI Methods	Example company
Healthcare machine learning	• Nubentos
	• Infermedica
Computer vision	• Valossa
	• Identifai
Natural language processing	• TextRazor
	• Geneaa
	• Linguakit
	• Cogito

AIaaS Business Models

If we narrow the developer-centric product down only to AIaaS, there are two AIaaS fundamental business models, horizontal and vertical, as shown in Figure 4-3.

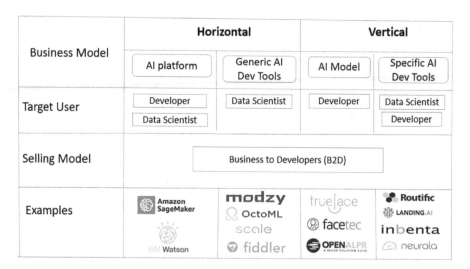

Figure 4-3. AIaaS business models

1. *Horizontal business model*: The AI solution can be applied to multiple industry sectors and domains.

    a. *AI Platform as Service*: This is an end-to-end Infrastructure and Platform as a Service to build and deploy AI models for various use cases and industry verticals. Examples are Amazon Sagemaker and IBM Watson.

    b. *Generic AI Tools as a Service*: A set of tools to help data scientists and engineers build, optimize, and deploy their AI models and datasets. Examples are Dataiku, DataRobot, H2O, Domino Data Lab, Modzy (model operationalization), OctoML (model deployment), Snorkel AI (dataset annotation), Scale AI (dataset annotation), and Super AI (dataset annotation).

2. *Vertical business model*: The AI solution is applied to a specific problem in a specific industry or domain.

    a. *AI Model as a Service*: An AI model or algorithm packaged as API endpoints, SDKs, or containers. Examples are FaceTec (liveness detection deployed as API and SDK), OpenALPR (license plate recognition deployed as API and container), Trueface (face recognition model packaged as SDK and container), and PicPurify (porn and gun detection deployed as API).

    b. *Specific AI Tools as a Service*: A set of tools to help data scientists and engineers build, optimize, and deploy their AI models and datasets for a particular industry. Examples are Routific (route optimization model building), Landing AI and Neurala (building manufacturing industrial inspection models), and Inbenta (building question-answer models for the banking industry).

Instead of building a horizontal end-to-end AI development platform or tooling, building an AI Model as a Service and eventually a vertical AI development tool that targets specific use cases in the industry vertical is better.

The reason is that building a horizontal platform or tooling that helps data scientists/AI engineers build generic AI models is challenging because of the following reasons:

1. Every AI use case is different. Building AI models for manufacturing has different challenges from building AI models for the healthcare industry and autonomous car companies. The data annotation method and AI model building and training methods are different. The deployment methods are also different. Any horizontal platform would need heavy reconfiguration and customization to handle new use cases.

2. Determining the target market segment is tricky. Many common complaints are that an end-to-end AI building platform is too complex for beginner and citizen developers but too restrictive for experienced technical persons. It doesn't solve the problems for both user segments.

3. Even if you successfully build a generic horizontal end-to-end AI platform, you will compete with infrastructure giants who have already built this AI tooling platform on top of their infrastructure platform and can easily charge their AI tooling platform for a low price, even free.

4. There is no dominant design of AI development tools yet. Novel AI development methods and paradigms are invented daily and published in prestigious conferences like *NeurIPS, ICML, ICLR, CVPR,* and *ICCV.* The research is also publicly available as open source projects. So why must a customer pay for development tools that adopt obsolete methods when novel methods are already available for free?

The best bet is to sell a combination of AI models and also a development tool to build and configure specific AI models. This will also depend on the use cases.

Why Selling to Developers

With the rapid adoption of SaaS and public clouds, it's clear that developers are driving innovation in enterprise software. The next trillion-dollar sector could be developer-driven.

Developers are at the center of today's technology-driven world. They've become key players in the business, using their skills to build products that can be customized for any need or situation. Developers are not just other customers. They have the power to change an organization and its products, so companies need their needs met to succeed on this new level playing field that we call development nowadays. In this section, we will discuss further why the developer market is lucrative, the challenges, and how to win the hearts of the developers.

The Developer Market Is Lucrative

The developer market is lucrative because of the following reasons:

1. *Market size*: The potential size of the market is big. There are millions of developers in the United States alone. Developers are also working in SaaS and app companies serving millions of users.

2. *Market validation*: Developers and their employers (SaaS and app companies) have an interesting problem to solve. In a digitally transformative, innovation-driven economy like now, companies are expected to build new technology to support their legacy systems as well as build new profitable business models. Developers are at the forefront of this war and must endlessly find the most efficient solutions to always be one step ahead of competitors. Cutting-edge technologies like machine learning can scale the business to another level, given that the developers can find the easiest way to apply and deploy them.

3. *Influence*: Developers are the new star of the business. Technology has given developers the power to change industries. They are no longer just coding away at computer screens but shaping businesses from within by influencing their content and products with expertise that equals business influence. There are many benefits to getting developers on board with your product, including the opportunity for them or their clients' companies to get funneled back into yours.

4. *Technology validation:* As a technology company selling B2D products, you are selling something that solves your problem, and you believe that it would be useful for other developers. This *dogfooding* mechanism can help B2D companies build much better relationships than B2B companies. B2D companies with good developer advocates can get their customers helping to find bugs and provide valuable technical feedback and feature development.

5. *Word-of-mouth marketing:* Developers (including data scientists, testers, and software architects) are groups of people who hold highly particular values. The values of meritocracy, transparency, and sharing are very important for them. Developers want to work with companies that provide them with quality products. If you offer an honest, valuable service for developers, they'll be happy enough to be your ambassador and boost word-of-mouth marketing.

AIaaS companies can always benefit from building products for developers.

The Characteristics and Challenges of the Developer Market

Despite the attractive benefits of selling to the developers' market or B2D, there are some characteristics of this market that we need to understand to be able to validate and sell the product successfully. It is helpful to use the familiar use cases in B2B and B2C as a baseline and compare them to B2D market models.

Most developer-centric markets (B2D) have characteristics that are uniquely different from the consumer-centric market (B2C), which has only one decision-maker, and from the business-centric market (B2B), which has several decision-makers. Actually, B2D contains some aspects of B2C and B2B.

B2D is similar to B2C in that

- Individual decision-making that leads to calls to action, such as self-service signups and credit card payments, takes priority over sales demos and contract negotiation.

- Inbound marketing strategies such as content marketing, social media marketing, community building, and partnerships are prioritized over inside sales and outbound marketing.

- Because the onboarding process is self-service and very low touch, it is easier to be data-driven in B2D.

But B2D is also similar to B2B in that

- The solution provided by the B2D company must first solve business problems. For example, the AIaaS product must automate some of the business processes.

- The buying decision-making process can still involve multiple stakeholders.

- Due to technical complexity, handholding and high-touch support are higher than in B2C, where support can be made more low touch.

In addition, the B2D market also has its own challenges, as follows:

- *DIY trait*: No matter how good your content, product, and relationship with the developers, developers are DIY (Do It Yourself) kind of persons. Their social status and pride are determined by the complexity of the code they develop with their own hands. This leads to the second point.

- *Not Invented Here (NIH) syndrome*: The NIH syndrome is prevalent among developers in software companies. They feel that the best developer-centric product is the one they created themselves. This is also motivated by the proliferation of the open source movement, which enables tech companies to build their own proprietary tech stacks based on the open source frameworks.

- *Intellectual property*: Many tech companies feel that purchasing and using ready-made B2D products such as AIaaS hinders them from building core technology values, which can be part of their Intellectual property (IP). Building core technology values is indeed a very important part of a tech company. For example

    - An automated recruitment SaaS company most likely develops their own *emotional analytics* engine as their core technology value.

    - The Salesforce automation SaaS company will develop its own *sales lead analytics* engine.

    - Planogram plan SaaS companies will tend to develop their own retail *object recognition* engine.

- *The paradox of selling tools to artisans*: Selling tools to artisans and builders such as developers is tricky:

  - If they cannot build the tool themselves, then it's more likely that their knowledge level is low and continual handholding is unavoidable, which makes scaling the business almost impossible.

  - If they can build the tool themselves, they wouldn't need our product. So we need to find the right market segment.

Key to a Successful Developer-Centric Product

To overcome some of the challenges of selling to developers, the following are the best practices from successful developer-centric companies. This applies to AIaaS as well:

1. *Friendly sandbox*: Provide a developer-friendly environment to play with your solutions. If the solution is AI development tools, the data scientists can build AI models on the sandbox. If the solution is an AI model, the developer can try the AI model by giving some inputs and receiving some outputs.

2. *Clear collaterals*: Provide clear and instructive documentation, guidelines, and video tutorials to help the developers build the applications using your tools and/or AI models.

3. *Build vs. buy business case*: Write a convincing time- and cost-saving ROI from adopting the solution.

4. *Select a non-core, tedious, or complex use case*: Select a use case that is not a core value for most SaaS companies, which is usually a tedious one, for example, a payment service, or complex to develop, which needs quite deep and long R&D, for example, AI development tools and computer vision models (face recognition, face liveness detection, speech recognition).

5. *Build strong moats*: Your solution must have a strong technical moat such as follows:

   a. Huge data was collected.

   b. Efficient and scalable systems and processes.

   c. Superior patented algorithms or AI models.

6. *Customizable*: The developer solution must be easy to customize and configure by developers themselves with minimal handholding.

7. *Agnostic deployment*: The developer solution must be easy to deploy to multiple platforms (Web, edge devices, smartphones, bare-metal machines).

The Mistakes of Developer-Centric Product Strategy

Understanding the challenges, there are several caveats when building developer-centric products. These are the common mistakes:

1. Targeting SaaS with a too niche market. B2D-oriented products like vertical AIaaS must target vertical SaaS with a large user base, for example, financial technology (FinTech) and marketing technology (MarTech), compared with SaaS in aviation, for example, with a small user base. After all, niches in SaaS usually have already developed their own core technology themselves because it is their main proposition.

2. The product competes head-to-head with open source with a large community.

3. The product is too complex to use for a developer with no easy interface.

4. Selecting the use case where the workflow and configuration variations are too high. The implication is potential handholding with developers and difficulty scaling. In this case, we must also sell the configurable tools and platform, which the user can adjust easily.

5. Selling a product that doesn't have clear benefits and/or is too easy to develop by decent developers.

6. The product does not deliver on the performance promised.

Five-Step AIaaS Validation

After building AI-first SaaS and selling it to the business users (B2B), we can further break down the AI models and platform to sell those to the developers (B2D) as well.

In this section, we will learn how to validate vertical AIaaS solutions, from assessing the maturity of the AI model, defining the vertical markets, defining the developer journey map, testing the market, and finally achieving Product-Market-Technology fit.

Suppose we can successfully validate and sell the vertical AIaaS (AI as a Service). In that case, we can also keep improving the maturity of the development platform and then, when the time comes, finally sell it as a vertical developer tool where the workflow and configuration, even the generation of new AI models, can be easily customized by the developer users (see Figure 4-4).

The validation steps described here are also a good exercise for AI startup founders to retrospect and understand more about the technical and business feasibility of the current AI product and its extension to be developer-oriented (Figure 4-5).

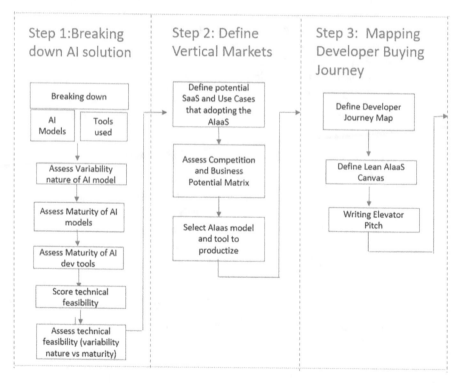

Figure 4-4. Steps 1, 2, and 3 of the AIaaS validation framework

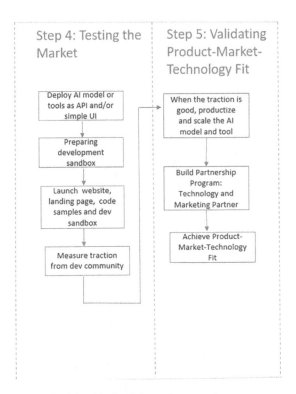

Figure 4-5. Steps 4 and 5 of the AIaaS validation framework

Step 1: Breaking Down the AI Solution

Considering the main goal of AIaaS is to sell either the AI model or the AI tools, we first need to understand the maturity of our current AI models and tools to build those AI models (Figure 4-6). For that, we need to break down all the models and tools to evaluate the variability inter-customer and then assess their maturity using a proprietary maturity assessment framework.

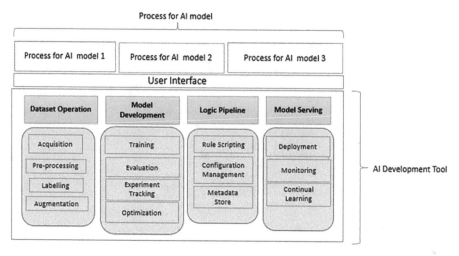

Figure 4-6. AI models and development tools

Some AI models need to tackle different data characteristics from customer to customer. For example, for face liveness detection, the image data will be relatively similar from customer to customer (just facial images), so one API endpoint with one face liveness detection model can be used by several customers. On the other hand, the image data for retail SKU image recognition will differ from brand to brand (shown in Figure 4-7), so multiple models must be trained and deployed for different customers.

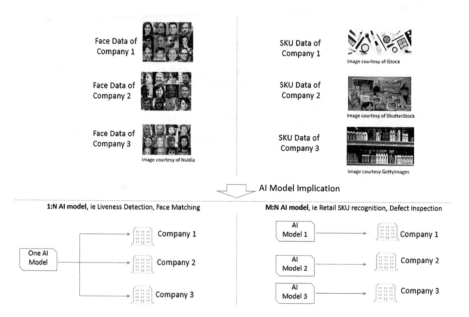

Figure 4-7. One-to-one model (low variability for data inter-customer) vs. one-to-many model (high variability for data inter-customer)

The implication of data varies from customer to customer because the data annotation and model training would differ for each customer. Therefore, the user must have the capability to train and configure their own AI model.

In addition to the variation of data characteristics from customer to customer, there is another challenge in the variation of logic, workflow, and rules of some AI models between customer and customer. Some AI models have a higher tendency to have different rules and logic compared with other AI models. An example is a Question and Answer (Q&A) chatbot model. If we are using classical NLP algorithms and not Large Language Models, we can have a variety of rules and logic to be implemented for different use cases and different customers. The implication is we must also provide a tool for the users to modify and configure the Q&A chatbot workflow and logic. To break down the AI models to be productized, we have to do the following steps:

1. The first thing that we need to evaluate is the variability of the AI model deployed between customers, which is based on these two things:

    a. *Data variability*: How the input data characteristics would be different from customer to customer

    b. *Logic and rules variability*: How the rules and logic would be different from customer to customer.

    Tabulate all the AI models to be productized and assess the variability of data and logic by using the following scale:

    a. Data variability

        i. *1 → low*: Few variations in data characteristics among customers.

        ii. *2 → medium*: There is significant variability in the data characteristics among customers.

        iii. *3 → high*: Every customer has different data characteristics.

    b. Rules and logic variability

        i. *1 → low*: Little variability of rules and logic among customers.

        ii. *2 → medium*: Significant variability of rules and logic among customers.

        iii. *3 → high*: Every customer has different rules and logic.

We tabulate and score the data and logic and rules variability like the example in Table 4-2.

Table 4-2. Variability of Data and Logic with AI Model Examples

AI Model	Input	Output	Data Variation per Customer	Rules and Logic Variation per Customer
Face matching	Two faces	Matching score	1	1
Planogram compliance	Product images on shelf	Compliance score	3	2
Route optimization	Drop points and expected time	Optimal route with time windows	2	3
Manufacturing defect inspection	Image of product	Defect/Not Defect	3	1

Then we determine inter-customer variability based on the following conditions (Table 4-3).

Table 4-3. Determining Inter-customer Variability of AI Models

Inter-customer Variability	Condition
Low	If data and logic variability < 2
Medium	If either data or logic variability > 2
High	If both data and logic variability > 2

2. After we understand the potential variability of each AI model, we then measure the maturity of the **AI models** by assessing the maturity of the process in each AI model development phase based on the following levels:

   a. *Level 1 (Initial):* The process in each stage is seen as unpredictable, inefficient, poorly controlled, and reactive.

   b. *Level 2 (Managed):* Best practices and standard operating procedures have been managed but not written systematically in each stage.

   c. *Level 3 (Defined):* Each stage has defined and written best practices and standard operating procedures.

d.   *Level 4 (Quantitatively Managed):* Quantitative objectives for quality and process performance are established and can be monitored manually.

e.   *Level 5 (Automated):* The process can be easily replicated, monitored, and automated with minimal human intervention.

3. Measure the maturity of the **AI development tools** to create the AI models in all phases, from the data operations and training pipeline to serving, by the following levels:

a.   *Level 1 (Basic):* The tool is available but scattered with no standardized documentation or operational procedure.

b.   *Level 2 (Systemized):* Standardized documentation and operational procedure are available, but the tools are still scattered with no integration between them.

c.   *Level 3 (Integrated):* The tools are integrated with proper documentation and operational procedure.

d.   *Level 4 (Customizable):* The tools can be easily configured and customized with a text-based command line.

e.   *Level 5 (Externalizable):* The tools have an easy-to-use and user-friendly UI that can be used by external developers or data scientists.

4. Using the following maturity templates (Figures 4-8 and 4-9), fill in the tool and AI model process maturity for each phase of AI development.

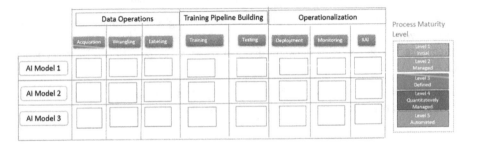

Figure 4-8. AI model process maturity template

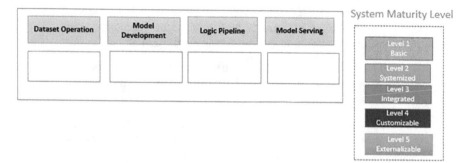

Figure 4-9. System maturity template

The maturity score of the end-to-end AI model process is then scaled as follows (max 40 points):

- *1 → low*: Process maturity score 1–10
- *2 → medium*: Process maturity score 11–20
- *3 → medium*: Process maturity score 21–30
- *4 → high*: Process maturity score > 31

The maturity score of the AI development tool is then scaled as follows (max 20 points):

- *1 → low*: Tool maturity score 1–5
- *2 → medium*: Tool maturity score 6–10
- *3 → medium*: Tool maturity score 11–15
- *4 → high*: Tool maturity score > 16

The maturity of AI models (in terms of process) and AI tools (in terms of systems) defines whether they can be marketed on a scale.

Select the AI models and AI tools that have the highest maturity level. The AI model with the highest maturity level is supposed to have an end-to-end automated process from data acquisition to how to explain the model result (XAIOps).

The AI tools with the highest maturity level are supposed to have an end-to-end system that external developers can easily configure.

As both the AI models and tools become more mature, we can eventually package and sell the AI models as API and SDK and development tools in one platform, so the customers can modify and configure the workflow, parameters, and performance of the AI models themselves. Some AI models with high levels of variability inter-customer must always include workflow and data configuration tools as a service.

Both maturities of AI models and AI tools determine the technical feasibility of AIaaS.

The AIaaS technical feasibility (see Table 4-4) is assessed as follows.

Table 4-4. AIaaS Technical Feasibility Based on Process and System Maturity

Process Maturity	System Maturity	Technical Feasibility
Low-Medium	Low	Not feasible
Low	Medium-High	Low feasibility
Medium-High	Medium-High	Medium feasibility
High	High	High feasibility

5. The last step is deciding whether to productize the AI model. The technical feasibility and AI model variability inter-customer determine (see Table 4-5) whether or not we shall productize and sell the AI Model as a Service.

Table 4-5. The Decision to Productize the AI Model or Not Is Based on Variability Inter-customer and Technical Feasibility

Variability	Technical Feasibility	Productize/Not
Low	Low	Go with notes
Low-Medium	Medium-High	Go
Medium-High	Low	Stop
High	Medium-High	Go

From the preceding table, we can infer that when the technical feasibility of the AI model is low and variability between customers is high, then we cannot productize it. When the technical feasibility of the AI model is low and variability between customers is low, we can still productize it with notes that the maturity (process and system) must be improved along the way.

CASE STUDY: BREAKING DOWN THE AI SOLUTION

Sarah and Carlos have been quite successful with their AI concierge SaaS. Inspired by the Amazon Web Services (AWS) successful story, where they sold their internal tools to the public in 2006[1] as a side business, but it turned out to be a quite successful business that contributed significant revenue, Sarah and Carlos are interested in selling the AI models and the tools they have developed for the AI concierge SaaS.

First, they are breaking down the AI models used in their AI-first SaaS:

- *Face verification and recognition model:* A computer vision deep learning model to verify faces (1:1 face matching) and recognize a face (1:N face matching)

- *Customer service QA model:* NLP question-answering deep learning model

- *Situational awareness model:* A computer vision deep learning model to recognize suspicious behavior and intruders

Then they are scoring the variability inter-customer for every AI model as follows (Table 4-6).

Table 4-6. Variability Inter-customer for the AI Concierge Models

AI Model	Input	Output	Data Variation per Customer	Rules and Logic Variation per Customer	Variability Inter-customer
1:1 face matching	Two faces	Matching score	1	1	Low
1:N face matching	Face vs. N faces	Nth similar face	1	1	Low
Customer service QA model	Queries	Answers	3	3	High
Situational awareness	CCTV frames	Potential intruders and crime	2	2	High

---

[1] https://techcrunch.com/2016/07/02/andy-jassys-brief-history-of-the-genesis-of-aws/

Based on the preceding table, Sarah and Carlos infer that the face matching model can be productized merely as an API, while the customer service QA and situational awareness models can only be productized if the model and workflow can be configured due to higher expected variability between customers.

The next step is they need to score the process maturities of the AI models in each operational phase with the following colored table (Table 4-7).

Table 4-7. Process Maturities of AI Concierge Models

	Process Maturity								Total
	Acquisition	Wranglling	Labeling	Training& Retraining	Testing& Validation	Serving	Monitoring	XAI	
Face Recognition	4	3	2	4	5	5	3	1	27
Customer Service QA	2	3	3	4	4	4	1	1	22
Situational Awareness	4	3	3	3	2	2	1	1	19

System Maturity Level

Level 1 Basic
Level 2 Systemized
Level 3 Integrated
Level 4 Customizable
Level 5 Externalizable

From the preceding table, the process maturity scale for each AI model is

- *Face recognition*: 3 → medium
- *Customer service QA*: 3 → medium
- *Situational awareness*: 2 → medium

Second, they must also break down the tools used to develop the AI models and score their system maturities. The result is tabulated in the following table (Table 4-8).

Table 4-8. AI Tool/System Maturity of the AI Concierge SaaS

Component	Maturity Level (1–5)
Dataset operations	3
Model development	4
Logic pipeline	4
Model serving	4
Total	17

From the preceding table, the tool maturity scale is **High**. This means that the tool used to do data operations, model plus logic development, and deployment for the AI concierge is highly configurable and can easily be used by external users.

The next step is Sarah and Carlos must assess the technical feasibility for all AI model candidates to be productized based on their process and system maturities using the template in Table 4-9.

Table 4-9. Technical Feasibility of AI Models for the AI Concierge SaaS

AI Models	Process Maturity	System Maturity	Technical Feasibility
Face recognition	Medium	High	**Medium feasibility**
Customer service QA	Medium	High	**Medium feasibility**
Situational awareness	Medium	High	**Medium feasibility**

We can see that all the AI models have medium technical feasibility. The last step is to assess which AI models are suitable for the variability between potential customers based on the template in Table 4-10.

Table 4-10. Technical Feasibility vs. Variability for Each AI Model

AI Model	Variability	Technical Feasibility	Productize/Not
Face recognition	Low	Medium	Go
Customer service QA	High	Medium	Go
Situational awareness	High	Medium	Go

Based on the preceding table, Sarah and Carlos are confident that their AI system and process can handle various variability for different customer use cases. Next, the commercial aspect will also be assessed after the technical aspects are considered.

Step 2: Defining the Vertical Market

The next step is to analyze the market to sell the AI models. We must define potential use cases in different verticals that will potentially adopt the AI models and/or tools. The steps are as follows:

1. Define potential use cases that will adopt the AIaaS. We must analyze the SaaS landscape in different verticals and see where AIaaS can be adopted. The potential use cases are then scaled as follows:

   - 4: > 4 use cases in more than three industry verticals.

   - 3: < 4 use cases in more than three industry verticals.

   - 2: > 4 use cases in less than three industry verticals.

   - 1: < 4 use cases in less than three verticals.

2. Assess the competition. Our main competition in the AIaaS space is direct competitors and also the in-house development team. The peril of selling to technical people like developers is that if the solution is easy for them to build, they will build it themselves unless there are significant complexity and obstacles. The development team will tend to build the AI solution in-house if the following conditions are met:

   a. There is a considerable number of public datasets available.

   b. The annotation does not need to be performed by subject matter experts.

   c. Many research papers, blogs, and other references explain how to build the AI model.

   d. The complexity of the model's architecture is relatively low if the input is structured data (transaction records, Excel tables, SQL). Unstructured data (images, videos, tweets, texts) is more complex than structured data.

   e. Compared with streaming data, the infrastructure needed to build and run the AI model is considerably light (non-streaming data).

We score the risk of the AI solution that has a tendency to be built in-house as follows (Table 4-11).

Table 4-11. In-House AI Model Build vs. Buy Scoring

Criteria	
Datasets available publicly (+1).	Most datasets are proprietary (+0).
Lots of references (+1).	Few references (+0).
Many open source AI models are available (+1).	Only a few open source AI models are available (+0).
Structured data (+1).	Unstructured data (+0).
Non-streaming data (+1).	Streaming data (+0).
Anyone can label (+1).	Only an expert/SME can label (+0).

- A score above 3 means that the AI solution is most likely to be developed in-house.

- A score between 0 and 3 means that the AI solution is less likely to be developed in-house due to the resource needed.

For the AIaaS product idea, scale the competitiveness on the following scale:

- 1: > 4 direct competitors and mostly to be developed in-house.

- 2: > 4 direct competitors and less likely to be developed in-house.

- 3: < 4 direct competitors and most likely to be developed in-house.

- 4: < 4 direct competitors and less likely to be developed in-house.

3. We then tabulate the scores of competition and business potential.

4. Based on the scores, we select the AIaaS product to sell.

CASE STUDY: DEFINE THE VERTICAL MARKET

After analyzing the maturity of the AI models and tools, Sarah and Carlos then analyze the potential vertical market for the AI models and/or tools.

1. They define the AI models' potential uses cases and industry verticals that can be targeted (Table 4-12).

Table 4-12. Potential Use Cases and Industry Verticals from AI Models in the AI Concierge SaaS

AI Model	Use Case	Direct User (SaaS and Apps)	End User (Industry)	Number of Uses Cases	Number of Industry Verticals
Face verification and recognition	Visitor onboarding	Visitor management systems	Hospitality, buildings	3	6
	Document matching eKYC	Border processing Mobile banking, P2P lending, trading	Immigration, airport Banks, financial services, trading firm		
Hotel customer service QA	Room service Concierge service	Hotel reservation app	Hospitality	2	1
Situational awareness	Intruder detection	Security application	Buildings, hospitals	1	1

2. Then they define the competitiveness of the AI models. First, they assess the tendency of the AI model to be developed in-house or not (see Table 4-13).

Table 4-13. The Tendency of AI Models to Be Developed In-House or Not

Criteria		Face Recognition	Service QA	Situational Awareness
Datasets available publicly (+1).	Most datasets are proprietary (+0).	I	0	0
Lots of references (+1).	Few references (+0).	I	0	0
Many open source AI models are available (+1).	Only a few open source AI models are available (+0).	I	0	0
Structured data (+1).	Unstructured data (+0).	0	I	0
Non-streaming data (+1).	Streaming data (+0).	0	0	I
Anyone can label (+1).	Only an expert/SME can label (+0).	I	0	I
Total		4	I	2

Then they assess the competitiveness scale: direct competitors who already sell similar AIaaS plus the in-house development tendency (Table 4-14).

Table 4-14. The Competitiveness Scale

AI models	Number of Competitors	In-House Development Tendency	Score
Face recognition	6	Yes	I
Service QA	5	No	4
Situational awareness	2	No	4

3. The last step is to tabulate the maturity, business potential, and competitiveness of each AI model (Table 4-15).

Table 4-15. The Total Score of System/Process Maturity, Business Potential, and Competitiveness of AI Models

AI Models	Business Potential Score	Competitiveness Score	Total Score
Face recognition	3	I	4
Service QA	I	4	5
Situational awareness	I	5	6

Based on the preceding scores, Sarah and Carlos decide that their situational awareness model has the best potential to be commercialized. The next step they will do is to define the journey map and proposition.

Step 3: Mapping the Developer Buying Journey

This step will define the developer buying journey and lean canvas for AIaaS. This step aims to define the growth strategy based on the proposition offered by this AIaaS.

The steps are as follows:

1. Define the developer buying journey map.

    The developer buying journey map is the process that the product managers, developers, and data scientists go through on the way toward buying developer products, such as API, SDK, and development tools. The goal of building the buying journey map is to better understand our customer's experience and expectations so that we can define proper propositions and marketing strategies for our developer product (see Figure 4-10).

Stage	Discovery	Evaluate	Learn	Build	Call to action
Who	Product Manager	-Developer -Product Manager	Developer	-Developer -Product	Developer Product Manager
Goals/Needs	Is this useful for me?	Will it meet my needs?	How does it work ?	Can I build a proof of concept?	How can I pay? Will it scale Can I give feedback?
Questions	1. What is it? 2. Is it add intelligence to my SaaS/App? 3. Is it useful for my users?	1. Does it look easy to use? 2. Is it look credible? 3. Is the price sensible?	1. Time to generate Output? 2. Is the Docs clear? 3. What is the support?	1. Speed to build MVP app 2. Speed to integrate Build vs Buy ? 3. Is the Minimum Algorithmic Performance met?	1. How I pay? 2. What is the pricing model? 2. How can I give feedback? 3. What is roadmap?
Activities : Thinking, Do	PM Thinking to add Intelligence into the SaaS/App	PM ask Dev To searching for suitable AIaaS, otherwise build inhouse	Dev test various AIaaS, check the docs and support	Dev building MVP by Integrate with AIaaS and Test the performance	PM and Dev decided what Pricing model to use
Internal Touchpoint	- Blog - Landing Page - Whitepapers - Soc media - API Marketplace	- Docs - Use Cases - Product Pages - Pricing Page	- Trial page - Quick Start Guide - Code Samples - Tutorials	- Sandbox - Reference Guide - Changelogs - Support	- Payment page - Product Roadmap - Partner program - Ticket pages - Showcase page
External Touchpoint	- Online Media/Press - Developer Groups - Referals	- Stack Overflow - Tech influencer	- Tutorial on Youtube, Udemy - Tech books and ebooks		

Figure 4-10. *Developer buying journey map*

In the developer buying journey map, we must define

- *Who:* The actors or the persons that will buy our AIaaS product.

- *Goals/needs:* The goals and needs of the actors in every stage.

- *Questions:* What questions do they have in mind at every stage.

- *Activities:* What our actors think and do at every stage.

- *Internal touch point:* The properties and content that your company owns and controls. Examples are the company website, developer hub, documentation, social media, public code repository, etc.

- *External touch point:* The properties and content that your company does not have direct control of, but they are the channels to reach existing users and potential customers. Examples are Stack Overflow, Product Hunt, developer events and hackathons, online tech blogs, and online tech magazines.

  The good thing if you already have an AI SaaS is that your product manager and your developer can be your valuable persons to get insights and feedback about their pains in finding ready-made AI solutions.

2. Define the lean AIaaS canvas. After we understand the pain points and the needs of the potential customers, we put the AIaaS idea into perspective and a guide to validate our hypothesis. We fill the following lean AIaaS canvas (Figure 4-11).

SaaS/Application Target	Dev User	End User
The SaaS/App target market	The developer user category	The user
Use Case	Industry	
What is the Use Cases of this AI model	In what industry the Use Cases can be applied	
AI model Input/Output	Model Deployment	
Input/Output of AI model	Where the AI model will be deployed?	
Current tool/practice in SaaS	Benefits/Outcome for Users	
What is the current practice in SaaS/Application target market	Cost/Time Saving, Potential Revenue, or other benefit for the developer and end users	
AIaaS Summary		
The summary of AIaaS solution we provide for our customers		

Figure 4-11. AIaaS lean canvas

The AIaaS lean canvas consists of the following components:

- *SaaS/app target market:* SaaS or application that can leverage our AI model. We are targeting the developers and product managers of this particular SaaS or application.

- *End user:* The target market of this SaaS or application.

- *Use case:* The use cases where the AI model can be applied.

- *Industry:* The industries where the AI model can be useful.

- *AI model input and output:* What data is given as an input and what is resulted as an output.

- *Model deployment*: How the AI model is going to be deployed, whether it is via API, edge device, or SDK.

- *Current tool/practice*: How the current SaaS performs the task manually.

- *Benefits for users*: The benefits of the AIaaS for the developers and end users.

- *AIaaS summary*: The summary of the AIaaS solution we provide to the customers.

3. Based on the previous lean AIaaS canvas, we write down the elevator pitch for our AIaaS solution in the following format:

    - *For **[SaaS and application providers]** who want to add proposition such as **[proposition for the SaaS]**. Our product is a **[name of AI model or tool as a service]** that provides **[what AI model or tool does]**. Unlike **[the conventional method/practice]**, our AIaaS enables **[value and functionality of AI model/tool]** that can be consumed by **[end users]** industries and enable them to **[benefits for end users]**.*

CASE STUDY: MAPPING THE DEVELOPER BUYING JOURNEY

Sarah and Carlos have chosen the situational awareness AI model to be productized as a service. Next, they must map the developer buying journey, define the lean AIaaS canvas, and write the elevator pitch (see Figures 4-12 and 4-13 for the Learn, Build, and Call to action stages of the developer buying journey).

Sarah and Carlos perform buying journey mapping of situational awareness AI as a Service in whiteboards with post notes or a collaborative whiteboarding software like Miro.

Stage	Discovery	Evaluate
Who	Product Manager of Surveillance, Smart city App	-Developer -Product Manager
Goals/Needs	Looking for solution for Improve USP for surveillance SaaS	Explore from different AIaaS providers
Questions	1. What is it? 2. Is it add intelligence to my SaaS/App? 3. Is it useful for my users?	1. Does it look easy to use? 2. Is it look credible? 3. Is the price sensible?
Activities : Thinking, Do	PM Thinking to add intruder And suspicious act detection	PM ask Dev To do search ready AI Because its hard R&D
Internal Touchpoint	- Internal Blog - Landing Page - Whitepapers - API Marketplace (AWS, RapidAPI)	- Docs - Use Cases - Product Pages - Pricing Page
External Touchpoint	- Surveiillance technology blogs - Towardsdatascience	- Medium blog - Tech influencer youtube channel

Figure 4-12. Discovery and Evaluate stages of the developer buying journey

Learn	Build	Call to action
Developer	-Developer -Product	Developer Product Manager
How does it work ?	Can I build a proof of concept?	How can I pay? Will it scale Can I give feedback?
1. Time to generate Output? 2. Is the Docs clear? 3. What is the support?	1. Speed to build MVP app 2. Speed to integrate Build vs Buy ? 3. Is the Minimum Algorithmic Performance met?	1. How I pay? 2. What is the pricing model? 2. How can if give feedback? 3. What is roadmap?
Dev finds no available Open Source, Searching options Finding solution, do trial	Developer builds intruder Detection MVP And integrate with surveillance app	PM and Dev decided what Pricing model to use
- Trial page - Quick Start Guide - Code Samples - Tutorials	- Sandbox - Reference Guide - Changelogs - Support	- Payment page - Product Roadmap - Partner program - Ticket pages - Showcase page
- Tutorial on Youtube, Tech blogs on Medium		

Figure 4-13. Learn, Build, and Call to action stages of the developer buying journey

The next step is for Sarah and Carlos to write down an AIaaS canvas to reiterate the value proposition of their product (Figure 4-14).

SaaS/Application Target		Dev User	End User
Surveillance, Visitor Management System, NVR software		Product Manager Backend developer, Fullstack developer	Security managers Office managers

Use Case	Industry
Intruder detection, blacklisting, suspicions behaviour detection	Building management, hospitals, hospitalities

AI model Input:Output	Model Deployment
CCTV Images : Intruder warning|Suspicious behaviour	Edge Device, Android

Current tool/practice in SaaS	Benefits/Outcome for Users
Simple movement detection, security staff still check what is the cause of the movement	- End User: Less cost for security staffs Improved security, less criminal risk. - Dev user: Less development cost for situation awareness AI model.

AIaaS Summary
The Situation Awareness AIaaS is an AI model to be integrated with surveillance and visitor management applications to detect intruder and suspicious behaviour of visitors

Figure 4-14. *Lean AIaaS canvas for situational awareness*

Based on the preceding lean AI canvas, Sarah and Carlos then write down the following elevator pitch:

For [surveillance SaaS and NVR providers] who want to add proposition such as [intruder detection, blacklisting]. Our product is a [situational awareness engine] that provides [AI models related to intrusion detection]. Unlike [the usual motion detection feature], our AIaaS enables [automatic intruder monitoring] that can be consumed by [building management, hospital, and hospitality] industries with the benefits of [reducing the cost of security staff and reducing criminal risk].

Step 4: Testing the Market

Here we define the AIaaS market demand and growth strategy even before we build the product completely. We must define the go-to-market (GTM) strategy that can validate the AIaaS needs and demands by creating the following checklists:

- Preparing a landing page with content about possible use cases of the AI model

- Showing sample codes or user interfaces for the developers to show how easy and seamless it is to use the AI models and/or tools

- Preparing a *call-to-action* page with trial pages for a development sandbox

---

CASE STUDY: TESTING THE MARKET

After Sarah and Carlos made a clear proposition defined in the AI lean canvas and elevator pitch, Carlos and his technical team set up the situational awareness AI model and configuration tool to be deployed on the Docker container and then deployed on the public cloud as a development sandbox to be accessed by developers from their website. Carlos is also preparing *to start the guide* and documentation.

Sarah and Carlos then prepare a website with a landing page.

They put the following on their landing page:

1. The narration of why intrusion and suspicious behavior detection is important for industries such as building management and hospitalities

2. The benefit of using the situational awareness AI engine for surveillance/visitor management system SaaS developers, NVR application developers, and CCTV manufacturers

3. Link to the developer sandbox where the developers can try the situational awareness AI engine for free during a trial period with limited features

4. Call-to-action page with contact forms and a pre-subscribe page where the developers can pre-pay the situational awareness AI model for the full features during some subscription period

5. Analytics tool to analyze the behavior of the users (developers) while tinkering with the sandbox and reading the documentation

Step 5: Validating Product-Market-Technology Fit

In this last step, when we have lots of traction from developers, as indicated in the following

1. Many developers are trying our AI as a Service models and/or tools in the sandbox.

2. Many developers are pre-subscribing to our AI models and configuration tools.

we can finally say that we have validated the product, market, and technology.

For the developer market, the market validation from building an MVP of the development sandbox is much more effective than testing it with surveys, FGD (focus group discussion), and interviews. We can analyze how they interact with the AI models, how they integrate them, and how they read the documentation and developer guides provided. If we have a steady growth of new users pre-subscription (i.e., 10% monthly), we have validated the AIaaS market.

As we have more users, we must scale the system with more features, better operationalization (DevOps and MLOps) and infrastructure capacities, and a better user interface (Chapter 7). We must also build better user management, API management, payment, and subscription systems. Also, expand the deployment models to other platforms such as Android and edge devices.

As we scale out the system, we can also scale up the go-to-market strategy by building a partnership program (which will be discussed in Chapter 9).

CASE STUDY: VALIDATING PRODUCT-MARKET-TECHNOLOGY FIT

After launching the situational awareness AIaaS landing page and developer sandbox, there are sufficient insights on how developers use and integrate the AI model with their applications. Sarah and Carlos then analyze the usage data to determine whether or not the market for this particular AI model is validated.

They see that the usage growth is significant, plus some developers decide to pre-subscribe to their AIaaS.

The growth of developers pre-subscribing to their AIaaS is 10% monthly. They conclude that the Product-Market-Technology fit has been met, so they decide to scale up the MVP to full-scale development and operationalization.

They are also preparing a more thorough and scalable go-to-market strategy with a partnership program.

Conclusion

Selling to a developer in the business-to-developer (B2D) market is quite a new business model and can be very lucrative if we can select the right product and market. AI as a Service (AIaaS) is selling AI models or AI development tools for the developer as a user and a part of the B2D business model.

Building AIaaS is an interesting endeavor if we already have AI-first SaaS. We need to break down the AI models and tools to develop the AI models in the first place and productize and sell them. But to select which AI models to productize is quite complex. We need to measure the technical and business feasibility first and then validate the product, technology, and market.

Key Takeaways

- Developers in today's world are key players who have the power to change an organization and its products.

- The B2D or business to developer is a business model in which the product is consumed by technical people who develop software.

- Developer-centric products include API (Application Programming Interface), SDK (Software Development Kit), software platform, software tool, and software framework.

- Developing and maintaining AI is a costly process that can be difficult for many startups or companies.

- AIaaS (AI as a Service) is a business model that explicitly targets the technical audience, such as developers and data scientists. The people who will implement and use AI solutions are typically technical.

- AIaaS is part of the B2D (business-to-developer) business model.

- The B2B model is when the buyer of a company sells to another company's buyers. ROI and value for end users are the largest deciding factors in this model.

- The B2D model features fast and efficient development plus less development cost.

- B2B targets strategic decision-makers, and B2D targets technical decision-makers.

- The most popular form of AI service is API because it is simple, easy to monetize, and quick for developers to make use of.

- AIaaS, or AI as a Service, is divided into horizontal and vertical models.

- The horizontal business model can be applied to multiple sectors and use cases, while the vertical business model applies only to one sector and/or use case.

- Instead of building a horizontal end-to-end AI development platform or tooling, it's better to build an AI Model as a Service and, eventually, a vertical AI development tool that targets specific use cases in the industry vertical.

- Selling to a developer is also challenging because developers like to develop everything by themselves.

- The key to successful B2D products is as follows:

  - Friendly sandbox

  - Clear collaterals

  - ROI-oriented business case

  - Selecting a non-core, tedious, or complex use case

  - Building strong moats

  - Customizable

  - Agnostic deployment

- Mistakes of B2D are as follows:

  - Targeting SaaS with a too niche market.

  - Competes head-to-head with open source with a large community.

  - The product is too complex to use for the developer.

  - Selecting the use case where the workflow and configuration variations are too high.

  - Selling a product that doesn't have clear benefits.

  - The product does not deliver on the performance promised.

- The five steps of AIaaS validation are

  1. Assessing the technical feasibility by breaking down AI solutions into AI models and development tools to develop the AI models and evaluate their maturity

  2. Assessing the business feasibility by assessing competition and potential

  3. Mapping the developer buying journey and value proposition

  4. Validating the market by building a landing page and developer sandbox

  5. Validating the Product-Market-Technology fit by analyzing the traction

AI Product Strategy

In the previous chapters, we learned how to validate AI products for B2B and B2D markets. After we validate the market, the next step is to build a sound product strategy essential to the overall process. The product strategy guides decisions regarding the vision and mission of the product, the outcome expected for the customers, the stakeholders involved in their development and marketing efforts, and other crucial aspects necessary for success, like desired feature sets.

In this chapter, we will learn about how to build an AI product and translate it into a roadmap by following the five-step AI product strategy lifecycle framework: First, we must define product vision and objectives. Second, we perform product discovery followed by collaborative requirements analysis, and then we do product prioritization. Finally, we evaluate the roadmap efficacy to measure whether or not our product roadmap is fulfilling our objectives.

The process is a collaborative effort comprising stakeholders directly or indirectly involved with the product. After finishing this chapter, you can create a robust and dynamic AI product strategy as a product roadmap.

We will also learn about AI product lifecycle management, which is the strategic process of managing a product lifecycle, from initial ideation to retirement, based on the advancement and AI technology hype cycle.

© Adhiguna Mahendra 2023
A. Mahendra, *AI Startup Strategy*, https://doi.org/10.1007/978-1-4842-9502-1_5

Product Strategy Fundamental

It's essential to clearly understand what your product should achieve and how that supports the organization. A clear objective will help you define all aspects of your product, including an end-to-end vision for success.

Product strategy is about defining what your product should achieve and how that supports the organization. The product strategy is represented through a roadmap that outlines an end-to-end vision for achieving this goal in full detail with specifics on getting there from where we are now. We will follow a five-step product strategy lifecycle framework that is suitable for enterprise AI products (Figure 5-1):

1. *Product visioning*: Building product vision, objectives, and principles.

2. *Product discovery*: Understanding customer problems and needs.

3. *Product requirements analysis*: Understanding the reasoning of the requirements deeply (5W1H – Why, What, When, Who, Where, How) and categorizing them into tactical, strategic, and disruptive features.

4. *Product prioritization*: We are prioritizing the features in the product roadmap.

5. *Roadmap efficacy evaluation*: Measuring the effectiveness of the product roadmap relative to product objectives. We can adjust the product objectives and the following steps if there is a discrepancy.

Steps 1–5 are continuously performed cycles during a product's lifetime (Figure 5-1).

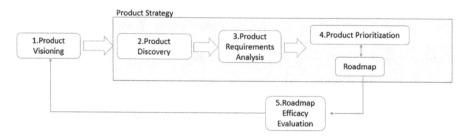

Figure 5-1. From product vision to product roadmap

Product Roadmap

A product roadmap is a strategic plan that outlines a series of tactical steps aligning with the company's goals to push forward in its planned direction.

Product roadmaps are plans of action that reflect product strategy. The goal is to outline all the necessary tasks related to developing and launching new products, service offerings, or feature sets for the company's portfolio and any promotional campaigns and go-to-market strategy needed.

The roadmap's purpose is to outline the plan for both the customer and the company. There are two purposes of the roadmap:

- *Giving the direction*: A product without a roadmap is directionless.

- *Giving clarity*: Lack of clarity results in stakeholders steering the product in multiple conflicting directions, with impact:

  - Sales growth is stagnant.

  - Gaps widen with competitors.

  - Lack of innovation and excitement.

  - High turnover due to low confidence in the product.

However, there is a prerequisite before we can define a good product roadmap. The product needs to have a solid Product-Market-Technology (P-M-T) validation first.

A product roadmap also has a different audience, internal and external. Anyone outside the product/AI and engineering/development team is considered an external audience. Therefore, we should write two different roadmaps: an external and an internal roadmap (Table 5-1).

Table 5-1. Roadmap, Audience, and Its Component

Component	External Roadmap	Internal Roadmap
Audience	Audience: customers, sales team, AM, BD/partnership.	Audience: product/engineering/AI team.
Delivery	Outlines outcome or value delivered to the customer (end user and developer user) in each release.	Outlines a detailed list of features delivered in each release, including internal features.
Features	Conceals internal features that do not directly impact customers.	Every feature committed in each release will be visible.
Reviewer	Various stakeholders reviewed what to share, how much to share, and when to share.	Reviewed and mutually agreed by both PM and engineering/AI team.
Feedback	Feedback was gathered from feedback forms, questionnaires, and user interviews.	Feedback gathered from customer services/ service delivery and PMs.

No matter what, a product roadmap is not a committed plan carved on rocks. We need to continuously adapt to changes and new situations in the business world. We must also never prepare the product roadmap in reactive mode. Every item added to the roadmap is carefully evaluated by the following criteria:

- How does it help customers' (end users and developers) business?
- How does it help in achieving product objectives?
- How does it help realize product purpose?
- Is it aligned with product strategy?

Define Product Vision, Strategy, and Roadmap

The product roadmap is a plan of action consisting of tactical steps to execute product strategy pushing the product ahead in the trajectory of planned direction in alignment with product vision while accomplishing short-term and long-term product objectives.

So to have a sound product roadmap, the first reasonable step is to define product vision, which is the statement of the value of your product, followed by defining product strategy, which represents the path to accomplish the product vision. Finally, we outline a product roadmap as tactical steps to execute the product strategy (Figure 5-2).

Figure 5-2. The product roadmap is built on the foundation of product vision and product strategy

Product vision is usually also company vision, especially if your company only has a single product.

Product vision defines the true purpose of the product or why the product exists. Product vision shows clarity on the overall direction of the product.

Two essential aspects drive product vision:

- *Product principles/purpose*: The set of principles of the product that is a core belief in the existence of the product. To define this, we need to answer these questions:
    - What is the core belief of the organization?
    - What is the true purpose and reason behind the creation of the product?
    - What is the future that the organization intends to create?
- *Product objectives*: The mission of the product. To define this, we need to answer these questions:
    - What are the tangible values for the customers?
    - What are the tangible goals for the organization?

Some examples of vision and mission from leading AI companies are shown in Figures 5-3 and 5-4.

Landing AI : We **believe** that companies with even limited data sets can realize the business and operational value of AI and move AI projects from proof-of-concept to full scale production.

Clarifai : We **believe** that they can demystifying and democratizing AI and machine learning for unstructured data

Carto: We **believe** will that location intelligence will ultimately transform and shape the future success of many companies and organizations.

Figure 5-3. The vision of several AI companies reflects the core belief of the organization

Landing AI : to **empowers** companies to jumpstart AI adoption, propel teams toward success and create practical business value today.

Clarifai : to **bring** The World's AI to developers everywhere.

Carto: is to **enable** every organization out there to solve spatial problems with the best data and analysis

Figure 5-4. The mission of several AI companies reflects the organization's objective

The product strategy is a high-level plan that describes what the company hopes to accomplish with its products and the steps to achieve that.

Product strategy consists of several sub-steps, as depicted in Figure 5-1:

1. Product discovery is a method to help product managers refine their ideas by exploring all possible options and strategies that solve customers' problems effectively. Product discovery is supposed to focus on user outcomes instead of features.

2. Product requirements analysis defines your new product's features and functions to fulfill the expected outcome. The outcome is this step's backlogs with requirements categories (tactical, strategic, and disruptive).

After the product strategy is defined, we write down a prioritized roadmap. The detailed process is depicted in Figure 5-5.

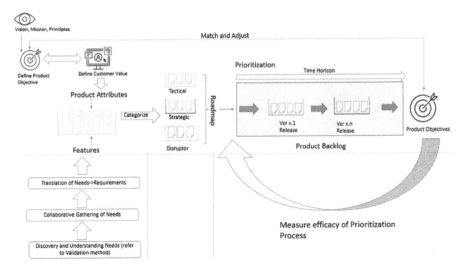

Figure 5-5. From vision to prioritization

This whole process aims to match the product roadmap with business objectives. In essence, what we do consists of the following:

1. Define our belief in vision, mission, and principles.

2. Define product objectives based on customer value by discovering their requirements.

3. Churn out product backlogs and categorize them into tactical, strategic, or disruptive features.

4. Prioritize the backlogs based on the current market conditions and trends.

5. Evaluate whether or not we have attained our objectives.

The following sections will discuss product discovery, requirements analysis, and prioritization.

Product Discovery

In many startups, the product backlogs and requirements are made based on the request of the customer or business development team, which is not an ideal case. The product team should not let customers dictate what to develop. Instead, they must discover the business challenges and problems (which can be translated into needs) of the customers and, along with the technical team, derive the optimal solution (requirements) that would address the business challenges (Figure 5-6). Finally, the requirements will be mapped into features consumed by the users.

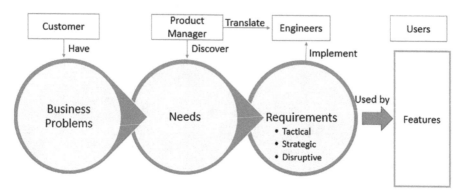

Figure 5-6. From business problems to needs to requirements to features

Understanding Customer Needs

Understanding customers is by delivering what they need and not what they ask, because what customers say they want and what they need are entirely different. Understanding customers identifies what they need to deliver outcomes beyond their expectations.

For AI products, we can use the SETDA framework to determine the customers' needs by considering which challenges, problematic or tedious cognitive tasks, can be assisted, augmented, or performed by AI in a more scalable way (Figure 5-7).

1. We categorize the cognitive challenges into three categories:

   • Generating revenue or a new business model

   • Reducing cost/improving operational efficiency

   • Reducing and managing risk

   These three challenges will be excellent outcomes if we manage to solve them using AI products.

2. For each potential outcome, we define the AI methods suitable to realize the outcome:

   i. *Sense*: The cognitive task is related to perceiving information from the world and transforming it into data.

   ii. *Explain*: Cognitive tasks related to summarizing, analyzing, and visualizing facts and data.

iii. *Think*: Cognitive tasks are related to correlating, predicting, and reasoning, something like insight.

iv. *Decide*: Cognitive tasks are related to making an optimal and rational decision.

v. *Act*: Cognitive tasks are related to actions that the computer can take (automation) on its own based on insights and decisions.

3. We then break down the outcomes into needs and requirements.

Outcome	SENSE (Perception)	EXPLAIN (Description)	THINK (Insights)	DECIDE (Decisions)	ACTION (Automation)
Generate Revenue& New Business Models	ID Verification	Summarize Contributing Factors of Failed Sales	Predict Churn / Predict Revenue	Optimize Investment Portfolio	Buy and Sell Stocks bots
Operational Efficiency	Monitor overproduction	Summarize Wasted material	Predict Estimated Time of Arrival Of goods / Predict Remaining Useful Life	Optimize Production Schedule	Assembly robots / Automated Forklifts
Risk Reduction	Monitor Security / Catching Fraud	Analyze Root Cause of accident	Predict Machine Breakdown / Predict Default Loan	Optimize Maintenance Schedule	Fire extinguisher robots

Figure 5-7. SETDA framework to discover AI outcomes

There are several tools to perform a *need understanding*, such as

- *Buying journey map*: Mapping the process where the customers go through their way toward purchasing the product.

- *Building in public*: Building a product or service with the audience and potential customers to understand their needs and wants.

- *Feedback forms*: A method of asking users for feedback about your products and services right after using them.

- *Pre-order test*: This is a validation method where the customers can buy a product that has not yet been released or produced. Customers can even be charged with a deposit or full payment for a non-existing product.

- *Questionnaire*: A mass survey to ask what people think about your products and services before you even start advertising them. Usually, this method is followed by a conjoint testing method.

- *User interview*: A method of interviewing users to gather their needs and validate product and feature ideas.

- *Prototyping*: A validation method to build a preliminary model of a product to test users' needs and the reaction of users toward proposed product features. In an AI-related product, a prototype must meet the Minimum Algorithmic Performance (MAP) or the minimum level of accurate intelligence required to justify real-world adoption while solving business problems.

- *User persona analysis*: A validation method to understand more about individual persona and their motivation.

- *UX testing*: A validation method to get people in front of your product and watch their behavior and reaction to the product.

Discovery of Needs

Ideally, as product developers, we know the customers' needs before they ask. This can be accomplished by using *need discovery*. There are several tools to perform a *need discovery*. Some example tools are

- *Demand profit pool*: A market segmentation method to organize customers into groups based on the demand and profitability they want to satisfy.

- *Value chain analysis*: A method of evaluating each of the activities in a company's value chain to understand how AI-driven software can improve them.

- *Value curve analysis*: A method of comparing products on a range of factors by rating them on a scale from low to high to define propositions against that of a competitor or industry norms.

- *Ethnographic research*: A market research method that originates from anthropology studies of users in real-life scenarios in their business process and industry.

- *Conjoint test*: A form of statistical analysis to understand how customers value different components or features of the product and services. This can help with pricing, marketing, and feature development strategy.

- *Context map canvas*: A tool to understand the world around our business and team, which we have zero control over. It is an excellent strategic tool for understanding competition, major trends, technology advancements, regulations, uncertainties, and customers' desires.

- *Scenario planning*: A method to identify a specific set of uncertainties and possible realities of what might happen related to your industry in the future.

- *PESTLE analysis*: A framework used to gain a macro picture of an industry, especially on the political, economic, social, technological, legal, and environmental factors that may impact the industry, and identify risk factors.

Discovering needs is different from *understanding* needs. In the latter, the needs are already recognized by the customers. Several methods for understanding needs are feedback forms, questionnaires and user interviews, and MVP (Minimum Viable Product), which we already learned in the previous section. The outcome is tactical requirements, defined as requirements that can guarantee the business will run and the customer will be happy now. In comparison, discovering needs is more about predicting the customer's needs or the market shifts in the future. The outcome is strategic requirements, defined as requirements that anticipate the customer's needs in the future and have the potential to grow the business.

To use every need discovery tool described earlier, we need to understand that the discovery of needs is also divided into two different categories:

- *Customer focus*: Know customers better than themselves and predict what they need before telling us.

- *Market focus*: Anticipate the market's overall direction and predict the shift or disruption in the market.

Each discovery tool mentioned earlier has a specific use, as shown in Figure 5-8.

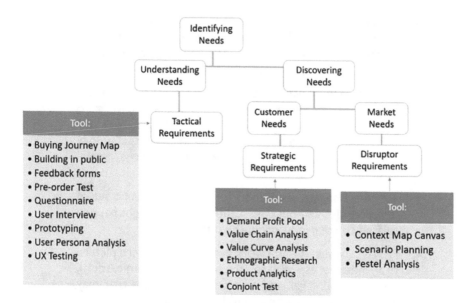

Figure 5-8. Tools to understand and discover customer needs

To understand or discover the customer's needs, the product manager must collaborate with other teams to gather insights. The collaborators are

- *Support team:* The feedback from the support team as a team closest to the user is valuable to get a sense of UI/UX and list down quality issues such as bugs and performance gaps.

- *Engineering team:* The feedback on the latest technology, integration methods, reducing TCO (Total Cost of Ownership), and infrastructure efficiency.

- *AI/data science team:* The feedback are the most accurate algorithms and efficient data and AI model pipeline.

- *Sales team:* The feedback is why and how the customers buy our products, competitors' features, and prices.

- *Business development:* The feedback concerns product growth strategy and new target segments.

- *Marketing:* The feedbacks are business trends, competition, and product value perception.

- *Management (VP and above):* The feedback is high-level strategic information such as industry trends, competitor strategy, political situation, and investment landscape.

We can use many different tools described earlier and use them in collaboration with other teams (Table 5-2).

Table 5-2. Collaborators and Tools for Need Discovery

Collaborators	Collaborate in	Tools
Support team	UI/UX intuitiveness Quality issues: bugs Performance gaps Feature request	End user interview Developer user interview UX testing
Engineering team/UX	Latest tool/library to improve outcome Tech integration TCO (Total Cost of Ownership) Efficiency	User interview Product analytics UX testing
AI/data science team	Machine learning value	User interview Product analytics UX testing
Business dev/partnership team	Product growth New target segment Pricing	Conjoint analysis Pre-order test
Market research/prod strategy/product marketing/ GTM	Trends and sunsets Competition Product value Pricing	Product analytics Conjoint analysis Context map canvas
Management	Product strategy Market shift Pricing	Context map canvas Scenario planning PESTLE analysis

After performing need discovery and understanding, we will do product requirements analysis and prioritization.

Translating Needs to Requirements

After collaborating with other stakeholders to gather needs, the product manager must translate them into requirements. This is difficult because each stakeholder has unique vocabulary and terminologies, and the product manager must also understand them.

For example, the end user will discuss user experiences such as UI design, workflow, and outcomes. In contrast, developer users will discuss developer experiences (DX), such as API structure, documentation, and development sandbox. The AI and data science team will speak about AI-related matters such as machine learning model accuracy, precision, recall, and the uncertainty monitoring method.

As for the internal teams, the sales and business teams will talk about pricing and the sales pipeline. The engineering/AI team will speak about technical feasibilities, TCO, and the latest technology stacks to add product value.

The product manager needs to translate the *need*, which is defined as a business challenge, pain, or business outcome expected from the user perspective, into *requirements* defined as specifications to be understood by the internal team (engineering and AI).

Usually, the requirements are written into a PRD (Product Requirements Document), which will describe why and what. For example, a FinTech wishes an online credit default prediction feature to predict the possibility of credit default from potential customers (what). It will speed up the process and reduce risk (why).

Product Requirements Analysis

In this section, we will learn how to define product requirements based on the needs of the customers using the tools we mentioned in the previous section. Product requirements analysis is a process to understand the requirements mapped out of the customer needs deeply.

Define Product Requirements

To define the product requirements, we must do these steps:

1. Understand the requirements. We must understand why the customers require a particular requirement. We can use this 5W and 1H framework:

   - *Why*: The actual purpose of the requirement

   - *What*: The outcome for the user

   - *When*: The time and frequency of user usage

   - *Who*: The user persona

   - *Where*: The place of usage

   - *How*: Usage mechanism

2. Categorize the requirements into three types by analyzing the current and future market and technology landscapes (see Table 5-3):

    a.   *Tactical requirements*: Short-term requirements (one-year time horizon) address customers' short-term business challenges. The tactical requirements related to AI usually solve the customers' direct operational and revenue problems using classical methods such as regression and mathematical optimization.

    b.   *Strategic requirements*: Near-long-term requirements (two to three years' time horizon), which bring entirely new value to customers. They don't explicitly request, and we must discover. More novel applied AI technologies from research institutions such as Google DeepMind, OpenAI, and Facebook AI Research (FAIR) can usually be utilized for these strategic requirements.

    c.   *Disruptive requirements*: A game-changer requirement (more than three years' time horizon) will create a new market and new normal. This requirement will make the old way of doing things irrelevant. This requirement will also typically need a groundbreaking technology, such as a completely different AI paradigm still in the research phase.

Table 5-3. Requirements Categorization

Aspect	Tactical	Strategic	Disruptive
Scope	Addressing the existing business challenge	Product growth Emerging opportunities	Anticipating market shift Disrupting the market
Product stage	Introduction Maturity	Early growth Later growth	Later growth
Customer value	Very clear	Partially clear Hypothesis needing validation	Unclear Continual validation
Time horizon	Short-term	Near-long-term	Long-term
Technology enabler	Established technology (e.g., regression, XGBoost, CNN, transformer deep learning)	Novel technology (e.g., generative adversarial network, TinyML, multimodal learning)	Groundbreaking technology (e.g., neurosymbolic AI, AGI, quantum machine learning)
Outcome	Steady revenue	Potential growth	Future sustainability

3. After categorizing the requirements (tactical-strategic-disruptive), we create the three-year product roadmap based on the product lifecycle (Figure 5-9):

   a. Determine your current product stage based on your product's sales revenue and the number of customers.

   b. If you are in an early stage of the product, validate the market and technology by focusing on the tactical requirements that solve the customer's business challenges.

   c. If you are in an early growth stage, the market has been validated, and you are increasing the adoption rate. Focus on defining the tactical and strategic requirements for the next year proportionally (70% tactical and 30% strategic as a rule of thumb) using customer and market discovery tools in the previous section.

   d. If you are in a later growth stage, the market is growing rapidly, but many competitors arise. You must focus on the following year's tactical, strategic, and disruptive requirements (70% tactical, 20% strategic, and 10% disruptive, as a rule of thumb).

   e. If you are in a maturity stage, the market is already saturated. You should only focus on tactical requirements and start to realign resources to develop the new product.

   f. When you are in a decline stage, you are preparing to deprecate the product. You are no longer concerned about new requirements, only supporting current users until the product's retirement announcement.

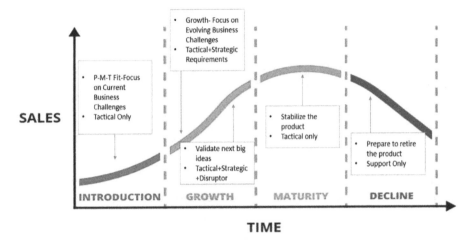

Figure 5-9. Product lifecycle and its requirements

4. Based on the list of requirements and their category from the previous step, we must prioritize the requirements for the next year (four quarters).

Product Prioritization

We have learned how product managers can collaborate with several collaborators for customer understanding and discovery, anticipate a market shift, and even disrupt the market. After the product manager has gathered customer needs and translated them into requirements, we must prioritize them. A product roadmap is a top-down approach that evolves from product vision and consists of product purpose and objectives. In product prioritization, we will shift the discussion from requirements to features. Requirements outline customers' needs that the product should address. Requirements allow engineers (developers and data scientists) to define how to address those needs by mapping the requirements into features (Figure 5-6).

Identification of Product Purpose and Product Objectives

The product vision is the product's foundation, consisting of product purpose and objectives. Product purpose explains why the product exists and the product's principle and value for the customers. Product objectives describe tangible values for the organization, such as

-   Increase in market capitalization
-   Expansion into a new market to align with market trends

- Development of new technology
- Increase in sales and revenue

We prioritize by identifying the right set of requirements that will accomplish the product objectives and remain aligned with the product vision.

From Product Objectives to Customer Values to Roadmap

The next important thing is defining customer values and aligning these with our product objectives. We must also consider the requirements we gathered from the users with various tools we learned from the previous section.

Based on the general framework depicted in Figure 5-5 on defining the vision to prioritize the features for the short-term roadmap, we continue with more detailed steps as follows:

1. Define product vision, mission, and principles.

2. Define the objectives of the product.

3. We define the themes based on the product objectives and the customer values we want to focus on in a year.

4. Break the product objectives down into product attributes that reflect the customer values.

5. List the features aligned with the customer requirements gathered using various tools mentioned in the previous section for each product attribute.

6. Weighting and prioritizing the features using the *scorecard system* will be explained in the next section. Steps 2–6 are depicted in Figure 5-10.

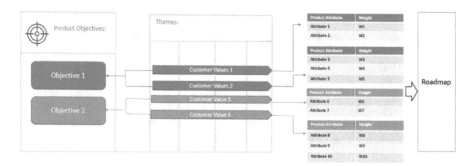

Figure 5-10. From product objectives to roadmap

Collaborative Weighted Scorecard Prioritization Method

There are several methods of product prioritization, such as the Kano model and RICE, but for a complex product such as AI-first SaaS, the prioritization method called the Collaborative Weighted Scorecard (CWS) method is arguably more relevant because of the following reasons:

1. In complex enterprise products employing innovative technology, attaining business value and technology feasibility is vital. We need a prioritization method that optimizes the balance between business value and effort to build the technology to satisfy business needs.

2. The cost of feature R&D for a deep tech–driven innovative startup is high; therefore, feature prioritization based on the trial and error method should be minimized. We must create a product strategy that aligns well with the developed features. Weighted scoring is an ideal prioritization methodology to align the features plan with the product strategy.

3. It instills a sense of ownership due to collaborations between stakeholders. Business, engineering, AI/data science, product, and operations are working together to share perspectives and define needs, requirements, product attributes, feature weightings, and business values.

4. It is quantitative and collaborative in nature, so it is more objective and minimizes HIPPO (Highest Paid Person's Opinion) syndrome or pressure from the sales team.

There are pros and cons to applying the Collaborative Weighted Scorecard for prioritization.

The pros are as follows:

- Better alignment and quantification of every stakeholder on product purpose, objectives, and strategies.

- Ensuring that feature prioritization is still in line with the product roadmap.

- The quantitative nature of the method provides a more rational and justified view of prioritizing product features.

- It works well on more complex enterprise products with a higher expectation of quality and governance.

The cons are as follows:

- It works best only if absolute clarity exists on what value and expectation to deliver to customers.

- Purely quantitative. It can mislead people to believe that the prioritization must be performed rigidly while actually not. Prioritization is a combination of qualitative and quantitative endeavors.

- Not suitable for a novel product where the market is not validated yet and quick agility to changes is needed.

- Basic features (must-haves) will never be scored high on the value index; hence, we must identify the basic features first.

The steps of how to do collaborative prioritization using a weighted scorecard are as follows:

1. Define the weights of each product attribute.

2. Measure the value of each feature against product attributes on a scale of 1–10.

3. Measure the cost of each feature on a scale of 1–10 with the following formula:

$$Cost = Man \, Weeks \, Needed \times \frac{100}{Man \, Weeks \, of \, the \, Most \, Complex \, Feature}$$

4. Group the value of the feature vs. cost in a 2 × 2 prioritization matrix.

5. Calculate the features using absolute value by using the following formula:

$$Absolute \, Value = \frac{Total \, Value \, of \, Feature \, x}{Cost \, of \, Feature \, x}$$

6. Rank the features by absolute value to determine the priority.

7. If necessary, combine with other prioritization methods such as Kano or RICE.

8. Decide the features to be developed for a particular time horizon.

Measuring the Efficacy of the Product Roadmap

A product roadmap is an incredibly critical element that determines the success of a product and even business sustainability. Consequently, the product manager must periodically measure the efficacy of the product roadmap. The effectiveness measurement is to see the impact of the roadmap on the product objectives.

The product manager should examine whether the product is on the right path to accomplish product objectives. It means they need to answer the following questions:

- Do we pick the right product attributes and weights?

- Do we pick the right features that deliver real customer values?

- Does delivering customer value have an impact on product objectives?

We can use the tool called Feature Usage Metrics, which is a tool to measure features and customer values.

The steps to building Feature Usage Metrics are as follows (see Figure 5-11):

1. Pick the top-ranked features we gather from the last release of the roadmap.

2. Identify their usage. We can use product analytics software or user interview to collect this data.

3. Features with top ranks presumably delivered more value to the customers and were used more.

4. If customers do not utilize the top-ranked features, then we need to answer these two questions:

   a. Are customers aware of these features?

   b. Do these features address real needs?

5. If the answer to the preceding two questions is yes, we must revisit product attributes and weightings.

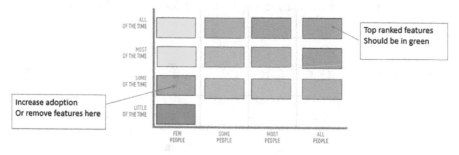

Figure 5-11. Feature Usage Metrics

CASE STUDY: DEVELOPING PRODUCT STRATEGY FOR SMARTCONCIERGE

After Sarah and Carlos successfully validated their AI concierge Product-Market-Technology (P-M-T) fit by building AI consulting for the hospitality business, they are now ready to go to the next phase, creating a product strategy for their AI startup. Creating a product strategy enables them to plan ahead of their startup's direction, which benefits not only the founders but also the employees and potential/existing investors. They follow the *five-step product strategy lifecycle framework* described in this chapter.

Step 1: Product Visioning and Objectives. They prepare product vision and objectives, leading to a roadmap for the next four quarters (one year). Sarah defines the product vision of their AI concierge startup: SmartConcierge, as follows (Figure 5-12).

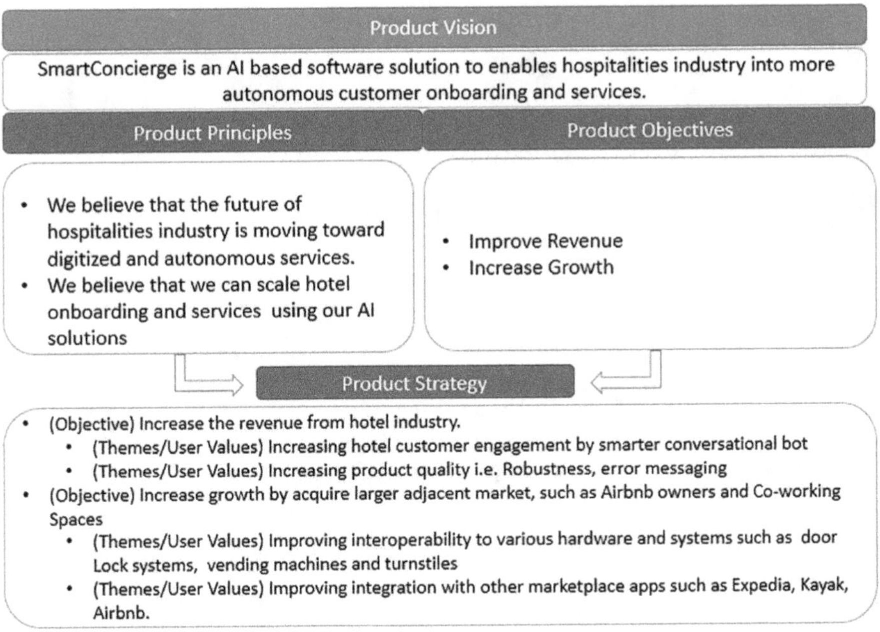

Product Vision
SmartConcierge is an AI based software solution to enables hospitalities industry into more autonomous customer onboarding and services.

Product Principles	Product Objectives
• We believe that the future of hospitalities industry is moving toward digitized and autonomous services. • We believe that we can scale hotel onboarding and services using our AI solutions	• Improve Revenue • Increase Growth

Product Strategy

- (Objective) Increase the revenue from hotel industry.
    - (Themes/User Values) Increasing hotel customer engagement by smarter conversational bot
    - (Themes/User Values) Increasing product quality i.e. Robustness, error messaging
- (Objective) Increase growth by acquire larger adjacent market, such as Airbnb owners and Co-working Spaces
    - (Themes/User Values) Improving interoperability to various hardware and systems such as door Lock systems, vending machines and turnstiles
    - (Themes/User Values) Improving integration with other marketplace apps such as Expedia, Kayak, Airbnb.

Figure 5-12. Product vision, principles, objectives, and strategy of SmartConcierge

Sarah and her team approach the product roadmap from two sides, top-down and bottom-up (Figure 5-13).

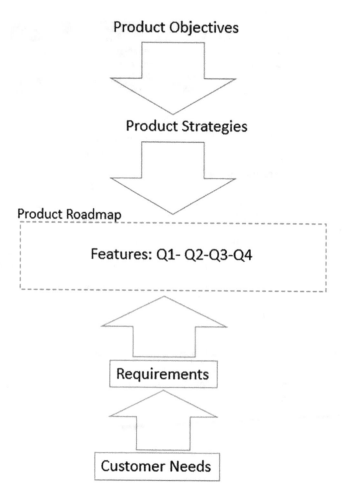

Figure 5-13. Top-down and bottom-up approaches to product roadmapping

The top-down approach defines product objectives as follows:

- Improve revenue.

- Increase growth.

After clearly stating product objectives, they define customer values or expected outcomes along with the timeline.

Step 2: Product Discovery. Based on various customer validation tools, the team decides on two themes that deliver customer values that will help the revenue improvement:

- Increase hotel customer engagement. Because the revenue primarily comes from hotels, there should be a way to engage them more.

- Improve product quality. This will help improve the hotel guest's trust; hence, the hotel decision-maker will also be more engaged.

One customer value will help with market growth: acquiring new markets other than hotels, such as Airbnb owners and coworking spaces.

The customer values are then mapped into product attributes (Table 5-4). The product attributes are given weights to mark their importance relative to customer values.

In parallel, the bottom-up approach is also performed by defining the market's needs and then translating them into requirements.

The requirements are gathered using different requirement-gathering tools explained in a previous section, as depicted in Table 5-4.

Table 5-4. Product Objective-Customer Value-Product Attribute-Weight

Product Objectives	Themes/Customer Values	Product Attributes	Weights
Improve revenue	Increase hotel engagement	Customer onboarding	2
		Hotel customer satisfaction	2
		Hotel customer safety	1.5
		Ancillary revenue	1
	Improve product quality	Robust systems	1
		Informative system	0.5
Increase market growth	Penetrate coworking space and Airbnb owner market	Hardware interoperability	1
		Integration with marketplace	1

Step 3: Requirements Analysis. The team then analyzes the requirements mapped from the market needs and market discoveries by 5W1H analysis. Based on the requirements, they now have a list of tactical, strategic, and disruptive features. The list of tactical features that will be developed for the next year is then tabulated and scored against the weights of each product attribute.

Step 4: Product Prioritization. The team performs feature scoring based on the customer values (see Table 5-5). Then they multiply the scores with the weights of each attribute to get feature values as follows.

Table 5-5. Scoring the Features Based on Customer Values

No.	Feature	Hotel Customer Onboarding (Weight: 2)	Hotel Customer Satisfaction (Weight: 2)	...	Customer Value Score
1	Room booking bot	10 x 2 = 20	8 x 2 = 16	...	49.5
2	Integration with hotel reservation software	9 x 2 = 18	8 x 2 = 16	...	52.5
3	ID verification and matching	9 x 2 = 18	7 x 2 = 14	...	62
4	Guest face enrollment	8 x 2 = 16	8 x 2 = 14	...	65
...	...	...	...	... ...	

Then calculate the feature cost by the following equation:

$$Cost = Man\ Weeks\ Needed \times \frac{100}{Man\ Weeks\ of\ the\ Most\ Complex\ Feature}$$

The most complex feature is predicted to be completed in 20 weeks. The feature costs are tabulated as follows (Table 5-6).

Table 5-6. Estimating the Feature Costs

No.	Feature	Man Weeks	Feature Cost
1	Room booking bot	13	65
2	Integration with hotel reservation software	7	35
3	ID verification and matching	20	100
4	Guest face enrollment	6	30
...	...	...	...

The team then plots the customer value vs. feature cost (effort), as shown in Table 5-7, and then plots it in the prioritization graph (Figure 5-14).

- *Quadrant IV* (high customer value, low feature cost): This is low-hanging fruit where the outcome is optimal with minimal effort. These are highly likely features to be developed.

- *Quadrant III* (high customer value, high feature cost): This feature is developed if it can be a strong differentiator/delighter.

- *Quadrant II* (low customer value, low feature cost): This feature is developed if it is a must-have feature.

- *Quadrant I* (low customer value, high feature cost): This feature should not be developed.

Table 5-7. Customer Value vs. Feature Cost

Feature Name	Description	Customer Value	Feature Cost
F1	Room booking bot	49.5	50
F2	Integration with hotel reservation software	52.5	35
F3	Guest ID verification and matching	62	100
F4	Guest face enrollment	65	30
F5	Room upgrade/upsell bot	60	55
F6	Integration with the door lock system via Bluetooth/face	64.5	45
F7	Situational awareness bot	52	80
F8	Integration with the vending machine via Bluetooth/face	59	40
F9	Integration with turnstiles with face recognition	47.5	35
F10	Integration with the employee attendance system with face recognition	40	40

The team plots the customer value vs. feature cost in the prioritization graph (Figure 5-14).

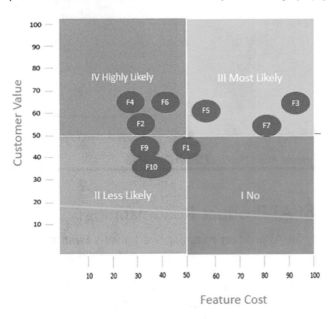

Figure 5-14. Prioritization graph of customer value vs. feature cost

Based on the preceding prioritization graph, the SmartConcierge team prioritizes the features as follows:

- Guest face enrollment (F4)

- Integration with the Bluetooth/NFC door lock system (F6)

- Integration with hotel reservation software (F1)

- Room upgrade/upsell bot (F5)

- ID verification and matching (F3)

- Etc.

Then they divide the features to be developed in the Q1–Q4 roadmap.

Step 5. Roadmap Efficacy Evaluation. After the features on the roadmap are successfully implemented, the team continually validates the market and analyzes the feature usage using Feature Audit Matrix (Figure 5-15). Many users should have frequently used the highly ranked features 1–10 as possible (which positively correlated with product objectives); otherwise, they must review their market needs, discovery, requirements, and prioritization processes.

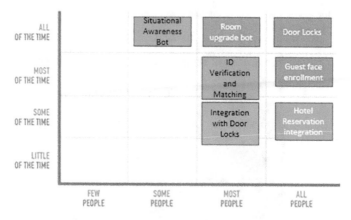

Figure 5-15. Feature Audit Matrix of SmartConcierge

Ten Sins of AI Product Roadmapping

When building an AI product roadmap, we have to avoid the ten most common mistakes:

1. *Prioritizing requirements based on the latest AI hype*: It is tempting to build requirements based on the latest untested but trendy AI methods fresh out of R&D labs. Technical AI product people are prone to this tendency.

2. *Prioritizing elusive requirements that are not feasible technologically*: AI products help humans automate or augment decision-making by replicating cognitive systems. Selecting far-fetched requirements that only happen in sci-fi movies is sometimes enticing.

3. *Prioritizing requirements based on revenue potential*: It is natural to focus on requirements with higher revenue potential. After all, revenue is the reason a product exists. But obsessing over the revenue aspect only causes us to lose sight of the long-term objectives.

4. *Prioritizing requirements of biggest customers*: The big company name in your customer list is significant in enterprise products. They may also contribute to the revenue, but unless your company is a consulting/service provider, focus on requirements that will satisfy the majority of your customers.

5. *Prioritizing requirements concurring with technical teams*: In a tech-dominated organization such as an AI startup, technical people like software engineers and AI specialists have a powerful influence and power to dominate in defining and prioritizing requirements. This should be avoided by focusing on requirements with maximum customer values first instead of technical team preference.

6. *Prioritizing requirements of the end user only instead of the buyer*: In an enterprise product, the end user and the buyer are two different people. For product managers, getting end user feedback is easier than for the buyer because there are many usage analytics tools and opportunities to interact with end users. But product managers also need to balance requirements prioritization by listening and gathering insights from the buyer or the decision-maker of the product.

7. *Prioritizing requirements without common themes*: The theme with customer value as output unifies the requirements for a particular period. The themes are the underlying how-to of product objectives. With themes, it is easier to define product attributes.

8. *Prioritizing requirements based on the pressures of the business team:* The business team is an essential team that communicates regularly with customers and usually acts as a customer's voice. But the business team has different KPIs from the product team, such as revenue and sales. So they are motivated to pressure the product team to deliver the customer's requirements with more significant revenue potential. This conflicts with the product manager's goal: to create a product with optimal value to as many customers as possible. The product manager must also align customer requirements directly with the whole product strategy.

9. *Prioritizing requirements based on what competitors are doing:* Watching what competitors are doing is necessary, but we should not establish our prioritization on competitors' features to check the box. Instead, we should focus on customer needs. We must use competitors' products as a benchmark and learn from them, but not blindly develop things they have been building.

10. *Prioritizing requirements based on the request of management:* It is common in any organization to accommodate the requirements defined by top-level management. But a good product manager must always challenge the management request with market and customer data and align their request with the whole product objectives and roadmap.

Conclusion

This chapter teaches about building product strategies for enterprise AI products. There is no rigid methodology for product strategy. We only provide a guidance or framework, which we think is the best for such complex products.

Building product strategy through a clearly defined roadmap is crucial for product success regardless of whether a particular product has an AI on it or not. The product roadmap starts by defining a high-level product vision, including objectives, missions, and beliefs. The product vision must always align with the customer and market needs. A product roadmap continuously evolves with changes in user needs and behavior, technological advancement, and business conditions. A product manager must always collaborate with multiple stakeholders to validate the tactical, strategic, and disruptive requirements through the market, business, technical, operational, and financial aspects.

Ultimately, a good product roadmap will deliver optimal customer value, eventually sustaining the company's business.

Key Takeaways

- Product strategy defines what a product must achieve and how to achieve it.

- A product roadmap is an outline of product strategy from product vision to requirements to features for a particular timeframe.

- The five-step product strategy framework consists of product visioning, discovery, requirements analysis, prioritization, and evaluation of roadmap efficacy.

- A product roadmap has different audiences, internal and external.

- A product roadmap must adapt to changes in the business world.

- Product vision consists of product objectives, missions, and principles.

- We can use the SETDA (Sense, Explain, Think, Decide, Act) framework to determine customer needs for AI products.

- There are several tools to perform *need understanding* and *discovery*.

- The product manager must collaborate with other stakeholders for *discovery* and mapping needs into requirements and prioritization.

- A product lifecycle has four states: introduction, growth, maturity, and decline.

- The requirements must be categorized into tactical, strategic, and disruptive based on their state in the product lifecycle.

- The requirements must be mapped into features and categorized into themes with customer values as outcomes.

- The Collaborative Weighted Scorecard prioritization method is suitable for enterprise AI products with heavy R&D and innovation.

- We can measure the efficacy of the product roadmap by using a method such as Feature Usage Metrics.

Human-Centered AI Experience Design

In the previous chapter, we learned how to create an AI product roadmap. This is a tool that product managers and engineers use to plan the features and functionality of AI-based products based on user needs and demands. The roadmap helps ensure that the products align with the company's strategy and vision. It can also be used to communicate with stakeholders about the planned features and their impact on the business.

In this chapter, we will explore the principles of human factors that make it easy and intuitive for users to interact with an AI application. These principles include embracing customer needs, imposing trustworthiness, being ethical, and amplifying human capability. We will also learn about design principles that serve as guidelines for creating user-friendly and valuable AI products

© Adhiguna Mahendra 2023
A. Mahendra, *AI Startup Strategy*, https://doi.org/10.1007/978-1-4842-9502-1_6

based on the research and work of experts such as Don Norman, Amber Case, and Motoharu Dei. These principles and the design thinking approach aim to create user-friendly and valuable AI products, which involve empathizing with the user, defining the problem, ideating solutions, prototyping and testing, and implementing the final solution.

By applying these principles and using design thinking, we can create a human-centered user experience design for AI products. AI user experience design is a process that focuses on the needs of users when creating products that rely on artificial intelligence. It considers how people will interact with AI-powered systems and aims to make those experiences as positive and easy as possible. By considering how users will input information, receive feedback, and navigate, designers can create intuitive interfaces that make using AI feel more natural. This is especially important in cases where AI is used to make decisions or recommendations, as users must have confidence in the system's accuracy and trust the results. In short, AI user experience design ensures users have an excellent overall experience when interacting with artificial intelligence. Finally, we will demonstrate these concepts through a case study with an example of how to design the human interface for an AI-first logistics application.

The Principles of Human Factors in AI

When it comes to artificial intelligence, human factors are essential for creating a successful product. Human factors refer to the various aspects of design that make an AI application easy and intuitive for users. Understanding user needs is critical in designing an effective AI solution, and translating AI capabilities into user-friendly solutions is essential to success.

By considering human factors, we can create AI applications that are truly helpful to users and solve their problems. In addition, by making our applications easy to use, we can help reduce user anxiety about using AI products and increase user adoption rates. Ultimately, incorporating human factors into our AI designs is the best way to ensure that our applications are beneficial and valuable to users.

There are several principles of human factors for AI products:

- Embrace customer needs.
- Impose trustworthiness.
- Be ethical.
- Amplify human capability.

Embrace Customer Needs

If we want to build AI applications that work, understanding customer needs should be at the top of our list. AI applications are designed to automate or augment human decision-making and to do this effectively. We need to understand what our customers' needs and problems are. This is especially important when it comes to cognitive loads or the amount of cognitive work that a person must do to complete a task. If an AI application is going to relieve some of that cognitive load, it needs to know the customer's problem in the first place.

Embracing customer needs is essential for any business looking to use AI applications. By understanding what our customers need, we can create applications that make their lives easier and help them achieve their goals. To embrace customer needs, we need to understand what the problem is, who has this problem, why this is a problem, and how humans solve one specific problem and then replicate the cognitive process to be performed by AI.

For example, in an AI-powered logistics application, the problem is it is challenging to plan the most efficient schedule and delivery route (what). The fleet managers have this problem (who). This is an impactful problem to solve because it can save delivery costs and time (why). An experienced fleet dispatcher intuitively knows how to build a delivery route with hundreds of vehicles and drivers with pencil and paper (how). This capability can be replicated in route optimization software such as *Routific* and *OptimoRoute*.

Amplify Human Capability

We also need to understand the strength of AI in performing tasks. AI is better at some tasks, and humans are better at others.

AI's real value is reducing human cognitive load and amplifying human capabilities.

Humans are powerful in cognitive tasks like thinking strategically and creatively, innovating things, connecting the dots, creating new concepts, and persuading people on a personal level.

Some tasks are better performed than AI, for example, analyzing huge and complex data, doing a repetitive job, and performing dangerous tasks for humans.

The key is to find an intersection of human strengths, user needs (tasks), and AI strengths, as shown in Table 6-1.

Table 6-1. Strength of Human vs. AI

	Strength	Task	Example
Human	• Thinking out of the box • Communicating persuasively • Innovating	Strategic, creative, intuitive, personal, reason	Building product plans Writing science fiction Writing songs Closing deals Negotiating
AI	• Doing repetitive things efficiently and precisely • Analyzing and processing a large amount of data • Generating new things (song, image, text, video, material, drug) given examples	Repetitive, data-intensive, dangerous, precise, logical	Summarizing Generating human-like text Forecasting Scheduling Allocating Recommending Sweeping the floors

Another important aspect is to differentiate between *augmenting* and *automating* tasks using AI. Augmenting means we are building assistive AI to help humans with their tasks, and automating means we are building autonomous AI to perform a particular task without human intervention. We need to understand the use cases and motivations for automating vs. augmenting some tasks (see Table 6-2). Here are some examples:

- *Assistive AI*: A doctor uses a computer system to help with diagnosis by providing relevant information and data to which the doctor may not have access. The system assists the doctor in making a more accurate diagnosis.

- *Autonomous AI*: A L5 self-driving car can navigate roads and intersections without input from a human driver. The car is performing the task of driving completely autonomously.

There are several aspects to consider regarding whether the AI system should augment or automate our tasks. We want the AI to augment the tasks with a high stake and that need to be regulated or too complex to handle by AI. We also do not want AI to automate the activity we enjoy, such as playing music.

Table 6-2. Augmenting vs. Automating

	Used When	Motivation	Example
Augmenting (assistive AI)	• Critical • High stakes and regulated • Enjoyable • Extremely complex • Technically infeasible • High value	• Reducing cognitive load • Greater control • Improved job satisfaction	• AI to help doctors with diagnostics • AI to help lawyers find conflicting legal clauses • AI to suggest portfolio optimization for investment managers
Automating (autonomous AI)	• Lack of ability and knowledge to do the task • Repetitive and boring • Low value • Dangerous	• Reduced human cost • Reduced risk • Improved safety • Reduced time to finish	• Autonomous guided vehicles for warehouse • Mine-sweeping robots

Based on the preceding table, we want to use AI to automate tasks that we lack the ability and knowledge to do, such as correcting grammatical mistakes and improving our paragraphs for someone untrained in a particular language. Secondly, we would also want the AI to automate repetitive and tedious tasks with low value, such as counting cars and people. Lastly, the automated task should be dangerous, such as cleaning and detecting land mines on the battlefield.

We can also categorize AI (*assistive* vs. *autonomous*) based on the SETDA framework previously explained. Assistive AI would only be able to help us *Sense, Explain, Think, and Decide*, while autonomous AI will help us *Decide* and do some *Actions* too (Figure 6-1).

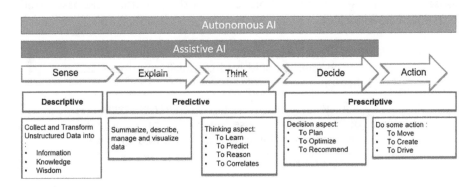

Figure 6-1. SETDA framework and AI type

Embrace Trustworthiness

AI trustworthiness is an essential factor to consider when designing AI products. An AI can be well-intentioned, robustly performing as we envisioned, explainable, transparent, and safe to use. We must embrace AI trustworthiness to build our confidence in these systems and ensure they are reliable.

There are several examples of why embracing AI trustworthiness is important. One is the case of a self-driving car. If a self-driving car is untrustworthy, it could lead to accidents and loss of life. Another example is in healthcare. If a patient's healthcare AI product is untrustworthy, it could lead to incorrect diagnosis or treatment.

Therefore, we must design AI products with trustworthiness in mind. Doing so can build confidence in these systems and ensure they perform as expected.

Be Ethical

Ethical AI is an important consideration for all AI applications. By incorporating ethical AI practices into our product design, we can ensure that our applications act fairly and do not expose user data. Some examples of ethical AI practices include privacy-preserving models and avoiding bias in decision-making.

Privacy is key in ethical AI. We must build models that cannot identify or infer details about individual users. This protects the user's privacy and helps ensure that their data is not used in harmful ways.

Another important consideration is *bias*. We need to ensure that our AI models do not discriminate against people based on race, gender, or sexuality. This is important for ensuring everyone has an equal chance of benefiting from AI's advantages. As AI continues to evolve and become more sophisticated, it is more important than ever that we ensure that it is used ethically and responsibly. With so much at stake, it is crucial that we take measures to ensure that the technology we develop does not have negative consequences for society as a whole. Some of the potential risks associated with unethical AI include

1. *Unfairness:* If an AI model is biased against certain groups of people, it could lead to unfair treatment and discrimination.

2. *Privacy infringement:* If data is not properly protected, it could be accessed and used without the concerned individual's consent. This could lead to a loss of privacy and personal information.

3. *Automated decision-making*: If AI models are given control over life-altering decisions, there is a risk that they could make inaccurate or harmful decisions without human intervention.

4. *Moral hazard: If AI systems are used to make decisions on behalf of humans, it could lead to a loss of responsibility and accountability on the part of humans.*

Therefore, ethical AI is important and necessary to avoid these potential risks.

User Experience Design of an AI Product

Applying design thinking is essential to design user-friendly and helpful AI products. Design thinking is a human-centered approach that helps identify user needs and envision innovative solutions. This approach allows AI products to be designed with the user in mind, making them more intuitive and valuable.

One example of an AI product using design thinking is Google Assistant. Its designers interviewed people who used digital assistants and found they wanted the assistant to be more personalized to their needs. As a result, Google Assistant was designed with features such as a customizable interface and personalized recommendations. Another example is Amazon Echo, which was developed based on the findings from user research. The team spoke to Amazon customers who used Echo and found out they wanted an assistant that could control all their smart devices at home. As a result, Amazon Echo was designed with features such as voice control and compatibility with different smart devices.

Thus, design thinking is useful for designing AI products as it considers both the users' needs and the company's business goals.

Another interesting example is how OpenAI developed their product ChatGPT. OpenAI developed ChatGPT using a "learn-as-you-go" approach, much like teaching a child. They started by showing the AI a wide range of Internet content and trained it to predict text patterns. Human feedback was then used to fine-tune the AI's learning, enabling it to understand and respond accurately to user needs in various scenarios. They designed a collaborative system where humans supervised and managed the AI, ensuring that it continually improved. This thoughtful approach resulted in ChatGPT, a smart AI tool that can write text, choose tools, and even quality-check human work. Essentially, OpenAI uses design thinking methods, which involve testing, refining, and seeking user feedback in a repetitive process to enhance the product.[1]

---

[1] www.ted.com/talks/greg_brockman_the_inside_story_of_chatgpt_s_astonishing_potential/c/transcript

Each of these products was successful because the designers took the time to understand the user needs and create a product that met those needs. By using design thinking, AI designers can create products that are both useful and enjoyable to use.

Principles of AI UX Design

Designers should keep a few fundamental principles in mind when it comes to user experience with AI products. First and foremost, the focus should always be on the human aspect – on solving problems for people – not on the AI algorithms and technology themselves. In addition, design thinking principles should be used to help create an intuitive, user-friendly interface. And finally, calm technology should be taken into consideration to ensure that the product does not require too much attention from users. By considering these things, designers can create delightful and user-friendly AI products.

Design Thinking

Design thinking is a human-centered methodology for creative problem-solving. It's based on the idea that if you can understand a person's needs and thoughts, you can develop better solutions to their problems.

Design thinking is very relevant to AI products. Many AI products are designed to solve specific problems, and it's essential to understand the needs of the people who will be using them. Empathy, expansive thinking, and experimentation are all essential aspects of design thinking that can help make AI products more user-friendly.

Empathy is the ability to understand and feel what someone else is feeling. When designing an AI product, it's important to put yourself in the shoes of the people who will be using it. What are their needs, and how do they think? What are their frustrations, and what are their hopes for the product?

Expansive thinking is the ability to see beyond the obvious. When designing an AI product, it's crucial to think about all the ways it could be used and all the possible applications. Can the product be adapted to meet the needs of different users? Can it be used in different situations? Is there potential for growth and expansion?

Experimentation is the willingness to try new things. Being open to change and willing to experiment with different ideas is essential when designing an AI product. Sometimes the best solutions come from trying something that initially seems like a bad idea.

Design thinking is essential for designing AI product experiences because of the high level of technicality involved in AI. Focusing on the user and their problem, rather than the technology itself, is essential to ensure that the product is effective and meets the needs of those using it. Additionally, aligning all team members in a common direction helps ensure that everyone is working toward the same goal and that no one is working at cross-purposes. Finally, using design thinking to validate whether or not AI should even be used to solve a given problem can help avoid unnecessary implementation of this complex technology.

To create an effective and innovative AI product, it is important to understand the design thinking process from Stanford (see Figure 6-2). This five-step process is based on empathy, definition, ideation, prototyping, and testing.

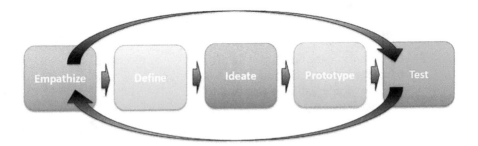

Figure 6-2. Stanford's design thinking process

The first step, *empathy*, is about understanding the user's needs and wants. You need to put yourself in the user's shoes and try to understand what they are looking for. For example, when developing an AI product, you need to consider what features the user would want and how they would want to use them.

The second step, *definition*, is about figuring out what you want your AI product to do. It would be best if you defined the product's goals and what problem it is trying to solve. This helps you determine what features to focus on and how to achieve your goals best.

The third step, *ideation*, is where you develop new ideas for your AI product. This step can be done by brainstorming with others or simply thinking about ways to improve your original ideas. It's essential to be creative and think outside the box during this step.

The fourth step, *prototyping*, is where you start implementing your ideas. This can involve creating a basic prototype of your product or just sketching out how it will work. It's important to have a rough idea of what the product will look like and how it will function before moving on to the next step.

The fifth and final step, *testing*, is where you put your prototype to the test. This involves testing out your product with real users and getting their feedback. It's important to listen to what users say and make changes based on their feedback.

AI UX Design Principles

Design principles serve as a guide to interaction design. For AI interaction design, we shall adopt Don Norman's six design principles, which are

1. *Visibility*: Make sure users know what the AI is doing and how it interacts with them. For example, the blue light ring turns on with Amazon Echo when the AI listens to you.

2. *Feedback*: Let users know the AI's actions due to their interactions. For example, with Google Home, after asking it to do something, it will read back what it heard and then either do what you asked or provide an error message.

3. *Constraints*: Place limits on what the AI can and cannot do to prevent users' confusion or frustration. For example, Google Home will only respond to certain questions and not others.

4. *Mapping*: A clear relationship between control and effect should be created to create a smooth user experience. In other words, users should be able to easily understand how they can control the product and what impact their actions will have. An example of this principle in action can be seen in the design of Amazon Echo. When interacting with Echo, users can speak directly to it to control various functions, such as playing music or setting a timer. The clear mapping between control (speaking) and effect (the desired action) makes it easy for users to know what to do and ensures a smooth interaction.

5. *Consistency*: Keep interface elements similar across different platforms and devices to avoid confusion on the part of users. For example, the layout of buttons in the Google Home app is very similar to that in the Google Home app for Android phones.

6. *Affordance (clarity): Use clear labels and instructions so that users know how to interact with the AI product. For example, the Amazon Echo app has clear instructions for connecting your Echo device and changing settings.*

Don Norman based these principles on his observations of how people interact with the physical world, where human-centered design is an approach that puts humans' needs, capabilities, and behaviors first. It designs around these things to accommodate them better.

Amber Case has proposed one additional principle for interaction design in the digital age: calm technology.[2] These principles can be applied to AI products to create a more user-friendly experience.

All of these principles are important when designing AI products. For example, if the goal of a product is to help people manage their schedules, then it should be designed with that purpose in mind. The interface should be easy to learn and use so people can get up and running quickly. Feedback must be clear so that users know what is happening as they interact with the product. Consistency ensures that users will have a predictable experience no matter which part of the product they use. Repetition makes it easy for people to remember how to use the product. And anticipation helps people plan their interactions and anticipate the consequences of their actions.

The calm technology principle is also vital for AI products. It refers to designs that minimize distractions and provide a sense of tranquility. This can be especially important for products that are used often or for long periods. For example, if someone uses an AI assistant to manage their calendar, they may not want interruptions while working on it. In this case, calm technology would ensure that the assistant does not pop up notifications or alerts that could distract them from their work.

Design principles from Don Norman and Amber Case provide a foundation for creating user-friendly AI products. By understanding these principles and applying them appropriately, designers can create products that are easy to use and offer a satisfying experience for users.

Another essential principle is actionable AI, which Motoharu Dei coins.[3] Actionable AI is an artificial intelligence technology that can provide specific actions a user can take to change the outcome. In the context of loan applications, for example, it could guide improving one's credit score or what documents to submit to be approved. By providing clear and actionable instructions, actionable AI can help users improve their chances of success and make the most out of artificial intelligence technology.

AI UX Design Process Framework

In this section, we will use design thinking as the base for our framework to design AI user experience from *empathizing* to *testing* the AI product idea. The step-by-step and outputs from each stage will be explained.

---

[2] https://calmtech.com/
[3] https://medium.com/@daydreamersjp/proposing-a-new-ai-concept-actionable-ai-6873abd6ceb5

1. Empathize

Empathize is the first phase in design thinking to understand more about the customer persona and problems.

Steps:

We will do the following steps in the *Empathize* phase:

1. *Hypothesize*: We must build a hypothesis of the enterprise user persona at the strategic, tactical, or operational level because each level has different needs, problems, success metrics, and objectives.

2. *Decide on the research methodology*: In order to decide on the research methodology to perform user research, one must first consider the hypothesis defined in point 1. Once these have been determined, the most appropriate research methodology can be selected. Questionnaires, in-depth interviews (IDI), focus group discussion (FGD), and contextual inquiry or ethnographic[4] research are all viable methods that can be used to understand the users deeply. Selecting the methodology that will provide the most accurate information to build an accurate user persona is crucial. Some of the critical questions that need to be answered are

   a. Who are the users?

   b. At what level are the users (strategic, tactical, operational)?

   c. What are their success metrics and objectives?

   d. What are their problems and pains?

3. *Acquire data*: Go out and perform data collection on real users.

---

[4] https://uxdesign.cc/contextual-inquiry-a-primer-14e2e0696fb9

4. *Data synthesis*: Data synthesis combines all the data acquired from the previous process to create a more complete and accurate understanding of the user persona, levels, needs, and specific problems. The information gathered from individual users is combined and analyzed to develop a more comprehensive view of the user's wants and needs. This can help identify patterns and commonalities among users that may not have been apparent from studying individual datasets. Synthesizing data can also help prioritize needs and determine the most important problems to be addressed.

Output:

The output expected from this step is we can get the persona of every enterprise user, such as:

- *Decisioning level*: Strategic, tactical, or operational
- Objective, problem, and pain
- Tasks and success metrics

We will use the persona data to create the hypothesis with the following format: *"We believe the [target users] whose decisioning level is in [strategic/ tactical/operational] in [target enterprise market] have [problems] in finishing [tasks] to achieve their goal in [most important objectives]."*

2. Define

Define is the second phase in design thinking to understand more about the user journey and tasks.

Steps:

We will do the following steps in the *Define* phase:

1. Detail the enterprise user persona and mental model. The sub-steps are as follows:

   a. Organize into persona groups:

       i. *Strategic user*: Those who make decisions that impact the overall direction of the company.

      ii. *Tactical user*: Those who carry out the strategic plans of the company. They may not make decisions, but they implement the decisions made by the strategic users.

      iii. *Operational user*: Operational users are those who carry out the day-to-day tasks of the company.

   b. Make the persona realistic by creating the character and their mental model. This is especially important for users who will be interacting with our products. We must ensure that the persona we create for these users is based on real-world data so that they act and think believably and naturally. If the persona and mental model are unrealistic, it can lead to negative user experiences. For example, suppose the persona we create for an AI product is too idealistic or unrealistic. In that case, users may feel they are not being taken seriously or treated as intelligent. This can cause them to lose trust in the product and even lead to them abandoning it altogether.

   c. Similarly, if the mental models we create are unrealistic, it can lead to confusion and frustration among users. For example, if the task we ask an AI product to perform is too complicated for users to understand, they will likely become confused and frustrated. This can lead them to abandon or misuse the product in ways that could have serious consequences.

2. Create an AI user journey map of the whole process to finish the core tasks. The sub-steps are as follows:

   a. Divide by user persona decision level (strategic, tactical, operational).

   b. Define their touchpoints to finish their core task.

   c. Define problems and opportunities at every touchpoint.

   d. Define how AI can help solve the problems in every touchpoint by automating or augmenting some of the cognitive tasks defined by the SETDA (*Sense, Explain, Think, Decide, Act*) framework (Table 6-3).

Table 6-3. Cognitive Tasks and Their Categories

	Sense	Explain	Think	Decide	Act
Cognitive task	See, hear, feel	Speak, describe, visualize	Calculate, predict, verify, reason	Allocate, schedule, plan	Write, drive, operate, move
Objects	Person, speech, odor	Tabular data, paragraph	Sales, temperature, traffic	Staff, equipment, vehicles	Machine, robot, drone, new songs, new material
AI techniques used	Computer vision, speech recognition	Speech generator, natural language processing	Machine learning, Bayesian network	Optimization algorithm, symbolic logic, reinforcement learning	Generative AI, autonomous systems

Output:

After performing the preceding steps, the output from this phase is a user persona canvas (Figure 6-3) and AI user journey map (Table 6-4).

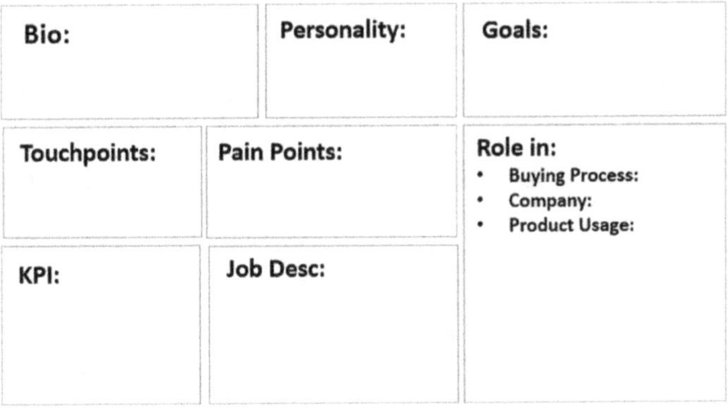

Figure 6-3. User persona canvas template

Table 6-4. AI User Journey Map Template

Journey	Touchpoint1	Touchpoint2	Touchpoint3
User goals			
Expectation			
Cognitive task			
Current practice			
Tools			
Current pain points			

3. Ideate

Ideate is the third phase in design thinking, which is brainstorming potential AI algorithms to solve a problem and the corresponding dataset needed to make those algorithms work. Ideation is integral to the design thinking process and can help teams develop innovative solutions to complex problems.

Steps:

We do the following steps in the *Ideate* phase:

1. From the user journey map in the previous step, we define AI opportunities for each cognitive task that can be automated or augmented by doing the following:

    a. Define the category of the cognitive task within the SETDA (*Sense, Explain, Thinking, Decide, Act*) framework.

    b. Determine the AI solution plan and its feasibility. AI solution planning and feasibility analysis is a methodology for selecting the best AI models and algorithms for a particular cognitive task. It involves understanding how often the AI model needs to be updated and the trustworthiness expectation, such as fairness, explainability, and robustness. It also includes understanding possible errors that may happen by human users or the systems and how to mitigate them. Lastly, it evaluates the minimum performance our AI solutions need to contribute to real business values. Therefore, the components of these sub-steps are

i. AI model and algorithm category

1. *Machine learning/deep learning*: Suitable for prediction, classification forecasting, and generative tasks

2. *Decision optimization*: Suitable for scheduling, allocation, and routing tasks

3. *Knowledge representation and reasoning*: Suitable for verification, validation, and audit tasks.

ii. *Model update*: How often should an AI model be updated to remain accurate and performant? The frequency at which an AI model is updated can depend on a variety of factors, such as

1. Changes in the inputs (environment): If the environment in which the model is being used is changing rapidly, it may be necessary to update the model more frequently to keep up with these changes. This is also referred to as data drift; a change of the input data distribution to the model is being applied. Some inputs change rapidly overtime, such as house prices in a particular city, smartphone images, customer behavior, etc.

2. Changes in the business process, rules, and regulations: This is also referred to as concept drift, defined as a change in the underlying concept or relationship that the model is attempting to learn. An example is in vehicle classification. Some pickup trucks that were previously classified as trucks are no longer classified as a truck due to regulations, so the definition of what constitutes a truck changes as a concept.

3. Degradation of AI model performance: Suppose the AI model's performance degrades quickly overtime (usually due to complexity, unavailability, low quality of the data, or data drift). In that case, updating the model more frequently may be necessary to keep its accuracy.

4. Accuracy vs. risk expectation: How critical are the AI models for the business? Model updates must be performed frequently if it involves a huge amount of money or life risks when the accuracy is compromised. An example is the predictive maintenance model for aircraft engines.

iii. *Trustworthiness aspects*: Trustworthiness is the level of trust expected of AI products to produce fair, unbiased, and explainable outputs. This is especially true for AI applications in critical use cases such as healthcare, finance, law enforcement, and aviation, where regulation, audit, and governance are strict. If an AI product has trustworthiness problems, it will eventually have legal issues. This is because people will not be able to trust the product to produce accurate results, which could lead to severe consequences in critical areas such as healthcare and finance. AI developers must ensure that their products are trustworthy to avoid these legal issues. Regarding errors in AI products, two types of errors can occur, human and system errors. Incorrect data entry, assumptions, or usage mistakes can cause human errors. On the other hand, system errors are usually caused by coding mistakes, unexpected software/firmware/API changes or updates, software glitches, or edge cases. No matter the type of error, it's important to have a plan for how to deal with it. We need to have procedures in place for catching and correcting human errors. We need to have the plan to recover from system errors and prevent them from happening again. So the components of this sub-step are

1. *Fairness and explainability*: Fairness refers to the idea that the outcomes of a model or algorithm should be unbiased and not disproportionately affect certain groups of people, while explainability refers to understanding and explaining how a model or algorithm makes its decisions.

2. *Risk and error*: Errors refer to mistakes or deviations from expected or intended outcomes, while risk refers to the potential negative consequences of an AI system or its deployment:

   a. Possible human and system errors

   b. Error risk and the path taken

iv. *Minimum Algorithmic Performance (MAP)*: The Minimum Algorithmic Performance (MAP) concept is essential for businesses looking to adopt AI products. MAP defines the threshold at which an AI product is considered minimally effective and still provides acceptable business value for the users. In other words, MAP helps businesses identify when an AI product is ready for use and can provide tangible benefits. An example of MAP in action is using machine learning algorithms for fraud detection. A business may set a MAP threshold of 90% accuracy for its fraud detection system. This means that the system must be accurate at least 90% of the time to be considered effective. Anything less, and the business may not see a return on its investment in the AI product. MAP can simply be standard metrics like accuracy, precision, recall, and F1 score, but in my experience, it is better that the MAP can be directly converted into some business performance metrics, such as on-time performance, cost reduction, time saving, revenue increase, etc. MAP can also be used as a value justifier, which justifies the ROI of the AI system. The precondition is that the MAP promised must be aligned with the technical and commercial feasibility.

2. Define dataset planning and its feasibility. Dataset planning and feasibility ensure that the condition of data availability and the possibility to be acquired, annotated, and validated is feasible. This includes having an annotator with the needed expertise available at a sensible cost and defining the Extract-Transform-Load (ETL) process well and feasibly. By planning and assessing the feasibility of a dataset operation, we can ensure that our AI product is production ready. So the components considered are

   i.   Data availability

   ii. Annotator availability and expertise

   iii. ETL process needed

   iv. Data validation

3. Define a feedback mechanism. We must define a feedback mechanism that will be useful for our AI product improvement. The feedback mechanism consists of two different methods:

   i.   *Implicit*: A measurement of how users behave when they are unaware that their actions are being monitored. This type of feedback is usually used to evaluate how users interact with an AI product to improve the design or effectiveness of the product. An example is measuring how long users finish a task or how often they misunderstand the data input instruction.

   ii. *Explicit*: When the user performs an action specifically designed to enable them to give feedback to the system. This might be something like rating a prediction quality. Another explicit feedback mechanism for AI products is *active learning*, which is a key part of the machine learning process that helps improve models' accuracy by only asking humans to label datasets that are most uncertain. This reduces the amount of time and data needed to improve the model. Additionally, active learning can be used in a few AI applications, such as image recognition and natural language processing. The use of active learning in these applications helps improve the product's accuracy and usability.

Output:

The output from this phase is an AI experience design canvas (see Figure 6-4).

Problem	Data	Process	Minimum Acceptable Performance
• What is the problem • Why is it a problem? • Whose problem it is?	• Source • Data availability • Annotator availability • Data transformation • Data Validation	• Which Process is augmented or automated • Current Practice • SETDA? • Step before this process • Step after this process • Who is augmented/automated	• How to evaluate AI model? • Which metrics used? • What is MAP ?
	Solution • AI Type • Is it feasible? • Has it been researched? • Output Expected		**User Persona** • User Type? • Job KPI • Typical Traits • Career Objective?

Value	Trustworthiness	Feedbacks	Model Update	Risk&Error
• The size of problem • Impact of AI • What is revenue/saving/uplift • What is the human baselines	• How to guarantee fairness • Explainability proposed	• Implicit • Explicit	• Frequency • Notification	• Human Error • System Error • Error risk • What path taken when error happens • How to monitor error

Figure 6-4. AI experience design canvas

4. Prototype

The next phase in design thinking is a *prototype*. Prototyping is a key part of the design thinking process. It helps us test our ideas and assumptions quickly and get user feedback. With feedback from users, we can then make changes to our prototypes and test them again. This cycle of feedback and iteration helps us create better solutions.

In the context of AI, end-to-end prototyping is especially important. Solutions that are built with AI (AI-first solutions) are quite complex. They need to perform their tasks well, but it's also important for them to make it clear to users what they can and can't do.

The main difference between traditional and AI-first applications is that the latter augment and automate a business process and a human cognitive capability. To make an AI-first application feasible as a business, we need to ensure it is production-ready and not only demo-ready.

In production AI, the last 20% takes 80% of the work.

Getting to the 80% drives a good demo, but the last 20% determines whether this AI-first application can be used in the real world or just for showing purposes.

The 80% is the usual UI/UX and basic AI models that satisfy the business needs (MAP, minimum acceptable performance).

The 20% is things such as dataset availability, ensuring the AI model remains accurate, edge case handling, human in the loop feedback mechanisms such as *active learning*, error handling, and explainability of the AI models.

So, if we don't consider the last 20%, there will be only a dispute in the end.

Let me reiterate: if 20% is not considered, the AI business will only become *the business of dispute.*

Most AI businesses fail because they did an excellent job in 80% but failed to validate the 20%.

The consequence is that even just for prototyping, it must be thorough.

We need to be sure that our AI algorithms are meeting the users' requirements, our model can perform well with the datasets we have, and they can handle the volume and variety of data we need to process. Prototyping allows us to test our algorithms on a small scale with limited data. This gives us a better idea of how well they will work. It is important to prototype your solution before committing to a full-scale implementation. Prototyping will allow you to test your assumptions about how AI solutions will be viable business- and technical-wise.

Steps:

We will do the following steps in the *Prototype* phase:

1. *Gathering a development team*: Build a small team consisting of a front-end engineer, back-end engineer, UI/UX designer, machine learning engineer, data engineer, and dataset annotators to plan and execute the prototyping phase.

2. Creating the user interface design and wireframe of the AI application MVP (Minimum Viable Product), which considers

   a. User input and validation

   b. Instructions

   c. *Feedback mechanisms*: Implicit and explicit

   d. Explainability and transparency

   e. Error handling

3. *Creating an AI model prototype*: It is important to build a prototype of the AI model before creating the full-fledged model for production. This prototype will help us test and verify the acceptability of the performance of the AI algorithm using ground truth data. The AI engineers involved in building the prototype must be experts in machine learning, mathematical optimization, symbolic logic, or knowledge representation and reasoning (KRR) models. The full-fledged AI model is created for production after the prototype is found to be acceptable.

4. *Creating a data operations (DataOps) pipeline prototype*: Data is a crucial part of any AI solution. Therefore, it needs to be defined well. There are two important sub-steps:

   a. *Manually collecting, annotating, and validating required datasets*: Datasets are the lifeblood of any AI, especially machine learning algorithms, including Large Language Models. The data's quality and accuracy can determine an AI product's success or failure. To build a viable AI product, it is essential to start with high-quality data. This data must be correctly annotated so the algorithms can learn from it. The data will not be useful for training the AI models without accurate annotation. Validation is also important to ensure that the data is correct and representative of the real world. Incorrect data can lead to faulty AI models that produce inaccurate results. It is, therefore, critical to take the time to get the right data and to annotate it accurately if we want to build a successful AI product. We treat the annotated dataset as a ground truth, which will help us evaluate and validate the AI model performance developed by machine learning engineers. After manual steps have been performed, the data annotation team collaborates with data engineers to do the next step.

   b. *Building a DataOps pipeline prototype, which is a framework that helps manage data*: It provides a backbone for streamlining the lifecycle of data acquisition, aggregation, annotation, preparation, management, and development for AI, machine learning, and analytics. The prototype of data operations must be developed by data engineers assisted by machine learning engineers and data annotators. This is important because it allows for better data management and helps ensure that the DataOps pipeline is realistic and ready for production.

5. *Creating a front-end prototype*: This is an implementation of a user interface (UI) design that lets users interact when using the AI product. This includes designing the layout of the UI, as well as developing interactive elements such as buttons, forms, and maps. The UI must be visually appealing and intuitive.

6. *Creating a back-end prototype responsible for the infrastructure used to host and run the AI product*: The infrastructure can include both cloud-based and on-premise servers, depending on the need and requirements. Other tasks include developing API that allows the front end, data platform, and AI models to communicate with the back end and developing the logic, workflow, and algorithm that power the AI product. In addition, the back end of an AI product may also include data processing and storage infrastructure, such as a database or data warehouse, to support the storage and manipulation of large datasets.

Output:

The output from this phase is as follows:

1. *Application mockup*: Web, mobile, or desktop application with a clean and instructive user interface

2. AI models

3. Dataset along with its ground truth data

4. *Data operations pipeline prototype*

The preceding components are the building blocks expected to satisfy user needs and help them augment or automate their cognitive tasks (Figure 6-5).

User-Interface-Cognitive Task

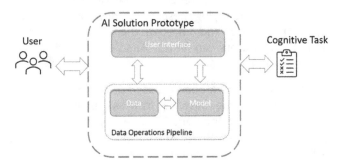

Figure 6-5. The AI solution prototype building blocks

5. Test

The testing phase is the phase in which the prototype is put in the hands of users (beta testing), and their feedback is analyzed to see if the AI performance is acceptable and provides real business value for the three types of users: strategic, tactical, and operational. Another way to test AI is by analyzing its performance against certain benchmarks or goals. This helps us determine whether the AI is meeting expectations and if there is room for improvement. Some examples of using AI testing include:

- Testing how well an AI can predict future events

- Testing how accurate an AI's image recognition is

- Analyzing how well an AI can recommend products or services

- Seeing how efficiently an AI can automate a task

Steps:

We will do the following steps in the *Test* phase:

1. The first step in the testing phase of an AI prototype is to put the prototype in the hands of users and let them interact with the user interface. This allows users to get a feel for how the AI works and how it can be used in their business.

2. After users have had a chance to interact with the prototype, they are then allowed to try out the AI models and judge their accuracy and business values. This step allows businesses to see if the AI can provide accurate results that are valuable to their operations.

3. After users have tested the AI models, any errors, unfairness, or inconsistencies in the results need to be analyzed. By identifying these issues, developers can work to correct them and improve the accuracy of the AI models. The users can fill the AI solution testing canvas as shown in Figure 6-6.

4. Once all issues have been corrected, comparing the test results with some baseline from a public dataset or competitors is important. This will give businesses a good idea of how well the AI solution performs compared with other solutions on the market.

5. Finally, the development and business teams must evaluate whether the AI solution can be used in a real-world setting. If it is determined that the AI solution provides real business value, businesses can begin using it in their operations. We define technical feasibility based on the preceding constraints from the AI model and dataset perspective. To determine the feasibility, we must consider the team capability, technology support, and infrastructure needed to build and operate the AI solution. The cost will be concluded to run and operate this AI solution. The main question is, can we make it commercially viable or not?

Before The First Interaction	During Interaction		After Interaction
Instruction • Is the the limitation and capability of the AI solution is clarified well ?	**Inputs** • Is the Input has validation mechanism ? • Is the input limitation clear?	**Fairness** • Is the AI has a notable bias?	**Monitoring** • Can you monitor the AI system performance?
Dashboard • Is the important metrics (Personal record, leader board) visible and easily understood?	**AI Model** • Is the AI model performance acceptable ?	**User Interface** • Is the User Interface is Intuitive?	
Interesting Items • Is the interesting items such as latest news, last activities and insights are displayed well?	**Errors** • Is human error notified or automatically corrected ? • Is system error notified? **Transparency** • Is the result from AI algorithm explained well ? • Is uncertainty and confidence level explained?	**Business Value** • Is the AI output helps you with your business goal ? • Is the AI output actionable?	**Feedback** • Is the AI system asking for feedback clearly? • Does this feedback improve their performance ? • Is the feedback actionable

Figure 6-6. AI solution testing canvas

CASE STUDY: USER EXPERIENCE DESIGN FOR AN AI-POWERED LOGISTICS PLATFORM

David, a seasoned veteran in logistics with more than 25 years of experience in operations and business development in logistics companies, with his friend Tom experienced in operations research and analytics for supply chain management and logistics, decided to build *Optitrax*, a startup that builds an AI-powered logistics application to optimize logistics operations. Following the framework in Chapter 3, David and Tom quit their jobs to start their venture by working as logistics technology consultants and establishing their consulting firm, developing an application powered by analytics for logistics operations, from inventory to last-mile logistics. They found problems in the niche market in last-mile logistics and thought that AI could really be applicable to boost logistics operations' efficiency.

After analyzing the market size and doing in-depth interviews, they finally found an early adopter, Safe Logistics, a medium-sized logistics company with a last-mile logistics business unit. They can convince this company to pay for the AI-first logistics application *Optitrax*, if they can prove that this solution is helpful with the metrics agreed upon by both. So they build a prototype with good experience design to validate the customer needs and requirements. They follow the design thinking process and perform these steps:

1.   Empathize

     Based on his years of experience running logistics operations, David has a preconceived notion that tactical and operational users can benefit from intelligent logistics applications powered by AI. He contacts his logistics industry networks to further validate his notion and does in-depth interviews, questionnaires, and focus groups with his ex-partners and colleagues. Then, he analyzes and synthesizes the data and talks with the potential users of Safe Logistics, a logistics company.

     He comes up with the hypothesis for two types of users as follows:

     •   Tactical users (fleet managers)

         *"We believe the **fleet managers** whose decisioning level is **tactical** in **logistics companies** have **inefficiencies** in finishing **logistics routing and scheduling** to achieve their goal in **minimizing operational cost and delivery time**."*

     •   Operational users (couriers)

         *"We believe the **couriers** whose decisioning level is **operational** in **logistics companies** have **forecasting problems** in finishing **logistics delivery** to achieve their goal in **minimizing delivery time and optimizing customer satisfaction**."*

         The persona based on the two types of users will be further detailed in the next step.

2. Define

   Combining the information gathered and synthesized from the in-depth interviews, questionnaires, extensive literature review in the last-mile delivery industry, and focus groups with personal experience managing logistics operations, David and his team create two different personas. One is the logistics manager (Figure 6-7), and the other is the courier (Figure 6-8).

Bio:

Andy, 35/Male

Logistics Manager, BS in Mechanical Engineering, works in courier Service

Personality:

MBTI: ENTP
DISC: C-D

Goals:

- Make sure delivery operations runs well
- Reducing operations cost
- No complaints from user

Touchpoints:

- Order Management
- Planning and Scheduling
- Dispatch Order

Pain Points:

- Hard to plan logistic operations accurately

Role in:

- Buying Process: Strong Decision Makers
- Company: Tactical
- Product Usage: Regular users

KPI

- Operation Cost
- Ontime Delivery
- Number of shipments

Job Desc:

- Planning and Managing delivery operations.
- Managing couriers.

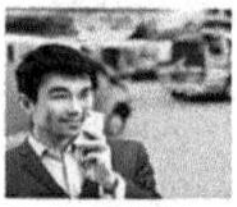

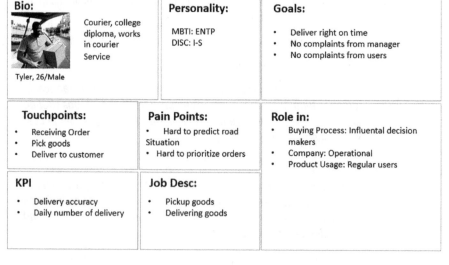

Figure 6-7. User persona canvas of a logistics manager

Bio:

Tyler, 26/Male

Courier, college diploma, works in courier Service

Personality:

MBTI: ENTP
DISC: I-S

Goals:

- Deliver right on time
- No complaints from manager
- No complaints from users

Touchpoints:

- Receiving Order
- Pick goods
- Deliver to customer

Pain Points:

- Hard to predict road Situation
- Hard to prioritize orders

Role in:

- Buying Process: Influental decision makers
- Company: Operational
- Product Usage: Regular users

KPI

- Delivery accuracy
- Daily number of delivery

Job Desc:

- Pickup goods
- Delivering goods

Figure 6-8. User persona canvas of a courier

The logistics manager and courier personas are the ones who will become the primary Optitrax regular users. They will have the most benefits from this AI application. Understanding their personas, including their age, personality, education level, job description, goals, KPI, role, and pain points, is instrumental in deciding which features and capabilities should be prioritized.

After creating the personas, David and his team create an AI user journey map for both tactical users (logistics managers; see Table 6-5) and operational users (couriers; see Table 6-7), which outlines the steps and cognitive tasks needed to complete the core task from start to finish.

By analyzing the user journey map, they will understand more about the touch points and their related tasks, along with current practices and pain points.

To find an opportunity where AI can be applied, they break down further the tasks into cognitive tasks according to the SETDA (*Sense, Explain, Think, Decide, Act*) framework (Figure 6-1). The goal is to understand whether the tasks can be categorized into cognitive tasks, which can be automated or augmented by AI. Usually, a task categorized as *Sense, Think,* and *Decide* is a low-hanging fruit for AI applications. Augmentation of the cognitive task using AI will greatly reduce the users' cognitive loads, reducing errors and improving efficiency. The cognitive tasks for the logistics managers and their AI opportunities are listed in Table 6-6.

Table 6-5. AI User Journey Map for the Logistics Manager

Journey	Getting Pick-and-Drop Orders	Route Planning	Dispatching Orders	Monitoring Orders
User goals	View and search for the latest orders.	To plan the route with optimal time and cost.	To give orders to couriers.	To monitor all orders and their status.
Expectation	Easily retrieve the latest orders from OMS.	Easily plan to route in the shortest amount of time.	Giving orders easily to all couriers.	Easily view orders in progress and delivered, along with the courier's performance.
Task	Open order list. View which orders are open for next week and today. Convert to Excel.	List down pick and drop points. Pick best couriers for areas. Pick best vehicles for particular packages. Arrange schedule, courier, fleet, and pick/drop points with Excel.	Prepare a list of couriers, delivery points, and times. Send the order list to courier via WhatsApp.	View dashboard. See orders already delivered. View orders in progress. View time to delivery.
Current practice	Manually retrieve orders from OMS and convert them to Excel.	Manually use Excel to schedule and route deliveries.	Copy and paste from Excel to Slack/Telegram.	Read reports in messaging (Slack/Telegram).
Tools	OMS Order sheet Excel	Excel	Excel, Slack, Telegram	Excel, Slack, Telegram
Current pain points	Time-consuming to view orders.	Tedious in planning the route and schedule manually using Excel.	Tedious to copy-paste to Slack and send one by one.	Do not have real-time visibility, and it is difficult to gather data for analysis.

3. Ideate

   After creating the personas and AI journey map for each persona based on questionnaires, interviews, and literary analysis of the last-mile delivery industry, David and his team start to brainstorm potential AI algorithms to solve the user problem by augmenting or automating some of their tasks. They also need to consider other important aspects such as datasets, trustworthiness, possible errors, and minimum acceptable performance (MAP). The steps are as follows:

1. Based on the user journey map depicted in Table 6-5, the team then categorizes the tasks into SETDA cognitive tasks for the logistics manager.

Table 6-6. AI Opportunities for Logistics Manager Tasks

Task	Cognitive Task (SETDA)	Inefficiencies/ Cognitive Loads	AI Opportunity	Non-AI Opportunity
View orders.	A	Time-consuming to view orders.		API to retrieve orders from OMS and view them.
Pick the best couriers for particular areas. Pick the best vehicles for particular packages.	T/D	Time-consuming to allocate couriers and packages manually using historical data.	Automatically matching best couriers to delivery areas.	
Plan the route and schedule and the delivery routes.	T/D	Tedious to plan the route and schedule manually using Excel.	Automatically route and schedule using AI.	
Prepare a list of couriers, delivery points, and times. Send the order list to courier via WhatsApp/Slack.	A	Tedious to copy-paste to WhatsApp and send them one by one.		Send all order tasks to the courier's smartphone.
View dashboard. View orders already delivered. View orders in progress. View time to delivery.	S/E	Do not have real-time visibility. Difficult to gather data for analysis.	Notified when there is an anomaly in deliveries that causes a delay.	Have a real-time dashboard where the whole operations can be monitored.

Based on these, AI can help with several tasks related to logistics management, such as

- Matching vehicles and couriers with delivery areas
- Automatically creating routes and schedules
- Notifying the logistics manager if there are any issues with delivery operations

In other words, AI can assist logistics managers by streamlining and automating various tasks and providing alerts for any problems during delivery.

The process is repeated from the courier's perspective, so the user journey map for the courier is defined in Table 6-7.

Table 6-7. AI User Journey Map for Couriers

Journey	Received Orders and Route	Delivering Package	Handover Package	Monitoring Remaining Orders
User goals	View the latest delivery orders from the dispatcher.	To deliver the packet to the customer.	To hand over the packet to the customer.	To monitor all orders and time left.
Expectation	Easily view delivery orders and their time windows.	Easily plan to route in the shortest amount of time.	Easily finalize Proof of Delivery task.	Easily view orders and time left and performance today compared with before.
Cognitive task	Open order list. View route suggested. Decide whether to follow the route suggested or not.	Delivering packages according to routes and time windows suggested.	Take a picture of the receiver's package, address, and residence. Check the package has been delivered.	Track the list of orders left. View performance.
Current practice	Read the list of orders in the WhatsApp group and decide whether to take it.	Use Google Maps to go to pickup/ delivery points.	Send a picture of the package and house via WhatsApp. Send a message to the logistics manager.	Remember what orders are left.
Tools	WhatsApp/Slack/ Discord	Google Maps	Phone camera, WhatsApp	WhatsApp/Slack
Pain points with current practice	Time-consuming to select and view orders.	No visibility of what orders should be prioritized based on the latest road condition.	Must manually send Proof of Delivery via WhatsApp.	Sometimes one doesn't remember how many orders are left.

Based on the preceding table, the tasks are listed, and then some of the tasks are categorized into cognitive tasks (either Sense, Explain, Think, Decide, or Act). Then, whether AI can be applied to augment the cognitive task is decided (Table 6-8).

Table 6-8. AI Opportunities for Courier Tasks

Task	Cognitive Task (SETDA)	Inefficiencies/ Cognitive Loads	AI Opportunity	Non-AI Opportunity
Open order list. View route suggested.	A	-	-	-
Deliver packages according to routes and time windows suggested.	E/T/A	Reroute in case of traffic, accident, or any situation changes (accident, force majeure, etc.) is very cumbersome.	Situational nowcasting (traffic, weather). Dynamic rerouting.	-
Take a picture of the receiver's package, address, and residence. Check that the package has been delivered.	A	-		-
Track the list of orders left. View performance.	A	-	-	-

From the preceding table, we can see two possible applications of AI: nowcasting potential traffic or weather changes and automatically rerouting in case it is needed.

The team is picking cognitive tasks that AI will augment or automate. Based on the previous tables, there are three possible AI opportunities:

    a. AI to match the courier with a delivery area (for the logistics manager)

    b. AI to route and schedule deliveries (for the logistics manager)

    c. Dynamic rerouting by nowcasting the changes of the situation (for the courier)

  2. Determine the AI solution plan and feasibility for the AI opportunities described. In this step, the team analyzes

    a. *Possible AI model and algorithms:* The team determines the most suitable algorithms or AI model for each opportunity. AI can help match couriers to delivery areas using unsupervised machine learning techniques such as clustering. Clustering groups couriers and delivery areas into separate clusters, each representing a delivery area. This can be useful when data is not readily available. When enough past delivery data is available, supervised machine learning methods such as SVM and AdaBoost can predict optimal assignments based on input features (e.g., courier performance and experience, delivery area characteristics).

For the optimization of delivery routing and scheduling, the team uses a combination of mathematical optimization algorithms such as linear programming, mixed integer programming, or heuristics such as the *Clarke-Wright savings algorithm* and machine learning techniques such as *neural networks* or *graph machine learning*. Graphs are useful for representing complex data with relationships between entities such as delivery points, vehicles, and routes. *Graph machine learning* algorithms can be used to learn from this data and make predictions or decisions based on the relationships in the graph, such as the most efficient routes based on distance, traffic, and the availability of delivery vehicles, also predicting the time it will take for a delivery to be completed.

For rerouting the courier due to new events such as accidents or traffic, it is necessary to use more dynamic algorithms that can quickly adapt to environmental changes. This could involve machine learning techniques such as *online learning* or *reinforcement learning* to update the model as new data becomes available continuously. Of the three AI models, the delivery rerouting has the highest complexity.

b.   *How often should the AI model be updated*: Three things are affecting model update frequency: how often the inputs (environment) and business process/regulations/rules are changing, how complex the AI model is, and how risky the model's inaccuracy is. For the courier matching algorithm, the machine learning model is quite simple, the environment and business process are also not changing rapidly (how often would the company change the couriers and delivery/pickup regions), and the risk of accuracy is not severe. The risk of mismatching the couriers with delivery areas is rather small. The AI models needed for automated routing and scheduling optimization are quite complex, involving machine learning and mathematical optimization. The inputs and business processes also vary from company to company. Therefore, frequent model update is necessary. Finally, for the courier rerouting, the model complexities are high, and the environmental inputs, such as traffic conditions and road closures, are also changing rapidly. Therefore, for this kind of model, a method like online learning is necessary, in which the model is trained and updated as new data becomes available rather than being trained on a fixed dataset.

c.   *Trustworthiness*: The team is analyzing the needed trustworthiness for each AI model that will be developed. The components are fairness, explainability, possible risks, and errors. The main consideration is especially if our AI models must deal with regulatory and audit processes. The Optitrax team is discussing that fairness and explainability are not crucial for the courier matching model as long as the model decision can be traced to how the courier is assigned to a particular delivery area in a proportional amount of work. The error risks are not very significant. If the AI model mismatches the right courier to the delivery area, the worst that can happen is the delivery will take more time. AI can help with delivery routing and scheduling by suggesting routes and schedules that consider various factors such as traffic, road closures, and weather conditions. The model's decisions don't need to be fair or easily explained as long as the inputs that influence the recommendations can be traced and understood. The risk of error is also not very severe. In the worst case, if the scheduling and routing are not optimal, an additional cost will be incurred, and customer satisfaction will be reduced (due to late delivery). As for the dynamic rerouting, explainability and fairness are not crucial as long as the courier is always informed about why the route is altered (Figure 6-9). The risk of error is also moderate, as wrong rerouting will only impact courier's time and cost.

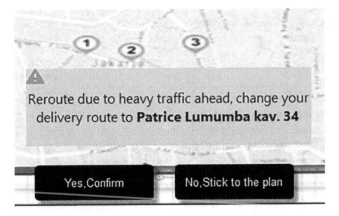

Figure 6-9. Courier delivery rerouting and its explanation

d.   *Minimum Algorithmic Performance (MAP)*: The main performance metrics of each algorithm need to be set first. For the courier–delivery area matching, the performance metric selected is on-time performance, which tracks the delivery times for a sample of shipments and calculates the percentage that was delivered within the desired time frame. After a discussion with the business team, the expected OTP is defined to be 90%. This is the MAP of the courier matching model. The performance metrics for delivery scheduling and routing optimization are reducing the distance traveled, planning time, and operational cost. The MAP is a 20% reduction in distance traveled, a 40% reduction in planning time, and a 20% reduction in operational cost after using the AI system. Lastly, the performance metrics for dynamic rerouting are decided to be fuel reduction. The MAP is fuel reduction of 20% and improving customer satisfaction by 20% after using the AI system.

The summary is shown in Table 6-9.

Table 6-9. Minimum Algorithmic Performance

AI Opportunities	Algorithms/ AI Model Used	Model Update	Trustworthiness	Minimum Algorithmic Performance
Courier matching	SVM, AdaBoost	Infrequent	The courier assigned proportionally.	90% OTP
Scheduling and routing optimization	Graph machine learning, neural network, and mixed integer programming	Infrequent	The input for routing and scheduling decision (traffic, road condition) can be explained.	20% reduction in distance, 40% in planning time, 20% in operational cost
Dynamic rerouting	Reinforcement learning	Online	Inform the courier why they should reroute.	20% fuel reduction 20% customer satisfaction improvement

2. *Dataset planning and its feasibility.* Another important thing is the planning and feasibility of data needed to feed to the AI system. The Optitrax team must be mindful of potential impediments like limited data and annotator resources to ensure smooth data operation. Several components need to be assessed, such as

    a. *Data availability.* The Optitrax team is analyzing the data availability. For logistics delivery applications, some of the data is always available from paid and public APIs. But some data must be annotated manually by a trained annotator. The data needed is the performance of each courier, the delivery time, weather, traffic, big events (concerts, sports, etc.), accidents, disasters (floods, typhoons), road closures, and other traffic regulations such as road classes for different vehicle types.

b. *Annotator availability and expertise*: The *Optitrax* team deter-
    mines the annotators needed and classification. The annotator
    may annotate data such as road closures and road classes,
    which change over time, but machine learning is not always
    used in delivery routing. Hence, annotators are not always nec-
    essary for developing delivery routing algorithms. One or two
    annotators are sufficient. Moreover, annotators do not need to
    have special qualifications for the logistics use case, except
    maybe some basic knowledge in logistics and deliveries.

c. *ETL (Extract-Transform-Load)*: The *Optitrax* team analyzes the ETL
    system needed. The *Extract* step involves collecting data from order
    management applications, spreadsheets, and APIs. The data might
    include information on delivery points, vehicle types, weather, traffic
    conditions, and other relevant inputs. In the *Transform* step, the data
    is preprocessed and formatted. In the *Load* step, the data is loaded
    into a database or in-memory database for further analysis. The
    Optitrax team decides that the ETL system is based on Kafka and
    Spark. Kafka is used to ingest data from various sources, which is
    then transformed by Spark. The processed data is then loaded into
    the target system, an in-memory Redis database.

d. *Data validation*: In this step, the *Optitrax* team defines a data
    validation mechanism where a data validator validates the an-
    notated data related to deliveries, such as the delivery time, OTP,
    and other data. Some outliers can be checked and verified to
    make sure the data is reliable for machine learning training.

3. *Feedback mechanism*: The *Optitrax* team defines implicit and explicit
    feedback mechanisms that could be used by delivery scheduling and
    routing applications to gather feedback from logistics managers and
    couriers. Some examples include

    a. Implicit feedback mechanism

        i. *User usage*: Tracking how often the logistics managers use
            certain features, such as courier matching, routing, and
            scheduling planning. We can track whether couriers use
            the dynamic rerouting feature or prefer to decide the route
            themselves.

        ii. *User behavior*: Tracking the user behavior to identify pat-
            terns and trends in how the application is being used, such
            as how long the logistics manager spent time matching
            the courier with the delivery area, planning the route, and
            dispatching the orders to the couriers. For the courier, the
            behavior could be tracked, for example, how they use the
            whole application, from receiving the orders to following
            the route or reroute suggested by the AI system.

b. Explicit feedback mechanism

   i. *Surveys:* The application could include surveys or polls that allow users to provide feedback on specific features or their overall experience with the application. For the logistics manager, these could be triggered after certain events, such as the completion of the whole delivery task at the end of the day. For the courier, this could be triggered after the completion of delivery to the customer at the end of the shifts.

   ii. *Rating and reviews:* Users could be given the option to rate or review specific features or the whole application after completing tasks.

   iii. *Active learning:* Active learning is a way to improve the accuracy of a machine learning model by involving a user in the learning process. This can be done by showing the user a series of predictions made by the model and asking them to rate the accuracy of each prediction. For example, in a logistics system, the user (e.g., a logistics manager) might be shown the system's predictions for which courier should be assigned to which delivery area and be asked to rate the accuracy of those predictions. This feedback can then be used to improve the model's performance. The feedback from the logistics manager will improve the accuracy of the courier matching model. An example of active learning is shown in Figure 6-10.

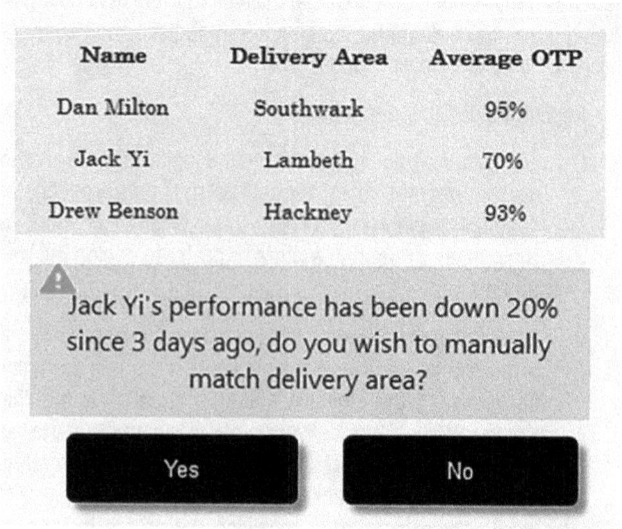

Name	Delivery Area	Average OTP
Dan Milton	Southwark	95%
Jack Yi	Lambeth	70%
Drew Benson	Hackney	93%

> ⚠ Jack Yi's performance has been down 20% since 3 days ago, do you wish to manually match delivery area?

Yes	No

Figure 6-10. Active learning for the courier matching machine learning model

iv.　*Customer support:* The application could provide a customer support channel, such as chat or email support, where
users can ask questions or provide feedback.

The AI user experience canvas is shown in Figure 6-11, which is a
summary of the *Ideate* phase.

Problem	Data	Process	Minimum Acceptable Performance
Problem: planning and executing delivery operations is time taking and inefficient For logistics manager: planning And monitoring is painful. For courier, finding the best route Is painful	Source of data is API (traffic, map, weather, distance matrix, Fuel price) All data is available. Annotation is needed only on road closures, special events, Road classes.	• Import Order (Manual). • Planning and dispatch courier, route and schedule (AI augmenting Think, Decide). • Reroute if unexpected events happened (AI automating Think, Decide). • Proof of Delivery (Manual).	• MAP for courier matching: The 90% courier reach OTP. • MAP for scheduling and routing: 20 % distance reduction, 40% planning time reduction, 20% cost reduction • MAP for dynamic rerouting: 2% reduction of fuel
	Solution • Courier Matching using SVM and XGBoost with high feasibility. Output is pair courier-delivery area. • Planning & scheduling using Neural Network, Mixed Integer Programming, high feasibility, Output Is optimized route and plan. • Dynamic Rerouting using Reinforcement, Learning, low feasibility, output is Reroute plan		**User Persona** • Logistic manager: Traits: Impatient, detailed, calculating KPI: operational efficiency, service satisfaction. • Courier: Traits: Adventurer, quick, impatient, action person. KPI: Ontime Performance, delivery cost, minimum complaints.

Value	Trustworthiness	Feedbacks	Model Update	Risk&Error
• Routing and Scheduling can save fuel cost and time to plan. • Dynamic Rerouting can save fuel cost and time to delivery • Human baseline is 4 hour to plan Route. • Rerouting can replace dispatcher.	• Courier matching result can be verified, low error risk • Routing and Scheduling result can be verified, low error risk • Dynamic routing can be verified, low error risk	Implicit: -User usage and behavior for route and schedule optimization, rerouting Explicit: - Survey, rating: After finishing tasks - Active learning: Everytime courier missing the OTP, check courier-delivery area matching ML model	• Model update is infrequent for Courier matching and route&schedule Optimization. • For dynamic routing It's online update	• Human error: Logistic managers misplaced time windows, courier went to wrong routes. • Human error risk : low

Figure 6-11. The AI user experience canvas of the AI logistics solution

4.　Prototype

Based on the preceding AI user experience canvas, which summarizes
the results from interviews and brainstorming sessions, the *Optitrax*
team develops a complete prototype for the AI logistics solution. The
steps they perform are as follows:

a.　The whole development team is gathered, from UI/UX designers
to data engineers and scientists. The whole prototyping process
must involve the whole team with the following RACI led by the
product manager as an accountable person (see Table 6-10).

Table 6-10. RACI of the Prototyping Team

Task	UI Designer	Software Engineer	Machine Learning Engineer	Dataset Manager	Data Engineer
UI design	Responsible	Consulted	Consulted	Informed	Informed
Collecting Annotating Validating dataset	Informed	Informed	Consulted	Responsible	Informed
Creating AI model prototype	Informed	Informed	Responsible	Consulted	Consulted
Creating DataOps pipeline	Informed	Consulted	Consulted	Consulted	Responsible
Creating front-end prototype	Consulted	Responsible	Consulted	Informed	Informed
Creating back-end prototype	Informed	Responsible	Consulted	Informed	Consulted

b. *Creating the user interface design:* Using the AI user journey canvas as a reference, the UI designer of *Optitrax* designs the end-to-end wireframe of the logistics solution.

c. *Creating the AI model prototype:* The machine learning and algorithm engineers are working with dataset annotators and data engineers to build an AI model prototype that meets minimum acceptable performance (MAP) defined in the previous step.

d. *Creating the data operations (DataOps) pipeline prototype:* The data engineers are building a data acquisition and integration platform that gathers real-time data from the API, such as mapping, distance matrix, weather, and traffic, which will be used as training data for the AI models.

e. *Creating front end:* The front-end software engineer then implements the user interface designed by the UI designer as a web application for logistic managers (Figure 6-12) and a mobile application for couriers (Figure 6-13).

Figure 6-12. Delivery management web application

Figure 6-13. Mobile app of couriers

     f.   *Creating back end*: The back-end engineer is building a proto-
type of cloud-based infrastructure with a database integrated
with AI models and a data platform.

5. Test

    After the end-to-tend prototype has been developed, it is the time to put it in the hands of users (beta test), where they can interact with and use it for real-world logistics operations. These are the steps in this phase:

    a. The *Optitrax* team shows the web and mobile application to the Safe Logistics team and teaches them how to use the application to manage their logistics operations.

    b. The Safe Logistics team consists of logistics managers and couriers. They test the *Optitrax* application to deliver to real customers by managing their orders.

    c. After the Safe Logistics staff have tested the platform, the test results are then compiled into the AI solution testing canvas (Figure 6-14) along with the score, which is rated from 1 (very bad) to 10 (excellent).

    d. The verdict is that the prototype has been deemed acceptable for production use. So it is technically feasible. But Safe Logistics wants the pricing to be less than the business value created (cost savings and time to plan and deliver).

    e. Now with that pricing and cost of scaling the marketing, development, and operation, David and Tom, as the Optitrax founders, must calculate whether Optitrax is a viable business as AI-first SaaS or not.

Before The First Interaction ▼	During Interaction ▼		After Interaction ▼
Instruction	**Inputs**	**Fairness**	**Monitoring**
• Is the the limitation and capability of the AI solution is clarified well ? **7 out of 10**	• Is the Input has validation mechanism ? **8 out of 10** • Is the input limitation clear? **7 out of 10**	• Is the AI has a notable bias? **8 out of 10**	• Can you monitor the AI system performance? **8 out of 10**
Dashboard	**AI Model**	**User Interface**	
• Is the important metrics (Personal record, leader board) visible and easily understood? **8 out of 10**	• Is the AI model performance acceptable ? **7 out of 10**	• Is the User Interface is intuitive? **8 out of 10**	
Interesting Items	**Errors**		**Feedback**
	• Is human error notified or automatically corrected ? **7 out of 10** • Is system error notified? **7 out of 10**	**Business Value**	• Is the AI system asking for feedback clearly? **8 out of 10**
• Is the interesting items such as latest news, last activities and insights are displayed well? **8 out of 10**	**Transparency**	• Is the AI output helps you with your business goal ? **8 out of 10**	• Does this feedback improve their performance ? **7 out of 10**
	• Is the result from AI algorithm explained well ? **7 out of 10** • Is uncertainty and confidence level explained? **7 out of 10**	• Is the AI output actionable? **8 out of 10**	• Is the feedback actionable **7 out of 10**

Figure 6-14. AI solution testing canvas results of Optitrax

Conclusion

This chapter focuses on designing a human-centered user experience for AI software products. When designing AI products, it is important to consider human factors such as customer needs, trustworthiness, ethics, and the amplification of human capabilities. Design thinking principles can be used to create problem-solving solutions for AI products. There are six AI UX design principles and five design thinking steps relevant to AI interaction design. The calm technology principle can also help minimize distractions in designing AI products.

Key Takeaways

- Building a user experience for AI products requires considering human factors such as customer needs, trustworthiness, ethics, and the amplification of human capabilities.

- AI can assist with or automate various tasks, with assistive AI able to provide assistance with Sense, Explain, Think, Decide, and Act and autonomous AI able to perform these tasks independently.

- Ensuring AI trustworthiness involves making the AI robust, explainable, transparent, and safe to use.

- Ethical AI prioritizes privacy and avoids bias.

- Design thinking is a valuable approach for creating solutions that solve problems from a human-centered perspective and is relevant for AI product design.

- There are several principles and steps to consider when designing AI products, including six AI UX design principles and five steps of design thinking, as well as the principle of calm technology, which aims to minimize distractions, and actionable AI, which provides specific actions for users to change the outcome.

Human-Centered AI Developer Experience Design

In the previous chapter, we learned how to build a human-centered AI experience design oriented toward the end user. In this chapter, we will learn how to design AI developer experience (DX), a methodology aimed at making the development process of AI-powered applications more straightforward and intuitive for developers. By focusing on the needs and preferences of developers, this approach can help streamline the creation of AI-based products and services. In addition, by providing a framework for incorporating

© Adhiguna Mahendra 2023
A. Mahendra, *AI Startup Strategy*, https://doi.org/10.1007/978-1-4842-9502-1_7

AI into applications, AI developer experience design can help reduce the risk of errors and glitches during development. In building a developer experience for AI products, design thinking is essential to create an intuitive and user-friendly experience that contributes to the AI product's robustness and trustworthiness. By empathizing with the needs and preferences of developers and using design thinking methodologies to guide the development process, teams can create an experience tailored to their target audience's needs. This allows for a more efficient and effective development process and an end product more likely to succeed. In this chapter, we will explore the role of design thinking in creating a successful developer experience for AI products and provide two case studies that illustrate its application in practice.

AI Products for Developers

As an AI product manager, one of the main goals is to develop products targeted to developers that make AI development and integration easy. Four main types of AI products are targeted toward developers: AI as a Service, AI as an Engine (AIaaE), AI toolkits, and AI Platform as a Service (Figure 7-1).

Figure 7-1. Four archetypes of AI products for the developer

The developer experience for AI as a Service, AI as an Engine, AI toolkits, and AI PaaS can differ depending on the specific service or toolkit and the intended use case:

- AI as a Service (AIaaS) is a cloud-based subscription model that allows businesses to access AI capabilities without needing in-house expertise or infrastructure. These services can include natural language processing, image recognition, and machine learning. Examples of AIaaS include FaceTec, Identifai, Onfido, OpenAI, and

Routific. These AIaaS providers allow developers to easily access and utilize AI without expensive infrastructure or specialized knowledge. Developers can access the AI capabilities provided by the service through API calls, which can be integrated into their applications or services. This allows developers to utilize AI capabilities without worrying about the underlying infrastructure or maintenance.

- AI toolkits are pre-built tools and libraries that developers can use to build, train, and deploy AI models. These toolkits can include platforms and libraries for machine learning, deep learning, computer vision, natural language processing, pre-trained models, data visualization tools, and development frameworks. Examples of AI toolkits include Landing AI, Clarifai, Roboflow, Viso AI, and Super AI. These toolkits provide developers with a way to build and deploy AI models without the need for extensive expertise in AI or machine learning quickly and easily. AI toolkits are also typically delivered as command-line tools that developers can use to build, train, and deploy AI models (i.e., Masterful AI). These toolkits often include libraries for machine learning, deep learning, computer vision, natural language processing, pre-trained models, data visualization tools, and development frameworks. Toolkit outputs can also be deployed to operating systems, containers, or virtual machines (VMs), allowing developers to run them in their preferred environment.

- AI as an Engine (AIaaE) refers to integrating AI capabilities directly into a product or application, typically as part of the product's core functionality. With AI as an Engine, businesses can build AI-powered products and services tailored to specific use cases and industries. Examples of AI engines include Trueface and Visionaire AI. These AI engines allow developers to add advanced AI capabilities to their products and services, allowing them to build cutting-edge applications that can be used in a wide range of industries. AI as an Engine is typically delivered as a Software Development Kit (SDK) that can be integrated into the developer's existing product or application. SDKs are tools and libraries that developers can use to access the AI engine's capabilities and integrate them into their products or services. These SDKs can also be delivered via *operating systems*, containers, or virtual machines (VMs) to provide flexibility for developers to run them in the preferred environment.

- AI Platform as a Service (AI PaaS) is a platform that provides a complete environment for developing, deploying, and managing AI applications, including data storage, compute power, and a suite of AI development tools. Examples of AI PaaS are Amazon Machine Learning, Azure Machine Learning, and IBM Watson. These platforms provide developers with a comprehensive environment for building and deploying AI applications, allowing them to focus on the development and integration of AI without worrying about the underlying infrastructure. AI Platform as a Service (AI PaaS) is typically delivered through API, SDK, and a graphical user interface (GUI). Developers can use the GUI to access the platform's capabilities and manage their AI models, while the API and SDK allow them to programmatically access the platform's capabilities and integrate them into their products or services. These platforms can also be delivered via operating systems, containers, or virtual machines (VMs), allowing developers to run them in their preferred environment.

Overall, the delivery method of an AI product to developer users can vary depending on the product itself. Still, most commonly, it is delivered through API, SDK, command-line interface (CLI), operating systems, containers, VMs, or GUI. These delivery methods are designed to make it easy for developers to access and use the AI capabilities provided by the product and to allow them to integrate AI into their products and services most efficiently.

Building an AI Platform as a Service (PaaS) can be daunting, requiring significant resources and expertise. It's a realm typically reserved for tech giants like Google, Amazon, IBM, and Microsoft. AI PaaS is beyond any startup capability and is not recommended to be developed by them, so we are not discussing it in this chapter. However, smaller companies still have opportunities to significantly impact AI by building an exceptional developer experience for AI as a Service, AI as an Engine, and AI toolkits. These AI products can provide similar and overlapping developer journeys, allowing developers to access advanced AI capabilities without requiring extensive infrastructure or maintenance. By providing developers with easy-to-use and flexible tools, companies can help bridge the gap between cutting-edge AI research and real-world implementation, making it possible for developers of all skill levels to create innovative and intelligent applications.

In summary, while AI as a Service, AI as an Engine, and AI toolkits can provide developers with powerful AI functionality, they can focus differently on the developer experience, with AI as a Service and AI as an Engine emphasizing ease of use and integration and AI toolkits emphasizing flexibility and control.

Principles of AI DX Design

When designing the developer experience for AI products, several key principles should be considered:

1. *Ease of use and integration: The AI product should be easy to use and integrate into a developer's workflow, with a clear and consistent user interface and minimal setup required.*

2. *Flexibility and control: The AI product should provide developers with the flexibility and control they need to tailor the product to their specific needs and use cases.*

3. *Comprehensive tools and capabilities: The AI product should provide a comprehensive set of tools and capabilities for developing, deploying, and managing AI models and data infrastructure.*

4. *Good documentation and support: The AI product should come with clear and comprehensive documentation and responsive support channels to help developers understand how to use the product and get help if needed.*

5. *Monitoring and visibility: The AI product should provide developers with visibility and insight into their AI models' performance and the underlying systems that support them to identify and debug issues and track performance.*

6. *Scalability and maintenance: The AI product should be able to handle large volumes of data and scale to meet the demands of the developer's use case. It also should be well-maintained and supported, with regular updates and bug fixes.*

7. *Collaboration and community: The AI product should facilitate collaboration and knowledge sharing among developers and encourage the participation of a community of users who can share their expertise and best practices.*

8. *Trustworthiness: Trust is a critical factor in any AI system, so the developer experience should include clear explanations of how the AI models work, how they were trained, what data they were trained on, and what the limitations and potential biases of the models are. This will help developers understand how the models are likely to behave in different situations and make informed decisions about when and how to use them.*

9. *Fairness: AI models can perpetuate and even amplify societal biases, so fairness must be considered when designing AI products. The developer experience should include tools and capabilities that help developers identify and mitigate biases in their models and ensure that the models are fair and unbiased.*

10. *Feedback*: The AI product should include feedback mechanisms, such as evaluation metrics, monitoring systems, and user feedback, to allow developers to measure the performance of the models, identify errors, and improve the models over time.

An example of a good developer AI product is GPT-3 from OpenAI, which excels in developer experience design, aligning well with the principles of good developer experience. Its easy integration, flexibility, comprehensive tools, and responsive support enable developers to build sophisticated applications effortlessly.

AI Developer Experience Process Framework

Design thinking is a user-centered approach to design that emphasizes empathy, prototyping, and testing to understand and solve problems. In designing a developer experience (DX) process, design thinking is essential because it allows the team to understand the needs and pain points of the target audience (developers) and create solutions tailored to their specific needs. The similarity between developer experience (DX) and typical user experience (UX) based on design thinking is that both design approaches are user-centered and start with understanding the needs and pain points of the target audience. Both processes also involve using prototypes and testing to validate the design concept with the target audience.

The difference is that developer experience (DX) specifically targets developers as users. At the same time, user experience (UX) can target any user. Developer experience focuses on improving the developer experience, while user experience enhances the overall user experience. Developers have different needs and pain points than other users, and the DX process is tailored to address these needs.

1. Empathize

The first phase of building AI product developer experience using design thinking is the Empathize phase. This phase is crucial in understanding the needs and pain points of our target audience, the developers using the AI product. The goal of this phase is to create a preliminary hypothesis of the developer persona that will shape the design of the AI product and improve the developer experience. The step-by-step and outputs from each stage will be explained.

Steps:

This is what is needed in the *Empathize* phase:

1. *Hypothesize: Hypothesize about the types of developers using our product and what they need to succeed in their AI development. The task will involve understanding the target audience and their roles, such as front-end developers, mobile developers, back-end developers, and data scientists, as a persona. To have a more detailed persona, we will also identify the development tasks, problems, and pain points these target developers face, such as AI development, integration, and performance. Therefore, the persona of the developers is defined as follows:*

   a. *Developer user:* What is the specific title and function of the developer?

   b. *Applications developer:* What is the application they develop?

   c. *Goals and motivations:* What are the goals and motivations of the developer using the AI product?

   d. *Pain points and challenges:* What are the developer's pain points and challenges when working with AI?

   e. *Metrics:* What metrics are used to measure the performance of the AI?

2. *Define data-gathering methods:* We will define data-gathering methods to support our hypothesis. We will also examine prominent product review platforms such as producthunt.com, unite.ai, futurepedia.io, and saashub.com. We will gain valuable insight into the current product landscape to locate potential gaps in market demand based on feedback and reviews. We will also conduct in-depth interviews and collect user analytics from the sandbox to understand their pain points, feedback, and success criteria.

Output:

The output of this phase will be an understanding of the benefits of AI tools or services, which will include information about the developer user of our target audience, such as front-end engineer, mobile engineer, back-end engineer, and data scientist. Additionally, we will gather information about the persona and problems and pain points developers face regarding AI development and integration, performance monitoring, and the types of applications they develop, such as SaaS, mobile, or ecommerce websites. We also collect information on the AI tasks they are working on, such as prediction, object recognition, forecasting, generation, optimization, and recommendation, as well as the specific tasks and metrics they use to measure success, such as latency and accuracy. To summarize, the following are the outputs expected from this phase (Table 7-1).

Table 7-1. Hypothesize the Developer's Need for AIaaS, AIaaE, or AI Toolkit

Components	Sample Data
Developer user	Front-end developer, mobile developer, back-end developer, data scientist
Applications developed	Accounting SaaS, ecommerce mobile app, CRM SaaS
Cognitive tasks	Recommending books, forecasting weather
Metrics	Click rate, prediction accuracy, classification accuracy
Business values	Improving revenue, reducing cost, reducing risk, increasing customer satisfaction

We will use the general persona data to create the preliminary hypothesis of the AIaaS, AIaaE, or AI toolkit along with its user developer persona with the following format: "We believe the [developer users] who develop [applications] will benefit from integrating the application with our [AI as a Service/AI toolkit] to [augment/automate] some [cognitive tasks] to optimize [metrics] which results in [business values]."

2. Define

The Define phase of design thinking for a developer product is focused on detailing the developer persona, mapping the developer experience journey, and understanding the tasks and mental models of the target audience. This phase aims to understand the developer's experience from initial engagement with the product to ongoing use and maintenance.

Steps:

We will do the following steps in the *Define* phase:

1. *Define the persona of the developers using the AIaaS, AIaaE, or AI toolkits. A developer persona is a fictional representation of a specific type of developer who will be using your product. Here are some of the key components of a developer persona:*

a. *Demographics:* This includes age, gender, education level, and job title.

b. *Applications developed: The type of applications they usually develop.*

c. *Type of developer user: The development title and function include back-end developer, machine learning engineer, or data scientist.*

d. *Technical skills: The developer's level of expertise in specific programming languages, frameworks, and technologies.*

e. *Goals: The developer's goals and objectives, such as increasing productivity, improving the quality of their code, or reducing development time.*

f. *Pain points: The challenges and frustrations the developer typically experiences, such as lack of documentation, poor tooling, or lack of support.*

g. *Integration method: The way developers prefer to integrate and interact with AIaaS, AIaaE, or AI toolkits, such as using an API to integrate AI functionality into an existing system, using an SDK to customize AI functionality to specific needs, using a CLI for command-line integration, using a GUI for graphical user interface integration, and using a WebSocket for real-time data streaming.*

2. *Map the developer's journey from their current state to their desired future state. There is a slight difference between the developer journey of AIaaS, AIaaE, and AI toolkits. The main difference is that in AIaaS and AIaaE, the developers focus more on integrating the AI service with their own applications. In AI toolkits, the developers are focused more on the AI model development using the AI tool and the integration with the existing workflows and technology stacks.*

Therefore, the stages of the developer journey for AIaaS and AIaaE are the signup process, learning how to use the product, trial and experimentation, integration with other tools, and ongoing monitoring and maintenance:

a. *Signup:* In the signup process, we focus on understanding how the developer first finds out about the product, what information they need to decide to use it, and what value they expect to gain from it.

b. *Learning:* In the learning process, we focus on how the developer acquires the knowledge and skills needed to effectively use the product, what resources they need, and what challenges they may encounter.

c. *Trial:* In the trial process, we focus on how the developer experiments with the product, what they are trying to accomplish, and what feedback they provide.

d. *Integration:* In the integration process, we focus on how the developer integrates the product into their existing workflow, what challenges they may encounter, and what changes they make to their application.

e. *Operationalization:* In the operationalization and monitoring process, we focus on how the developer maintains the AI models developed, what metrics they are monitoring, and what challenges they may encounter.

While the stages of the developer journey for AI tools are the same in signing up, learning, and trial, the operationalization step is replaced with development and integration with existing workflow. To summarize, the following are the stages of the developer journey for AI tools:

a. *Signup:* The signup process is the first step for developers to register for the AI tool. It should be simple, user-friendly, and secure.

b. *Reading instruction:* Developers must read through the product documentation and instructions to understand the features and how to use the tool.

c. *Trial:* Developers will have the opportunity to test the tool, either through a free trial or a sandbox environment, to ensure it meets their needs.

d. *Development:* Developers can start building AI models using the tool, taking advantage of pre-built models and libraries and easy-to-use interfaces.

e. *Integration:* The tool should provide integration options like REST API, SDK, CLI, web-based UI, and event-driven to integrate with existing systems and workflows easily.

3. The next step is to understand the mental models of the target audience. This includes understanding the developer's assumptions, beliefs, and expectations about the product and their goals and motivations for using it. This information is used to create a developer experience journey map, which visually represents the developer's journey, highlighting key stages, pain points, and opportunities for improvement. By understanding the developer's journey and mental models, we can identify areas for improvement and design a more effective and satisfying product experience for the developer. This can ultimately lead to better product adoption and usage, improved developer satisfaction, and, ultimately, better business outcomes.

Output:

The output of this phase is a developer persona canvas (Figure 7-2) and a developer experience journey map for AIaaS and AIaaE products (Table 7-2) and an AI toolkit product (Table 7-3), which is a visual representation of the process that developers go through when interacting with an AI product.

Developer User	Applications Developed	Demographics
The specific job and function In development area such As backend, front end engineer	Applications developed such as SaaS, Mobile App	Characteristics such as age, gender, education, and job title
Technical Skills	**Pain Points**	**Goals and Motivation**
Expertise in languages, frameworks, and technologies	Challenges and frustrations faced	What a developer wants to achieve and what drives them such as increasing productivity, Reducing development time
Metrics	**Integration Method**	
Quantifiable measurements used to evaluate the performance of a developer	Preferred way of interacting with AI services or tools	

Figure 7-2. Developer persona canvas

As an AI product developer, creating a persona canvas is essential in understanding your target audience and designing a product that meets their needs. It is a visual tool that helps you identify key characteristics such as technical skills, experience, pain points, and behavior patterns of your product's developers. By creating a developer persona canvas (Figure 7-2), you can better tailor your product to the specific needs of your target audience, increasing the chances of success.

Table 7-2. Developer Journey Map for AIaaS and AIaaE Products

Developer Journey	Signup	Reading Instruction	Trial	Integration with Other Apps	Operation
User goals	Understand what AIaaS can accomplish.	Understand the basic functionalities.	To evaluate the API or SDK and decide whether this is suitable or not.	To integrate the API/SDK with their own apps.	Seamlessly smooth operation.
Expectation	Understand what it should do.	Understanding of benefits, limitations, and whether the API/SDK can easily integrate with their apps.	To be able to easily use the API or SDK to create simple working apps.	To be able to integrate the API/SDK with their own applications easily.	To be able to monitor system performance and be notified when something happens, such as error, maintenance, and update.
Task	Read description. Try some demo.	Read Getting Started guides. Read technical specifications. Read example codes.	Follow along with the tutorials. Perform trial with different inputs and parameters. Evaluate performance.	Evaluate sample codes. Pick boilerplate codes. Embed the boilerplate code into their apps.	View performance dashboard. View usage and its charge. Read release notes.
Components	Landing page Demo Use cases	Getting Started guide API reference Data sheets Data acquisition guide	API sandbox Installation SDK	API client libraries SDK client libraries	Performance dashboards Usage dashboards Release notes
Pain points	Hard to understand the value of the AIaaS.	Documentation is hard to understand.	Unable to create simple AI-powered working apps.	Unable to integrate with other applications.	Error without explanation during operations.

The developer journey map for AI as a Service and AI as an Engine is focused on seamlessly integrating existing applications and ensuring smooth operation. On the other hand, the developer journey for AI toolkits is centered around the development and integration with current workflows and technology stacks, providing developers with the flexibility to build and train their models (Table 7-3).

Table 7-3. Developer Journey Map for AI Toolkits

Developer Journey	Signup	Reading Instruction	Trial	Development	Integration with Existing Workflow
User goals	Understand what AIaaS can accomplish.	Understand the basic functionalities.	To evaluate the API or SDK and decide whether this is suitable or not.	To use the tool as part of the model development process.	To integrate the tool with the current AI model development environment/stack.
Expectation	Understand what it should do.	Understanding of benefits, limitations, and whether the API/SDK can easily integrate with their apps.	To be able to easily use the API or SDK to create simple working apps.	To be able to successfully develop an AI model according to the expectation.	To be able to integrate the AI tool with current workflow and environment successfully.
Task	Read description. Try some demo.	Read Getting Started guides. Read technical specifications. Read example codes.	Follow along with the tutorials. Perform trial with different inputs and parameters. Evaluate performance.	Develop the AI model using the tool provided. Evaluate and monitor the tool's benefit, cost, and efficiency.	Try the tool. Use the tool to be integrated with the current workflow. Monitor the benefit of the tool.
Components	Landing page Demo Use cases	Getting Started guide API reference Data sheets Data acquisition guide	API sandbox Installation SDK	API client libraries SDK client libraries	Integration end point
Pain points	Hard to understand the value of the AIaaS.	Documentation is hard to understand.	Unable to create simple AI-powered working apps.	Unable to integrate with other applications.	Unable to integrate seamlessly with current AI workflow.

The developer journey map for AI toolkits is a set of steps developers go through when working with these tools. It is designed to help developers understand how to build and integrate AI models into their applications. The developer journey typically starts with installing and setting up the toolkit and then building, training, and validating the models using the provided APIs and SDKs. Once the models are built, developers will then integrate them into their existing workflows and technology stacks. The journey also includes ongoing maintenance and monitoring of the models and updating them as necessary.

One key aspect of the developer journey for AI toolkits is the flexibility it provides to developers. Unlike AI as a Service and AI as an Engine, where the models are pre-built and provided by the provider, developers using AI toolkits can build and train their own models. This allows them to customize the models to their specific use case and incorporate domain-specific knowledge. Additionally, the integration process with existing workflows and technology stacks is designed to be as smooth as possible, allowing developers to easily add AI capabilities to their existing applications.

This journey map helps identify pain points and opportunities and guides the rest of the design thinking process. It also helps understand the mental models of the developers, which is essential in creating a product that is aligned with their needs and expectations.

3. Ideate

The Ideate phase in the design thinking process for AI products targeted toward developers is a crucial step in development.

First, we must address the difference between AIaaS, AIaaE, and AI toolkits. AI as a service (AIaaS) and AI as an Engine (AIaaE) differ regarding their target user and usage. AIaaS is typically targeted toward developers or end users, where the AI model is packaged as a service that can be consumed through an API. An example is OpenAI, where they sell GPT for developer users or ChatGPT for end users. The user experience is focused on ease of use, accuracy, and quality of the results. The main goal is to provide a ready-to-use AI solution that can be integrated into an existing application or workflow.

On the other hand, AI as an engine (AIaaE) is targeted toward developers and data scientists, where the AI model is packaged as an engine that can be integrated into an existing application or workflow. The user experience is focused on performance, scalability, and flexibility. The main goal is to provide a robust and customizable AI solution that can be fine-tuned to fit specific use cases.

AI toolkits, on the other hand, are targeted toward developers and data scientists who want to build their own AI models. The user experience is focused on ease of use, flexibility, and control. The main goal is to provide a set of tools and libraries that can be used to build, train, and deploy AI models.

Therefore, the steps and output for each product will be different as they cater to different user needs and use cases. AIaaS and AIaaE will have steps and output focused on user experience and integration, while AI toolkits will have steps and output focused on development and customization.

It is crucial to identify and understand the potential use cases for the AI models packaged as AIaaS and AIaaE and the developers using them. In this phase, the following steps should be taken to ensure a successful outcome of AIaaS and AIaaE developer experience (DX) design:

Steps:

1. *Identify applications:* The first step in the Ideate phase is identifying the applications that can leverage the AI models packaged as API and SDK. This includes understanding the tasks and problems the AI models will solve and the data types that will be used as input.

2. *Determine deployment:* Determine how the AI models will be deployed. This includes understanding the various deployment options such as Web, mobile, virtual machines, or bare-metal servers. It also has to determine which deployment option is the most suitable for the specific use case and the developers using the AI models.

3. *Define input-output:* Define the input and output of the AI models. This includes understanding the types of data that will be used as input and the types of outputs that will be generated. It also includes determining the input and output data format and any preprocessing or post-processing that needs to be done.

4. *Understand in-house development challenge:* Understand the developer's challenge if they instead build their own AIaaS/AIaaE in-house.

5. *Define AI type:* Define the type of AI that will be used. This includes understanding the different types of AI models, such as machine learning, decision optimization, rule-based systems, expert systems, and knowledge representation and reasoning models. It also includes determining which type of AI is the most suitable for the specific use case.

6. *Define performance monitoring:* Define the performance monitoring of the AI models. This includes understanding the metrics that will be used to measure the performance of the AI models, the minimum acceptable performance, and how the AI models will be monitored. It also includes understanding how the results of the AI models will be explained to the developers.

7. *Define version update:* Define the version update of the AI models. This includes understanding how the AI models will be updated and the frequency of the updates. It also includes understanding how to notify developers that the AI models have been updated to ensure that it does not violate Hyrum's law. Hyrum's law emphasizes the importance of designing APIs for AI services that are easy to use and hard to misuse. This means providing clear documentation, well-defined interfaces, error messages, and constraints to limit unintended consequences. By doing so, AIaaS/AIaaE providers can prevent errors, security vulnerabilities, and other issues that may negatively impact their customers' experience.

8. *Define parameter optimization and data post-processing:* We define and understand what parameters or hyperparameters of the AI models that developers themselves can optimize. Parameter optimization that users can handle during inference time is important and necessary because it enables developers to fine-tune model performance based on specific use cases and real-time data. This allows for greater flexibility and adaptability of machine learning models and more efficient and accurate results.

9. *Define workflow:* We define which workflow this API/SDK runs in the application and what task has been automated or augmented.

10. *Define feedback:* We define the feedback given by the AI models. This includes understanding both implicit and explicit feedback given by the AI models. Implicit and explicit feedback are two types of feedback that are commonly used in machine learning:

    a. *Implicit feedback:* This type of feedback is not explicitly provided by the user or data source but is inferred from the data itself. It can come from various sources, such as user behavior or data characteristics, and is typically used when obtaining explicit feedback is not feasible or too expensive.

b. *Explicit feedback*: This type of feedback is provided by the user or data source, such as through surveys, ratings, or labels. It is typically used when the goal is to train a machine learning model to accurately predict a specific output, such as a classification or a numerical value.

Self-supervised learning and *active learning* are two techniques that can be used to improve the performance of machine learning models using these types of feedback:

- *Self-supervised learning*: This technique uses unlabeled data to train a model to predict a certain output. By doing so, the model can learn to identify key features of the data without relying on explicit labels. Self-supervised learning can be integrated with the implicit feedback mechanism to train the models.

- *Active learning*: This technique uses explicit feedback to identify errors in the model's predictions and then uses these errors to select new training data to improve the model's performance. *Active learning* can be integrated with the explicit feedback mechanism to improve the models.

Furthermore, many different types of feedback can be used to train machine learning models, and the choice of feedback will depend on the specific application and use case. For example, in a natural language processing system, feedback could come in explicit labels (such as correct/incorrect classifications) or implicitly (such as the user's engagement with the system). In a recommendation system, feedback could come from user ratings or user interactions with the system.

11. *Define risks and errors*: Explain what potential errors can be caused by the developers, environment (input images from different cameras), and systems, including edge cases that may happen. This will help developers understand how to mitigate these risks and handle errors when they occur.

Output:

The output of this Ideate phase is the development design experience canvas for AIaaS and AIaaE products (Figure 7-3), which will summarize all of the preceding points in a single, easy-to-use visual representation. This canvas will serve as a valuable tool for developers, helping them understand the AI product's key components and how it can be integrated into their existing workflows.

Applications	Deployment	Workflow	Performance Monitoring
• List of apps can use this SDK/API based AI model ? • Is it difficult to build this AI Model	• Mobile Platform • VM/Bare Metal • Web	• In which workflow in the application this API/SDK runs? • What task has been automated or Augmented?	• Which metrics used? • What is MAP ? • How AI model performance is monitored? • Accuracy/optimal Result • Explainability • Fairness
	AI Type	**Input and Output**	**Inhouse Development Challenge**
	• AI Type • Is it ML, DO, KRR	• Input • Output	• Model development • Data acquisition and annotation • Model maintenance
Parameter Optimization	**Feedbacks**	**Risk and Errors**	**Version Update**

• What parameter can be modified by developers?	• Implicit
	• Explicit
	• Active learning
		• What error:
		  • Developer
		  • Systems
		  • Input environment
			• Model and app update
			• Frequency
			• Notification mechanism (Hyrums law)

Figure 7-3. AI developer experience design canvas for AIaaS and AIaaE

AIaaS or AIaaE typically provides a ready-to-use AI model that can be integrated into an existing application or workflow. The developer journey for these types of AI products involves understanding the input and output of the model, as well as the different use cases and applications where the model can be applied. The output of the Ideate phase for AIaaS or AIaaE would typically be a canvas outlining the input and output of the model, as well as the different use cases and applications where the model can be applied.

On the other hand, an AI toolkit is a set of tools and frameworks developers can use to build and train their AI models. The developer journey for an AI toolkit focuses on the development process, including understanding the different AI models and ecosystems that can be developed, assisted, or optimized. The output of the Ideate phase for an AI toolkit would typically be a detailed document outlining the different AI models and ecosystems that can be developed, assisted, or optimized using the toolkit, as well as the different workflows and use cases that the toolkit is designed for.

These are the steps and output for ideating AI developer experience for AI toolkits.

Steps:

1. Identify the AI models and supporting infrastructure that can be developed, assisted, or optimized using the AI toolkits. This includes determining the type of AI models that can be created, such as machine learning, large language model, decision optimization, rule-based systems, expert systems, or knowledge representation and reasoning. The supporting infrastructure includes data acquisition, annotation, and AI model optimization or monitoring.

2. Define the deployment options for the AI models developed using the toolkits. This includes identifying the deployment options available, such as Web, mobile, virtual machines, or bare-metal servers.

3. Define the input and output of the AI toolkits. This includes identifying the data types and inputs the toolkits can handle and the outputs they can produce.

4. Understand in-house development challenge. Understand the developer's challenge if they instead build their own AI tools in-house.

5. Define the potential cost- and time-saving benefits of using the AI toolkits.

6. Define how the AI toolkits support trustworthiness aspects such as robustness, fairness, and explainability.

7. Define the scope of the development workflow covered by the AI toolkits. This includes identifying which stages of the development process are supported and which are not.

8. Explain how to monitor the performance and cost of the models developed using the toolkits. This includes identifying the metrics that will be used and the minimum acceptable performance.

9. Define the compatibility of the AI model builder to common tech stacks, including deep learning libraries and hardware providers.

Output:

Once all of these steps have been completed, the result is the development design experience canvas for AI toolkits (Figure 7-4), which summarizes all of the key points and provides a clear and concise overview of the AI toolkit ideation components and how developers can use them.

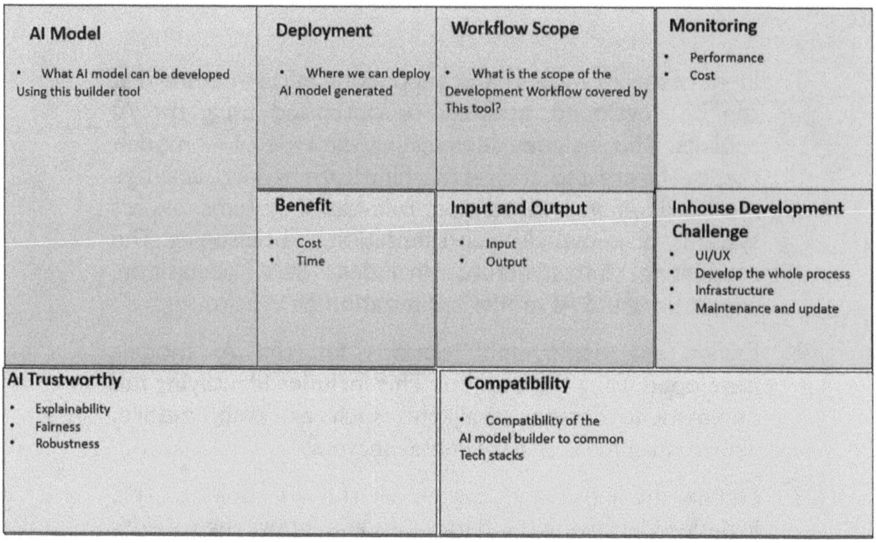

AI Model	Deployment	Workflow Scope	Monitoring
• What AI model can be developed Using this builder tool	• Where we can deploy AI model generated	• What is the scope of the Development Workflow covered by This tool?	• Performance • Cost
	Benefit • Cost • Time	**Input and Output** • Input • Output	**Inhouse Development Challenge** • UI/UX • Develop the whole process • Infrastructure • Maintenance and update
AI Trustworthy • Explainability • Fairness • Robustness		**Compatibility** • Compatibility of the AI model builder to common Tech stacks	

Figure 7-4. AI development experience canvas for AI toolkits

4. Prototype

In the Prototype phase of design thinking for AI products targeted to developers, the development team conducts brainstorming sessions to develop a prototype of the AI product. This team typically includes the product manager, front-end engineer, back-end engineer, machine learning engineer, and data engineer. The prototype is based on the product hypothesis, developer persona, developer journey map, and developer experience canvas previously gathered during the Ideate phase. In terms of creating the prototype, there are two different methods for creating prototypes for AI as a Service (AIaaS) and AI as an Engine (AIaaE) and AI toolkits.

For AIaaS and AIaaE, the team creates a user interface (UI) design for API endpoints, command-line interfaces (CLI), or Software Development Kits (SDKs) that package the AI models developed by AI experts. These AI models can include large language models, computer vision deep learning models, decision optimization models, and more. The prototype must take into account several key considerations.

Step:

1. Before the user interaction, the development team should focus on providing easy-to-understand documentation and instructions for the AI product prototype. This includes clear explanations of the API endpoints, CLI, or SDK and any parameters or hyperparameters that can be configured. It should also include instructions on how to set up the developer sandbox and any prerequisites that need to be met before using the prototype.

2. During the user interaction, the development team should focus on creating an intuitive API and SDK for the developer sandbox. This includes designing error-handling mechanisms and notifications to make it easy for developers to understand and diagnose any issues that may arise. The team should also consider what parameters and hyperparameters can be configured and how they can be accessed and modified within the developer sandbox.

3. After the user interaction, the development team should focus on providing developers with the tools and information they need to monitor and explain the results of the AI models. This includes metrics, performance monitoring capabilities, and fairness and explainability mechanisms. The team should also consider how the AI models can be integrated with other applications and how implicit and explicit feedback, including active learning mechanisms, can be implemented as part of the prototype.

In addition to these, for AI toolkits, the team should focus on providing an intuitive GUI or CLI for building and optimizing AI models, data operations, or operational infrastructure. The team should also consider how the results of the AI toolkits can be deployed and integrated into existing development workflows and how compatibility with common technology stacks can be ensured. The team should also provide tools for monitoring and calculating the benefits of using the AI toolkits instead of in-house development, such as cost and time savings.

Output:

A working prototype of the AI product, including the API or SDK and any necessary documentation, that can be accessed or open-sourced for developers to test and experiment with.

5. Test

The testing phase in *design thinking* is when the prototype is put in the hands of real users to gather feedback and validate the solutions developed during the previous phases of *Empathize*, *Define*, and *Ideate*. This phase is crucial in AI product development targeted to developer users because it allows the development team to understand how their solutions perform in a real-world context and identify any pain points or areas for improvement.

For AIaaS (AI as a Service) and AIaaE (AI as an Engine) products, the Test phase can involve deploying the API or SDK to a small group of developer users and gathering feedback on the ease of use, performance, and accuracy of the AI model. This can include evaluating metrics such as response time, error rate, and user satisfaction. It can also involve gathering feedback on the documentation, developer portal, and other developer-facing aspects of the product.

For AI toolkits, the testing phase can involve providing developer users with access to the toolkit and gathering feedback on its usability, functionality, and overall effectiveness. This can include evaluating metrics such as user engagement, task completion time, and user satisfaction. Additionally, it can also include gathering feedback on the documentation, tutorials, and other developer-facing aspects of the product.

It is important to note that during the testing phase, the team should also validate their assumptions about the users and the problem they are trying to solve. This can be done by observing the users during testing, conducting user interviews, and analyzing the feedback data.

The steps for design thinking's Test phase in the developer experience (DX) process for AIaaS/AIaaE and AI toolkits are as follows.

Steps:

1. The first step in the testing phase is to provide the developers with a playground or sandbox to access the prototype's user interface. This allows them to understand how AI works and how it can be used in their development projects. Their behavior and feedback are helpful for us to improve our AI products.

2. Next, developers can test and interact with the AI product. The products are tested in three phases (before, during, and after interaction with the product).

For AIaaS/AIaaE, the components are as follows:

- Before the user interaction

- *Documentation*: Before using the API/SDK, developers should have access to clear and comprehensive documentation that includes examples of how to use the API/SDK. This can help ensure that developers understand the API/SDK's capabilities and how to use it effectively. OpenAI API is renowned for its excellent and well-structured developer documentation, which has been widely recognized and appreciated.

  - *Dashboard*: The usage dashboard can provide developers with insight into how the API/SDK is being used, such as the number of hits, billing information, and credit top-ups. This can help developers better understand the usage of the API/SDK and make informed decisions about how to use it.

  - *Usability*: The user interface and overall developer experience of the API/SDK should be intuitive and easy to navigate. This can help developers quickly and easily find the information they need to use the API/SDK effectively.

- During the user interaction

  - *Functionality*: The API/SDK should work as intended and meet the minimum acceptable performance requirements. Developers should be able to use the API/SDK to accomplish the tasks they need to complete.

  - *Performance*: The API/SDK's response time and scalability should be satisfactory. Developers should not have to wait long for responses, and the API/SDK should be able to handle many requests.

  - *Errors*: Human and system errors should be handled gracefully. Human errors should be notified and automatically corrected, and system errors should be notified.

  - *Transparency*: The API response should be based on an AI algorithm, and the response should be well explained. Also, uncertainty and confidence levels should be explained.

- *Integration*: The API/SDK should be easy to integrate with other applications using mechanisms such as WebSockets and webhooks.

- *Flexibility*: Developers should be able to change certain parameters or configurations of the API/SDK, such as input-output, threshold, hyperparameters, model, and evaluation metrics.

- *Deployment*: The API/SDK should be easy to deploy to various platforms, such as the Web, Android, and ARM.

- After the user interaction

  - *Monitoring*: The API/SDK's performance, such as accuracy and latency, should be monitorable.

  - *Update feedback*: The API/SDK should ask for feedback clearly, and this feedback should be used to improve the API/SDK's performance. Feedback should be actionable, and any updates to the model should be communicated clearly.

For AI toolkits, the components are as follows:

- Before user interaction

  - *Functionality testing*: This tests that the AI toolkit includes all the features and capabilities developers expect.

  - *Compatibility testing*: This tests that the AI toolkit is compatible with the developer's existing development environment and tools.

  - *Documentation testing*: This tests the quality and clarity of the documentation provided to developers to ensure that it is easily understood and provides clear instructions for using the toolkit.

- During user interaction

  - *Usability testing*: This tests how intuitive and easy the GUI of the AI toolkit is to empower the developers in building AI systems.

  - *Integration testing*: This tests how well the AI toolkit integrates with other systems and applications that the developer is using.

- *Performance testing*: This measures how well the AI toolkit performs regarding response time and scalability to ensure it can handle the expected volume of usage.

- *Debugging and troubleshooting*: This allows developers to debug and troubleshoot issues that may arise using the AI toolkit.

- After user interaction

  - *User feedback testing*: Measures developers' satisfaction with the AI toolkit and what areas can be improved.

  - *Maintenance testing*: This tests the AI toolkit's ability to be maintained and updated overtime to ensure that it continues to meet the needs of the developer audience.

  - *Bug reporting and tracking*: This allows developers to report issues they encounter while using the AI toolkit and track the progress of these issues as the development team addresses them.

3. Finally, the development and business teams must assess the technical feasibility of these AI products in a real-world setting. This includes evaluating user satisfaction, the team's capabilities, the technology and infrastructure required, and the cost of building and operating the AI product. The final goal is to determine whether the AI product is commercially viable.

Output:

For AIaaS/AIaaE, the output of this test process should be a scorecard of the API/SDK's testing performance. The scorecard can be used to make improvements to the API/SDK and to ensure that it continues to meet the needs of developers. The scorecard of the AIaaS/AIaaE is depicted in the AI testing canvas (Figure 7-5).

Before The First Interaction ▼	During Interaction		▼ After Interaction
Documentation • Is the API/SDK documentation clear and include examples ?	**Functionality** • Is the API/SDK works as intended? • Is the Minimum Acceptable Performance satisfied?	**Integration** • Can it easily integrated with Other applications using Websocket, Webhook or other mechanism?	**Monitoring** • Can you monitor the API performance (ie Accuracy, latency) ?
Dashboard • Can the API/SDK shows the usage Such as number of hits, billing and credit Top ups?	**Performance** • How good is the response time ? • How good is scalability?	**Flexibility** • Can we change some parameters or configuration Of this API/SDK? Ex. Input-Output, threshold, hyperparameters, model, evelution metrics	**Update Feedback** • Is the API/SDK asking for feedback clearly?
Usability • Is the user interface and overall Developer experience of API/SDK is Intuitive and easy to navigate?	**Errors** • Is human error notified or automatically corrected ? • Is system error notified? **Transparency** • Is the API response based on AI algorithm explained well ? • Is uncertainty and confidence level explained?	**Deployment** • Can we deploy the model easily to any platform such as Web, Android, ARM ?	• Does this feedback improve their performance ? • Is the feedback actionable • Is the model update Communicated clearly?

Figure 7-5. AI product testing canvas for AIaaS/AIaaE

Likewise, for the AI toolkit, the output is the scorecard of AI toolkit testing performance, which is depicted in the AI testing canvas (Figure 7-6).

Before The First Interaction ▼	During Interaction		▼ After Interaction
Documentation • Is the AI toolkit documentation is clear and include examples ?	**Functionality** • Can developer use the tool to create or optimize working AI models ?	**Integration and Interoperability** • Can the tool integrated With other tool and workflow?	**Monitoring** • Can developer monitor the performance of model/data/ pipeline created?
Dashboard • Can the AI toolkit shows information like models created, usage per day, Average performance?	**Performance** • How good is the accuracy , size and latency of the AI models created?	**Template Library** • Can developer easily select predefined algorithms, models, data and pipelines ?	**Feedback** • Is the performance metrics, error analysis, Visualization can be provided by the AI tools?
Usability • Is the user interface and overall Developer experience of the AI toolkit is Intuitive and easy to navigate?	**Testing** • Can developer test the models, data and configurations to work as expected? **Version control** • Can developers easily version control the model or data?	**Metrics** • Can developer easily set The metrics to evaluate the Model, pipeline or data created/improved by AI tools?	

Figure 7-6. AI product testing canvas for the AI toolkit

It is also important to note that this is a cyclical process. Testing should be done repeatedly to make sure that the AI product is continuously improving. To improve the developer's experience, the AI product should be tested by different groups of developers and in different use cases. This can help identify potential issues that may not have been discovered during initial testing.

CASE STUDY 1 (AI AS A SERVICE): DEVELOPER EXPERIENCE DESIGN FOR IDENTITY VERIFICATION

Identifax is an identity verification AIaaS company founded by Barbara, a former bank risk manager, and Nguyen, an accomplished computer vision engineer with experience in developing biometrics systems. Barbara and Nguyen met while working at a large bank, where Barbara was a risk manager responsible for implementing robust identity verification systems and Nguyen was developing eKYC software.

They quickly realized a gap in the market for an easy-to-use and reliable eKYC (electronic know-your-customer) identity verification system (Figure 7-7). They decided to leave the bank to start their own company, Identifax.

Figure 7-7. eKYC identity verification

The company aimed to create an eKYC identity verification AI as a Service (AIaaS) for developers to build identity verification features for their mobile and web applications.

1. *Empathize*: The first step in the development process was the Empathize phase, where Barbara and Nguyen researched their potential customers' needs and hypothesized. They interviewed developers and businesses in various industries to learn about the challenges they faced when implementing identity verification in their products. They also reviewed the existing identity verification solutions on the market and identified gaps in functionality and usability. The output of this phase is the table and hypothesis in the following (Table 7-4).

Table 7-4. Developer Persona of eKYC AIaaS

Developer user	Back-end developer
Applications developed	Mobile banking, loan application, insurance claim
Cognitive tasks	Matching faces, checking face liveness, character recognition from ID
Metrics	Face matching accuracy, liveness detection accuracy, OCR accuracy
Business values	Increased new user onboarding, reduced personnel cost, reduced onboarding time

The Identifax team then creates the preliminary hypothesis as follows:

We believe that the ***back-end engineers*** who develop ***mobile banking or FinTech applications*** will benefit from integrating the application with our ***AI as a Service*** to automate some ***face and ID matching*** to attain optimal face matching accuracy and OCR detection accuracy, which increases ***the number of users onboarded, reduces the number of personnel, and decreases new customer time to onboard***.

2. *Define:* The developer persona is detailed further in the second phase, and the developer experience journey is mapped. The Identifax team analyzes the developer user and comes up with a more specific developer persona hypothesis on the following:

    - *Developer user:* The developers using Identifax are mostly back-end or mobile application engineers looking for easy-to-use API and SDK of face matching and OCR solutions.

    - *Applications developed:* Most are developing banking or financial technology applications, where identity verification of the new users is crucial.

    - *Demographics:* Most of the developers targeted by Identifax are male, with an undergraduate degree in a technical subject such as computer science, engineering, and physics. The average age is below 30 years old, and as banking and fintech industries are high-risk industries, the applications are developed mainly by senior back-end developers with experience of more than five years.

    - *Technical skills:* The back-end engineers are primarily experts in back-end webs such as server-side programming, database, RESTful API, containerization technology such as Docker, and cloud platforms such as Amazon Web Services, Microsoft Azure, and Google Cloud.

- *Pain points*: The pain points of back-end engineers developing AI for identity verification are handling large amounts of facial and identity data, developing and deploying complex machine learning models based on the data, scaling their models to meet demand, maintaining and updating models, and understanding complex biometrics-related machine learning algorithms.

- *Metrics*: The metrics of the back-end engineers developing banking and FinTech solutions are the development cost, the latency, and the accuracy of identity verification machine learning models.

The next thing is that the Identifax team brainstorms to ensure a smooth journey for the developer using their product and the different stages a developer would go through when integrating the identity verification AIaaS into their workflow:

1. *Signup*: The developers realize that they need the identity verification module when the product managers having discussions with the business development managers and risk managers are given the requirements to onboard the new users as seamlessly and safely as possible. The developers realize that developing their identity verification machine learning model is complex, costly, and time-consuming. Therefore, they start to search for ready-made APIs and SDKs. After searching around, they find the Identifax landing page, explaining the benefits, use cases, and USPs of Identifax AIaaS that can be accessed through API and SDK. The important principle of this step is that the CTA (call to action) must be obvious and direct: to click the free trial button to enable the developer to access the developer sandbox.

2. *Learning*: In this phase, the developers are tasked with familiarizing themselves with the API and SDK documentation, including sample programs written in various programming languages such as Java, Python, and JavaScript. This step is crucial as it allows developers to understand how to effectively access and utilize the API and SDK to achieve their desired outcomes. By studying and comprehending the documentation and sample programs, developers can gain the necessary knowledge to integrate the API and SDK into their projects effectively.

3. *Trial*: In this step, the developers are trying out some API sandbox to try API requests and get responses accordingly on some real images. The available APIs are *face matching* with an enrolled face on the database, facial liveness detection, and ID recognition.

4. *Integration*: After the developer tinkers with the APIs and tries some requests, adjusting some parameters (i.e., thresholds) and getting responses, they can integrate the APIs with their own applications.

5. *Operationalization*: The developer can monitor the API's usage and performance.

The Identifax team creates a developer persona canvas and journey map based on the brainstorming sessions and findings.

3. *Ideate*: In this stage, the Identifax team brainstorms and elaborates on the technicality of the developer experience aspects of eKYC services, such as the AI algorithms, deployment, and application type.

    a. *Identify applications*: The Identifax team lists the applications needing AI-based eKYC solutions:

        i. *Banking and financial services*: Account opening, loan applications, and other financial transactions

        ii. *Telecommunication*: SIM card activation, customer onboarding

        iii. *Government services*: ID card issuance, voter registration, tax compliance

        iv. *Healthcare*: Patient onboarding, verification of insurance coverage

        v. *Ecommerce*: Customer onboarding, fraud prevention, age verification

    b. *Determine deployment*: The API and SDK of AI-based eKYC can be deployed on the Web and mobile (Android and iOS). Hence, the team must prepare mobile SDKs for face liveness and ID OCR as boilerplate codes for various platforms such as iOS and Android. The mobile SDKs are useful for integrating the API with mobile applications. The main interaction with the FinTech and banking application users is mostly through a smartphone. The developer can integrate active liveness mechanism available as a mobile SDK, for example, asking the users to blink, hold still, or shake their head for ID verification in mobile applications to make sure the users are not spoofing the system using printed face or mask (Figure 7-8).

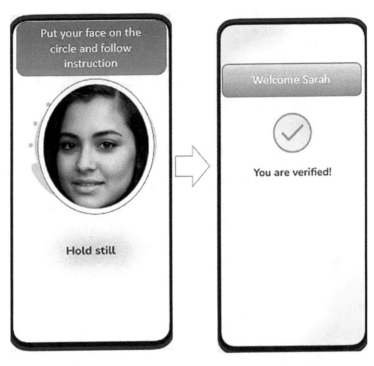

Figure 7-8. Active liveness to check human face liveness in mobile applications

c. *Define input-output*: The API input is the image of the user's face, and the input of the SDK is the video of the user taken with various poses. The output is that the face is matched or not matched with the liveness score. A low score (0–5) means the face is probably a spoof. A high score (>8) means the face is more likely an actual living person. This score can be adjusted accordingly by users.

d. *Understand in-house development challenge*: Some of the challenges of developing AI-based eKYC in-house are as follows:

   i. Building AI models based on computer vision, especially related to facial liveness detection and ID recognition, is challenging and needs lots of research and development.

   ii. Data availability to train and validate computer vision models needs large amounts of high-quality labeled data. Acquiring and preparing such data can be a significant challenge.

   iii. Training AI models requires a significant amount of computational power.

iv. AI models such as eKYC require ongoing maintenance and updates to remain effective. The company must possess MLOps tools and capabilities.

e. *Define AI type*: There are three main AI models for eKYC. The Identifax AI team brainstorms the AI type used as follows:

  i. *Face matching*: Deep neural network such as the Siamese network

  ii. *Liveness detection*: An ensemble of several deep neural network models, such as the *Siamese network* and sequential CNN (*convolutional neural network*)

  iii. ID OCR: A combination of deep neural network models such as CNN and ViT (*Vision Transformer*)

f. *Define performance monitoring*: Performance monitoring regularly assesses machine learning models' accuracy and reliability to ensure they meet a minimum acceptable performance level. The minimum acceptable performance for the face matching model would be high accuracy in matching faces to the correct individual. For face liveness detection, the minimum acceptable performance would be accurately identifying whether the detected face is real or fake to prevent fraud or unauthorized access. For the ID OCR model, the minimum acceptable performance would be a high level of accuracy in reading and interpreting text on identification documents, to prevent errors or fraud in the verification process.

g. *Define version update*: Version update in the context of machine learning models for face matching, face liveness detection, and ID OCR involves updating the models with new data or improved algorithms to enhance their accuracy and performance (fine-tuning). The frequency of updates will depend on the availability of new data and the evolving needs of the application. The updated version of the models should be made available to the developers and users, with clear documentation of the changes made and their potential impact on the performance of the models. This will help developers stay informed of the updates and make any necessary adjustments to their application, thereby avoiding any violations of Hyrum's law, which is a phenomenon that occurs when an implementation relies on assumptions that are not explicitly guaranteed by the interface specification. For face matching, the model may require updates when there are changes in the subject's appearance due to aging or trend changes in hairstyle or trends in accessories like glasses or masks (e.g., during a pandemic). For face liveness detection, updates may be required

when new types of spoofing attacks are identified or when changes in the system's hardware or software components affect the
detection performance. The frequency of updates may depend on
the rate of false positives or false negatives and the rate of change
in the input data. For ID OCR, the frequency of updates may depend on the quality and diversity of the input data, the required
accuracy, and the rate of change in the input data. The ideal time
for updates may be determined by the rate of error in recognizing
characters or words or the frequency of changes in the ID formats
used. Generally, updates should be performed regularly to ensure
the model remains accurate and reliable over time.

h. *Define parameter optimization*: Some parameters that developers can optimize and adjust during inference time for various
machine learning models include threshold values, input image
size, and confidence scores. For a face matching machine learning model, developers can adjust the threshold value, which determines the minimum level of similarity required to classify two
faces as a match. Depending on the use case, this parameter can
be adjusted to increase the model's sensitivity or specificity. In
addition, developers can adjust the input image size to optimize
performance and reduce computational requirements. For a liveness detection machine learning model, developers can adjust
the confidence score, which determines the minimum level of
certainty required to classify a face as a live detection. This parameter can be adjusted to increase or decrease the sensitivity
of the model. Additionally, developers can adjust the input image
size and the number of frames required for liveness detection.
For an ID document OCR machine learning model, developers can
adjust the input image size to optimize performance and reduce
computational requirements. They can also adjust the confidence
score, which determines the minimum level of certainty required
to classify a particular character or word. Additionally, developers
can adjust the language and font settings to improve accuracy
and reduce errors.

i. *Define workflow optimization*: The eKYC machine learning models
such as face matching, liveness detection, and OCR of ID documents are integrated into the user verification process of an application in industries such as banking, finance, and ecommerce.
These models automate the tasks of comparing the face in the
photo to the face on the ID document, verifying the user's physical
presence, and extracting relevant information from the ID document. This automation allows for a more efficient and secure user
verification process, reducing the risk of fraud and improving the
user experience.

j. *Define feedback:* The implicit and explicit feedback for eKYC AI as a Service, such as face matching, liveness detection, and ID OCR, are critical for improving the accuracy and reliability of the models. *Self-supervised learning* can be integrated with the implicit feedback mechanism to train the machine learning models using unlabeled data, while *active learning* can be integrated with the explicit feedback mechanism to improve the machine learning models using user feedback to identify errors and train the models with new data. For example, in face matching, implicit feedback comes from the similarity between faces, and explicit feedback comes from user input on the accuracy of the match. At the same time, *self-supervised learning* can be used to train the model on unlabeled data, and *active learning* can be used to improve the model using user feedback. For liveness detection, implicit feedback comes from the data characteristics of the images presented to the model, and explicit feedback comes from user input on the success of the verification process. For ID OCR, implicit feedback comes from the consistency and similarity of the characters recognized by the model. In contrast, explicit feedback comes from user input on the accuracy of the OCR result. In both cases, *self-supervised learning* can be used to train the model on unlabeled data, and *active learning* can be used to improve the model using user feedback.

k. *Define risks and errors:* eKYC AI services, such as face matching, liveness detection, and OCR ID, carry inherent risks and errors that can arise in their use. Here are some examples:

   i. *Face matching:* One risk is that the model can produce false positives or false negatives, meaning that it can incorrectly identify a person as a match or not identify a person who is a match. Errors can arise due to poor image quality, lighting or pose changes, and facial feature variations.

   ii. *Liveness detection:* One risk is that the model can be fooled by fraudsters who use advanced techniques to mimic live person behavior, such as using high-quality videos or 3D masks. Errors can arise due to poor image quality, background noise, and variations in facial expressions.

   iii. *ID OCR:* One risk is that the model can produce incorrect or incomplete results, meaning it can misread or miss parts of the ID document. Errors can arise due to variations in text and font, poor image quality, and background noise.

These risks and errors can have serious consequences, such as identity theft or fraud, if not managed carefully. It is important to continuously monitor and evaluate the eKYC AI services' performance to mitigate these risks and provide feedback and corrections when errors occur. It is also important to use secure and reliable systems to ensure that personal data is protected and used only for its intended purpose. Finally, it is important to establish clear policies and guidelines for using eKYC AI services to ensure they are used responsibly and ethically.

4.   *Prototype*: In this stage, the development team of Identifax conducts a brainstorming session to develop the prototype of the eKYC AIaaS:

   a. *Before the user interaction*: The development team focuses on providing easy-to-understand documentation and instructions before any interaction. They want to ensure their product is accessible to a wide range of developers, with clear explanations of the API endpoints, CLI, or SDK and any configurable parameters or hyperparameters. They also provide instructions on how to set up the developer sandbox and any prerequisites that must be met before using the prototype.

   b. *During the user interaction*: The team works hard to create an intuitive eKYC AIaaS API and SDK for the developer sandbox. They design error-handling mechanisms and notifications to make it easy for developers to understand and diagnose any issues that may arise. They consider what parameters and hyperparameters can be configured and how they can be accessed and modified within the developer sandbox. The team wants to create a product that is user-friendly and easy to work with.

   c. *After the user interaction*: The team shifts their focus to providing developers with the tools and information they need to monitor and explain the results of the eKYC AI models. They provide metrics, performance monitoring capabilities, and fairness and explainability mechanisms. The team also considers how the AI models can be integrated with other applications and how implicit and explicit feedback, including active learning mechanisms, can be implemented as part of the prototype. They work tirelessly to create a product that is not only functional but also ethical and responsible.

5.   *Test:* After the eKYC AIaaS prototype was developed, the Identifax team decides to test it with a small number of developer users as API sandbox and mobile SDK. The goal is to gather feedback on the AI model's ease of use, performance, and accuracy. To evaluate the product's performance, they measure response time, error rate, and user satisfaction metrics:

- Before the user interaction, the team provides clear and comprehensive documentation for the API/SDK, including examples of using it effectively. They also include a usage dashboard that allows developers to track the usage of the API/SDK and make informed decisions about how to use it. The user interface and overall developer experience of the API/SDK are designed to be intuitive and easy to navigate.

- During the user interaction, the team focuses on ensuring that the API/SDK works as intended and meets the minimum acceptable performance requirements. They evaluate the functionality, response time, scalability, error handling, transparency, integration, flexibility, and deployment capabilities of the API/SDK for each AI model. They also ask for feedback on the performance of the API/SDK and make any necessary improvements to the model.

- After the user interaction, the team monitors the API/SDK's performance, such as accuracy and latency, and continues gathering developer feedback. They use this feedback to improve the product, such as updating the AI model and enhancing the user experience. The team also continues to ensure that the API/SDK is easy to deploy to various platforms and can be integrated with other applications using mechanisms such as WebSockets and webhooks.

The team also considers how the AI models can be integrated with other applications and how implicit and explicit feedback, including active learning mechanisms, can be implemented as part of the prototype for each AI model.

Through this process, the Identifax team created a successful eKYC AIaaS MVP and, later, a fully commercial product with face matching, liveness detection, and ID OCR that met the needs of developers. The feedback they received allowed them to improve the product and make it more accessible to a broader range of users for each of the AI models. The team was proud of the hard work and dedication that went into creating the eKYC AIaaS product, and they looked forward to its continued success.

CASE STUDY 2 (AI TOOLKIT): DEVELOPER EXPERIENCE DESIGN FOR A NO-CODE COMPUTER VISION PLATFORM

Gunther and Franz were both driven by a passion for technology, and they shared a vision of a world where anyone could create powerful machine learning models. Gunther, a former sales VP at SAP GMBH, had a talent for identifying customer needs and bringing products to market. Franz, a computer vision consultant with PhD in computer science, was an expert in machine learning and had a knack for solving complex technical problems.

However, they also understood the challenges faced by businesses and developers who lacked the resources or technical expertise to build and deploy deep learning models for computer vision problems.

To address this issue, Gunther and Franz founded Visionix, a low-code computer vision AI tool that would make it easy for anyone to build and deploy powerful deep learning models. They used design thinking principles to identify the pain points of businesses and developers and create a solution to address their needs.

One of the key challenges that they identified was the complexity of building and deploying deep learning models. Many developers, even seasoned data scientists, lacked the skills and experience to build and train models effectively. Businesses often struggled to find the resources to hire data scientists and build their models. Gunther and Franz believed that by making deep learning more accessible and easier to use, they could empower businesses and developers to achieve their goals without requiring extensive technical expertise.

To solve this problem, they created a no-code platform with a drag-and-drop graphical user interface to simplify the data annotation and model training process (Figure 7-9). The platform also included a suite of pre-trained models that users could use as starting points for their models, saving time and resources.

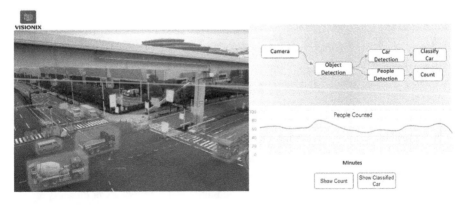

Figure 7-9. Visionix no-code computer vision platform

One of the key advantages of Visionix was its ability to quickly deploy models in the cloud, on-premise, or on mobile devices. This allowed businesses and developers to deploy models in the best environment.

Underlying the platform was a powerful deep learning engine that provided users access to state-of-the-art computer vision models. The engine was built using the latest deep learning and computer vision research, ensuring that Visionix's models were accurate and effective.

Overall, Gunther and Franz aimed to democratize deep learning and make it accessible to businesses and developers of all sizes. By creating a low-code platform that simplified the process of building and deploying deep learning models, they aimed to unlock the full potential of AI and empower businesses to achieve their goals in new and exciting ways.

The step-by-step of their design thinking process from ideation to validation is as follows:

1. *Empathize*: Gunther and Franz initiated the development process with the Empathize phase. They researched to comprehend the requirements of their potential customers and hypothesized the types of developers who would benefit from their product, Visionix. They interviewed developers and businesses from a wide range of industries to gain insights into the difficulties they faced when developing, deploying, and operating computer vision–based deep learning models in their products. Additionally, they scrutinized the current computer vision builder toolkits available in the market and identified inadequacies in functionality and usability. The outcome of this phase is the table and hypotheses mentioned in the following (Table 7-5).

Table 7-5. Developer Persona of the No-Code Computer Vision Platform

Developer user	Data scientist, back-end developer
Applications developed	Any applications that require computer vision models
Cognitive tasks	Object detection, object recognition, object tracking
Metrics	Accuracy, latency, model size
Business values	Cost and time efficiency for developing and deploying computer vision models and improved accuracy and productivity for businesses that use them

The Visionix team then creates the preliminary hypothesis as follows:

We believe that the ***data scientists and software engineers*** who develop ***any applications that need computer vision models*** will benefit from integrating the application with our ***AI toolkit*** to automate some ***object detection, object*** *recognition, and object tracking* to *optimize the accuracy and latency of computer vision models,* which results in an *increasingly shorter time for computer vision model development.*

2. *Define:* The Visionix team details the developer persona and maps the experience journey in the second phase. They analyze the developer user and generate more specific hypotheses on the following developer persona:

    a. *Developer users:* Visionix is used by data scientists or back-end engineers seeking an easy way to develop computer vision models quickly.

    b. *Applications:* The platform is used to develop applications for various use cases, such as image recognition for inventory management, ecommerce SKU analysis, or object detection for surveillance.

    c. *Demographics:* Users are typically under 30 years old; have a technical undergraduate or master's degree in computer science, engineering, or physics; and are predominantly male or female.

    d. *Technical skills:* The data scientists using Visionix are experts in machine learning and have experience building and optimizing machine learning models using various machine learning frameworks.

    e. *Pain points:* Users face challenges managing large amounts of computer vision data, annotating and selecting data for model development, deploying complex models, scaling to meet demand, maintaining and updating models, and monitoring performance.

    f. *Metrics:* The primary metrics of interest are the time and development cost for annotating and building deep learning computer vision models.

    User experience design is a crucial part of any successful software development process. The Visionix team is aware of this and is currently focused on brainstorming ways to ensure a smooth journey for developers using their product. The team has identified five key stages of the developer journey for the AI tool: signup, reading instruction, trial, development, and integration. Each stage is designed to make the experience as user-friendly, efficient, and intuitive as possible:

    a. The signup stage is the first step in the journey and is critical to ensuring a positive user experience. The Visionix team is working hard to make the signup process as simple and secure as possible, with streamlined registration procedures to minimize potential roadblocks.

b. The reading instruction stage is equally important. It provides developers with the necessary product documentation and instructions to understand the features and how to use the Visionix no-code computer vision platform. The team is carefully crafting these materials to ensure they are easy to understand and follow.

c. The trial stage allows developers to test the Visionix platform in a free trial or sandbox environment to ensure it meets their needs and requirements. This stage is a critical part of the user experience, allowing developers to test the platform and provide feedback before committing to using it.

d. The development stage begins the actual work, and the Visionix team is committed to making it as straightforward and efficient as possible. The no-code interface, combined with pre-built models and libraries, makes it easy for developers to create advanced no-code computer vision deep learning models easily.

e. Finally, in the integration stage, the Visionix team is focused on providing flexible integration options, allowing developers to easily integrate their models into their existing development workflow and infrastructure.

3. *Ideate*: At this stage, the Visionix team is fully immersed in the technical intricacies of developing a low-code computer vision building tool that addresses the many challenges associated with creating, annotating, training, and deploying AI algorithms. To accomplish this goal, the team has identified several key technical aspects of the platform:

a. *Identifying AI models and supporting infrastructure*: The Visionix team has defined the platform's focus as helping developers build basic computer vision models, such as object detection, classification, tracking, and object segmentation using various deep learning techniques.

b. *Deployment options*: The Visionix platform can deploy computer vision models into the cloud using REST API and WebSocket or into any container, such as Docker and Kubernetes, enabling deep learning models to be deployed to any on-premise servers.

c. *Input and output*: The Visionix platform takes image and video data as input and outputs insights, such as object location, number, and behavior.

d. *In-house development challenges*: Developing computer vision models using deep learning is challenging because of the need to annotate images, mix and match different neural network architectural designs, experiment, optimize hyperparameters, and deploy the model, all coded and scripted in an unintuitive manner.

e. *Cost- and time-saving benefits:* The cost of using the no-code computer vision platform is lower because fewer data scientists are needed and development time is shorter because the entire end-to-end process from annotating images to monitoring the model can be handled by one platform.

f. *Trustworthiness:* The computer vision models produced by the Visionix platform can be explained through an image saliency mechanism.

g. *Scope of development workflow:* The Visionix platform builds a black box for any application where insight generation and decision-making can be built on that black box.

h. *Performance and cost monitoring:* The success metrics used are accuracy, size, and development time.

i. *AI model builder compatibility:* This no-code deep learning computer vision platform supports machine learning libraries like TensorFlow and PyTorch and runs on Nvidia and Intel OpenVINO.

j. The Visionix team is dedicated to providing developers with a powerful, easy-to-use, cost-effective low-code computer vision building tool that overcomes the technical challenges of building advanced computer vision models. With the capabilities of the Visionix platform, developers can focus on the creative aspects of computer vision model development while the platform handles the technical intricacies.

4. *Prototype:* The development team of Visionix has embarked on a new project to create a low-code computer vision platform. The team began brainstorming and outlining the project's objectives, features, and technical requirements. The team prioritized ensuring their product would be user-friendly and accessible to a wide range of developers:

a. Before the interaction stage, they focused on developing easy-to-understand documentation and instructions to clearly explain the graphical user interface, API endpoints, and command-line interface. The team also provided instructions on using the drag-and-drop GUI and any prerequisites to be met before using the prototype to annotate and build computer vision models.

b. During the interaction stage, the team focused on creating an intuitive drag-and-drop GUI that allows developers to quickly annotate, mix and match deep learning models, and modify pre-processing algorithms such as data augmentation. They designed error-handling mechanisms and notifications to help developers understand and diagnose any issues that may arise. The team also considered the types of experimentations that model developers can analyze to create a product that is user-friendly and easy to work with.

c. After the interaction stage, the team shifted their focus to providing developers with comprehensive auditing and monitoring tools built into the Visionix platform. These tools enable proactive application performance management and make detecting issues in real time easier. Visionix provides dashboard tools to monitor events and metrics in the cloud. At the same time, its automated infrastructure and no-code capabilities enable the implementation of a responsive and fast computer vision development, update, and upkeep strategy. The platform also includes powerful diagnosis tools, system alerts, and automated health checks, enabling developers to detect issues early. When problems are identified, Visionix provides integrated tools for remote troubleshooting, fast rollbacks, and disaster recovery.

5. *Test.* After developing the Visionix no-code computer vision prototype, the development team wanted to test it with a few developer users as a web application that could be accessed from anywhere. The main goal of the testing was to gather feedback from the developers about the ease of use and performance of the low-code computer vision platform. To evaluate the prototype, the team measured metrics such as time to annotate images and train, validate, and deploy computer vision models and how easy the Visionix platform was to use. The Visionix team analyzed the testing results in three stages: before, during, and after the developers' interaction with the Visionix platform.

a. Before the user interaction stage, the development team conducted functionality testing to ensure that Visionix includes all the features and capabilities developers expect. They also tested compatibility to ensure that the Visionix platform is compatible with the developer's existing development environment and tools. Finally, the team conducted documentation testing to ensure that the documentation provided to developers is easily understood and provides clear instructions for using the no-code computer vision platform.

b. During the user interaction, the team conducted usability testing to measure how intuitive and easy to use the GUI of the Visionix no-code platform is for developers to build AI systems. They also tested integration to measure how well Visionix integrates with other developers' development libraries and infrastructures. In addition, the team conducted performance testing to measure how well the Visionix platform performs in terms of response time and scalability to ensure that it can handle the expected volume of usage. The team also tested the debugging and troubleshooting mechanisms of the platform.

c. After the user interaction, the team tested user feedback to measure developers' satisfaction with Visionix and what areas could be improved. They also conducted maintenance testing to measure the capability of Visionix models to be maintained and updated overtime, ensuring that it continues to meet the needs of developers. Finally, the team conducted bug reporting and tracking testing that enables developers to report issues they encounter while using Visionix and track the progress of these issues as the development team addresses them.

Through this process, the Visionix team created a successful no-code computer vision tool that met the needs of developers. The feedback from developers enabled the team to improve the product and ensure that it is a user-friendly, high-performance platform easily integrated with other development libraries and infrastructures.

Conclusion

This chapter teaches how AI developer experience (DX) design can help examine the creation of AI-based products and services while providing a framework for incorporating AI into applications. Using the design thinking principle, focusing on developers' needs and preferences helps create user-friendly high-quality AI products that meet their requirements. The feedback from users enables teams to improve existing products and ensure they meet end user expectations. Two case studies of AI as a Service and AI toolkits are presented.

Key Takeaways

- The developer experience for AI services can differ depending on the specific service or toolkit and the intended use case.

- AI services can be provided in various ways such as AIaaS, AI toolkits, AIaaE, and AI PaaS, which can be delivered through different methods, including API, SDK, CLI, operating systems, containers, VMs, or GUI. These services aim to provide developers with an easy and flexible way to access advanced AI capabilities without worrying about the underlying infrastructure.

- By providing developers with easy-to-use and flexible tools, companies can help bridge the gap between cutting-edge AI research and real-world implementation, making it possible for developers of all skill levels to create innovative and intelligent applications.

- When designing the developer experience for AI products, key principles should be considered, such as ease of use and integration, flexibility and control, and comprehensive tools and capabilities.

- Good documentation and support, monitoring and visibility, scalability and maintenance, collaboration and community, trustworthiness, fairness, and feedback are essential components that should be included in the developer experience.

- The developer experience for AI products should aim to provide developers with tools that allow them to understand how the AI models work, identify and mitigate biases, measure the performance of the models, and improve them overtime.

- Design thinking is important for designing a developer experience (DX) process, as it allows the team to understand developers' needs and pain points and create solutions tailored to their specific needs.

- The *Empathize* phase is the first step in building an AI product developer experience using design thinking. This phase involves hypothesizing about the types of developers using the product, defining data-gathering methods, and gathering information about the developer persona, problems, and pain points. The output of this phase is an understanding of the benefits of AI tools or services for the target audience, including the developers' specific needs and pain points.

- The *Define* phase of design thinking for a developer product focuses on detailing the developer persona, mapping the developer journey, and understanding the target audience's tasks and mental models. The output of this phase is a developer persona canvas, a developer journey map, and an AI toolkit product, which helps developers understand how to build and integrate AI models into their applications while identifying pain points and opportunities for improvement.

- The *Ideate* phase for AI products targeted toward developers involves different steps and outputs for AIaaS, AIaaE, and AI toolkits. Understanding each product's target user and usage is crucial for identifying potential use cases and designing a successful developer experience (DX). For AIaaS/AIaaE, the output of this phase is a canvas with the input/output of the model and its potential use cases. For AI toolkits, the output of this phase is a document detailing the different AI models that can be developed using the toolkit and the workflows and use cases it supports.

- In the *Prototype* phase, the development team creates a user-friendly design for the AI product's interface, with clear documentation and error-handling features. They also develop tools for monitoring and measuring the product's benefits. The output of this phase is a functioning prototype, including the GUI, API or SDK, and necessary documentation, which developers can test and use. The *Prototype* phase is essential in the design thinking process for AI products targeted toward developers, where the development team creates a prototype based on the product hypothesis, developer persona, developer journey map, and developer experience canvas.

- The *Test* phase is crucial in AI product development targeted to developer users. It allows the development team to understand how their solutions perform in a real-world context and identify areas for improvement. The *Test* phase for AIaaS/AIaaE and AI toolkits involves different components, such as documentation, usability, functionality, and integration testing. It should be a cyclical process to ensure continuous improvement and to identify potential issues in different use cases.

Building an AI Platform

As an AI startup, it is essential to have a clear strategy for designing, developing, and operating an AI platform that can meet market demands. In the previous chapters, we learned about validating AI products from various perspectives. This chapter will explore the details of building a successful AI platform that involves designing, developing, and operating the AI system. Building an AI platform is a complex process that requires careful consideration of many factors. We will explore the importance of the three pillars of AI platform design: system design, process design, and team design. We will provide a comprehensive framework that unifies these pillars into a single approach to building an effective AI platform. Measuring the maturity of an AI platform is also an essential aspect of the building process. We will discuss how to assess the platform at different stages, from initial development to optimized operation. This chapter will also discuss the challenges and best practices of building an AI platform. We will explore common issues and provide practical solutions to ensure success. To illustrate how the framework and best practices discussed in this chapter can be applied in practice, we will provide a case study of designing, developing, and operating an eKYC AI as a Service platform. This case study will provide real-world examples of the key considerations and decisions in building an effective AI platform. By the end

© Adhiguna Mahendra 2023
A. Mahendra, *AI Startup Strategy*, https://doi.org/10.1007/978-1-4842-9502-1_8

of this chapter, you will have a comprehensive understanding of what it takes to build a successful AI platform and the steps involved in designing, developing, and operating such a system.

Introduction

Artificial intelligence (AI) is increasingly being integrated into modern software platforms known as AI platforms. However, the development and deployment of an AI platform can be a complex and challenging task. To successfully build and deploy a scalable and robust AI platform, it is important to understand the cycle of how to architect, develop, and operationalize an AI software platform (Figure 8-1).

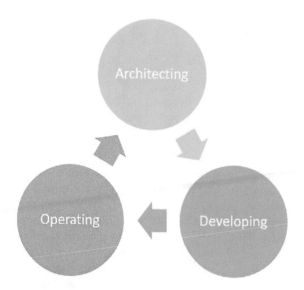

Figure 8-1. Architecting, developing, and operating cycle

Conway's law is one concept underpinning the AI platform's success. This law states that a system's design reflects the communication structures of the organization that builds it. In other words, the organizational structure and communication between teams as part of the overall process can significantly impact the design and effectiveness of the AI platform.

In designing the AI platform, other books and frameworks only focus on one pillar. However, this chapter presents a unified framework emphasizing the importance of the three pillars of AI platform design: system, process, and team design (Figure 8-2). Each pillar has its unique set of requirements and characteristics that contribute to the overall success of the AI platform.

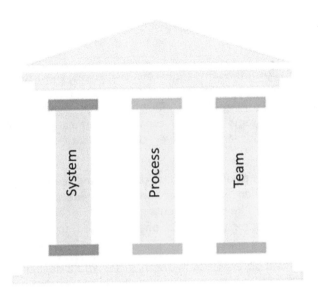

Figure 8-2. Three pillars of AI platform design

System design focuses on the technical infrastructure required for the AI platform. For example, the data layer (data pipelines), experimentation layer (model training and testing), and deployment layer (model serving) must adhere to established systems engineering principles.[1] The principles ensure the optimal functioning of these elements, creating scalable, maintainable, and fault-tolerant AI platforms and facilitating cutting-edge AI solutions.

Process design emphasizes implementing proper AI model development and operationalization, which crystallized into ModelOps/MLOps practices, such as version control, automated testing, and continuous deployment.

Team design refers to the organizational structure, communication, and collaboration between the various teams building and operating the AI platform.

This chapter will explore each pillar in more detail and guide how to build and operate a scalable and robust AI platform. By understanding the importance of each pillar and the interconnection between them, we can design and deploy AI solutions that meet the highest standards of quality and reliability.

---

[1] https://link.springer.com/book/10.1007/978-3-030-13431-0

Key Components and Layers of an AI Software Platform

Building an AI platform presents significant challenges, given the complexities involved in creating a system that can handle large amounts of data and perform complex computations efficiently in a dynamic environment. Furthermore, AI systems must be capable of emulating human cognitive capabilities, which adds another layer of complexity to the development process.

Focusing on the three pillars of system, process, and team design is essential to address these challenges. This section will provide an overview of an AI software architecture's key components and layers, including the concepts of process and team topologies, which offer a unified approach to building a software platform.

These concepts will be explored in depth, giving you a deeper understanding of their importance and how they contribute to developing a robust AI platform. The ideal AI software platform must be designed to handle the complexities of large-scale data processing while remaining flexible, scalable, and secure. The process of building and operating an AI platform requires a deep understanding of the technology involved and the ability to navigate the complexities of building a system that can adapt to changing business needs and remain effective overtime, which consists of the team structure.

AI Platform Design

Six Layers of the AI Platform

An AI platform consists of a complex system of interconnected components working harmoniously to deliver AI-based solutions.

Understanding the AI platform architecture and its six layers is crucial for a successful AI platform because they represent a structured approach to building a complex system of interconnected components that work together to deliver AI-based solutions.

Each layer is designed to handle a specific platform aspect, from the underlying infrastructure required to support it to the tools and mechanisms necessary to deploy and manage AI models.

By breaking down the platform into these individual layers, AI teams can ensure that each component is developed and optimized for its specific purpose, resulting in a more efficient and effective platform overall. Additionally, the layering approach allows for easier maintenance and scaling of the platform as it grows and evolves. Overall, the six layers provide a framework for building a robust and scalable AI platform to deliver user value (Figure 8-3).

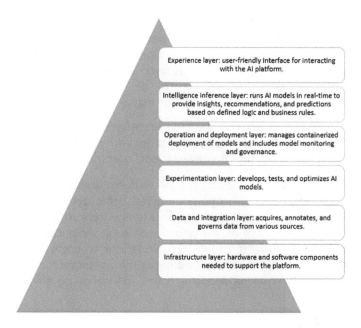

Figure 8-3. Six layers of an AI platform

1. The first layer is the infrastructure layer, which includes the hardware and software components needed to support the platform, such as *compute* and virtualization.

2. The second layer is the data and integration layer, which deals with the acquisition, annotation, quality control, governance, storage, and integration of data from various sources.

3. The third layer is the AI model experimentation layer, where the actual AI models are developed, tested, and optimized. This layer includes feature engineering, model development, model testing, model interpretability, and model management.

4. The fourth layer, the operation and deployment layer, deals with the tools and mechanisms required to manage the containerized deployment of various models and other components across the platform. This layer also includes model monitoring and governance.

5. The fifth layer is the intelligence inference layer, which runs the AI models in real time to provide insights, recommendations, and predictions based on defined logic and business rules. This layer includes an inference pipeline on runtimes, such as business process management and rules and logic management.

6. Finally, the sixth layer is the experience layer, which provides a user-friendly interface for interacting with the AI platform, such as a GUI, API, or conversational user interface.

By understanding the six layers of the AI platform architecture, developers can ensure that each layer is properly designed, optimized, and integrated to create a robust and scalable AI platform. This can help ensure that the platform can handle large volumes of data, perform complex computations efficiently, and provide valuable insights and recommendations to users. Additionally, a well-designed AI platform can provide a competitive advantage for organizations by improving decision-making, reducing costs, and increasing efficiency.

MLOps/ModelOps

MLOps (machine learning operations) is a set of practices and technologies used to build, deploy, and manage machine learning models in production.

Similarly, ModelOps is an approach that focuses on automating the development, deployment, and monitoring of all types of AI models, including machine learning, decision optimization, and symbolic logic models. MLOps and ModelOps aim to make the process of building and operating AI models more efficient, reliable, and scalable (Figure 8-4).

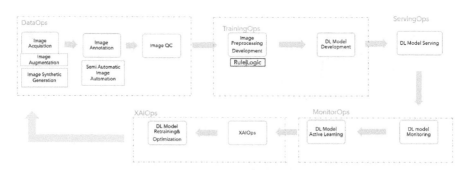

Figure 8-4. MLOps process applied to computer vision

The components of MLOps and ModelOps include data operations (DataOps), such as data acquisition/ingestion, ETL (Extract, Transform, Load), and annotation, followed by model experiments where the feature engineering, model development, and testing are performed (TrainingOps).

Next, there is continuous integration/continuous delivery (CI/CD) of model deployment and serving (ServingOps), followed by model monitoring and governance (MonitorOps). The newest trend includes XAI (explainable AI) into the cycle (XAIOps). These components ensure that AI models are built and deployed correctly and can be updated and managed overtime.

MLOps and ModelOps are similar in that they both aim to automate and streamline the process of building and deploying AI models. However, ModelOps is a broader term encompassing all types of AI models, while MLOps focuses specifically on machine learning models. MLOps often involves more advanced techniques such as hyperparameter tuning, transfer learning, and model interpretability.

In this section, we will focus more on the MLOps process of building AI products because machine learning is currently one of the most popular methods used in AI development. For example, predictive analytics relies heavily on machine learning, while computer vision applications are often based on deep learning, a branch of machine learning.

Embracing MLOps is important because it helps ensure that AI models are built and deployed correctly, can be updated and managed overtime, and can provide reliable and scalable results. This is crucial for building high-quality AI products that can meet the needs of businesses and end users.

MLOps is interrelated with the six layers of AI platform architecture discussed earlier because the MLOps components are integral to building and deploying AI models within the framework of the six layers. The data and integration layer is responsible for data acquisition and annotation, which are key components of MLOps. The AI model experimentation layer encompasses the feature engineering, model development, and testing components of MLOps. The operation and deployment layer is responsible for model deployment and serving, which are critical components of CI/CD in MLOps. Finally, the intelligence inference layer and experience layer are where the AI models are used and experienced by end users, making them important for monitoring and governance of the models.

LLM, VLP, and LLMOps

Most advanced generative AI products such as GPT, CLIP and DALL-E[2] from OpenAI rely on machine learning methods, specifically a type of model known as transformers, which belong to the broader class of large language models (LLMs) and Vision-Language Pretraining (VLP). These models are characterized by their ability to process and generate human-like text as well as image, a significant advancement from traditional machine learning models.

---

[2] https://openai.com/product

Traditional machine learning models are often tailored for specific tasks, ranging from spam detection to image recognition. Their learning process is primarily based on identifying patterns in the training data, and they require explicit feature engineering where relevant features are manually selected and fed into the model. While these models have been successful in many applications, they often struggle with tasks that involve understanding and generating natural language due to the inherent complexity and ambiguity of human language.

LLMs are trained on vast amounts of text data, enabling them to generate coherent and contextually relevant text based on a given prompt. Models like GPT-4,[3] a well-known example of an LLM, are designed to predict the next word in a sequence, having been trained on a diverse range of Internet text. They can answer questions, write essays, summarize texts, translate languages, and even generate Python code. However, they primarily operate in the textual domain and lack the ability to interpret or generate visual content.

On the other hand, VLP models, like DALL-E and CLIP from OpenAI, are designed to understand both textual and visual data. These models are pretrained on a large corpus of paired image-text data, allowing them to generate images from textual descriptions, answer questions about images, and even provide textual descriptions of images. This cross-modal understanding significantly expands the capabilities of AI models, bridging the gap between visual and textual data.

The integration of LLMs and VLPs could potentially lead to even more robust AI models capable of understanding, interpreting, and generating information across both textual and visual domains, much like humans do. These multimodal models can have wide-ranging applications, from more interactive and capable virtual assistants to advanced content creation tools.

When it comes to operations, MLOps (machine learning operations) is the discipline of AI model development and operations. It aims to unify ML system development and ML system operation, intending to shorten the ML lifecycle and provide high-quality, reliable ML products.

However, with the rise of LLMs and VLPs, there's an increasing need for large language model operations (LLMOps) and Vision-Language Pretraining operations (VLPOps), respectively. These operations are specialized subsets of MLOps that focus on the unique requirements and challenges of deploying and maintaining LLMs and VLPs. This includes managing the vast computational resources these models need, handling the diverse and large-scale data required for training, and implementing measures to mitigate potential ethical and fairness issues these models might raise.

---

[3] https://openai.com/research/gpt-4

Team Topologies

Conway's law states that the design of an organization's system will reflect the organization's communication structure. In other words, the organization's structure will impact the design of the system it creates. This is highly relevant to building AI platform architecture because it highlights the importance of team design in the overall architecture of the platform.

Team topologies is a concept that builds on *Conway's law*[4] and offers a framework for designing teams that can effectively build and operate modern software systems, including those with machine learning components. It is based on three main ideas:

1. *Simplify the team's cognitive load*: Teams should be designed to minimize the complexity of the system they work on, reducing the amount of cognitive overhead required to understand and work on the system.

2. *Enable fast and safe changes*: Teams should be designed to allow for fast and safe changes to the system they work on, enabling the team to deliver value quickly and respond to changing requirements.

3. *Build a foundation of effective communication*: Teams should be designed to promote effective communication and collaboration within the team and with other teams involved in the system.

The team topologies framework emphasizes four types of team interactions: stream-aligned teams, platform teams, enabling teams, and complicated subsystem teams. These teams work together to create an architecture optimized for the organization's needs and the product being built.

Stream-aligned teams are responsible for the end-to-end delivery of a particular product or service. Platform teams provide foundational services that are leveraged across multiple stream-aligned teams. Enabling teams are responsible for supporting and improving the flow of work across all teams. Finally, complicated subsystem teams work on highly specialized areas of the system that require deep expertise.

---

[4] https://teamtopologies.com/

Here's an example for team topologies for a machine learning product such as *fraud analytics*:

- The *stream-aligned team* for *fraud analytics* includes the data acquisition team responsible for obtaining high-quality fraud data, data analysis team for identifying fraud patterns and anomalies, and fraud machine learning team for building and maintaining the machine learning models for various fraud patterns.

- The *platform team* includes the infrastructure team responsible to build the data streaming acquisition, data transformation, data labeling, feature store, computing environment, and data storage and the MLOps team to develop MLOps components from model experiments to model serving.

- The *enabling team* includes the data governance team for ensuring data protection regulations and the security team for platform security.

- The *complicated subsystem team* includes the fraud explainability team and the machine learning model optimization team.

The team topologies concept defines three interaction modes for teams: collaboration, X as a Service, and facilitating. Collaboration involves teams working closely, while X as a Service involves consuming or providing something with minimal collaboration. Facilitating consists of helping (or being helped by) another team to clear impediments.

Here are some examples of how the fraud analytics team might use the three different interaction modes:

- *Collaboration*: The fraud data acquisition team and fraud data analysis team work collaboratively to ensure the data being collected is of high quality and analyzed effectively to identify patterns and anomalies. The fraud machine learning team and machine learning model optimization team work collaboratively to improve the machine learning models continuously.

- *X as a Service*: The infrastructure team provides a machine learning model serving infrastructure for the fraud machine learning team to deploy their models to production, with minimal collaboration required. The data governance team provides data policies and guidance on data ethics to the other teams as a service, with minimal collaboration required.

- *Facilitating*: The MLOps team facilitates the deployment of the machine learning models by helping the fraud machine learning team clear any impediments in the deployment pipeline. The security team facilitates the platform's security by providing guidance and support to the other teams to ensure the platform remains secure.

Team topologies is highly relevant to building and architecting a robust AI platform because it provides a structured approach to designing teams that can work effectively within modern AI systems' complex and dynamic environment. It helps ensure that teams are optimized for the specific requirements of the system they are building while promoting effective communication and collaboration between teams.

MLOps processes must embrace team topologies to effectively manage the complex interactions between teams and components within a machine learning system. By designing teams and communication structures that are optimized for the system's specific requirements, MLOps teams can effectively manage the entire process of building, deploying, and maintaining machine learning models.

An example of building a team for a machine learning product using team topologies might involve creating a cross-functional team that includes data scientists, software developers, and DevOps engineers. The team would be designed to minimize the cognitive load by focusing on specific tasks related to the machine learning component while also enabling fast and safe changes to the system through Agile methodologies and continuous integration/continuous delivery practices. The team would also be designed to facilitate effective communication and collaboration between team members and with other teams involved in the overall AI platform architecture.

Unifying All

To build a successful end-to-end AI platform, it is important to understand the six layers of AI platform architecture and the process of building and operating AI models, known as MLOps. The MLOps process consists of data operations such as data acquisition/ingestion, ETL, annotation, and model experiments, where feature engineering, model development, and testing are performed. This is followed by CI/CD of model deployment and serving. By integrating MLOps into the six layers of AI platform architecture (Figure 8-5), organizations can ensure that the models are built and deployed consistently, with best practices for testing and monitoring.

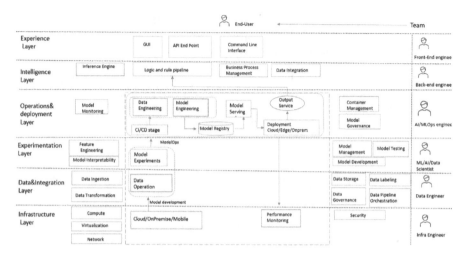

Figure 8-5. Unified architecture, process, and team design

Additionally, the importance of team structure in building and operating an AI platform cannot be overstated. Due to Conway's law, I believe that team topologies lends itself well to building and operating AI platforms. Team topologies is a set of organizational patterns that aim to improve communication and collaboration between teams while enabling teams to work more effectively and efficiently. By incorporating team topologies into the MLOps process and the six layers of AI platform architecture, organizations can ensure that the teams are structured and operate effectively, with clear roles and responsibilities, communication processes, and feedback loops for continuous improvement.

It is important to note that all these elements must be integrated into a unified design, process, and teaming framework. By understanding and implementing this framework, organizations can build end-to-end AI platforms that are scalable, efficient, secure, and capable of delivering high-quality results. With a well-designed AI platform and a team that is structured and operates effectively, organizations can ensure that their AI models are built and deployed in a consistent and repeatable manner, with best practices for testing and monitoring, and that they meet the evolving needs of the organization overtime.

Challenges in Building an AI Platform

Building an AI platform comes with its challenges that must be overcome to ensure success. The first challenge is that training and inferencing AI is expensive. This is due to the need for powerful computing resources and specialized hardware, such as GPUs, to handle the vast amounts of data involved in AI training and inference. Additionally, maintaining these resources can be expensive, leading to higher overall costs.

The second challenge is that collecting data is complex and expensive. To train AI models, a significant amount of high-quality data is required. Collecting this data can be a complex and time-consuming process, and the cost of data acquisition can also be high.

The third challenge is that AI is inherently probabilistic, non-stationary, and non-deterministic. This means that AI models can be highly sensitive to changes in the input data and can produce different results depending on the data that is presented. This introduces a level of uncertainty into the AI system, making it difficult to rely on the results with absolute certainty.

The fourth challenge is that AI is an effort to replicate human thinking and operates in a dynamic environment where we cannot control the input. This means that AI systems must be able to handle unpredictable inputs and adapt to changes in the environment. We have edge cases, which are the situations where the model performs unexpectedly due to encountering data that falls outside the norm of what it was trained on. For example, a computer vision model may struggle to identify objects in images with low lighting, or a natural language processing model may struggle to accurately identify sentiment in reviews with unusual language or slang. Edge cases are important to consider and address as they can significantly impact the performance of machine learning models in the real world. Creating a reliable AI systems that can consistently produce accurate results is challenging.

The impact of these challenges is significant. The reliability of AI is still questionable, and there is a risk that models can decay overtime due to changes in the data or environment (Figure 8-6).

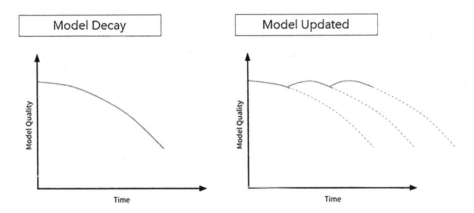

Figure 8-6. Machine learning model quality must be updated over time

Edge cases, or situations that are outside the normal range of inputs (Figure 8-7), can also be difficult for AI systems to handle. Additionally, the high cost of AI development and deployment can be a barrier for many organizations.

Figure 8-7. Sample of an edge case, where Tesla mistakes horse and buggy as trucks. The image is taken from `https://futurism.com/the-byte/tesla-mistakes-horse-buggy-murderous-semi-truck`

Careful attention must be paid to the system architecture, MLOps process, and team to overcome these challenges. System design should be optimized for performance, flexibility, interoperability, trustworthiness, and scalability. MLOps processes should be designed to ensure efficient and effective training and inferencing and robust data quality control and validation. Team design should be optimized for collaboration, flexibility, trustworthiness, and scalability.

In summary, building a successful AI platform requires careful consideration of the challenges involved and a well-designed approach to the system architecture, MLOps process, and team. By addressing these challenges and creating a solid foundation for AI development and deployment, organizations can overcome the barriers to success and create reliable, effective AI systems.

Ideal AI Platform Design

Despite the challenges described earlier, the ideal AI platform design must consider five factors for success: performance, flexibility, interoperability, trustworthiness, and scalability.

- Performance refers to the ability of the AI platform to handle large volumes of data and process it quickly and efficiently, delivering accurate and reliable results in real time or near real time. An example of this success factor for an AI platform would be the ability to process and analyze customer behavior data to make accurate real-time recommendations for personalized products or services.

- Flexibility involves the ability of the AI platform to adapt to changing business requirements and evolving technology trends, supporting multiple programming languages and frameworks and integrating with other systems and tools. An example of this success factor for an AI platform would be the ability to easily incorporate new data sources and change the AI models based on the new requirements.

- Interoperability refers to the ability of the AI platform to work seamlessly with other systems and tools, allowing for easy data sharing and collaboration. An example of this success factor for an AI platform would be the ability to integrate with third-party data sources and analytics tools.

- Trustworthiness involves designing the AI platform with reliability, security, and privacy in mind, ensuring robust data governance and compliance mechanisms, and providing tools and processes for monitoring and mitigating risk.

- Scalability involves the ability of the AI platform to scale up or down as needed to handle changing workloads, adding or removing computing resources and distributing workloads across multiple nodes or clusters. An example of this success factor for an AI platform would be the ability to quickly expand data processing capabilities to support a surge in customer demand during peak seasons.

The three pillars of the AI platform design, system design, process design, and team design, must adhere to these five success factors.

System design must be optimized for performance, flexibility, interoperability, trustworthiness, and scalability.

Process design must be optimized for efficiency, flexibility, trustworthiness, and scalability. And team design must be optimized for collaboration, flexibility, trustworthiness, and scalability.

For example, the identifai.id eKYC biometrics AI as a Service platform adheres to these success factors by utilizing a high-performance computing environment with distributed data storage and processing capabilities, allowing for real-time facial recognition and biometrics identification. The platform is flexible and scalable, allowing for integration with various data sources and analysis tools to enhance fraud detection and compliance monitoring capabilities. The platform is interoperable, seamlessly integrating with third-party verification systems and customer relationship management tools. The platform is trustworthy, implementing robust data governance and compliance mechanisms and providing clear roles and responsibilities for team members. The platform's team design fosters collaboration, flexibility, trust, and scalability, with cross-functional teams working together to improve the platform's capabilities and address customer needs continuously.

To summarize, the ideal AI platform design requires a combination of the five success factors – performance, flexibility, interoperability, trustworthiness, and scalability – across the three pillars of system design, process design, and team design. The success of an AI platform depends on its ability to optimize each of these factors, as exemplified by the identifai.id eKYC biometrics AI as a Service platform.

Architecting an AI Platform

Building an AI software platform requires careful consideration of various factors, including accuracy, cost, scalability, fault tolerance, and reliability. To achieve these objectives, it is necessary to measure the maturity of the AI platform and adhere to Conway's law while applying data-centric principles. In addition, identifying the AI product archetypes and requirements is essential. This involves designing the architectural layers of the AI platform and aligning them with the team design, utilizing the principles of team topologies. Finally, evaluating technology choices, including buying or building a framework, is critical to building a successful AI software platform. This section will explore these topics in greater detail to help architects and product managers understand how to build an effective AI platform.

AI Product Archetypes and Their Architectural Complexity

This section will reintroduce several AI product archetypes referring to products incorporating AI technology.

The first category is AI-enabled products, which use AI to enhance their functionality. These products can be further categorized into AI-first solutions, where AI is the application's core, and AI-powered solutions, where AI is an optional feature.

Examples of AI-first solutions include ChatGPT, Exceed AI, and Grammarly, while AI-powered solutions include HubSpot, Shutterstock, and Canva.

Another category of AI-enabled products is AIaaS or AI as a Service, which allows users to access AI services via the cloud. Examples of AIaaS platforms include FaceTec and Identifai ID.

AIaaE or AI as an Engine is another category of AI-enabled products that refers to AI engines that can be deployed on devices via SDKs. Examples of AIaaE products include Trueface and Nodeflux Visionaire.

The second category is AI toolkits, products that help in AI development. These products can be further categorized into data tools, such as annotation, versioning, and synthetic data generators, and modeling tools, such as experimenting, training, workflow orchestration, packaging, serving, optimization, and monitoring. Examples of data tools include Scale, Labelbox, and Pachyderm, while modeling tools include Weights & Biases, MLflow, and Comet.

Each AI product archetype has six layers with varying levels of complexity. These six layers are infrastructure, data, experimentation, deployment, intelligence, and experience. For AI-enabled products, the complexity scores are as follows (Table 8-1).

Table 8-1. AI Product Archetype and Its Complexity by Layers

AI Product Archetype	Infrastructure	Data	Experimentation	Deployment	Intelligence	Experience
AI-First						
AI-Powered						
AIaaS						
AIaaE						
Data Tools						
Modeling Tools						

In the preceding table, each AI product archetype is listed along with a score for each of the six layers of complexity. The scores range from light green (lowest complexity) to dark green (highest complexity). The scores are based on the level of complexity for each layer for each specific AI product archetype.

Measuring the Maturity Level of Your AI System

Designing a software systems architecture for an AI platform can be a complex and challenging process. It is important to measure the maturity level of the AI systems, from the initial stage to the optimized stage, based on the six layers previously described. This helps understand the progress and identify the areas that need improvement (Figure 8-8).

Figure 8-8. The maturity level of an AI system

The maturity level of an AI system is

1. *Initial*: The infrastructure layer is in the early stages of development, with limited resources and little automation. The data layer is not well-established, with limited data sources and basic data management processes. The data annotation procedure and system are non-existent. The experimentation layer is not yet developed, with ad hoc model testing and no clear approach to model selection or evaluation. The deployment layer is not yet established, with no clear approach to deploying models to production. The intelligence layer is limited, with simple models, standard logical pipeline, and limited automation. The experience layer is not yet developed, with no clear approach to user experience design, error handling, or feedback gathering.

2. *Managed*: The infrastructure layer is managed and monitored, with some automation in place. The data layer is well-established, with a clear data management process and growing data sources. The experimentation layer is being developed, with some standardization in model selection and evaluation. The deployment layer is in the early stages of development, with some standardization in deployment processes. The intelligence layer is expanding, with a growing range of models and some capability to perform pipeline automation. The experience layer is being developed, with some attention to user experience design, error handling, and feedback gathering.

3. *Defined*: The infrastructure layer is well-defined, with clear strategies for automation and scaling. The data layer is well-established, with clear data management processes and a wide range of data sources. The experimentation layer is well-established, with standardized model selection and evaluation approaches. The deployment layer is well-established, with clear processes for deploying models to production. The intelligence layer is expanding rapidly, with a wide range of models and significant pipeline automation capability. The experience layer is well-established, with clear attention to user experience design, error handling, and feedback gathering.

4. *Quantitatively managed*: The infrastructure layer is monitored and optimized, with data-driven decision-making guiding further development and scaling. The data layer is monitored and optimized, with clear metrics for data quality and management processes. The experimentation layer is monitored and optimized, with clear metrics for model performance and model selection. The deployment layer is monitored and optimized, with clear metrics for model deployment and production performance. The intelligence layer is monitored and optimized, with clear metrics for model performance and pipeline that can be automated. The experience layer is monitored and optimized, with clear metrics for user experience design and feedback gathering.

5. *Optimized*: The infrastructure layer is highly optimized and automated, with efficient infrastructure and system architecture that can handle high traffic and data volumes with ease. The data layer is highly optimized, with advanced data management processes and a wide range of high-quality data sources. The experimentation layer is highly optimized, with advanced model selection and evaluation processes and a wide range of high-performing models and automated model hyperparameterization. The deployment layer is highly optimized, with advanced deployment processes and high levels of production performance. The intelligence layer is highly optimized, with advanced model development and pipeline automation processes that are constantly improving. The experience layer is highly optimized, with advanced user experience design, error handling, and feedback gathering processes that are constantly improving.

To understand where we are in the maturity level of an AI system based on the six layers, we need to measure with the following steps:

1. Evaluate each layer separately.

   - *Infrastructure layer*: Evaluate the state of the hardware and software infrastructure that supports the platform, including the availability, scalability, and reliability of resources such as compute, virtualization, storage, and networking.

   - *Data layer*: Assess the quality, quantity, and diversity of data that can be processed by the platform, as well as the mechanisms in place for data processing, transformation, labeling, cleaning, quality control, governance, and storage.

   - *Experimentation layer*: Evaluate the platform's ability to do model mix and match, support different types of experimentation (i.e., champion-challenger testing, A/B testing, multi-armed bandit testing), and evaluate model performance.

   - *Deployment layer*: Assess the platform's ability to deploy models to production and perform shadow deployment, including the speed and efficiency of the deployment process, the level of automation, performance monitoring, and the frequency of updates.

- *Intelligence layer*: Evaluate the level of sophistication of the platform's AI models, including their accuracy, speed, and ability to adapt to changing conditions.

- *Experience layer*: Assess the user experience of the platform, including the ease of use, accessibility, and effectiveness of the interface.

2. Once each layer has been evaluated, assign a maturity level to each layer based on the following scale:

   - *Initial*: Basic infrastructure is set up, with no clear strategy for how to scale or optimize the layer.

   - *Managed*: Infrastructure is managed and monitored, with some optimization and scaling strategies in place.

   - *Defined*: The layer has a well-defined strategy for optimization and scaling based on specific business needs and usage patterns.

   - *Quantitatively managed*: Performance metrics are actively monitored and optimized, with data-driven decision-making guiding further development and scaling.

   - *Optimized*: The highly optimized layer has efficient infrastructure and processes that can easily handle high traffic and data volumes.

3. After assigning a maturity level to each layer, you can determine the overall maturity level of the platform by taking the average of the maturity levels across all layers.

Measuring the maturity level of an AI platform is an ongoing process as the platform continues to evolve and new challenges arise. Organizations can focus on optimizing the platform to achieve the desired outcomes as the platform matures. This may involve implementing new features, refining existing models, or integrating new technologies.

Therefore, measuring the maturity level of an AI platform is an essential step in designing a software architecture for the platform. By evaluating various aspects of the platform and identifying areas that require improvement, organizations can allocate resources more effectively and optimize the platform for maximum performance.

Best Practices of Architecting an AI Software Platform

Architecting an AI platform involves addressing important aspects such as accuracy, cost, scalability, fault tolerance, security, and flexibility. However, building AI platforms also involves challenges such as edge cases, model decay, reliability, and trustworthiness. To address these challenges, several best practices can be followed.

One of the best practices is to embed Conway's law into the system by designing team topologies to optimize communication and collaboration between various teams involved, including data scientists, machine learning engineers, software engineers, and DevOps engineers. Another best practice is to build a data flywheel by making the process data-centric. By making the process data-centric, the focus is on optimizing the whole process from annotation to training and inferencing.

A data-centric platform can help solve edge cases and accuracy decay by using techniques that optimize data as input to AI models, such as data augmentation, feature engineering, ensemble models, regularization, and active learning.

Data augmentation can increase the amount and variety of data used to train the model. Data augmentation can address edge cases by creating new synthetic data that can help improve the performance of AI models in rare or underrepresented scenarios. At the same time, feature engineering can carefully select and engineer more robust features for edge cases. Ensemble models can combine the predictions of multiple models with improving accuracy and robustness, and regularization techniques can prevent overfitting to the training data and improve generalization to new data, including edge cases. Active learning involves iteratively selecting samples from the most informative or uncertain dataset and using them to train the model. Active learning can help the model adapt to edge cases and improve its performance overtime.

Furthermore, a data-centric platform can help build a data flywheel that optimizes the entire annotation, training, and inferencing process. This involves creating a closed-loop feedback system where data is constantly fed back into the system to improve accuracy and performance. The focus is on collecting high-quality data, cleaning and preparing it for training, selecting the best models and hyperparameters, and iteratively improving the models overtime. This process can help improve the accuracy of the model and reduce the impact of edge cases and accuracy decay. The more we have the data, the more accurate the machine learning system.

In short, architecting an AI platform requires addressing important aspects such as accuracy, cost, scalability, fault tolerance, security, and flexibility. Building a data-centric platform and following best practices such as embedding

Conway's law, using data augmentation techniques, building ensemble models, and using active learning can help address challenges such as edge cases, model decay, reliability, and trustworthiness. Furthermore, a data-centric platform can help build a data flywheel, optimizing the whole process from annotation to training and inferencing and improving the accuracy of the model overtime.

Designing the AI Platform Architecture

Designing an AI platform based on the six layers (infrastructure, data, experimentation, deployment, intelligence, experience) requires careful consideration to ensure scalability, accuracy, maintainability, fault tolerance, flexibility, and security. Here are the step-by-step methods for designing the architecture of an AI platform:

1. *Define the system requirements*: This involves identifying the business use cases and requirements to establish the necessary components of the AI platform. Consider factors such as data sources, performance requirements, user interface, and compliance with the AI platform's necessary features, functionalities, and performance criteria. It is important to clearly understand the requirements up front to guide the design process and ensure that the final product meets user needs.

2. *Design the system architecture*: This involves identifying the subsystems and components of the AI platform and how they interact. The architecture should be designed with scalability, maintainability, and fault tolerance in mind.

   a. *Design the infrastructure layer*: Determine the hardware and software infrastructure to support the AI platform. This includes selecting appropriate cloud services, server configurations, and network infrastructure.

   b. *Build the data layer*: Develop a data strategy and architecture that includes data acquisition, data storage, data labeling, data processing, and data management. Consider factors such as data quality, security, governance, and privacy.

   c. *Create the experimentation layer*: Develop a process for model selection, training, evaluation, and iteration. Consider techniques such as hyperparameter optimization, cross-validation, and ensemble modeling.

d. *Deploy the AI models*: Develop a deployment pipeline that includes packaging, deployment, and monitoring. This should include considerations for version control, scalability, and reliability.

e. *Develop the intelligence layer*: Develop the algorithms and models pipeline facility that will be used in the AI platform. Consider factors such as accuracy, interpretability, and explainability.

f. *Build the experience layer*: Develop the AI platform's user interface and user experience (UI/UX). Consider factors such as accessibility, feedback (implicit and explicit), ease of use, and design consistency.

3. *Choose appropriate technologies*: The choice of technologies used in the AI platform can significantly impact its performance, reliability, and scalability. It is important to carefully evaluate and choose appropriate technologies, including buy vs. build, which we will discuss in the next section.

4. Identify the teams involved in building, maintaining, and operating the AI platform and designing the system architecture in a way that optimizes communication and collaboration between them.

5. *Implement and test the system*: Once the system architecture has been designed and appropriate technologies chosen, the system can be implemented and tested. Testing should be performed at multiple stages of development, including unit testing, integration testing, and system testing, to ensure that the system meets the requirements and performs as expected.

6. *Deploy and monitor the system*: After the system has been tested and verified, it can be deployed and put into production. Ongoing monitoring and maintenance are crucial to ensure that the system continues to perform optimally and meets user needs.

Implementing an effective and robust artificial intelligence (AI) platform necessitates the adoption of established best practices. Specifically, using the systems engineering approach, data-centric approach, Conway's law, and team topologies principle can ensure the development of a scalable, maintainable, and fault-tolerant AI system. Adherence to these principles can offer a comprehensive framework for designing and implementing AI platforms that meet the evolving demands of modern technology. As such, it is crucial for practitioners in the field of AI to prioritize the application of such best practices in their development efforts.

For example, in an AIaaS platform like Identifai, the infrastructure layer may involve using cloud services such as Amazon Web Services (AWS) or Microsoft Azure. The data layer may include data processing techniques such as data augmentation (augmenting half/full mask to the face). The experimentation layer may involve techniques such as active learning and ensemble modeling. The deployment layer may include containerization and Kubernetes for scalability. The intelligence layer may involve deep learning models such as FaceNet for face matching. Finally, the experience layer may include the development of a user-friendly dashboard for customers to access the AI services.

For an AI-first application like ChatGPT, the infrastructure layer may involve using cloud services such as Microsoft Azure to host the application. The data layer may involve natural language processing (NLP) techniques to process user input. The experimentation layer may involve the use of language models based on transformers such as GPT-3 for generating responses. The deployment layer may involve the use of APIs for integration with other applications. The intelligence layer may involve techniques such as sentiment analysis for understanding user emotions. Finally, the experience layer may include the development of a chatbot interface for users to interact with the AI.

Evaluating Technology Choices

Designing and building an AI platform requires careful consideration of the tools and frameworks used in each of the six layers: infrastructure, data, experimentation, deployment, intelligence, and experience. These tools can be open source or paid and may involve building from scratch or purchasing pre-made solutions. To ensure the platform is built effectively, it is important to clearly understand the available options and how they align with the business requirements and use cases. The selection process should involve identifying the strengths and weaknesses of each tool, evaluating their performance and scalability, and considering their compatibility with the overall system architecture. Additionally, a decision must be made whether to buy or build the necessary tools and framework, which involves balancing factors such as cost, time to market, and the level of customization required. By following a structured approach to tool selection and considering both buy and build options, it is possible to build a robust and effective AI platform that meets the business's unique needs.

The following is a step-by-step structured approach to tool selection and considering buy vs. build for an AI platform:

1. *Identify business requirements*: Understand the AI platform's business requirements and use cases. This will help identify the platform's necessary components, including the required tools and frameworks. Consider scalability, accuracy, fault tolerance, flexibility, and security.

2. *Evaluate available tools*: Conduct research to identify the tools and frameworks available for each layer of the AI platform. Consider both open source and proprietary options and tools that can be bought or built in-house. Evaluate each tool based on its features, performance, and cost.

3. *Assess buy vs. build*: Based on the evaluation, determine whether buying an existing tool or building one in-house using open source software stacks is more cost-effective. Consider factors such as the time and resources required to build a tool, the level of expertise available in-house, the unique selling proposition offered, intellectual property, and the Total Cost of Ownership.

4. *Test and validate*: Once the tools have been selected, test and validate them to ensure that they meet the requirements of the AI platform. Conduct testing at multiple stages of development, including unit testing, integration testing, and system testing.

5. *Monitor and update*: After integrating the tools into the AI platform, monitor their performance and functionality regularly. Update them to ensure they meet the business and technical evolving needs.

6. *Consider scalability*: Consider the scalability of the tools and frameworks chosen. Determine whether they can handle the expected increase in data and usage overtime. Ensure that the tools can be easily scaled up or down as needed.

The rule of thumb is that if you want unique technology differentiation, then it is better to build from scratch in-house than buy ready-made solutions. The observation on several AI startups on the buy vs. build for our AI product archetypes is as follows (Table 8-2).

Table 8-2. AI Product Archetype: Buy vs. Build

AI Product Archetype	Infrastructure	Data	Experimentation	Deployment	Intelligence	Experience
AI-first	Buy	Buy	Build	Build	Build	Build
AI-powered	Buy	Buy	Buy	Buy	Buy	Build
AIaaS	Buy	Buy	Build	Build	Build	Build
AIaaE	Buy	Buy	Build	Build	Build	Build
Data tools	Buy	Build	N/A	N/A	N/A	Build
Modeling tools	Buy	N/A	Build	Build	Build	Build

An AI-first product company tends to build almost everything in-house because they must have strong technology propositions compared with their competitors. This is why an AI-first product such as ChatGPT is developed exclusively in-house.

On the other hand, the AI-powered product company can use a ready-made platform for data and model engineering (from data acquisition to model training/testing) because AI is only an option/additional feature for them.

Note that these recommendations are based on a general assessment of cost vs. value and may vary depending on each organization's specific needs and resources. It is important to carefully evaluate the costs and benefits of buying vs. building for each layer of the AI platform, considering factors such as time to market, customization, and maintenance.

Developing an AI Platform

With the rapid development of machine learning algorithms and deep learning techniques, the potential applications of AI are endless.

However, software development for AI software using machine learning differs from that of traditional non-AI software, requiring special consideration.

This section will explore the key differences between the two and examine the software development principles for AI software platforms.

We will explain in more detail the ten stages of AI software development. We will also discuss the AI software maturity model and how to measure AI software development process maturity. Finally, we will delve into the AI software development process, including MLOps, and highlight the ten stages of developing AI software. By understanding these topics, software developers will be better equipped to design, build, and deploy robust and effective AI software that meets the needs of their clients or organizations.

Why AI Software Development Is Different from Traditional Software Development

AI software development is different from conventional non-AI development due to several reasons:

1. Traditional software development relies on predefined logic and rules, while AI software development involves creating algorithms that can learn and improve overtime. This requires a different approach to problem-solving, testing, and quality assurance, as the behavior of the AI software is not always predictable.

2. AI software development involves dealing with large datasets and complex models requiring specialized skills and tools. The development process involves coding, extensive data preparation, and feature engineering to create effective machine learning models.

3. AI software development requires continuous monitoring and optimization to ensure that the models remain accurate and effective overtime. Discovering, managing, and versioning the data needed for machine learning applications is much more complex and difficult than other types of software engineering. This is because the data needs to be collected, cleaned, and labeled to ensure high-quality and unbiased data, which can be time-consuming. Additionally, model customization and model reuse require very different skills than are typically found in software teams.

4. Developing machine learning models requires specialized knowledge in statistics and mathematics and domain-specific knowledge.

5. AI components exhibit greater interaction complexity than non-AI software components, making them more difficult to manage as separate modules. Models in AI systems may be intertwined in intricate ways, leading to non-monotonic error behavior that is hard to predict and diagnose. This complexity calls for specialized software development practices and tools to handle the intricacies of AI systems.

6. The probabilistic and dynamic nature of the input environment causes edge cases and unexpected behavior, which can be challenging to predict and manage.

These factors make AI software development a specialized and complex process that requires unique skills and expertise. The following section will discuss how to deal with the preceding challenges from a software development perspective.

The Principles of Software Development for an AI Software Platform

To overcome these challenges, several solutions can be implemented.

First, we must embrace machine learning operations (MLOps) and use specialized tools and frameworks (i.e., Neptune, Valohai, Iguazio)[5] that can help streamline the development process and ensure accuracy and efficiency while reducing model decay.

Implementing version control and data management techniques can also help manage the complexity of data used in AI software development, ensuring that data is accurate, up to date, and easily accessible to developers.

Conducting thorough testing and validation is also essential to ensure that AI models are accurate, effective, and safe, including testing for edge cases and unexpected behavior and validating the model's performance against relevant benchmarks.

In addition, implementing active learning mechanisms can help subside edge cases,[6] while applying trustworthy and responsible AI through the development of XAI mechanisms can enable root cause analysis and ensure transparency and explainability.

Implementing monitoring and alerting mechanisms can detect and mitigate issues in the platform, ensuring that AI models remain accurate and effective overtime. Adopting Agile and DevOps methodologies can enable flexibility, collaboration, and continuous integration and deployment, which are essential for AI software development.

Finally, fostering cross-functional and interdisciplinary teams is crucial to ensure a comprehensive approach to AI software development that accounts for real-world applications. Such teams should include data science, machine learning engineering, data engineering, software development, and domain knowledge experts. By bringing together individuals with diverse skill sets, it becomes possible to consider all aspects of AI software development and ensure that models are built to meet the needs of users and stakeholders. This approach is aligned with the principles of team topologies, which emphasizes the importance of creating teams optimized for specific tasks and empowered to collaborate effectively.

---

[5] https://neptune.ai/blog/end-to-end-mlops-platforms
[6] https://link.springer.com/article/10.1007/s10462-022-10246-w

Understanding AI Software Development Stages

The development of an AI software application involves a series of stages that are critical to its success (Figure 8-9).

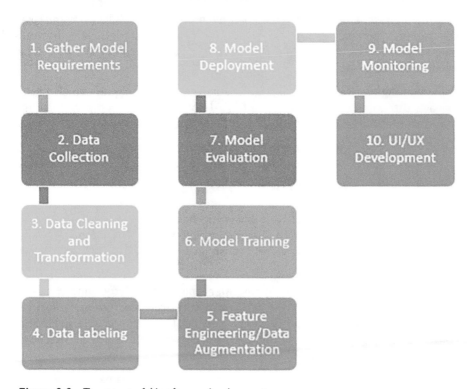

Figure 8-9. Ten stages of AI software development

The stages of AI software development are as follows (Figure 8-5):

1. *Gather model requirements*: This stage involves identifying the specific goals of the AI software application, including the type of data to be used, the intended users, and the desired outcomes. The goal is to establish a clear understanding of the problem to be solved by the AI software application.

2. *Data collection*: The second stage involves gathering and preparing the necessary data for the AI software application. This involves identifying data sources, collecting and cleaning the data, and preparing it for use in the application.

3. *Data cleaning and transformation*: Once the data has been collected, it must be cleaned and transformed to ensure that it is accurate, complete, and in the correct format for use in the AI software application. This may involve data normalization, imputation, and other techniques to ensure that the data is consistent and reliable.

4. *Data labeling*: In this stage, data is labeled to provide a clear understanding of the features and attributes of the data. This labeling is important for training and validating AI models.

5. *Feature engineering/data augmentation*: This stage involves transforming the labeled data into a format suitable for use in AI models. This may involve data augmentation techniques to increase the diversity and quantity of labeled data and feature selection to identify the most important features of the model.

6. *Model training*: The next stage involves training the AI model on the prepared data. This includes selecting appropriate machine learning algorithms, tuning model hyperparameters, and evaluating model performance.

7. *Model evaluation*: In this stage, the trained model is evaluated to assess its performance and suitability for the intended use case. This may involve various metrics such as accuracy, precision, recall, and validation against external data.

8. *Model deployment*: Once the model has been evaluated and validated, it can be deployed into a production environment. This may involve packaging the model and integrating it into the software application.

9. *Model monitoring*: After deployment, the model must be monitored to ensure that it remains accurate and effective overtime. This may involve performance monitoring, error detection, and retraining of the model as necessary.

10. *UI/UX development*: Finally, the AI software application's user interface and user experience (UI/UX) must be designed and developed. This includes accessibility, ease of use, and design consistency.

Measuring the Maturity Level of an AI Software Development Process

To develop effective and efficient AI software, it is important to have a structured approach incorporating best practices and standards. The Carnegie Mellon Capability Maturity Model (CMM)[7] provides a framework for assessing the maturity of an organization's software development process. Based on this model, we can define the five stages of AI software development process maturity (Figure 8-10).

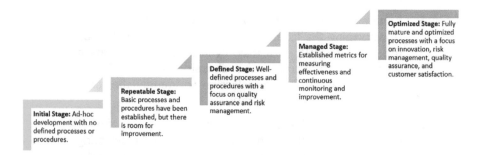

Figure 8-10. Maturity level of an AI software development process

- *Initial stage*: In this stage, the organization is just starting to develop AI software. There are no defined processes or procedures, and development is typically ad hoc. There is little documentation, and the development team is focused on individual tasks rather than a coordinated effort.

- *Repeatable stage*: In this stage, the organization has established basic processes and procedures for AI software development. There is documentation, and the team is beginning to work together in a coordinated effort. However, the processes are not yet fully mature, and there is still room for improvement.

- *Defined stage*: In this stage, the organization has well-defined processes and procedures for AI software development. There are guidelines and standards that the development team follows, and there is a focus on quality assurance and risk management. The team is working in a coordinated effort, and there is an emphasis on continuous improvement.

---

[7] https://resources.sei.cmu.edu/asset_files/technicalreport/1993_005_001_16211.pdf

- *Managed stage*: In this stage, the organization has established metrics for measuring the effectiveness of its AI software development processes. The development team is focused on meeting these metrics and is continuously monitoring and improving its processes. There is a focus on risk management, quality assurance, and customer satisfaction.

- *Optimized stage*: In this stage, the organization's AI software development processes are fully mature and optimized. The development team is continuously improving its processes and has established a culture of innovation and creativity. There is a focus on metrics, risk management, quality assurance, and customer satisfaction, and the team is working in a coordinated effort to achieve the organization's goals.

Measuring AI Software Development Process Maturity

We can use the ten stages of AI software development defined earlier to measure the maturity of an organization's AI software development process. Each stage represents a specific set of practices and procedures the development team should follow. By assessing the organization's practices against these stages, we can identify areas for improvement and develop a plan for achieving higher maturity levels.

Applying the Measurement Framework to Your Process

To use the measurement framework for your AI product, follow these steps:

1. Identify the ten stages of AI software development and the practices and procedures associated with each stage.

2. Assess your organization's practices against each stage.

3. Identify areas where your organization can improve and develop a plan for achieving higher maturity levels.

4. Continuously monitor and evaluate your organization's practices and procedures to ensure they remain effective and efficient.

5. Continuously strive for higher maturity levels, always seeking to improve your organization's practices and procedures.

AI Software Development Process

Developing an AI software platform involves various steps and considerations, from setting up the development environment and infrastructure to building testing and validation pipelines. Here is a detailed breakdown of the process:

- *Setting up the development environment and infrastructure*: This involves setting up the development environment, including the necessary software and hardware components. The infrastructure needs to include hardware resources such as computing power, storage, and memory. Cloud-based services like Amazon Web Services, Google Cloud Platform, and Microsoft Azure provide hardware resources on demand, which can be scaled up and down depending on the needs of the product.

- *Implementing the data pipeline, model training, model serving, and monitoring components*: The data pipeline involves collecting, cleaning, labeling, and transforming data. Open source tools such as Apache Kafka and Apache Beam can be used for data ingestion and streaming. Model training involves selecting an appropriate algorithm, choosing hyperparameters, and training the model. Popular open source machine learning frameworks include TensorFlow, PyTorch, and MXNet. Model serving involves deploying the model for use in production, either as a REST API or in a serverless architecture. Kubernetes and Docker are popular open source tools for model serving. Model monitoring involves tracking the model's performance, including metrics such as accuracy, precision, and recall. Open source tools like Prometheus, Grafana, and Elastic Stack can be used for monitoring.

- *Implementing MLOps mechanisms in the software*: MLOps involves applying DevOps principles to machine learning, including version control for models, automated testing, and continuous integration and deployment (CI/CD) pipelines. Model version control can be achieved using Git, while automated testing can be implemented using tools like Pytest or Nose. This involves setting up a pipeline for testing and validating the AI platform. This includes unit testing, integration testing, system testing, and testing for edge cases and unexpected behavior. CI/CD pipelines can be set up using Jenkins, Travis CI, or CircleCI. The pipeline can be triggered automatically every time new code or models are committed to the repository. Automated retraining involves using continuous learning and active learning mechanisms to improve the performance of the model overtime. There are also ready-to-use end-to-end MLOps platforms such as Neptune, Valohai, Iguazio, and ClearML that can be used.

- *Developing the user interface and integration interfaces*: Developing a user interface (UI) involves designing and building a user-friendly interface for users to interact with the AI platform. This can be achieved using popular front-end frameworks like React or Vue.js. Integration interfaces allow the AI platform to integrate with other systems and platforms, such as web services or databases. This can be achieved using REST APIs or other integration mechanisms.

Overall, developing an AI software platform requires combining technical expertise, domain knowledge, and an understanding of best practices in software engineering and MLOps. By following a structured approach and using open source tools and frameworks, developers can create robust and effective AI software platforms that meet the needs of users and organizations. Several good references exist for a more detailed approach to machine learning development.[8,9]

Operationalizing an AI Platform

Operationalizing an AI platform refers to the process of deploying an AI system into production so that it can be used to perform real-world tasks or provide value to users. This involves integrating the AI system into the existing infrastructure of an organization or application, testing and validating the system, and ensuring that it is performing as expected. Operationalizing an AI platform involves taking the model from a proof-of-concept or experimental stage to a production-ready state, where it can perform real-world tasks and provide value to users.

The success of an AI software platform relies heavily on the coordination and collaboration of various teams involved in the development and operationalization process. The machine learning team plays a crucial role in developing the models that power the platform. Still, they must work closely

---

[8]www.oreilly.com/library/view/designing-machine-learning/9781098107956/
[9]https://link.springer.com/book/10.1007/978-1-4842-7413-2

with data engineers, software developers, tech operations, and other domain experts to ensure that the platform meets end users' needs. Coordinating the work of different teams can be challenging, but using team topologies can help ensure that teams are structured and aligned for optimal performance.

Aligning MLOps processes with team topologies is also crucial for the success of an AI software platform. MLOps processes manage the entire lifecycle of machine learning models, including development, training, deployment, and monitoring. When these processes are aligned with team topologies, it can ensure that the appropriate teams are responsible for each step of the process and that communication and collaboration are optimized.

In this section, we will explore the use of team topologies in managing and operationalizing AI software platforms. We will discuss how to build effective teams using team topologies for different AI product archetypes and provide examples of how MLOps processes can be aligned with these team structures. By aligning MLOps with team topologies, we can ensure that the development and management of AI software platforms are optimized for success.

Team and Task

Developing and operationalizing an AI platform requires a team with diverse skills and expertise. The team must work collaboratively to ensure the AI platform is successfully designed, built, and deployed. The following are the key team members and their tasks for the development and operationalization of an AI platform using the MLOps/ModelOps process:

- *Product manager*: A product manager defines the product vision, strategy, and roadmap. They work closely with the subject matter experts, machine learning scientists, and the MLOps engineer to define product requirements and ensure that the product meets the needs of its intended users.

- *Subject matter expert*: A subject matter expert is a domain expert who understands the business problem that the AI platform is trying to solve. They work with the product manager and the machine learning scientists to define the scope of the problem, provide feedback on the model's outputs, and ensure that the platform meets the business needs.

- *Data labeler*: Data labeling is a crucial part of the AI development process, and a dedicated data labeler team is responsible for this task. They annotate data for training, testing, and validating machine learning models. They ensure the data is accurate, consistent, and labeled according to predefined guidelines.

- *Front-end software engineer:* A front-end software engineer is responsible for developing the user interface of the AI platform. They ensure that the user interface is intuitive, responsive, and easy to use for end users.

- *Machine learning scientist/data scientist:* Machine learning scientists are responsible for developing and training the machine learning models that power the AI platform. They use various algorithms, techniques, and tools to build, test, and optimize the models. They work closely with the subject matter experts and the data engineering team to ensure that the models are accurate and effective.

- *Machine learning/MLOps engineer:* A machine learning/ MLOps engineer is responsible for implementing the MLOps/ModelOps process. They design and build the AI platform's data pipeline, model training, model serving, and monitoring components. They also ensure that the platform is scalable, reliable, and secure.

- *Data engineer:* A data engineer is responsible for designing and building the data infrastructure that supports the AI platform. They ensure that the data is ingested, cleaned, transformed, and stored in an efficient, scalable, and secure way.

- *DevOps/infrastructure/back-end engineer:* They are responsible for designing and building the back-end infrastructure that supports the AI platform. They ensure that the platform is deployed on reliable and scalable infrastructure, that the platform is secure, and that there are mechanisms for backup and disaster recovery.

- *TechOps engineer:* A TechOps engineer is responsible for ensuring the platform is operational 24/7. They monitor the platform for errors, issues, and performance degradation. They work with the MLOps engineer to ensure the platform is retrained and updated regularly to maintain accuracy and effectiveness.

- *Customer success:* This team is responsible for ensuring that the AI product meets the needs and expectations of customers. They work closely with customers to understand their requirements, provide guidance on product features and usage, and address any issues or concerns that arise. Customer success team members may have a background in sales, marketing, or customer support and should have strong communication and problem-solving skills. Their role is crucial for the success of the AI product, as it helps ensure customer satisfaction and retention.

Though MLOps is a good process for streamlining the AI system production and operationalization, most AI teams are working separately with minimal alignment. There must be a way for them to align and collaborate well even with minimum communication. Team topologies is the answer. Aligning the team with team topologies is crucial to ensure that each team member understands their roles and responsibilities. It also ensures that each team member has the necessary tools, processes, and communication channels to collaborate effectively.

Coordinating the Different Teams with Team Topologies

Team topologies is a modern organizational approach that helps companies build better teams to deliver quality products and services (Figure 8-11). In this approach, different teams are created based on the nature of their work and how they interact with other teams:

- The stream-aligned team is responsible for delivering the product and services to customers, and it works closely with other teams to ensure that the product meets the market needs.

- The complicated subsystem team focuses on building complex software components that are difficult to understand or manage.

- The platform team is responsible for building and maintaining the core platform infrastructure, which other teams can use to develop their products.

- The enabling team focuses on providing tools, services, and support to other teams so they can work effectively.

Interaction mode is another important concept of team topologies. In this approach, different teams interact with each other based on the nature of their work:

- X as a Service means that teams provide services to other teams to focus on their core work.

- Collaborating means that teams work together to achieve common goals.

- Facilitating means that teams provide tools and resources to other teams, so that they can work more efficiently.

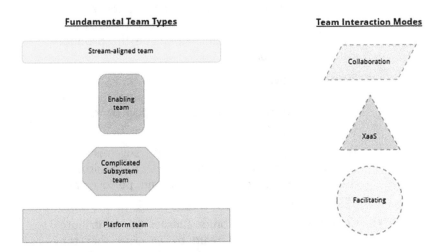

Figure 8-11. Team type and interaction mode of team topologies

Aligning the MLOps process and the team using team topologies is a good idea because it helps streamline the AI software development process. MLOps is a set of practices and tools that enable data scientists and machine learning engineers to develop, deploy, and monitor machine learning models at scale. By aligning the MLOps process with team topologies, companies can ensure that each team clearly understands their role in the development process and can work together effectively to deliver quality products.

In the context of the AI platform, the generic team topologies can be structured as follows:

- *The stream-aligned team*: This team is responsible for delivering customer value by aligning all teams to a clear, well-understood mission.

  - *Product manager*: The product manager is a critical member of the stream-aligned team. They are responsible for defining the product vision and roadmap and ensuring that all teams are aligned to the same goals.

  - *Subject matter expert*: The subject matter expert can provide valuable input on customer needs and market trends, which can help shape the product vision and roadmap.

  - *Front-end software engineer*: The front-end software engineer can contribute to developing the user interface, which is a critical component of the customer experience.

  - *TechOps engineer*: The TechOps engineer can contribute to the stream-aligned team by monitoring the platform for errors, issues, and performance degradation.

  - *Customer success*: Customer success can contribute to the stream-aligned team by ensuring that the AI product meets the needs and expectations of customers. In AI products, where sometimes the customer expectation is unrealistic (i.e., comparing the AI capability to the human cognitive capability), good customer service will help channel feedback from the customer to the internal team and vice versa.

- *The complicated subsystem team*: This team is responsible for developing and maintaining the complex subsystems that underpin the AI system.

  - *Machine learning scientist/data scientist*: The machine learning scientist/data scientist is a critical member of the complicated subsystem team. They are responsible for developing complex models that power the AI system.

- *The platform team*: This team is responsible for developing and maintaining the platform on which the AI system runs.

    - *DevOps/infrastructure/back-end engineer*: The DevOps/infrastructure/back-end engineer is a critical platform team member. They are responsible for building and maintaining the AI system's infrastructure.

    - *Machine learning/MLOps engineer*: The machine learning/MLOps engineer can contribute to the platform's development by ensuring that the models are properly deployed and monitored and that the infrastructure is in place to support the AI system.

    - *Data engineer*: The data engineer is responsible for building and maintaining the data pipeline, a critical component of the AI system.

- *The enabling team*: This team provides the tools and processes that enable the other teams to do their jobs effectively.

    - *Data labeler team*: The data labeler team can contribute to the enabling team by providing high-quality labeled data necessary for developing and training the AI system.

CASE STUDY: BUILDING AN EKYC AI AS A SERVICE PLATFORM

Identifai ID is a startup that provides AIaaS solutions for biometrics-based eKYC API and SDK for digital verification and identification. Their product includes face recognition, face liveness detection, OCR ID, and demography recognition deployed as API and SDK.

They are designing, developing, and operationalizing the AI platform based on the framework described in this chapter by the unifying system, process, and team design to ensure that the platform is scalable, maintainable, and fault tolerant. The framework emphasizes the importance of adhering to established best practices such as the systems engineering principle, data-centric approach, Conway's law, and team topologies principle. By following this comprehensive framework, the team can design and develop an AI platform that is optimized for real-world use and can effectively address the needs of the target application or system. Additionally, the team will be better equipped to overcome potential challenges that may arise during the operationalization of the platform, such as data integration or model accuracy issues.

These are the steps they are following:

1. *Designing the AI platform based on the six layers:* Identifai ID designs their AI platform using the six layers of AI application development: data, model, training, optimization, execution, and feedback. They carefully consider the complexity of each layer, especially in facial liveness detection, which is a challenging problem.

   - The data layer includes collecting, processing, and cleaning data. Identifai ID uses various data sources, such as public databases and private datasets, to ensure data accuracy and privacy.

   - Identifai ID builds machine learning models in the model layer to perform the biometrics-based eKYC process. They use deep learning techniques to achieve high accuracy and performance.

   - Identifai ID trains their models in the training layer using labeled data and algorithms, such as convolutional neural networks and recurrent neural networks.

   - In the optimization layer, Identifai ID optimizes their models for efficiency and performance using techniques like hyperparameter tuning and pruning.

   - In the execution layer, Identifai ID deploys their models as APIs and SDKs to provide their eKYC solutions to customers.

   - Identifai ID continuously monitors their models in the feedback layer and collects customer feedback to improve their system.

2. *Designing the MLOps process:* Identifai ID designs their MLOps process to ensure efficient model development, testing, deployment, and monitoring. They use Git for version control, Jenkins for continuous integration and deployment, and Kubernetes for container orchestration.

   - *MLOps process applied for their eKYC product:* Identifai ID uses the MLOps process to improve their eKYC product continuously. They test and validate their models using real-world data and customer feedback and deploy new versions of the models as necessary.

   - *Technology stack selection:* Identifai ID considered building and buying options for their technology stack. They opted to use a mix of open source and proprietary technologies to achieve the best balance of cost, performance, and support. For their face recognition component, they selected the OpenCV library to perform the initial feature extraction and then used the Face-Net model from Google's TensorFlow framework to perform the final face recognition step. They used an ensemble of special-ized convolutional neural networks (SCNN) and the Inception network for face liveness detection.

For OCR ID and demography recognition, they used U-Net for segmentation and RCNN for character recognition. They integrated these components as a pipeline into their AI platform and used an API gateway to provide a unified interface for their customers.

3. *Team topologies*: Identifai ID implemented the stream-aligned team topology, which focused on delivering a high-quality eKYC product while responding quickly to customer needs. The team was struc-tured as follows:

    - *Product manager*: Responsible for defining the product road-map, features, and user experience

    - *Subject matter expert*: Responsible for understanding the bi-ometrics and regulatory requirements of eKYC and guiding the team in developing solutions to meet those requirements

    - *Data labeler team*: Responsible for labeling the large volumes of data needed to train and validate the AI models

    - *Front-end software engineer*: Responsible for designing and developing the user interface for the Identifai ID portal and customer-facing APIs

    - *Machine learning scientist/data scientist*: Responsible for de-signing and training the AI models for face recognition, liveness detection, OCR ID, and demographic classification

    - *Machine learning/MLOps engineer*: Responsible for implement-ing the MLOps process, deploying models to production, moni-toring their performance, and retraining them as necessary

    - *Data engineer*: Responsible for managing the data pipeline, integrating various data sources, and ensuring data quality

    - *DevOps/infrastructure/back-end engineer*: Responsible for building and maintaining the cloud infrastructure, managing security and compliance, and ensuring high availability and scalability of the platform

    - *TechOps engineer*: Responsible for managing the APIs and SDKs, providing technical support to customers, and ensuring smooth integration with customer systems

    - *Customer success*: Responsible for managing customer expec-tations and gathering valuable feedback

The team was organized into feature teams that focused on delivering specific features of the eKYC product, such as face recognition or OCR ID. Each feature team consisted of members from different functional areas, such as machine learning, data engineering, and front-end development. The team used Agile methodologies to enable rapid iteration and collaboration and had daily stand-up meetings to ensure everyone was aligned and any issues were quickly addressed.

By implementing the stream-aligned team topology, Identifai ID delivered a high-quality eKYC product that met its customers' needs while responding quickly to changing market and regulatory requirements.

To manage the project's complexity and ensure that each team member clearly understands their roles and responsibilities, Identifai ID adopts the team topologies approach. The stream-aligned team is responsible for managing the end-to-end delivery of the product, including the development and deployment of the AI models, data pipelines, and APIs. The complicated subsystem team is responsible for developing and maintaining the complex facial liveness detection component. The platform team is responsible for developing and maintaining the API infrastructure, while the enabling team is responsible for developing and maintaining the SDKs.

Identifai ID also focuses on customer success and ensures that their AIaaS product meets the needs of their customers. They conduct user testing and gather feedback to improve their product's accuracy and efficiency. They also provide customer support to address any issues customers may encounter during onboarding or while using the product.

To conclude, Identifai ID is a successful AI startup that designs, develops, and operationalizes an AIaaS biometrics-based eKYC API and SDK for digital verification and identification. They use a six-layer AI platform design, MLOps process, build vs. buy framework, and team topologies to ensure their product's successful development and delivery. By focusing on customer success and continuously improving their product, Identifai ID has become a trusted and reliable solution for digital verification and identification.

Registering IP of an AI Product

In recent years, there has been a remarkable surge in the patenting of artificial intelligence (AI) technologies, indicating the growing recognition of AI's significance and potential. According to the World Intellectual Property Organization (WIPO), the number of AI-related patent applications worldwide witnessed an impressive 193% increase between 2013 and 2017. Furthermore, WIPO's examination of corporate acquisitions in the AI sector revealed that since 1998, 434 companies have been acquired, mostly occurring after 2016.

Today, AI and machine learning have emerged as driving forces behind innovation across numerous industries. Companies that recognize these technologies' substantial value are prudently safeguarding their intellectual property to secure a competitive advantage. Within this context, the United States Patent and Trademark Office (USPTO) has issued guidelines outlining what can be patented in the realm of AI and machine learning.

To obtain a patent for your AI innovation, it must fall under specific categories such as machine, method, article of manufacture, or composition of matter. However, it must not be related to laws of nature, physical phenomena, or abstract ideas. While some machine learning algorithms and AI inventions may be deemed abstract ideas and fail to gain patent protection, it is possible to patent the sequence of stages in your method. Under US patent law, this is because an algorithm is defined as a series of mathematical steps and operations.

It is important to note that while the software itself can be copyrighted as a finished product, machine learning methods are often considered abstract. To navigate this landscape successfully, best practices derived from software patents can be applied when seeking an AI (machine learning) model patent.

Here's a breakdown of these practices in simpler terms:

1. *Focus on the structure of the machine learning model in the claim*: Highlight your machine learning model's unique design and architecture when describing your invention. Explain how it differs from existing models and what makes it innovative.

2. *Identify the training and execution phases*: Determine whether your invention primarily relates to the training phase, where the model learns from data, or the execution phase, where it applies what it has learned to make predictions or decisions. It could be relevant to both phases as well.

3. *Claim the training process*: Clearly state the steps in training your model, including any specific techniques or algorithms used. This demonstrates the originality and value of your approach to training the AI model.

4. *Emphasize the preparation of input data*: Explain how you gather, clean, and preprocess the data before feeding it into the model. Highlight any unique methods or strategies you employ to ensure the quality and relevance of the input data.

5. *Cover the input mapping to the model:* Describe how the input data is transformed or mapped to work effectively with your AI model. This can involve techniques like feature engineering or data preprocessing to optimize the model's performance.

6. *Claim the post-processing and interpretation of output data:* Outline the steps involved in processing and interpreting the output generated by the model. This could include any additional computations or analyses performed on the results to extract meaningful insights.

7. *Draft different claim sets for training and execution phases:* Create separate sets of claims that specifically address the unique aspects of your invention in the training and execution phases. This ensures that you cover all relevant aspects and increases the chances of obtaining comprehensive patent protection.

8. *Avoid claiming conventional application to existing data:* Be careful not to make claims involving applying an existing model to existing data without substantial innovation. Please focus on the novel elements and improvements you have made to the AI model or the overall process.

Registering IP for AI products involves several steps:

1. Conduct a patent search to assess the novelty of your AI product.

2. Document and describe your inventions, identify patentable aspects, and consult with IP professionals.

3. File patent applications, prosecute, and defend your patents.

4. Maintain and monitor them.

Seeking legal advice and working with experienced IP practitioners enhances your chances of successfully protecting your AI inventions.

How to Scout Top AI Talents and Compete with Big Tech

In the rapidly evolving field of artificial intelligence (AI), attracting and retaining top talent is crucial for the success of any AI startup. However, competing with established big tech companies such as Google, Meta, OpenAI, Tesla, and others in terms of salary, facilities, and career development can be a daunting task. To overcome these challenges, it is essential to adopt a strategic approach to scouting and hiring the best AI talents as follows:

1. *Stay updated with latest research:* To identify promising AI talents, it is imperative to stay well-informed about the latest advancements in machine learning and AI in general. Regularly read research papers from top universities, research labs, and conferences, keeping an eye on emerging trends and breakthroughs. This will help you understand the cutting-edge techniques and areas relevant to the products you are building.

2. *Identify relevant authors:* Once you come across research papers relevant to your products, focus on identifying the authors who contributed to those papers. Ideally, look for PhD students as they possess in-depth knowledge and expertise in their respective fields. Master's students can also be valuable contributors. Consider sponsoring their PhD studies at the best universities near your geographical location, emphasizing the importance of relocation to your organization.

3. *Leverage value proposition:* Recognize that you may not be able to match the salary, facilities, and career development opportunities offered by big tech companies. Instead, compete by highlighting the unique value your startup provides. Emphasize the impact and value for societies that AI talents can make by working with your organization. Stress that they won't be mere cogs in a machine but will have the autonomy to make important decisions, collaborate with universities, choose conferences to attend, and publish papers. Additionally, emphasize their involvement in real-world AI deployment, exposing them in an end-to-end process from research to deployment using the MLOps or LLMOps process.

4. *Offer freedom and intellectual stimulation:* Attract talented AI professionals by offering them the freedom to explore and work on interesting projects during their spare time. Create an environment that encourages experimentation and innovation, allowing them to pursue their passion and curiosity. Emphasize the opportunity to work on diverse and impactful projects that go beyond profit-oriented goals prevalent in big tech companies.

5. *Communicate value and impact effectively*: Communicate the value and impact your AI startup is making to the world. Highlight the societal benefits, ethical considerations, and the opportunity to contribute to cutting-edge research and technological advancements. Demonstrate that your organization is driven by a mission to solve important problems and make a positive difference, fostering a sense of purpose and fulfillment among AI talents.

By implementing these tips, your AI startup can attract and retain exceptional talents, creating a competitive advantage even when compared with big tech giants.

Conclusion

This chapter explains the intricacies of building an AI platform requiring a multidisciplinary approach combining machine learning, software engineering, and data management expertise.

Developing an effective AI platform involves several key steps, including defining the problem, collecting and cleaning data, building and testing models, deploying them, and monitoring and maintaining their performance overtime.

MLOps provides a framework for managing the entire lifecycle of AI models, from development to deployment and beyond. It includes processes such as version control, automated testing, continuous integration and deployment (CI/CD) pipelines, model serving, monitoring, and automated retraining.

Aligning MLOps processes with team topologies ensures that each team member clearly understands their roles and responsibilities and has the necessary tools, processes, and communication channels to collaborate effectively. The stream-aligned, complicated subsystem, platform, and enabling teams provide a flexible framework for building interdisciplinary teams that can effectively develop and manage AI platforms.

To create a successful AI platform, it's essential to unify the system, process, and team design, which requires establishing clear goals and objectives, developing an architecture that accommodates the complexities of AI software, incorporating MLOps methodologies and best practices, and establishing clear roles and responsibilities for each team member, as well as effective communication channels and collaboration tools.

By following these best practices and adopting a flexible, interdisciplinary approach to building AI platforms, organizations can maximize the potential of AI technology and deliver innovative solutions to real-world problems.

Key Takeaways

- AI software development requires a different approach than traditional software development due to creating algorithms that can learn and improve overtime like human cognitive systems.

- Unifying system, process, and team design is crucial for creating a successful AI platform.

- The ten stages of AI software development include model requirements, data collection, data cleaning and transformation, data labeling, feature engineering, model training, model evaluation, model deployment, model monitoring, and UI/UX development.

- MLOps is a crucial process to streamline the production and operationalization of AI systems. It involves the implementation of version control for models, automated testing, continuous integration and deployment (CI/CD) pipelines, model serving, model monitoring, and automated retraining.

- Aligning the MLOps process and the team using team topologies is essential for effective collaboration and communication. This involves organizing the team into stream-aligned, complicated subsystem, platform, enabling, and customer success teams.

- Developing AI software platforms involves setting up the development environment and infrastructure; implementing the data pipeline, model training, model serving, and monitoring components; building testing and validation pipelines; and developing user interfaces and integration interfaces.

- We can use the Carnegie Mellon CMM to measure AI software development process maturity, which includes five stages: initial, repeatable, defined, managed, and optimized.

- To ensure trustworthy and responsible AI, it is crucial to develop XAI mechanisms for root cause analysis (XAIOps), ensure transparency and explainability of the model's decision-making process, and apply active learning mechanisms to subside edge cases.

- When selecting technology stacks, teams can use the build vs. buy framework to determine which components to build and which to acquire externally.

- The team members in AI development include the product manager, subject matter experts, data labelers, front-end software engineers, machine learning scientists/data scientists, machine learning/MLOps/LLMOps engineers, data engineers, DevOps/infrastructure/back-end engineers, TechOps engineers, and customer success specialists.

- It is important to foster interdisciplinary teams, including data scientists/machine learning experts, machine learning engineers, data engineers, software developers, and domain experts, to ensure that all aspects of AI software development are considered and that models are developed with real-world applications in mind.

Go-to-Market Strategy for an AI Startup

The previous chapters explored the essential steps in validating, developing, and operationalizing an AI product. This chapter will delve into the crucial topic of the go-to-market (GTM) strategy for an AI startup. Similar to any other product, launching an AI product requires a well-defined strategy to make it a successful and sustainable business. We will discuss the significance of the GTM strategy for businesses and the unique challenges that AI startups face while devising their GTM strategy.

We will delve into the importance of a go-to-market strategy for three types of AI products: AI (as a) Solution, AI as a Service, and AI (as a) Toolkit. Launching an AI product requires careful planning to avoid wasting time, risks, and costs associated with failed launches or internal misunderstandings.

Therefore, it's crucial to understand the key components of a successful go-to-market strategy and how they differ for AI products. Additionally, we will provide a case study for each of the three types of AI products to help illustrate how to apply these principles in practice. By the end of this chapter,

© Adhiguna Mahendra 2023
A. Mahendra, *AI Startup Strategy*, https://doi.org/10.1007/978-1-4842-9502-1_9

you will clearly understand the importance of a GTM strategy for an AI product and the key differences between the GTM strategies for AI products and general products.

Background

Previous chapters have distinguished between AI-powered SaaS and AI-first SaaS, where the former adds intelligence to workflows and the latter is AI-centric and nonfunctional without AI. AIaaS targets developers and data scientists, while AI-first SaaS caters to end users. These distinctions are essential for discussions on AI startups. This chapter discusses the importance of a go-to-market strategy for AI startups. Despite AI's hype and enthusiasm, launching an AI product requires careful planning to avoid costs, risks, and misunderstandings. We highlight the unique approach needed for AI startups and compare it with a general go-to-market strategy.

When bringing a new product to market, it's important to have a clear go-to-market (GTM) strategy. Unlike a long-term marketing or product strategy, a GTM strategy is a short-term plan that spans 6–18 months and is guided by a longer-term product and marketing strategy. However, a well-executed GTM strategy can lead to increased market awareness and ensure that you don't waste time and resources on a product that isn't necessary. By launching your product into a new market, repositioning your brand, or increasing sales of existing products, a strong GTM strategy can bring countless benefits to your business.

For example, here's the journey of Blue Yonder, a successful AI company that Panasonic acquired in 2021. The company was founded in 2008 by Professor Michael Feindt, a particle physicist passionate about applying artificial intelligence to solve real-world business problems. Blue Yonder's unique proposition is using AI and machine learning to help businesses make smarter decisions and optimize their operations, such as forecasting demand, optimizing inventory, and pricing products. Panasonic acquired Blue Yonder for $7.1 billion to enhance their portfolio of solutions for the supply chain, manufacturing, and logistics industries.

Blue Yonder's GTM (go-to-market) strategy provides end-to-end solutions that allow businesses to optimize their operations through AI-powered decision-making. The company targets specific industries, including retail, manufacturing, and logistics, and offers a range of products and services that cater to the unique needs of each industry. The crucial part of their GTM strategy is building long-term partnerships with clients like Microsoft and Accenture and investing in research and development to create new solutions that cater to evolving market trends and customer requirements. This helps them develop personalized solutions that match each client's unique needs.

Another important aspect of Blue Yonder's GTM strategy is its focus on digital transformation. The company recognizes that many traditional industries are struggling to keep up with the rapid pace of technological change and aims to help these industries transition to a more data-driven, AI-powered future.

This focus on digital transformation aligns with Panasonic's broader strategic goals of becoming a leader in the digitalization of manufacturing, logistics, and retail industries. From Panasonic's perspective, the acquisition of Blue Yonder represents an opportunity to accelerate their digital transformation efforts by leveraging Blue Yonder's expertise and technology.

By integrating Blue Yonder's AI-powered solutions into their existing portfolio of products and services, Panasonic can offer more comprehensive solutions that help clients optimize their operations and improve their bottom line.

Now, if we are to see the other side, several examples of AI startups have failed to enter the market. Ansaro, a SaaS that aimed to revolutionize the recruiting industry through innovative AI technologies,[1] is one example. The company was established in 2016 and received $2.25M from institutional investors and $750K from friends and family but ultimately failed to gain market traction (Figure 9-1).

Ansaro encountered several challenges with their go-to-market strategy. Firstly, they were slow to pivot and failed to question their initial product plan, wasting time and resources. Secondly, they focused on the wrong pain point, pitching new hire quality improvement to CHROs instead of hiring efficiency to recruiters. Lastly, they tackled a problem that required a long time to measure results, making it difficult to demonstrate ROI to HR buyers. The moral is that even with innovation and funding, AI startups can face difficulties in a highly competitive market.

---

[1] www.forbes.com/sites/valleyvoices/2018/01/29/how-ai-is-changing-the-game-for-recruiting/?sh=68063351aa23

Figure 9-1. Ansaro hiring AI software

A GTM strategy is essentially the "game plan" that describes how each functional team will contribute to launching a new product feature or service to the target customer to gain a competitive advantage. It specifies how the company will communicate and deliver the feature's value to potential customers, buyers, and other market influencers. A go-to-market strategy aims to provide a powerful, winning total customer experience to attract, win, and retain the most desirable customers while generating high sales and market share growth at the lowest possible cost.

A strong go-to-market strategy always includes multiple driving factors. These factors include value proposition, positioning, distribution model, customers, distribution channels, and price. However, we must remember that AI startups may have multiple target markets. There could be B2C, B2B, and even B2G target markets. The difference in the target market plays a big role in deciding which approach to use, what message we want to deliver, what pricing strategy we want to apply, and what the distribution channel looks like.

Talking about AI solutions, AI as a Service, and AI as a Toolkit, this chapter will discuss the needs of a specific target market, how to generate a value proposition and message that resonates with the target market, the pricing model, and how to create a customer journey map. At some point, we will also emphasize how to develop an API and SDK that are user-friendly and flexible and how to create an impeccable marketing strategy. Similar to the previous chapters, this chapter includes several case studies. The three business models are believed to facilitate a comprehensive discussion of the GTM strategy for AI startups.

This chapter aims to provide founders, product managers, business managers, and executives of AI startups with a comprehensive understanding of the essential elements of an effective go-to-market strategy. Through case studies and step-by-step guides throughout the chapter, you will learn how to develop and execute a GTM strategy that positions your AI products in the market, attracts customers, and drives revenue growth. In particular, the following subjects are going to be discussed in this chapter:

1. Defining your target audience and customer personas

2. Identifying your unique value proposition and messaging

3. Understanding the needs and pain points of developers

4. Creating a scalable sales and marketing infrastructure

5. Leveraging digital marketing channels and social media

6. Building strategic partnerships and alliances

7. Measuring and optimizing your GTM strategy for continuous improvement

This chapter provides a clear roadmap for creating a successful GTM strategy in the competitive AI marketplace. You will learn key takeaways and steps for bringing AI products to market and achieving business objectives. It covers building a unique value proposition and creating an effective marketing strategy and includes case studies of successful implementations by Nodeflux and Visionaire.

Introduction to the Go-to-Market Strategy for AI Startups

Product, channel, message or value proposition, and market are the four primary elements of a GTM strategy (Figure 9-2). We can all agree that to have an effective and relevant message, we must fully comprehend what customers find appealing about our products. In developing a GTM strategy for a product, we must ensure that we only sell products that the customer indeed requires so that we can be certain that someone is willing to purchase them.

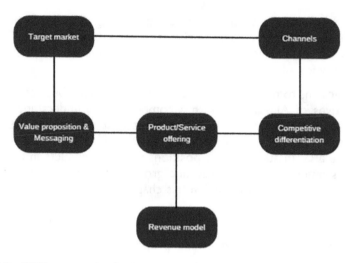

Figure 9-2. GTM strategy visualization

Therefore, if we want to sell products in large quantities, we must be prepared and map out the needs and expectations of our potential customers, which we can only obtain by working closely with them and listening attentively to what they say.

To effectively communicate with customers, businesses must identify and develop channels that serve as distribution points for their products and services. This requires a solid understanding of the target audience's preferred channels and potential channels that could be used in the future.

Focusing efforts solely on customer channels is important, considering factors such as geography, demography, and psychology. For instance, it would be futile for startups to sell AI products in regions with inadequate infrastructure or limited Internet connection and budget. By identifying the right channels and markets, businesses can focus their efforts and increase their chances of success. Briefly, the extent to which we comprehend customer needs, expectations, and behavior is crucial to the success of any GTM strategy. We must conduct a thorough investigation into what the customer desires. This is the fundamental basis for every successful GTM strategy.

In this section, we will examine the necessity of having a go-to-market strategy for an AI startup and dig deeper into the descriptions of each type of AI product discussed in the previous section. It is hoped that once we understand what makes a good go-to-market strategy, we will be able to anticipate the topics that will be further emphasized in the book.

The Importance of a Go-to-Market Strategy for AI Startups

Launching a product without a well-developed strategy is a mistake that should be avoided. After a new product is introduced to the market, there may be a temptation to consider the job done. However, when companies lack a clear and unified strategy for their AI product, it can lead to various issues. These issues may include miscommunication between internal teams, an underdeveloped pricing model, difficulties for the marketing team to create an effective message, and potential customers unaware of the product's existence. Therefore, it is crucial to have a solid strategy in place before launching a new product to ensure its success.

All of the factors mentioned earlier may result in tension between the team and key stakeholders, hindering the business's ability to collaborate. Therefore, having a strategy in place can foster the business's growth potential when launching a new product. A GTM (go-to-market) strategy is essential for any startup and becomes even more critical for AI startups. Here are some reasons having a GTM strategy is important for AI startups:

- *Helps identify the target audience*: AI startups will always target a specific demographic. A GTM strategy assists in identifying the target audience and their particular needs. It allows startups to comprehend their customers better and tailor their marketing efforts to meet their needs.

- *Guides product development*: A GTM strategy aids startups in comprehending the market they are entering, their competitors, and their unique value proposition. This knowledge guides product development and ensures the startup is constructing a product that meets the target market's needs.

- *Optimizes marketing efforts*: A GTM strategy outlines the marketing channels and tactics that are most effective for reaching the target audience. This helps startups optimize their marketing efforts and use their resources efficiently.

- *Attracts investors*: Before investing, investors want to see a clear path to market for a startup. A well-developed GTM strategy can increase a startup's appeal to investors and its likelihood of receiving funding.

- *Increases revenue*: A well-executed GTM strategy can assist startups in reaching their intended audience and generating revenue more quickly. Additionally, it can help them build a solid brand and reputation, resulting in long-term success.

In conclusion, it is almost impossible for AI startups to be successful without a GTM strategy. It aids in determining whom to market to, directs product growth, enhances promotional efforts, brings in capital, and boosts sales. AI startups may have trouble breaking into the market and reaching their objectives without a well-defined GTM strategy.

Description of Different Types of AI Products

The business model or type of AI product will ultimately determine how we will sell the product to the market. This is because a different model will significantly shape how the product will be sold to the market.

To better understand the challenges faced by several AI business models and their target market, we will get to the description of each one, understand their consequences, and get through some case studies relevant to the business model and the target market.

AI (as a) Solution

Many people agree that machine learning is one of the fastest-growing software areas, making it popular as part of SaaS or a product. As machine learning becomes more advanced, it can automate or augment cognitive tasks in enterprises across industries. Using machine learning helps enable any software to learn from every task or transaction, improving intelligence and efficiency along the way. Furthermore, as an AI-first application solution, this business model can dig deeper into insights and data, which will help you with the competition.

In this section, we will talk about AI solutions. In the previous chapters, we learned that two AI business models target end users: AI-powered SaaS and AI-first SaaS. AI-first solutions are products or services designed with AI as the primary focus to enhance user experience through AI capabilities. AI-powered solutions, on the other hand, refer to products or services that use AI to improve certain aspects, but AI is not necessarily the main focus. The main difference is that AI-first solutions prioritize AI, while AI-powered solutions use AI to enhance existing products or services.

We refer to these two business models as AI (as a) Solution. This AI business model is selling AI-first application solutions where AI is empowering the application, such as AI-powered CRM and AI-powered logistics software. AI solutions' target market is B2B, such as corporates, or B2C, such as end users.

The target market has a substantial impact on their purpose and orientation. AI solution business models focus on streamlining business processes, generating revenue, or reducing expenses by leveraging AI.

We will explore this business model by understanding Optitrax (Optitrax.co) as an example.

Optitrax is a cutting-edge software solution that empowers users to create and optimize delivery routes while considering a wide range of individual parameters, such as vehicle preferences, capacity, delivery times, customer service windows, historical traffic data, and work order specifications. Optitrax caters to a diverse range of use cases and industries that are focused on exceptional delivery services.

Optitrax offers an AI-powered solution for fast-moving consumer goods (FMCG) delivery to streamline operations and optimize deliveries. This solution addresses common challenges in FMCG delivery, such as inefficient driver tracking, suboptimal delivery times, and high delivery costs. By using individual parameters such as vehicle preferences, capacity, delivery time or customer service windows, historical traffic data, and work order specifications, Optitrax can provide an optimized delivery route for FMCG businesses. With this innovative software, FMCG companies can save time and money while ensuring efficient and timely delivery to their customers.

AI as a Service

AI-based software depends on hardware, such as GPU-based processing, which can be expensive to buy and maintain.

Instead of in-house development, individuals and companies can use Artificial Intelligence as a Service (AIaaS), a third-party artificial intelligence (AI) outsourcing service. They can experiment with AI to attain different goals with minimal initial cost and risk. Experimentation can assist the user in testing various machine learning algorithms based on natural language processing, computer vision, or generative adversarial network (generative AI). This AI business model sells their product through API calls, which can be integrated into users' applications, with developers as their target users.

AI as a Service targets software houses or system integrators (SIs) and individual developers. Aside from delivering AI through API, providing it through SDK could become an added value.

The main challenge is to build a developer-friendly API/SDK.

Identifai is a great example of an AI as a Service model. Identifai is an eKYC solution software developed by Nodeflux. This product focuses on identifying and verifying individuals through face recognition. Aside from face recognition, Identifai has developed several machine learning models, such as face liveness detection and ID OCR. They are mixing their marketing method between account-based marketing for the middle and bottom funnels and pull marketing for the upper funnel.

AI (as a) Toolkit

AI (as a) Toolkit or AI toolkits are pre-built tools and frameworks that enable developers to build, train, and deploy AI models without substantial AI or machine learning knowledge. AI toolkits are frequently deployed as a command-line interface (CLI), which can support the developers. The toolkits could include several things, such as data annotation and augmentation tools, machine learning and deep learning experimentation tools, and machine learning workflow and orchestration tools. The toolkit results can be deployed to operating systems, containers, or virtual machines (VMs).

In AI toolkits, the developers are focused more on the development using the AI tool and the integration with the existing workflows and technology stacks. The developer journey map for AI toolkits is a set of steps developers go through when working with these tools. It is designed to help developers understand how to build and integrate AI models into their applications.

The developer journey typically starts with installing and setting up the toolkit and then building, training, and validating the models using the provided APIs and SDKs. Once the models are built, developers will integrate them into their existing workflows and technology stacks. The journey also includes ongoing maintenance and monitoring of the models and updating them as necessary.

Unlike AI as a Service and AI as an Engine, where models are pre-built and offered by the provider, developers can construct and train their models using AI toolkits. This enables companies to tailor the models to their use case while incorporating domain-specific knowledge. Furthermore, the integration process with existing workflows and technology stacks is intended to be as seamless as possible, allowing developers to simply add AI capabilities to their existing applications.

An example of this AI business model is Visionaire. This computer vision integration platform enables the integration of any deep learning vision model to any camera to be deployed to a low-processing, low-bandwidth device.

Go-to-Market Strategy for AI (as a) Solution

This AI business model refers to an application or platform that uses AI to solve a specific business problem, is designed for a particular industry, and is sold as a software solution. This model targets end business users as the primary market. For a successful go-to-market strategy, identifying the target market is crucial. By doing so, the development team can create solutions that meet the target audience's specific needs, reducing development time and cost. Customized solutions can differentiate companies from their competitors and offer more appealing solutions to potential customers. Tailoring AI (as a)

Solution to a specific target market can also lead to a higher ROI as the solution is more likely to be adopted and used by the target market, resulting in increased revenue and profitability.

Identifying the Target Market

Developing AI (as a) Solution without understanding the target audience can lead to an irrelevant or ineffective product that doesn't solve the intended problem. By understanding the target audience's needs, developers can ensure that the AI solution addresses the target market's specific challenges and pain points and meets the expectations of potential customers. In previous chapters, we have defined in detail how to validate the target market, but in the GTM context, we repeat the process as follows:

1. *Define the problem*: The first step is defining the problem the AI solution intends to solve. This will help identify the potential markets for the solution.

2. *Conduct market research*: Conducting market research helps identify the target market by collecting and analyzing data on customer behavior, preferences, demographics, and other relevant factors.

3. *Analyze competition*: Analyzing the competition helps understand the existing solutions available in the market and how they meet the target audience's needs.

4. *Segment the market*: Segmentation involves dividing the target market into smaller groups based on shared characteristics, such as age, gender, income, or interests. This helps identify each segment's specific needs and preferences and tailor the solution to meet their needs.

5. *Develop buyer personas*: Buyer personas are fictional representations of the ideal customers based on market research and segmentation analysis. They help understand the target audience's needs, pain points, motivations, and preferences.

6. *Validate the target market*: Validating the target market involves testing the solution with a sample group of the target audience to ensure that it meets their needs and preferences.

Understanding the target audience is critical to the success of AI solutions. By identifying the target market and understanding their needs, developers can tailor the solution to meet the specific requirements and preferences of the target audience. Additionally, understanding the target audience can help developers anticipate future needs and trends, enabling them to create more innovative and relevant solutions.

However, B2B (business-to-business) end users have unique needs and requirements that differ from those of B2C (business-to-consumer) end users. Here are some of the key needs of B2B end users:

- *Efficiency*: B2B end users are typically focused on efficiency and productivity. They need AI (as a) Solution to help them automate tasks, streamline processes, and reduce operational costs.

- *Scalability*: B2B end users need AI (as a) Solution that scales with their business needs. This means that the solution should be able to handle large volumes of data and users as the business grows.

- *Customization*: B2B end users often have specific requirements and workflows that off-the-shelf AI solutions may not address. They need solutions customized to their specific needs and integrated with their existing systems.

- *Security*: B2B end users are concerned about data security and privacy. They need AI solutions that provide robust security features like encryption, access control, and data backup.

- *ROI*: B2B end users are focused on AI (as a) Solution's ROI (return on investment). They need solutions delivering measurable benefits, such as increased revenue, reduced costs, or improved customer satisfaction.

Understanding the needs of B2B end users is essential for developing effective AI solutions for businesses. By addressing these needs, developers can create solutions to help businesses achieve their goals, increase efficiency, and stay competitive in their industries.

Developing a Unique Value Proposition

To develop a successful AI (as a) Solution business model, it is important first to identify the target market and understand the competition. Understanding the competitive landscape can help identify gaps and opportunities in the market. After this step, the next is to define the unique value proposition (UVP) for the AI solution.

This clear and compelling statement describes the specific benefits and values the solution provides to the target market.

The UVP should differentiate the solution from competitors and focus on the benefits and outcomes that customers care about.

Once the UVP is defined, crafting clear, concise messaging that resonates with the target market is essential. The messaging should focus on the benefits and outcomes that customers care about, use language that the target market understands, and resonate with their emotions and motivations. A unique value proposition and messaging that resonates with the target market is crucial to building a successful AI solution business model (Figure 9-3).

Figure 9-3. Defining a unique value proposition

Finally, testing your messaging with your target market and iterating based on their feedback is important. You can use surveys, focus groups, or other methods to gather feedback on your messaging and adjust as needed. By following these steps, you can develop a unique value proposition and messaging that resonate with your target market for your AI solution business model. Remember to focus on the benefits and outcomes your customers care about and continuously test and iterate to ensure your messaging is effective.

Designing a Customer Journey Map

B2B-oriented AI startups should consider creating a customer journey map, which outlines the customer journey across the touchpoints used for a given stage or set of stages. This explains the touchpoints or steps a customer takes to complete a specific task and the digital channels and content utilized.

Here are some steps you can follow to create a customer journey map for an AI solution business model:

1. *Identify the stages of the customer journey*: The first step is identifying the various stages of the customer journey. This may include awareness, consideration, purchase, and post-purchase. For an AI solution business model, additional stages may include onboarding, training, and ongoing support.

2. *Define customer personas*: Understanding your customer's needs and expectations is key to creating a customer journey map. Define customer personas that represent your ideal customers, based on demographics, behavior, goals, and pain points.

3. *Map out customer touchpoints*: Next, identify the various touchpoints that a customer may have with your business during each stage of the journey. These touchpoints may include website visits, social media interactions, customer service calls, and product demos.

4. *Gather customer feedback*: To better understand the customer experience, gather feedback from your customers. This can be done through surveys, interviews, or online reviews. Use this feedback to identify pain points and areas where you can improve the customer experience.

5. *Identify opportunities for AI solutions*: Once you have identified the touchpoints and pain points in the customer journey, look for opportunities to integrate AI solutions. For example, AI chatbots can be used to provide instant customer support, while AI-powered personalization can create a more personalized experience for the customer.

6. *Create a visual representation*: Finally, create a visual representation of the customer journey map using tools like flowcharts or diagrams. This will help you visualize the customer journey and identify areas where you can improve the customer experience.

In summary, designing a customer journey map for an AI solution business model involves identifying the various touchpoints and interactions that a customer has with your business, defining customer personas, gathering customer feedback, and identifying opportunities to integrate AI solutions. A visual representation of the customer journey map can help identify improvement areas and create a more personalized customer experience.

Developing a Marketing Strategy to Reach the Target Market

Developing a marketing strategy for an AI (as a) Solution business model involves understanding your target market, creating a unique value proposition, identifying the best channels to reach your audience, and measuring the effectiveness of your efforts.

Although reaching the customer directly as a marketing method could help AI solutions reach many audiences, sales representatives will be needed eventually. As we approach the middle of the funnel, the customer will require detailed information about the products, which can only be provided effectively by a sales development representative (SDR) or salesperson.

In targeting B2B customers, especially for a complex product based on AI, a high-touch marketing approach is typically the most effective strategy. This approach involves deploying a field sales force to personally engage with potential customers and help them understand the product. A high-touch marketing approach is particularly suitable for AI solutions because AI can be complex and challenging to sell. Direct assistance through a high-touch approach can help customers better understand the value and benefits of the product, leading to increased adoption and sales.

Here are some steps to help you develop an effective marketing strategy:

1. *Identify your target audience*: Consider who will benefit most from your AI solution. This could include businesses in a particular industry or individuals with a specific problem that your AI solution can solve. Once you've identified your target audience, research their demographics, interests, and pain points to understand how to market to them effectively.

2. *Analyze your competition*: Research your competitors in the market and analyze their marketing strategies. Pay attention to their messaging, target audience, and the channels they use to promote their solutions. Determine what differentiates your AI solution from theirs, and use that information to create a unique marketing strategy. You can use web applications such as Rank Signals and SpyFu to analyze your competitor's marketing strategy.

3. *Identify your unique selling proposition (USP)*: Your USP is what sets your AI solution apart from your competitors. It's important to clearly define your USP so you can communicate it effectively to potential customers. Some possible USPs for an AI solution product might include faster processing times, more accurate predictions, or better data security.

4. *Set marketing goals and KPIs*: Identify specific marketing goals and KPIs that align with your overall GTM strategy. For example, you might aim to generate a certain number of leads, achieve a certain conversion rate, or increase brand awareness within a particular industry.

5. *Develop a content marketing plan*: Create a content marketing plan that targets your identified audience with relevant and informative content. This could include blog posts, infographics, case studies, or webinars. Ensure your content aligns with your USP and addresses the pain points of your target audience.

6. *Build a social media presence*: Determine which social media platforms your target audience uses most frequently, and create a presence on those platforms. Share your content on social media, engage with your audience, and use paid advertising to reach a wider audience.

7. *Utilize email marketing*: Create a marketing campaign targeting your identified audience with personalized and relevant messaging. This can include newsletters, product updates, and promotional offers. Use your email campaign to nurture leads and keep them engaged with your solution.

8. *Consider paid advertising*: Use paid advertising such as Google Ads, Facebook Ads, or LinkedIn Ads to reach a wider audience and generate leads. Ensure your ads are targeted to your specific audience and use clear messaging highlighting your USP.

9. *Measure and optimize*: Track your marketing KPIs and adjust your strategy accordingly. Use data to optimize your marketing campaign and improve your ROI. Continually test and refine your messaging, content, and channels to maximize your marketing effectiveness.

You can create a marketing strategy for your AI solution business model if you follow these steps. That strategy will effectively reach the target market for your AI solution. Remember that you should continuously adjust your strategy in light of the results to guarantee that you are achieving your professional objectives.

CASE STUDY I (AI AS A SOLUTION): OPTITRAX

Optitrax is an AI-powered logistics optimization software company with solid demand in the logistics industry. The company's innovative approach to logistics optimization, powered by AI, has resulted in significant demand for their services (Figure 9-4).

Figure 9-4. Optitrax: AI-based logistics platform

This case study examines how Optitrax developed and implemented a comprehensive GTM strategy leveraging AI-powered solutions to drive sales growth and expand their customer base. They used the Awareness-Consideration-Conversion funnel as follows (Figure 9-5).

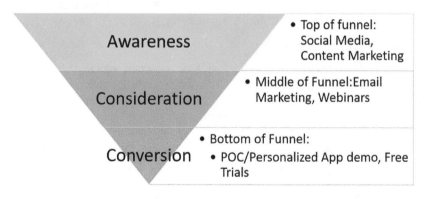

Figure 9-5. Optitrax sales funnel

Optitrax faced several challenges when developing their GTM strategy, including the following:

- The need to differentiate their AI-powered solutions from competitors in a crowded market.

- Educating potential customers on the value of AI-powered logistics optimization solutions is challenging.

- The need to establish partnerships and distribution channels to reach potential customers effectively.

Optitrax developed a comprehensive GTM strategy that leveraged their AI-powered solutions as a key differentiator and value proposition, including the following components:

1. **Market research and analysis**

   Optitrax conducted extensive market research and analysis on industries that do logistics and delivery services, identified potential customers, understood their pain points, and developed messaging highlighting the benefits of their AI-powered logistics optimization solutions.

2. **Targeting and segmentation**

   Using the insights gained from market research, Optitrax developed a targeting and segmentation strategy focused on specific industries, such as manufacturing, distribution, and transportation. The company also segmented their target customers by size, region, logistics, and delivery challenges.

3. **Messaging and positioning**

   Optitrax developed a messaging and positioning strategy that emphasized the benefits of their AI-powered logistics optimization solutions, including real-time data insights, courier matching, accurate demand forecasting, and route optimization. This messaging helped educate potential customers on the value of AI-powered logistics optimization solutions.

4. **Partnerships and distribution channels**

   Optitrax partnered with 4PL providers, software integrators, and consulting firms to provide customers with a comprehensive logistics optimization solution leveraging AI-powered technology. The company also developed a channel strategy for direct sales, partnerships, and online distribution.

5. **Customer acquisition and retention**

> Optitrax developed a customer acquisition and retention strategy, including targeted advertising, content marketing, and customer referrals. The company also developed a customer success program to ensure customers received maximum value from their AI-powered solutions.

Optitrax's AI-powered solutions were crucial to their successful go-to-market (GTM) strategy. The strategy involved targeted advertising and content marketing, which generated a high volume of leads and partnerships that helped them reach new customers across various industries. Optitrax's customer success program also improved retention rates and increased customer lifetime value. Optitrax's GTM strategy and AI-powered solutions allowed the company to differentiate themselves from competitors, effectively reach potential customers, and achieve significant sales growth in the logistics industry.

Go-to-Market Strategy for AI as a Service

This section focuses on AIaaS, which refers to AI services delivered as API or SDK specifically designed for developers. We will delve into developers' problems and difficulties and identify the best strategies to develop flexible API and SDK with detailed documentation. Additionally, we will examine the customer journey map of the developer journey.

Understanding the Needs and Pain Points of Developers

No matter what type of product or business model you have, it is essential to have a deep understanding of your target market. For instance, if you are selling an AI as a Service product and your marketing message only emphasizes the benefits, like "This product is a leading innovation that allows a cost reduction of 80% within one week," it may not resonate with your target audience, the developers. While this message may seem quantitative and clear, it fails to address the developers' specific problems. This ineffective messaging often comes from a lack of comprehensive understanding of the target audience. Therefore, understanding your target audience and their pain points is critical to crafting a message that resonates and drives conversions.

Selling AI products to developers is challenging because of the technology's complexity. To market to developers effectively, you need to invest in educating them on how to use the product and its potential. Case studies and blogs can be helpful for inspiring developers, while comprehensive documentation and code samples are essential to help them understand and try your product quickly. Therefore, providing resources that offer clear instructions and support is crucial to facilitate developers' adoption of your AI product.

Developers care about the technical aspects of AI models, such as integration, accuracy, and operational conditions. They also value simplicity and reliable support from the product team. However, it's important to consider their psychology and how the product can trigger their emotions. For example, developers may feel satisfied when they can create a highly polished and intelligent product in a short amount of time.

Adopting a bottom-up approach is important when selling AIaaS products to developers, as the product will be integrated into applications targeted toward end users. This approach has two key aspects – enablement and inspiration:

- Enablement focuses on the product's capabilities and how it can be developed into different forms to complete tasks efficiently. For example, providing clear documentation and code samples demonstrating how to integrate the AIaaS product can help enablement.

- Inspiration, on the other hand, focuses on sparking new ideas for developers through marketing collateral. For instance, providing case studies or success stories of how other developers have used the product can inspire developers to explore new possibilities.

Therefore, by combining enablement and inspiration, you can effectively sell AIaaS products to developers and encourage them to integrate your product into their applications.

When developers come across an AI as a Service product, they typically ask three questions to assess its suitability for their needs:

1. Can the model only be deployed on a specific platform like Web, Android, or iOS?

2. Is there a specific integration mechanism provided by the product?

3. What are the programming languages compatible with the product?

By answering these questions, developers can determine whether the AI as a Service product fits their project requirements. Therefore, companies must provide clear and concise answers to these questions to market their AI product to developers effectively.

These questions can be used to segment developers so that we can be more specific in determining the type of developer suitable for our products. So far, there are challenges in the implementation of AI as a Service faced by developers, including

1. *Integration challenges*: Integration between the AI model that we sell and the existing system and workflow of the developer is often challenging. The problem revolves around compatibility issues with the programming language or the framework used and difficulties with integrating the service through API and SDK. To solve this problem, we can do the following:

    *   Provide comprehensive documentation and support so that developers understand how to integrate their workflow with the models we sell, including detailed documentation on API endpoints, input/output formats, error messages, and responsive support via email, chat, or forums.

    *   Build an ecosystem of partners. The trained partners can help the developers for a project fee.

    *   Flexibility and customization provide developers with options for customizing input/output formats, selecting models or algorithms, and adjusting parameters.

2. *Data quality issues*: In the world of AI, the quality and quantity of the dataset used are crucial to the effectiveness of the resulting product. Insufficient datasets can lead to inaccuracies that decrease the product's effectiveness. For example, using only European facial images when marketing a product in Asia would not be appropriate. To solve this problem, we can establish data quality metrics that can help check the data quality and identify any potential issues that may affect the accuracy and reliability of the AI model. Additionally, developers can use data augmentation techniques to train the model further and improve its accuracy and reliability. Developers can ensure that their AI product is accurate and effective for the intended target market by establishing data quality metrics and utilizing data augmentation techniques.

3. *Scalability*: The processing of large-scale data is often a primary concern for developers using AI models. In addition to the challenges of managing bandwidth and memory usage, data processing is a critical factor that can affect the quality of the output generated. Several solutions can be used to address this issue:

   - Firstly, cloud computing platforms can be utilized to enable AI models to handle large datasets.

   - Secondly, optimizing AI models can enhance scalability by reducing their computational complexity and memory requirements.

   - Lastly, offering APIs, SDKs, or containers can allow developers to deploy their models to a scalable serving infrastructure easily.

   These solutions help alleviate the challenges associated with large-scale data processing and enable developers to utilize AI models.

4. *Model interpretability and explainability*: AI models can be challenging to interpret and explain due to their complexity, making it difficult for developers to communicate with non-technical stakeholders or ensure transparency and fairness in the model's decisions. To address this issue, explainability models can be used to help developers understand how the AI model works and detect any problems with the input data. The AI model's transparency and interpretability are improved by providing explainability models, which builds trust and facilitates communication between technical and non-technical stakeholders. This ultimately ensures the effective use of AI technology in various industries.

5. *Deployment and maintenance*: Once an AI application is developed, deploying and maintaining it can be a challenge. Developers must ensure that the application runs smoothly, monitor performance, and make updates as needed.

The preceding items focus on technical aspects of the product, but it's also important to consider the pain points associated with particular use cases or industries. To recognize these pain points, the following factors can be utilized to examine the audience's needs:

- *Demographic factors*: Demographic factors such as gender, age, education, and geographical region can lead to distinct methods of message capture.

- *Professional factors*: This factor relates to the developer's profession, including company size, industry, and job experience.

- *Usage factors*: This factor is essential as it relates to understanding how developers use our products in frequency, use cases, and required AI capabilities. Use cases vary across different industries, and it is crucial to identify pain points and relevant solutions specific to each industry. For example, in the banking industry, digital account opening requires face verification, necessitating facial recognition technology to authenticate the identities of prospective consumers. Conversely, facial recognition may be utilized in the mining industry to increase productivity or identify personal protective equipment worn by workers rather than to authenticate identities.

- *Business process factor*: In providing AI solutions as a service, it is crucial to understand the business processes of the target audience. By doing so, we can identify existing barriers in their processes and how our AI technologies can be used to address these issues. This analysis should be conducted not only at the corporate level but also at the department level to ensure accuracy. Understanding the target audience's business processes is essential for the successful implementation of AI solutions as a service.

In addition to conducting extensive user research, incorporating data from third-party sources, such as whitepapers, industry publications, and trend reports, can enhance identifying areas of difficulty. Identifying pain points is not a linear process. It requires continuous evaluation and experimentation to establish their significance and prioritize which issues will significantly impact the developer's decisions.

Developing a User-Friendly and Flexible API and SDK

APIs and SDKs vary in quality, and to be effective, they must be user-friendly and intuitive, allowing developers to understand and utilize their capabilities efficiently. This section will discuss key steps for creating a user-friendly API or SDK for your AI as a Service (AIaaS) platform.

1. Clear Documentation

Clear documentation is crucial for developers to utilize AI as a Service effectively. The product documentation should provide clear explanations and demonstrations of how to use APIs, SDKs, models, and algorithms. The documentation should also cover how to troubleshoot common problems. It's essential to update the documentation to reflect product updates and improvements regularly. This helps developers effectively use the AI as a Service platform and achieve their desired outcomes.

2. Integration

A well-defined API or SDK that adheres to programming standards is essential for easily integrating an AI as a Service product into a developer's code or project. The integration process should not require significant amounts of code or configuration, and the API or SDK should be user-friendly and intuitive. By simplifying the integration process, developers can more effectively incorporate AI as a Service products into their projects and applications.

3. Flexibility

An AI as a Service product should be versatile and configurable to accommodate multiple use cases and circumstances. Developers should be able to customize AI models, algorithm parameters, and settings to suit their needs. The product should also offer pricing and customization options to meet user requirements and budgets. This flexibility allows developers to tailor the AI as a Service product to their use case, ensuring optimal performance and outcomes.

4. Consistency

Consistent behavior across versions and platforms is crucial for AI as a Service products to reduce confusion and boost developer productivity. Developers should be able to update and migrate their applications using a consistent UI and API across different versions and platforms. Backward compatibility is also important to ensure that older applications work seamlessly with newer versions. By maintaining consistency, AI as a Service products can improve developer efficiency and reduce potential errors or disruptions during updates or migrations.

5. Excellent Assistance

Responsive and helpful support is essential for AI as a Service solutions to assist developers in resolving issues and answering queries. This support can include FAQs, online forums, and expert support, among other options. Developers need fast and responsive help to address bugs and other issues to ensure they can continue working on their applications. By providing adequate support, AI as a Service providers can foster strong relationships with developers and increase customer satisfaction.

6. Compatibility

An AI as a Service solution should be interoperable with multiple programming languages, frameworks, and platforms to improve adoption and reach a broader audience. It should include APIs and SDKs for Python, Java, and JavaScript to support creating AI applications for different use cases and platforms like cloud, mobile, and edge computing. Straightforward and user-friendly documentation makes APIs and SDKs accessible to developers, which we will discuss in detail in the next section.

What Makes a Great Documentation?

Clear and user-friendly documentation is crucial in conjunction with API/SDK friendliness. Developers use APIs and SDKs to interface with platforms and products; good documentation is essential for effective use. Consistent naming standards, well-documented code, and clear error messages can improve the usability of your product. Suppose the API or SDK is challenging to use or has insufficient documentation. In that case, developers may encounter difficulties integrating with your platform, leading to frustration and potentially discouraging them from using your product.

While designing documentation for an AI product, it is essential to consider the overall developer experience (DX), which includes onboarding, documentation, support, and UI design. Many standard practices must be adhered to while composing documentation that prioritizes DX. Here is the best approach:

- Prioritize usability by organizing the documentation logically and using clear headings and subheadings. The documentation should also be easy to search, read, and navigate. Use simple and accessible language that is easy for users to understand.

- Provide practical and specific guidance by offering step-by-step instructions on how to use the product. Use real-world examples to demonstrate how the product can be used in different scenarios.

- Accommodate developers' different learning styles by providing documentation in multiple formats, such as video tutorials and written guides. This ensures that the documentation is accessible to developers with varying learning preferences.

- Regularly update the documentation as the product evolves to remain current and accurate. This may involve modifying instructions, adding new sections, or updating images and videos.

- Seek developer feedback to identify improvement areas and optimize the overall user experience. This feedback can help refine the documentation and ensure it meets the needs and preferences of the developer community.

FaceTec is an example of an AIaaS company that stresses DX in their documentation. FaceTec provides developers with a range of APIs and SDKs, and their documentation is designed to be user-friendly, with clear headings, an intuitive navigation system, and extensive, step-by-step instructions on how to use their products. FaceTec also offers a range of learning methods, such as a comprehensive wiki, guides, video tutorials, and webinars. In addition, their website provides resources such as developer support and a dedicated FAQ section, thus improving the DX.

In conclusion, documentation is crucial to create a favorable developer experience for AI technologies. By focusing on usability, offering practical assistance, supporting a range of learning styles, maintaining up-to-date documentation, and requesting developer input, documentation can contribute to an amazing DX and eventually lead to product success.

Determining the Pricing Model and Packaging That Appeals to Developers

To build a successful AI product, it's crucial to determine a suitable pricing model and packaging strategy that appeals to developers. This section explores various pricing models and packaging strategies and provides guidance on identifying the best approach for your AI product. Crafting an effective pricing and packaging strategy can help your product stand out, attract developers, and achieve long-term success.

Packaging Strategies for AIaaS

This section will explore popular packaging methods that AI as a Service providers may consider. Packaging involves bundling AI-related services and products to create an attractive customer offering. Strategies may include grouping related services into packages, marketing individual services as standalone products, or developing customized offerings based on individual customer needs. The aim is to provide customers with clear and appealing options that meet their specific requirements and preferences. Determining proper packaging strategies can be challenging, but offering competitive and attractive offerings in the market is essential.

a. *All-in-one solution*: An all-in-one solution is a pre-packaged offering that provides customers with a complete range of AI services and products. This bundling method can simplify the purchasing and integration process, especially for new businesses seeking to offer a comprehensive solution. For instance, an AI startup providing a machine learning platform for the healthcare industry can bundle the platform with natural language processing, computer vision, and predictive analytics tools to provide a complete solution for healthcare providers.

b. *Standalone product*: Standalone products refer to individual AI services or solutions that are packaged independently and sold separately. This packaging method can benefit new businesses that want to give customers more flexibility in selecting the needed services. For example, a company that offers a natural language processing tool for customer support may package its tool as a standalone product and allow customers to add other AI services as needed. This would enable the startup to expand its market and attract more customers.

c. *Personalized services and products*: Customized solutions involve developing tailored offerings to meet each customer's unique needs, which are then packaged and sold to those customers. This packaging approach can benefit new businesses that want to differentiate themselves from competitors by providing personalized solutions to their clients. For example, a startup offering an AI-powered tool for inventory management could create customized solutions for customers based on their specific inventory requirements, such as demand forecasting, pricing optimization, and waste reduction.

Pricing Models for AIaaS

Pricing AI as a Service can be challenging for startups. Here are some common pricing structures for artificial intelligence that can be helpful for companies selling this type of product:

1. *Subscription-based pricing*: This model charges customers a recurring fee on a monthly or yearly basis, providing companies with steady revenue and customers with predictable costs. It is commonly used for AIaaS products, often combined with a free trial period to attract prospective buyers. For example, a startup providing a predictive analytics platform for ecommerce might price monthly memberships based on the number of users or transactions. CloudMinds and H2O.ai are AIaaS companies that offer subscription-based pricing models. CloudMinds charges customers based on the number of robots and devices connected to their AI-powered robotics platform, while H2O.ai charges customers based on the number of users and data scientists utilizing their AI platform.

2. *Usage-based pricing*: In this model, customers are charged based on the amount of the product they consume, making it attractive for AI solutions provided as a service. This pricing method is beneficial for new AI startups offering pay-as-you-go services, as it charges clients according to the value they receive from the product. For example, a startup offering a natural language processing tool for customer support could charge clients based on the number of requests the tool processes. OpenAI and Mighty AI are AIaaS companies that use different pricing models. OpenAI charges customers for their language processing technology API based on the number of API requests made, while Mighty AI charges customers for their training data platform based on the volume and complexity of the data they upload. OpenAI uses a usage-based pricing model, while Mighty AI uses a volume- and complexity-based pricing model. Paperspace offers plans based on the number of GPU hours used each month.

3. *Tiered pricing*: This model allows businesses to offer different service levels at different price points, catering to customers with varying needs and budgets. When combined with a free trial period, it can be an effective pricing strategy as it enables potential customers to try the product before committing to a purchase. For example, a startup offering a platform for image recognition could offer tiered pricing based on the number of images processed per month or the level of accuracy required. Clarifai and IBM Watson are AIaaS companies that offer tiered pricing models. Clarifai charges customers for their computer vision platform based on the number of API calls made each month, while IBM Watson charges customers for their AI platform based on the level of support, security, and customization required. Both companies use a tiered pricing model to offer different service levels at different price points to cater to their customers' varying needs and budgets.

Determining the right pricing and packaging strategy for an AI as a Service product is not a one-size-fits-all solution. Factors such as the target market, product attributes, and competition can all affect the most appropriate approach. Startups should remember that their pricing and packaging methods may evolve as their business grows.

To price and package their AIaaS product appropriately, firms need to know their target market and competitors. By staying current with market trends and consumer needs, startups can offer attractive products that meet customer desires and generate consistent revenue.

Customer Journey Mapping

Once pain points and pricing and packaging models have been identified, the next step is to analyze the customer journey. Understanding how customers interact with our products at each stage can reveal bottlenecks and areas for improvement. For example, if our marketing efforts are only reaching a small audience, there may be an issue with the awareness stage. We can then prioritize touchpoints, create engaging content, and attract more customers to our products.

In AIaaS, developers are a priority, and their needs should be met at each stage of their customer journey. This journey includes searching for solutions, comparing products, identifying offered solutions, and making a purchase (Figure 9-6). This process is not always linear and can occur at different rates. Our goal is to design each stage comprehensively with relevant promotion materials and be available to answer any questions they may have.

Figure 9-6. Typical customer journey map

There are several points along the developer journey, such as **Find**, **Assess**, **Absorb**, **Develop**, and **Scale**. Mapping out these touchpoints helps organizations identify shortcomings or friction in the developer journey, creating a better overall experience.

The following image summarizes how each stage affects the developer's decision-making process. You can also see a significant difference between the customer journeys for developers and users in general in the product development mindset and the ease of use when trying our product for the first time. Let's detail each stage or journey on the developer's side, from definitions to examples of appropriate content (Figure 9-7).

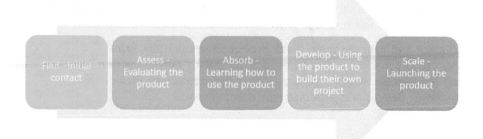

Figure 9-7. Developer's user journey

Find

Developers first encounter a product or service at the Find stage, assessing if it meets their needs and is trustworthy. At this stage, the goal is to generate excitement and provide resources such as demos, case studies, SEO, newsletters, and external touchpoints such as events and media placement.

Assess

At the Assess stage, developers evaluate the product for "red flags" and determine if it meets their needs. The goal is to address any concerns and keep them interested. High-quality resources like product pages, documentation, forums, and messaging tools can help.

Absorb

At the Absorb stage, developers test the product to ensure it meets their needs. The goal is to build their confidence in the product with high-quality, error-free documentation highlighting potential pitfalls. Resources like Getting Started guides, quick start guides, tutorials, and code samples help developers effectively use the product.

Develop

During the development touchpoint, the organization aims to keep developers interested and motivated to scale their products. Communication is crucial, so organizations should keep versioning and changes well-documented. Sandboxes and tools, such as test servers and interactive playgrounds, can help developers test the product efficiently. Quick response to questions via forums is important to keep developers encouraged.

Scale

The Scale stage is when developers launch their product or service and aim to reach more users. At this stage, organizations must ensure that their product meets the developer's and their users' needs. Developers' feedback should be considered, and any issues should be resolved promptly. Reference guides may include your API or SDK information and integrating your product with other technologies.

The developer journey is crucial for successful software products or services. Mapping the contact points between Find, Assess, Absorb, Develop, and Scale can improve the overall experience. Quality resources, product pages, documentation landing pages, FAQs, use cases and case studies, forums, community messaging tools, GitHub, and Stack Overflow can aid developers. At the same time, organizations must keep them motivated and ensure their product meets needs. A smooth developer experience leads to a better experience for all.

Developing a Marketing Strategy

The customer journey mapping from Find to Scale stages is connected, and success in one stage can impact the next. Effective marketing tactics that accommodate each stage are required to achieve long-term customer loyalty and advocacy, leading to a growth cycle. In the context of AIaaS, these tactics might include the following:

1. Create technical content:

    -   Publish a technical blog post that explains how to use a specific feature of the AIaaS product.

    -   Release a technical white paper that dives deep into the architecture and performance of the AIaaS product.

    -   Share code samples demonstrating how to integrate the AIaaS product into a specific programming language or framework.

2. Utilize demonstrations and proofs of concept:

    -   Create a demo video that shows the AIaaS product in action, highlighting key features and benefits.

    -   Offer a POC allowing potential customers to try the AIaaS product with their data.

3. Utilize communities for AI and ML:

    -   Join online communities such as Kaggle, GitHub, and Stack Overflow and share technical content related to the AIaaS product.

    -   Answer questions from community members and engage in discussions about the AIaaS product.

4. Offer free trials:

    -   Provide a limited-time free trial of the AIaaS product that allows potential customers to test its capabilities.

5. Collaborate with AI-focused businesses:

    -   Partner with a cloud hosting provider to offer the AIaaS product as part of their AI-focused services.

    -   Collaborate with an AI consulting firm to create a case study demonstrating the AIaaS product's effectiveness.

- Participate in AI conferences and events:
    - Attend an AI-focused conference and set up a booth to showcase the AIaaS product.
    - Host a workshop or presentation to demonstrate the capabilities of the AIaaS product and provide technical tips and tricks.
6. Utilize influencer marketing:
    - Partner with a data scientist or researcher with a large social media following and create a sponsored post promoting the AIaaS product.
    - Ask an AI influencer to create a video tutorial that shows how to use the AIaaS product.
7. Offer technical support:
    - Provide 24/7 technical support through email, chat, and phone for customers who need help using the AIaaS product.
    - Create a knowledge base or FAQ page addressing common issues and questions about the AIaaS product.

You can also engage customers through surveys and feedback sessions to gain insights and identify improvement opportunities. You can publish on a regular basis case studies and success stories that highlight the benefits of your products and services and how customers have used them to achieve their business objectives.

Your marketing strategy should focus on providing technical resources, free tools, and resources to convert potential customers into leads, personalized support and resources to convert leads into paying customers, and educational and training programs to help customers improve their AI skills and knowledge. By doing so, you can establish yourself as a leading AIaaS provider and cultivate a base of loyal AI developer community customers.

CASE STUDY 2 (AI AS A SERVICE): IDENTIFAI

Identifai is a product from Nodeflux, an AI company focusing on computer vision. Identifai provides face liveness detection, face matching, and ID optical character recognition as an identity verification service using deep learning technology (Figure 9-8).

Figure 9-8. Identifai Identity verification AIaaS

Liveness detection is a computer vision–based security technology that helps prevent fraud in biometrics authentication systems, particularly those that use facial recognition. It works by verifying that the biometrics input being provided is from a live, present individual and not a photograph or other artificial representations. In the banking and FinTech industries, liveness detection is crucial for preventing identity theft and fraud, as facial recognition technology is increasingly being used for identity verification and authentication. Without liveness detection, bad actors can use static images or videos to trick the system into granting access to sensitive financial information.

These AI models can be used in eKYC solutions for various use cases, including digital account openings, SIM card changes, driver verification for online ride-hailing, and social assistance through facial recognition. It's important to prioritize explainability when selling these analytics because they will be used in verification and validation processes.

Identifai eKYC has developed an advanced explainable artificial intelligence (XAI) capability that facilitates the interpretation and elucidation of facial feature analysis, encompassing aspects such as liveness detection and identification decision-making – leveraging cutting-edge XAI methodologies fostering trust and accountability in the eKYC system (Figure 9-9).

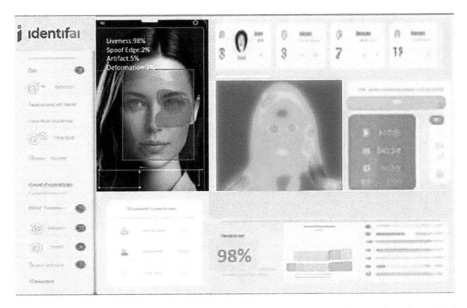

Figure 9-9. Identifai's USP is XAI capability can explain liveness decision based on facial features

XAI (explainable AI) capabilities provide decision-making transparency, which is crucial for FSI (Financial Services Industry) where accountability for activities such as opening account and disbursing funds are required.

Identifai's team believes that understanding developers' pain points is crucial before promoting a product. They conduct research to identify the audience's fears, needs, and desires to ensure that their products meet current demand. Identifai transforms these pain points into their product's unique selling proposition, such as developing explainable AI to explain liveness detection and face recognition results.

XAI for liveness detection in banking addresses multiple pain points, including fraud prevention by accurately detecting spoofing attacks and deepfake images, compliance with anti-money laundering and know your customer regulations through transparency and interpretability, and improving customer experience with a seamless onboarding process that reduces the need for in-person verification.

Identifai's team also determines the appropriate packaging and pricing based on the user's business characteristics. For example, in the banking industry, pricing is based on the number of people who register in a day. To convey this information to the appropriate audience, Identifai focuses on designing the customer journey, recognizing that digital channels play a critical role in each stage.

In the Find stage, Identifai promotes content centered on use cases via paid channels and organic media releases.

In the Assess stage, Identifai provides a product sheet and documentations that describe technical specifications and guide on how to use the eKYC platform (Figure 9-10).

Figure 9-10. The documentation page of Identifai

Identifai also offers a variety of content on their website, including demos, code samples, and a Getting Started guide. When a lead is attracted to Identifai, the sales team contacts the individual to inquire about their specific needs.

This high-touch marketing approach is sometimes important for products with a high technicality, such as Identifai, which targets developers.

Once leads become customers, Identifai conducts in-depth interviews and monthly product performance reviews to upsell or retain users. This enables developers or customers to provide feedback and contribute to product development or market validation.

Identifai understands that identifying pain points is a continuous process, particularly if the conditions of competition are getting tougher. Therefore, creating a unique selling proposition is essential to differentiate their products and stand out in the market.

Go-to-Market Strategy for AI (as a) Toolkit

AI toolkits are collections of software tools and frameworks that help developers and data scientists build and deploy AI applications. A GTM (go-to-market) strategy is important for AI toolkits because it enables companies to effectively bring their AI toolkits to market by identifying the target audience, understanding their pain points, and communicating the unique value proposition of their toolkit.

Understanding the Needs and Pain Points of Developers and Data Scientists

As mentioned in the previous chapters, AI toolkits allow developers to create, train, and deploy AI models using various platforms and libraries for machine learning, deep learning, computer vision, natural language processing, pre-trained models, data visualization, deployment, and development frameworks. These toolkits make it easy for developers with limited experience in AI or machine learning to build data acquisition, augmentation, and annotation pipelines, experiment with different models, and deploy them on various platforms. The main advantage of these products is that they enable users to create their own AI models based on their business needs without starting from scratch. Examples of AI toolkits are Landing AI, Viso AI, Clarifai, and Masterful AI, as well as data tools such as Snorkel and Scale AI.

AI (as a) Toolkit is a platform where users can experiment to develop customized AI solutions based on their business needs. This differs from AI as a Service products, which are more packaged and targeted toward a specific use case. Developers and data scientists are the primary target audience for AI toolkits. So it is important to understand what factors these segments consider when selecting an AI toolkit product:

a. *Time constraints*: AI toolkits can help developers build and deploy AI models faster with pre-built models, tools, and templates.

b. *Technical complexity*: AI toolkits can provide libraries and frameworks that abstract away complex algorithms and mathematical concepts, allowing developers without a background in data science to build AI models more quickly.

c. *Data management*: AI toolkits can include data visualization tools that make managing and cleaning large datasets easier for developers.

d. *Deployment issues*: AI toolkits provide infrastructure and deployment frameworks that make it easier to deploy AI models in production environments without extensive infrastructure expertise.

e. AI toolkits can update and improve their libraries and frameworks to keep developers and data scientists up to date on AI development.

To ensure the AI (as a) Toolkit product is successful, we need to understand who will use it. In this case, our users are developers and data scientists. These users have unique requirements and challenges that we need to consider. For example, factors like ease of use and compatibility with existing systems can influence a developer's decision to use our product. To determine this, the following steps must be taken to create personas to identify developers' and data scientists' pain points in more detail:

a. *Industry sector*: AI developers are employed in various industries, including healthcare, finance, retail, and manufacturing. You can better comprehend the unique challenges and pain points by segmenting by industry sector. AI developers face various contexts.

b. *Job title*: Depending on their specific organizational roles, artificial intelligence developers may have various job titles. Some specialize in data preprocessing, while others focus on model experimentation or deployment. By segmenting by job title, you can understand various AI developers' specific skill sets and expertise.

c. *Experience level*: Artificial intelligence developers may have varying experience levels, ranging from entry level to senior positions. Understanding the specific challenges and pain points developers face at various stages of their careers can be facilitated by segmenting by experience level.

d. *Geographic location*: Developers and data scientists are located worldwide, and their geographic location can affect their specific challenges and pain points. For instance, developers in developing nations may have less access to high-quality training data or resources. In contrast, those in developed countries may need to deal with higher AI performance due to intense competition.

e. *Company size*: Developers and data scientists may work for large corporations or small startups or as independent contractors. Understanding the various work environments, cultures, and expectations placed on AI developers can be facilitated by segmenting by company size.

f. *Programming language preference*: Developers and data scientists may have varying preferences for programming languages, such as Python, R, or Java. By segmenting developers based on their preferred programming language, you can determine which tools and resources they need to be successful.

To create products with specific applications, we begin by analyzing the industrial sector. For instance, when developing a product that utilizes computer vision, we identify the markets and industries that can benefit from this technology and the business processes that can be improved. With this knowledge, we can develop targeted marketing strategies and tailor our product development to meet the needs of our target audience. By understanding our target audience's goals, challenges, and pain points, we can create products and services that are more appealing to them.

Developing a User-Friendly and Comprehensive AI Toolkit

To ensure significant AI toolkit product adoption, the user-friendliness of AI products is an important consideration, followed by flexibility. Creating a single tool that caters to only one specific use case or industry requirement would waste money spent on research and development. In previous chapters, we covered the topic of AI product design. One of the main points that we went over was how creating an AI model as a toolkit ultimately needs to have the flexibility to be applied to various industries while also being closely related to a few specific use cases. If we develop an AI model for face recognition, for example, we need to think about the user and the use cases. The model can be used by law enforcement agencies, property owners who need round-the-clock monitoring, and city governments for urban supervision. These are only a few of the many possibilities that may arise from a single model. To make AI toolkits more user-friendly, it's important to consider factors beyond just developing multiple models:

1. *Emphasize usability*: Software developers and data scientists can find AI toolkits difficult to use. To solve this problem, make sure that your toolkit is user-friendly. This can be achieved by creating a simple and easy-to-use interface, providing detailed documentation and guides, and simplifying the installation and setup process as much as possible.

2. *Pre-built templates*: To help users overcome the learning curve when using your AI toolkit, you can provide pre-built models and pipelines as templates. This will enable users to get started more quickly and easily. Offering a variety of templates that cover different industries and use cases will be beneficial.

3. *Make available various development frameworks and library resources*: Provide development frameworks and libraries for common programming languages such as Python, Java, and JavaScript so that it is simple for developers to incorporate your AI toolkit into their existing workflows. This will make it easier for developers to use your AI toolkit.

4. *Offer data visualization tools*: The results that data scientists obtain from their AI models can be easily interpreted and visualized with the assistance of data visualization tools. Think about providing users with various tools that can be employed in producing charts, graphs, and other types of visualizations.

5. *Maintain scalability and flexibility*: As the requirements of your users evolve, they may require AI solutions that are both more powerful and more adaptable. Make sure that your toolkit is scalable enough to meet these requirements, and offer Application Programming Interfaces (APIs) to developers so that they can integrate your AI solutions with the applications and systems they already use.

6. *Offer support and training*: Even if you provide your users with an easy-to-use and comprehensive AI toolkit, they may still run into difficulties or need additional training. In this case, you should provide support and training. Help users get the most out of your AI toolkit by providing various support options, such as email support, community forums, in-app help, and training programs and resources.

By adhering to these steps, you can create an AI toolkit that is comprehensive and user-friendly. This toolkit will cater to the requirements and concerns of data scientists and software developers. This can help differentiate your product in the market and provide a valuable solution for those looking to construct and deploy AI models quickly and easily.

Determining the Pricing Model and Packaging That Appeals to Developers

When packaging an AI toolkit, it's important to consider the target audience's needs and the type of toolkit being developed. For instance, a deep learning toolkit may require more computational resources, which can be better suited for containerization or a virtual machine. Alternatively, a toolkit designed for beginner developers may benefit from a GUI or IDE packaging, while a more advanced toolkit may be better suited to a CLI or containerization approach. Once the packaging model is chosen, the next step is to determine the pricing model. Generally, there are three standard pricing models for AI toolkit products:

1. *Utilization-based pricing*: This pricing model can be attractive for data scientists and developers who may not require extensive use of the AI toolkit but may experience usage spikes. They can save money over time by paying only for what they consume.

2. *Price based on subscription*: This pricing model frequently appeals to developers and data scientists who employ the AI toolkit often. It also ensures they can always access the most recent updates and features.

3. *Different tiers*: Providing tiers can be an effective way to appeal to a greater variety of customers. For instance, offering a free tier with basic functionality can attract new users. More advanced features in higher-priced tiers can appeal to those requiring more robust functionality.

Some AI toolkit brands, such as Hugging Face, provide a free and open source version of their platform but charge for enterprise-level features and support. Others, including DataRobot, offer tiered pricing based on the number of users and the required level of support. Pricing and packaging of an AI toolkit should ultimately be determined by the needs of the target audience and the product's unique value proposition. The pricing strategy you choose for your AI toolkit should consider the value you provide to your target audience, the cost of developing and maintaining your product, and your competition. Here are some pricing strategies that could work well for different packaging options:

1. *Command-line interface (CLI)*: Considering that CLI is a common packaging option for AI toolkits, you may want to consider a competitive price for your product. Users could pay a monthly or annual fee to access your toolkit under a subscription-based model. Alternatively, you could offer a tiered pricing structure based on the number of users, the level of support provided, or the toolkit's features.

2. *Graphical user interface (GUI)*: A GUI could make working with the command line easier for developers and data scientists unfamiliar with it. This could make your product more appealing to novices, which may be willing to pay more for an intuitive interface. You could use a model in which users pay a one-time fee to gain access to your GUI toolkit.

3. *Integrated Development Environment (IDE)*: An IDE could be bundled with the AI toolkit to provide developers with a comprehensive development environment for working with the toolkit and creating AI models. Users could pay a monthly or annual fee to access your IDE toolkit, similar to CLI's subscription-based model.

4. *Containerization*: Containerization is an effective way to package and deploy AI models. It allows developers to use the same environment to run AI models on different machines and operating systems. Pricing can be based on the number of containers used, or a flat rate can be offered for a specific number of containers. Subscription-based pricing can also be an option.

5. *Virtual machine*: Similar to containerization, packaging an AI toolkit in a virtual machine can provide developers with a consistent environment to build, train, and deploy AI models. Users could pay a monthly or annual fee to access your VM toolkit under a subscription-based model.

How well AI toolkits do on the market depends significantly on how much they cost and how they are packaged. AI toolkits are complicated and high-tech products that need to be priced and packaged carefully to ensure they meet the intended audience's needs. Pricing and packaging strategy includes several factors that affect how the toolkit is seen, how it competes with other similar products, and how well it can make money.

One important thing to consider is whom the product is meant for, which can change depending on the industry, company size, and use case. Enterprise-level companies may have very different needs than small businesses. For example, a large organization may need scalability, reliability, and the ability to work with other systems. On the other hand, small businesses may want something that is easy to use and cheap and has a shorter learning curve. So a well-thought-out pricing and packaging strategy should consider how different audiences have different needs and tastes.

When making a good pricing strategy, it's also important to look into how competitors set their prices. By understanding industry standards and customer expectations, companies can find places where their AI toolkit may offer unique value that can be sold. Lastly, it's important to test and change the pricing model to ensure it fits what customers want and the market needs. Getting customer feedback and tracking how they use your product can show you where prices or packaging may need to be changed.

Designing a Customer Journey Map

AI (as a) Toolkit and AI as a Service differ in control and customization, development and maintenance effort, scalability, cost-effectiveness, and time to market resulting in different customer journeys. For AI toolkit products, the customer journey starts with research and evaluation, followed by installation, configuration, development, testing, deployment, and maintenance. In contrast, AI service products focus more on evaluation, integration, and scaling, with less emphasis on the development effort.

The customer journey for an AI toolkit product begins with research and evaluation of the various AI toolkits available. Customers may have specific needs they wish to fulfill, so they would seek out toolkits corresponding to those needs. After selecting a toolkit, customers must install and configure it. Next, customers must design, develop, and test their AI models or applications, which can require significant time and resources. Lastly, the client must deploy and maintain the AI solution in their environment, which may require ongoing effort and expense. We can use the following framework to design a customer journey so that we can provide appropriate collateral and services at each stage that the user goes through:

- *Awareness:* Like every product, the user's journey starts with finding the service that fits their needs. Therefore, our task in this phase is to utilize various touchpoints to build awareness of our brand and services. This activity can be in the form of social media posts that highlight the advantages of the services we have by previously defined pain points, blogging articles optimized through SEO, paid channels such as GDN or SEA for targeted users, making videos or webinars that focus on product introduction or services, and industry reports regarding the latest trends and use cases for the services we have.

- *Investigation and evaluation*: Once a potential user has discovered our AI toolkit product, they may compare it with similar products from different brands. As a product owner, it's important to provide content showcasing our product's unique benefits and features to ensure it's the best choice for solving their problems. For example, we can create product comparison tables that make it easy for users to see how our toolkits compare with others on the market. We can also create whitepapers or case studies demonstrating how our AI model can be used in various industries and share endorsements or reviews from satisfied customers to build trust and credibility. All of this content motivates users to understand the value of our solutions and choose our product.

- *Selection*: After a user expresses interest in our AI toolkit, they move on to evaluate the product's technical details, such as algorithms, precision, hardware, and software compatibility. This phase is called a POC or proof of concept, where the user will test and evaluate the AI model's accuracy and performance. It is essential to provide expert support or advice to the user, especially if they encounter problems during the process, to ensure that their technical needs and customization options are met. Good communication between the user and support team is essential, as many AI startups fail during this stage due to their products failing to meet customer expectations.

- *Installation and arrangement*: The installation begins after the user has tried the model. The POC is going well during this stage, and the consumer has decided to use our product. It is critical that we provide a detailed user manual guide that describes how to install or configure our model in various software and hardware. At this time, a how-to video instructional could be one of the supporting resources. Don't forget that the help forum or chatbot must be prepared to answer any issues the user may encounter during the procedure.

- *Design and development*: After installation and configuration, the user creates and tests the AI models or applications. This phase can take a long time, depending on the project's complexity and the customer's available resources. Although the customer has already committed to the product, they may still analyze its efficiency and precision. To help with this, providing documentation and download links that give users guidance and access to the AI tools and allow for customization is essential. We should also offer example codes or templates to make it easier for users to create AI-based applications or integrate the AI models into their products.

- *Deployment*: After developing and evaluating the AI models or apps, clients can deploy them within their environment. In this phase, we must provide multiple documents, such as instructions and checklists, to help the client install our AI model into their environment. It's important to provide support resources if any issues arise during this process.

- *Maintenance*: After the AI system has been deployed, the customer is responsible for its maintenance to ensure continued accuracy and performance. This requires ongoing effort and resources, such as software updates, hardware upgrades, and troubleshooting. As the selection process has passed and the customer has committed to the product, ongoing technical support and maintenance services are necessary. We can provide documentation or a knowledge base with articles offering troubleshooting help or detailing new features and updates. It's also important to communicate any changes to algorithms, precision, or customization to existing clients through email updates.

Let's take an example of a provider offering AI as a Toolkit, specifically for face recognition, gesture analysis, and demographic recognition for surveillance cases. Suppose a business wants to upgrade the security of their facilities by adding these analytics to their security system. To do so, they start by researching and evaluating various AI toolkits in the market. During this phase, they consider factors like the toolkit's precision, functionality, compatibility, and cost-effectiveness.

Once they find the right toolkit, they move to the installation and configuration phase, installing the software and configuring it to work with their security system. The toolkit provider may offer technical help or training to assist customers during this phase.

Next, they move to the design, development, and testing phase, using the AI toolkit to create their face recognition model, with gesture recognition and demographic recognition. This phase requires a significant investment of time and resources to ensure that the model identifies persons accurately and functions reliably.

After creating the model and the analytics pipeline, they move to the deployment phase, installing the AI model's system in their environment, which may require ongoing maintenance and updates.

Overall, the customer experience for an AI toolkit product goes through various phases, including research, evaluation, installation, configuration, design, development, deployment, and maintenance, each with different time and resource requirements. The duration of each phase may vary depending on the project's complexity and the client's available resources.

Building a Partnership Strategy

A channel is how a business communicates with its customers and shares information. Unlike traditional media like TV or newspapers, channels facilitate two-way communication between businesses and customers, making them more effective for sales. Channels can be direct, indirect, or direct-to-customer sales channels. With the increasing demand for AI-based products and services, businesses must establish effective distribution channels to reach their target audience and offer excellent customer support. For AI toolkits, it's especially important to have distributors and system integrators on board to ensure successful product integration. Before exploring partnerships with distributors and system integrators, let's first understand the three common channel classifications used in many industries:

1. *Direct channel*: This is the traditional way where a company directly sells its products or services to customers through a sales force. It is best used for big ticket sales that require complex processes.

2. *Indirect channel*: Intermediaries such as agents, resellers, and distributors provide value-added services such as installation, support, and configuration to increase the reach and consolidate services into unified products.

3. *Direct-to-customer channel*: Businesses can directly sell their products or services to customers without intermediaries through methods such as direct mail, telephone, or the Internet. This can reduce costs and reach a wider audience, but there may be limitations such as the absence of customer support and customization options.

The nature of your product plays a significant role in determining the most suitable sales channel for it. For instance, AI as a Toolkit is too complex to be directly sold to customers, while SaaS products like Workplace and ClickUp are simple enough to be marketed online. Since the effective adoption of AI solutions requires personalized assistance and technical support, low-cost channels like direct sales are not the best fit for promoting this kind of products.

When deciding which sales channel to use for your product, it's important to consider four key factors:

- The first is the complexity and customizability of the product, as more complex and customizable products often require more involved distribution methods.

- The second factor to consider is the clarity of the product's advantages, as this can impact the effectiveness of different sales channels.

- The third factor is the level of risk and uncertainty involved in the product, as more risky or uncertain products may require more specialized distribution channels.

- Finally, the level of difficulty of the negotiations involved in selling the product should also be taken into account.

  By taking these factors into consideration, you can select a distribution method that is compatible with your product and maximizes your sales.

In this section, we will discuss two types of sales channels that play a critical role in the success of AI products as toolkits during the go-to-market (GTM) stage: distributors and system integrators. However, before diving deeper, let's first understand the differences between these two types of channels. A distributor is an intermediary who purchases items from principals and resells them to end users or other channel partners. In contrast, a system integrator is an intermediary who combines hardware, software, and other components to produce a full solution for end users. The following are some important distinctions between distributors and system integrators:

1. *Product offering*: Typically, distributors offer a wide selection of items from numerous principals, whereas system integrators design bespoke solutions employing specific products and technology.

2. *Sales process*: Distributors normally sell products, whereas system integrators sell full solutions that match the specific demands of their customers. They frequently collaborate with customers to understand their needs and build and deploy solutions to satisfy those demands.

3. *Value-added services*: While distributors may provide technical support, training, and warranty services, system integrators often provide a broader range of services, such as design, installation, configuration, and continuing support.

4. *Customer relationships*: While distributors have a vast customer base, they may not have as deep a relationship with their customers as system integrators, who frequently work directly with customers over a longer period of time to design and execute solutions that match their individual needs.

5. *Margin*: Typically, distributors have smaller margins than system integrators, who may charge greater fees for value-added services and customization work.

Ultimately, while distributors and system integrators both play key roles in the channel, their focuses and business models are very different. Distributors are concerned with selling products, whereas system integrators are concerned with selling entire systems and offering value-added services to their clients.

Partnership with Distributors

When selling a product such as an AI toolkit, it is crucial to choose the appropriate distributor. These are some important factors to consider while choosing a distributor:

1. *Expertise and experience*: Search for a distributor with knowledge and experience in your business and product area. Distributors with a demonstrated track record of selling and promoting similar items can help you reach your target audience more successfully.

2. *Market reach*: Evaluate the market reach of the distributor and their ability to penetrate your target markets. You can increase your market presence more rapidly with the assistance of distributors who have an extensive network of connections and established ties with key clients and suppliers.

3. *Financial stability*: Engaging with a financially reliable distributor who can handle a high volume of sales and offer consistent payment terms is essential. A financially unstable distributor could affect your sales income and cash flow. Thus, it is essential to perform due diligence before choosing a choice.

4. *Customer service and support*: Look for a distributor that offers excellent customer service, including technical support, training, and after-sales service, to ensure customer satisfaction and retention.

5. *Marketing and promotion*: Ensure your chosen distributor can effectively sell and promote your product. They should have a strong marketing and sales team that can create targeted campaigns, generate leads, and build brand recognition.

6. *Product knowledge and training*: Verify that the distributor thoroughly understands your product and can provide excellent training to their sales team. A distributor with a well-trained sales force can better convey the characteristics and benefits of your product, resulting in increased sales.

7. *Compatibility and fit*: Assessing the compatibility and fit between your organization and the distributor is crucial. The distributor must share your values and culture and be willing to collaborate with you to reach your sales objectives.

To successfully sell an AI toolkit, it is essential to choose the right distributor carefully. This decision is critical to reaching target customers, building market presence, and maximizing the product's potential. Conducting proper research and thoroughly evaluating potential distributors is important to establish a mutually beneficial partnership. Considering these factors, you can select a distributor that will help you sell your AI toolkit more effectively.

Partnership with a System Integrator

AI toolkits require careful system integrator (SI) partner selection. First, the SI should know AI and related technologies. This ensures high-quality service. Another factor is the SI's product modification ability. Businesses need a SI partner to customize AI as a Toolkit. The SI should also have worked with similar companies in the same industry to understand the particular issues businesses face.

AI products as toolkits require more personalized sales approaches compared with low-cost channels such as direct-to-customer. System integrators can help ensure the proper integration of AI solutions. Therefore, when selecting a system integrator partner, startups that offer AI toolkits should consider the following factors:

1. *Technical expertise*: Technical expertise is the first and most significant factor to consider. The system integrator you select should have experience designing and integrating AI technologies. They should be well-versed in the most recent AI technologies, tools, and platforms and be able to recommend the best solutions based on your requirements.

2. *Industry knowledge*: Industry knowledge is another crucial thing to consider. The system integrator should be knowledgeable about your industry, company procedures, and difficulties. This will allow them to adapt their solutions to your demands better.

3. *Track record*: It is critical to examine the system integrator's track record to establish their capacity to execute high-quality work. Look for testimonials, case studies, and references to assess their prior performance and dependability.

4. *Cultural fit*: A partnership with a system integrator entails tight collaboration and communication between teams. To have a seamless and fruitful working relationship, ensure that the partner's culture corresponds with your own.

5. *Support and maintenance*: Consider the system integrator's support and maintenance services next. To ensure the success of their AI system, they will need to provide ongoing support and maintenance. Check to see if the system integrator provides these services and has a process to deal with faults and changes.

Selecting the right system integrator is critical to deploying AI as a Toolkit. A competent system integrator will have both technical expertise and experience in the industry, enabling them to design, customize, and integrate AI solutions effectively. By carefully considering these factors, businesses can choose the right system integrator to deploy and integrate AI as a Toolkit. Properly selecting a system integrator will ensure the successful deployment and integration of AI, resulting in improved efficiency, better decision-making, and a competitive edge.

Developing a Marketing Strategy

In a previous section, we explained that AI as a Toolkit differs from AI as a Service regarding target audience and product characteristics. AI as a Service targets end users from specific businesses or developers and prioritizes usability, cost savings, and rapid deployment as the value proposition, while AI as a Toolkit targets developers and data scientists and prioritizes customization, control, and the ability to create more complex AI applications. As a result, this affects how value propositions and messages are crafted, marketing channels are chosen, marketing materials are developed, and measurement is done.

A marketing strategy is a crucial part of the go-to-market (GTM) strategy. After developing a product, the focus shifts toward how to make it known to the target audience, generating interest and driving purchases. Identifying the target audience is essential to both the GTM and marketing strategy stages, but the purpose is different. In the GTM strategy stage, it's about identifying the target audience for the entire product development process, while in the marketing strategy stage, it's about exploring the appropriate message framework for the selected channel and target market. To create a marketing strategy, several steps need to be taken.

The first step to creating a marketing strategy is to identify what you want to achieve. For example, for an AI toolkit product, the goals could be to get more developers to use it, keep current customers happy, and be recognized as a leader in the AI industry. You can set specific goals like getting a certain number of new customers, making sure current customers use the toolkit more, or writing articles about the product in industry publications or social media. For instance, you might set a goal to gain 500 new customers in the next six months to increase adoption among developers or write two blog articles every month to establish the brand as an AI thought leader.

1. *Develop a marketing message:* The marketing message for an AI toolkit product should focus on how the product can help developers create intelligent applications faster and more efficiently than they could with other tools. The message should emphasize the toolkit's ease of use, versatility, and compatibility with different programming languages and platforms. You may also want to highlight unique features that differentiate the product from competitors. Example: Our AI toolkit empowers developers to create intelligent applications faster and more efficiently. Its ease of use, versatility, and compatibility with multiple programming languages and platforms make it the perfect tool for any AI project. Our AI toolkit is designed by experts in the AI space and backed by years of research and development. With its cutting-edge features and intuitive interface, it's the tool of choice for developers who want to stay ahead of the curve.

2. *Select marketing channels*: To effectively market an AI toolkit product to developers, it's important to choose the appropriate marketing channels based on their behavior and preferences. Online communities such as Twitter and LinkedIn may be effective in reaching developers who are active on social media, while webinars and tutorials can help educate developers about the benefits of the toolkit and how to use it effectively. Additionally, content marketing through blog articles and whitepapers can establish the brand as a thought leader in AI.

3. *Create marketing materials*: The marketing materials for an AI toolkit product may include product demos, tutorials, code examples, and case studies demonstrating the toolkit's capabilities and how it can be used to solve real-world problems. The materials should be high quality, engaging, and consistent with the brand's voice and style. You may also want to create videos or visual content to showcase the product's features and functionality. Example: Product demos that showcase the toolkit's features and functionality, tutorials and code examples that show how to use the toolkit to solve real-world problems, and case studies that demonstrate the toolkit's impact on businesses and organizations.

In essence, education should be a priority, and you need to explain how your product works and its benefits as an AI toolkit. However, digital marketing may not be the best option if your target audience is the government. Instead, you can partner with an organization that has an extensive network in the government or join an association to distribute your message effectively. By tailoring your approach to your target audience, you can maximize the effectiveness of your marketing strategy and promote your AI product successfully.

CASE STUDY 3 (AI TOOLKIT):VISIONAIRE

Visionaire AI (visionaire.ai) is a product developed by Nodeflux, a leading computer vision company. It is an AI toolkit that integrates and deploys various computer vision AI models, such as face recognition, license plate recognition, crowd estimation, and vehicle classification. Nodeflux has identified that the product is too complex to be marketed directly to end users who may not have adequate knowledge of AI development and integration to appreciate its value. Hence, they have targeted their marketing efforts toward developers and data scientists, who are the main users of this product. Visionaire is an AI toolkit product that offers various computer vision models that can be customized to meet users' unique needs (Figure 9-11). These models include object detection, object recognition, event recognition, and face recognition for images and video streaming.

Figure 9-11. Visionaire computer vision integration engine

Visionaire offers a highly flexible solution to deploy computer vision models that cater to various platforms, including Web, virtual machines, or bare-metal machines via containers (Docker). This ability to deploy on multiple platforms makes it easier for engineers to develop, test, and deploy models compatible with different types of cameras. By providing a solution that is not restricted to a specific hardware or software platform, Visionaire enables engineers to focus on developing their models without worrying about compatibility issues. The use of containers (Docker) ensures that the deployment of computer vision models is streamlined, as it allows for the creation of a portable and consistent environment for model deployment. This approach eliminates the need for additional setup or configuration, thereby increasing efficiency and reducing errors. Here are some possible use cases where Visionaire could be utilized:

- *Object detection*: A retail store wants to detect product placement on shelves to optimize stock levels and prevent stockouts.

- *Object recognition*: A manufacturer wants to inspect products on the assembly line to identify defects and reduce waste.

- *Event recognition*: A security company wants to detect and recognize abnormal behavior in surveillance footage to prevent security breaches.

- *Face recognition*: A government agency wants to verify the identities of individuals at border checkpoints to improve security and prevent illegal entry.

The Nodeflux team recognized that their AI toolkit product, Visionaire, was too complex to be marketed directly to end users who might not possess the necessary knowledge of AI development and integration to grasp its value. In response, they aimed to provide more than just a product but a solution that could seamlessly integrate into existing systems.

This led to the development of Visionaire as an integration platform, enabling easier adoption and implementation of computer vision AI models such as face recognition, license plate recognition, crowd estimation, and vehicle classification, among others. Over time, Nodeflux learned that the main problem in the Indonesian market was integration. Many existing CCTV systems were installed, and replacing them would be a huge task. Nodeflux knew that if they could integrate their product easily with existing systems, they would have a much better chance of success.

They worked hard to ensure that Visionaire could integrate easily with existing CCTV systems, regardless of the brand.

They also made sure that their computer vision models could be deployed on various platforms such as the Web, virtual machines, or bare-metal machines via containers like Docker.

This allowed maximum flexibility for their users, regardless of their technical expertise. Nodeflux's efforts paid off. Visionaire quickly became the go-to solution for many industries, from government agencies to retail businesses. They had created a product that was powerful and easy to use and integrate. They had made computer vision technology accessible to the masses.

Today, Nodeflux continues to innovate and improve its products, always aiming to make them more user-friendly and accessible. They are proud to have made a difference in the lives of many people and businesses across Indonesia, and they know that they have much more to offer.

As Visionaire aims to provide a flexible and integrated computer vision solution to various industries, it becomes clear that they cannot do everything alone. They need partners to assist them with deploying, marketing, distributing, and packaging various analytics to solve many business problems. To address this, Nodeflux has implemented a signature partnership model called Nodeflux Catalyst, which offers three options to partners. These options include technology partners, value-added resellers, and distributors. The technology partners focus on supporting additional technologies and integration methods, while value-added resellers add value to Visionaire's platform to create an end-to-end solution to specific business problems. Meanwhile, distributors are responsible for increasing product reach in specific markets and acting as Visionaire's field sales team in different geographies.

Regarding the marketing strategy, Visionaire has focused on combined online and offline approaches. The offline approach is mostly through events such as exhibitions and in-person events. Due to highly complex and customized products, Visionaire requires high-touch marketing. Field sales are essential in explaining the product and how it works, leading to calls to action that lead to meetings or the website. Furthermore, SEO optimization focuses on education and commercial intent. While digital marketing and events are marketing channels for up-funnel leads, the contribution of field sales and other teams is crucial for sales.

In summary, Visionaire's journey has shown that the product's characteristics significantly affect how it is marketed and sold. Direct-to-consumer channels and self-service approaches would be disastrous for Visionaire if they were the main marketing strategies. Providing an end-to-end solution to a business problem is also a significant undertaking. Therefore, other entities are needed to create a comprehensive solution that the market can adopt.

Conclusion

AI startups face unique challenges when bringing their products to market. Therefore, it's essential to select an appropriate go-to-market strategy. There are three AI products: AI as a Solution, AI as a Service, and AI (as a) Toolkit. Each requires a unique approach to the go-to-market strategy.

For AI solutions, the go-to-market strategy should be comprehensive and focus on creating value, establishing a sales and marketing strategy, and identifying channels to reach the target customers. Customer support and appropriate pricing are also essential.

For AI as a Service, the strategy should focus on providing a robust platform that integrates well with the customers' existing infrastructure, is easy to use, and offers clear documentation, API documentation, and support. The sales and marketing approach should focus on developers and businesses looking to enhance their products with AI capabilities.

For AI toolkits, the strategy should focus on providing versatile and sophisticated tools that can handle complex data processing tasks and enable developers to build sophisticated AI models. Detailed documentation, tutorials, and support must be provided. The sales and marketing approach should focus on technical audiences who are looking for advanced AI capabilities to build their models.

The go-to-market strategy is not a stage worked on in the middle of a company's journey but is an initial foundation to observe how relevant the product is to solving business problems. The product character drives all existing elements, from the target customer, value proposition, and channel to the pricing model.

Partnerships are critical for AI startups to succeed. They can help with limited resources, market access, and technical capabilities. AI startups can partner with technology companies to integrate or develop new products, consulting firms for customized solutions, research institutions for expertise, or other AI startups to collaborate on new products or services. Investors and venture capital firms can also provide funding and mentoring. AI startups should ensure the partnership is a good fit for their goals and values and mutually beneficial and bring complementary skills and resources. Overall, partnerships are essential to the go-to-market strategy for AI solutions, AI as a Service, and AI toolkits.

Key Takeaways

- A successful go-to-market strategy for AI products requires a nuanced approach considering the product type and target market needs.

- Understanding the product's complexity, sales and marketing approach, and customer support needs is crucial for achieving business success in offering AI as a solution, service, or toolkit.

- A go-to-market strategy for AI startups varies based on the product type, which affects audience segmentation, pricing, packaging, distribution, and marketing strategy.

- Providing clear documentation, tutorials, and support to help customers seamlessly integrate the platform is essential for AI as a Service.

- The sales and marketing approach for AI as a Solution should focus on highlighting the product's benefits and identifying channels that reach the target customers.

- AI as a Toolkit requires detailed documentation, tutorials, and support to help developers get started with the platform.

- Pricing and packaging should be appropriate for the target audience.

- Direct-to-customer channels may only be suitable for up-funnel needs, and field sales still play a crucial role due to the complexity of AI products.

- The differences between AI product types require different messaging frameworks to communicate effectively with the target audience.

- Providing exceptional customer support, identifying effective marketing channels, and appropriately pricing and packaging the product are critical to business success.

- Developing a comprehensive strategy that addresses the target customers' needs is crucial for sustainable growth and success.

- Partnerships can provide AI startups with critical resources, access to new markets and customers, and opportunities for collaboration and innovation.

- Partnering with other AI startups can lead to developing new products or services, sharing technical expertise, and pooling resources to overcome common challenges.

- When pursuing partnerships, AI startups must ensure that the partnership is a good fit for their business goals and values and is mutually beneficial.

- The product's characteristics drive all existing elements from the target customer, value proposition, and channel to the pricing model and should be considered when developing a go-to-market strategy for AI startups.

AI Startup Exit Strategy

As discussed in the previous chapters, building a successful AI startup is no easy feat. It requires a deep understanding of complex technology, its operationalization, a sound business model, and the ability to navigate complex market dynamics. But once a startup has gained traction and is on the path to success, the founders need to start thinking about their exit strategy.

This chapter will explore the various exit options available to AI startups and why founders must plan their exit in advance. We will also discuss why companies seek to acquire AI startups and the factors that impact their acquisition decisions.

Furthermore, we will provide practical advice for AI startup founders on identifying potential acquirers, evaluating their strategic value, navigating the due diligence process, negotiating a fair deal, and transferring ownership. Clear communication with customers and partners throughout the exit process is also essential, and we will discuss strategies for managing those relationships.

Using case studies, we will provide a real-world example of AI startups that have successfully exited and share the lessons learned along the way. By the end of this chapter, you will better understand the exit options available to AI startups, the factors that influence acquisition decisions, and how to prepare for a successful exit.

© Adhiguna Mahendra 2023
A. Mahendra, *AI Startup Strategy*, https://doi.org/10.1007/978-1-4842-9502-1_10

Introduction

The demand for AI solutions is increasing rapidly, resulting in the emergence of new AI companies.

By 2030, the global AI market is projected to contribute US $15.7 trillion to the global market, presenting a significant opportunity for businesses to drive innovation and create value.

AI adoption enables businesses to automate routine tasks, increase productivity, and make accurate predictions and recommendations in all industry sectors.

However, the potential benefits of AI must be balanced with the risks and challenges associated with bias, privacy violations, and employment impact. Despite these challenges, many companies, from tech giants like Google, Microsoft, and Amazon to startups like Nodeflux, Aire, AlphaSense, and Formation AI, are investing heavily in AI research and development to remain competitive in the market.

In addition to the examples of emerging AI startups, generative AI is also taking the world by storm. ChatGPT, Midjourney, and DALL-E are notable examples of generative AI startups gaining industry attention. ChatGPT, a language model trained by OpenAI, has been widely adopted for text generation tasks such as writing, customer service, and content creation. Midjourney's generative AI platform offers various services, including voice cloning and audio production, while DALL-E, also developed by OpenAI, generates images from textual descriptions. These examples demonstrate the growing influence of generative AI on various industries and highlight the potential for further innovation and disruption in the future.

This chapter discusses the exit options for AI startups, including acquisition and merger, and how to achieve a successful exit. We examine the strategic acquirer for AI companies, which could be any company interested in acquiring the AI company for strategic reasons aligned with their business goals. Furthermore, we provide strategies for increasing the likelihood of a positive outcome, drawing on case studies benchmarking 58 AI companies worldwide.

The Gold Rush of AI

The increasing adoption of artificial intelligence (AI) by businesses has led to a surge in the acquisition of AI startups. AI startups are considered attractive acquisition prospects, particularly after the pandemic, as companies seek to benefit from AI and machine learning technologies. Major corporations such as Google, Microsoft, and IBM have invested billions of dollars in AI companies across every industry and business function imaginable. This gold rush of AI is driven by the potential for productivity gains and cost savings, with companies rushing to capitalize on AI's benefits before their competitors. China and the European Union have also made significant investments in AI, reflecting the global importance of this technology.

Numerous AI firms have been acquired for different reasons. For example, Microsoft acquired Nuance, an AI-based technology company that provides speech recognition and voice transcription services, for $19.7 billion.

Facebook acquired Scape Technologies, a computer vision firm that uses AI to build a real-time 3D globe map using conventional pictures and videos, for $40 million. IBM acquired Turbonomic, an AI-powered Software Resource Management startup, to improve performance and save costs through AIOps.

Apple acquired Xnor.ai, a Seattle-based business focusing on the optimal application of AI in peripheral devices such as cell phones and drones. For $200 million, IBM acquired Databand.ai to enhance the trustworthiness of their AI products.

These acquisitions are designed to integrate AI technology further into core platforms and advance AI application development.

Exit Strategies of AI Startups

AI startups have different exit strategies that they can pursue to cash in their investments and efforts. One of the most common exit strategies is an initial public offering (IPO). However, this is rare for AI startups as it requires significant financial resources, a well-established track record, and a stable business model. Examples of AI startups that have successfully gone public include Darktrace, Babylon, and SentinelOne.

Another exit strategy for AI startups is an acquisition by larger companies. This has become a popular option, allowing AI startups to take advantage of the acquiring company's resources, network, and market presence. Examples of successful acquisitions of AI startups include AI.Reverie acquired by Facebook, VisionFactory by Google, Emotient by Apple, and Semantic Machines by Microsoft.

The acquisition is often the best option for AI startups because AI technologies are constantly evolving and becoming obsolete rapidly. Being acquired by a larger company provides the startup with access to the resources necessary to keep up with the latest advancements and stay competitive.

On the other hand, acquiring an AI startup also has several advantages for the acquirers. Firstly, it allows the acquirer to quickly access new technologies, expertise, and talent that can enhance their existing product offerings or help them enter new markets. This access to new technology and expertise can give the acquirer a competitive advantage over their rivals by assisting them to stay ahead of the curve in innovation and cutting-edge technology.

Additionally, acquiring an AI startup can be a faster and more cost-effective way for a company to gain access to new AI technology or expertise compared with developing these capabilities in-house. Moreover, it can help mitigate risk by reducing the time and cost associated with developing new technology or capabilities in-house and by providing a ready-made solution already tested in the market. Some examples of companies that have benefited from acquiring AI startups include Facebook's acquisition of Wit.ai for natural language processing capabilities, Google's acquisition of DeepMind for deep learning expertise, and Microsoft's acquisition of Semantic Machines for conversational AI technology.

I believe the acquisition is the best way to exit an AI startup. Therefore, the rest of the chapter will focus on successfully planning and executing an exit strategy through acquisition.

Why Companies Acquire

Companies acquire other companies, including AI startups, to build on their strengths and weaknesses and achieve their business strategy. This method, also known as business acquisition or takeover, involves taking control of the interest and management of a targeted company. A company's management team needs to analyze the market and consider how acquiring a company, including AI startups, can help achieve their business goals. Acquiring AI startups is often a strategic decision, as the startups may have unique technologies, talent, or intellectual property aligned with the acquirer's business strategy.

Established companies often acquire AI startups as a strategic move to strengthen their market position by leveraging the startups' capabilities and competencies in AI. One reason for the acquisition is the long-term bet to accelerate the overall business growth, as seen in Google's acquisition of DeepMind, Amazon's acquisition of Zoox, and Microsoft's acquisition of Lobe.

Another reason is to strengthen the core AI platform by enhancing existing AI capabilities, such as Tesla's acquisition of DeepScale, ServiceNow's acquisition of Element AI and Loom Systems, and Skyfii's acquisition of CrowdVision.

Companies may also acquire AI startups to add AI capability by integrating AI to have a stronger proposition in the market, as demonstrated by SAP's acquisition of Qualtrics.

Another motive for acquisition is to acquire talented individuals who can contribute to the development of the acquiring company, such as Apple's acquisition of Camerai. Companies may also acquire credentials such as ISO, standard, permit, certification, or license, which can increase their credibility in the market.

Acquiring base markets and IP (intellectual property) can enhance the acquirer's valuation. Finally, acquiring institutional knowledge is also a possible reason for the acquisition. Functional knowledge in banking, manufacturing, or other areas is precious if the acquiring company's management team lacks SME.

Technical know-how in AI operationalization is another valuable type of institutional knowledge that companies may seek through the acquisition.

In addition to the preceding reasons, another factor driving the acquisition of AI startups is the exclusive access to valuable datasets and partnerships that can help the acquiring company gain a competitive advantage in the market. Acquiring an AI startup can provide the acquiring company access to new and unique datasets that are not publicly available, giving them a head start in developing cutting-edge AI models. Furthermore, acquiring AI startups can also provide exclusive partnerships with other companies, research institutions, or government agencies, which can help the acquiring company stay ahead of the competition. For instance, Facebook's acquisition of Wit.ai and Google's acquisition of DeepMind provided access to new technologies and expertise and helped secure exclusive partnerships with leading research institutions in the field of AI.

The Importance of an Exit Plan

In the world of tech startups, it's often said that *companies are not bought but sold*. This means that the founders of startups need to have an exit strategy planned from the beginning. They must always be ready to optimize all the essential aspects that can make their startup more attractive to potential acquirers.

The importance of planning an exit strategy cannot be overstated because failing to do so will leave the money on the table or, worst, leave the startup with zero value.

Instead of waiting for an acquirer to make an offer, founders should actively seek out potential acquirers who align with their startup's strategic values and will appreciate its full range beyond just the financial aspect. In doing so, founders can optimize their exit strategy and secure the best possible deal for their startup at the right time.

Without an exit strategy, founders may find themselves stuck with a company that has become stagnant or is no longer profitable, without any clear way to liquidate their investment. To avoid this, founders must consider their company's financial and strategic values, such as its intellectual property, unique selling proposition, and potential market share. By doing so, they can target the most appropriate acquirers and maximize the value of their startup.

One of the essential aspects of optimizing the value of a startup is targeting suitable acquirers. This requires founders to understand their industry and what acquirers seek in a startup. By identifying these factors early on, founders can tailor their company to be as attractive as possible to potential acquirers. This means focusing on building a strong brand and a unique product while keeping an eye on potential acquirers and their seeking.

It's easy for founders to get lost in the day-to-day operations of their startup and forget about the end game of AI startups. However, planning for an exit from the beginning is crucial. This means clearly understanding the startup's value, targeting suitable acquirers, and being ready to sell at the right time. Ultimately, a well-planned exit strategy can be the difference between success and failure for a tech startup.

Many founders of AI startups are missing out on potential success by waiting too long to sell their companies. In the fast-paced world of AI, products can become obsolete quickly due to changes in technology and the market. If founders do not sell at the right time, they risk losing everything they have worked for. They must take action and sell the AI startup when the time is right, or they may be left with nothing.

I believe that any AI startup founder must find the potential acquisitor as early as possible and sell when they are at the top of the game instead of selling when they have to.

Factors Impacting AI Startup Acquisition

The success of an AI startup acquisition depends on various factors that can impact the outcome. In our analysis of around 36 AI startups that have been successfully acquired, we have identified some of the most critical factors that can make a difference:

- *Strategic fit:* Avoid competing with big tech giants. Instead, find a strategic case where they can acquire an AI startup that will increase their strategic value, for example, Microsoft's acquisition of Semantic Machines for conversational AI technology. The data also shows that only a small percentage (19%) of AI companies are acquired by companies within the same industry, as exemplified by the acquisition of Aidence, an AI-based radiology imaging company, by RadNet, a medical imaging company. This suggests that strategic match is more critical than industry similarity regarding AI acquisitions.

- *Focus on vertical products*: Most of the AI startups (87%) in the study focus on vertical products, which are specialized for specific industries. Strategic acquirers for these products are companies seeking to enhance their business with a specialized, vertical AI product. Only 13% of the companies in the study focus on horizontal products. An example is Gap's acquisition of CB4 Analytics, a vertical AI-based retail analytics serving the retail market.

- *The management team*: The management team must consist of senior subject matter experts such as senior business executives and AI specialists with PhD and track records (as in publications and patents) and real-world implementation experience. An example is Apple's acquisition of Emotient, whose co-founders were PhDs with expertise in AI, and the management also consists of experienced industry executives.

- *High-value business case*: The AI product must solve high-value business cases (i.e., add revenue or reduce cost significantly). An example is AppDynamics, an AI-based SaaS company for performance management and IT operations analytics that Cisco acquired in 2017 for $3.7 billion. AppDynamics's AI-powered platform helps businesses monitor and optimize the performance of their applications, which is a critical function for many enterprise companies. The acquisition helped Cisco expand their IT management and analytics tools portfolio, and the high-value business case made AppDynamics an attractive target for acquisition.

- *Robust*: The MVP (Minimum Viable Product) mindset doesn't work well for AI, and founders must prove that the AI product works and can handle edge cases better than humans. An example is Vicarious, which developed a robust AI platform that uses the computational principles of the human brain to process information and learn from experience. Its technology can handle complex robotics tasks with excellent accuracy. In 2022, Vicarious was acquired by Intrinsic, an Alphabet company.

- *Reputable customers*: Most successfully acquired AI startups have a brand name as their customers, and due to the AI complexity, most AI startups are acquiring customers and early adopters through consultative sales. An example is CB4, a retail analytics startup that Gap acquired, that has retail brand names as their customers, such as Levi's, Circle K, BestMarket, and Ace Hardware.

- *Reputable investor*: Successful AI startups are backed by prestigious global investors (Warburg Pincus, Goodwater Capital, Greylock Partners, Sequoia). This will attract other venture capital confidence to invest in your company by having world-known investors on your company track record. An example is AppDynamics, which has been invested in by Greylock Partners and acquired by Cisco.

- *Region*: A strategic acquirer is usually from the same area. This is due to the easiness of due diligence and the founders-acquirer background similarity. For example, BasisAI is a Singaporean AI startup acquired by Aicadium, a Singaporean AI technology company, because they are in the same Singapore technology ecosystem.

- *Strong intellectual property (IP) protection*: Having robust IP protection, such as patents and trademarks, can increase the startup's value and make it more attractive to potential acquirers. For example, Clari DeepMap, which Nvidia acquired, has 32 patents, with 16 already granted.

- *Scalability*: The ability to scale the technology and business model is critical for the startup's long-term success and makes it more attractive to potential acquirers.

- *Culture fit*: The cultural fit between the startup and the potential acquirer can play a significant role in the acquisition's success, as it can impact the integration of the two companies and the retention of key talent.

- *Financials*: A strong financial performance, including revenue growth and profitability, can make the startup more attractive to potential acquirers and increase the company's value.

- *Market traction*: Demonstrating traction in the market, such as through brand name customer acquisition and retention, can increase the startup's value and make it more attractive to potential acquirers. For example, BasisAI has good customer growth. They already signed a contract with DBS, UOB, OCBC, ComfortDelGro, Singapore Airlines, Accenture, PwC, Amazon, and Singapore government as customers before being acquired by Aicadium, partly because of their fast customer growth in a short time.

- *Blue ocean competition:* An AI startup operating in a blue ocean competitive landscape with innovative and unique AI technology can be an attractive target for acquisition by a tech company looking to gain a competitive edge in the market. An example is Heron Systems, an AI startup that builds autonomous agents and multi-agent systems for modern war-fighting problems acquired by Shield AI. Their military technology is considered to be in a relatively blue ocean space, with only a few competitors.

Identifying Potential Acquirers

AI startups are looking for potential acquirers willing to pay a premium price for their products as the AI industry continues to expand at an astounding rate. Finding companies interested in buying your AI startup can be tricky, but it is doable with the appropriate strategy.

Our internal survey found that only 13% of acquired AI companies produce solutions exclusively applicable to horizontal markets. The remaining 87% are engaged in solutions focusing on vertical markets and are highly specialized for those markets. Specialized solutions are attractive to strategic acquirers who want to strengthen their position in a specific market or industry. Additionally, specialized solutions often solve high-value business cases, impacting an acquisition's outcome.

When it comes to vertical AI startups, the typical strategic acquirer is a corporation that wants to acquire a specialized artificial intelligence product to improve their business. This type of acquirer is known as a vertical product acquirer. For example, a leader in the clothes retail business, Gap, decided to purchase CB4 Analytics, an artificial intelligence (AI)–based retail analytics startup, to achieve a competitive advantage in the retail industry.

Interestingly, just 19% of AI companies are purchased by other businesses operating in the same sector. This suggests that prospective purchasers are not always restricted to a single sector of the economy. The majority of artificial intelligence startups, according to the findings of the study, are typically bought by businesses operating in other fields. It suggests that the market for AI startups is not limited to a specific industry. Companies from various sectors are interested in acquiring AI startups to enhance their existing products or expand their market presence. This also highlights the importance of a strategic fit between the AI startup and the acquirer rather than industry similarity alone. Additionally, it emphasizes the need for AI startups to think beyond their own industry and be open to potential acquirers from various sectors.

Hence, to find potential acquirers for an AI company, it is vital to focus on businesses attempting to penetrate your industry but haven't found a way in.

This will help you find potential acquirers. Because they know they must be present in the market to maintain their competitiveness, these businesses are likelier to pay the highest rates.

1. *Industry leaders and established players*: One way to identify potential acquirers for your AI startup is to look at industry leaders and established players in your niche. These companies may be interested in acquiring your technology to enhance their offerings or to gain a competitive advantage. For instance, if you have developed an AI-based tool for customer service, then call center market leaders such as Zendesk, Freshworks, or Genesys may be potential acquirers.

2. *Private equity firms*: Private equity firms have the financial resources to acquire startups and can provide the necessary capital for growth and expansion. They often have expertise in specific industries and can provide valuable guidance and support to the startups they acquire.

3. *Strategic partners*: Strategic partners are companies you have worked with or are currently working with to develop and market your technology. These companies may have a vested interest in acquiring your startup to gain access to your technology or to eliminate competition. For instance, if you have developed an AI-based market analysis tool, the market research consulting you have partnered with to test and market your product may be a potential acquirer.

4. *Bigger competitors*: Bigger competitors are ideal AI startup acquirers as they offer resources and expertise to develop and scale the technology. They provide access to larger customer bases, distribution networks, infrastructure, and established processes. This accelerates growth in the fast-moving AI market. Larger competitors also provide financial resources, stability, and long-term innovation, which keep the startup competitive and push AI technology boundaries.

5. *Customers*: Customers can be potential acquirers of AI startups as they have firsthand experience with the startup's technology and see the benefit of acquiring it to gain exclusive access to that technology. Customers may also want to eliminate competition, expand their product offerings, or see an acquisition as a natural next step in their relationship if they have invested in the AI startup through funding or partnerships.

In addition to understanding each potential acquisition's pros and cons (Table 10-1), it's essential to understand your organization's goals and priorities in the exit process and know what traits and criteria you're looking for in potential acquirers. This can include cultural fit, ability to buy, motivation, competence in M&A, and alignment of values. By considering these factors and using a targeted approach to identify potential acquirers, you can increase your chances of finding the right acquirer for your AI startup.

Table 10-1. Potential Acquirers and Their Pros and Cons

Potential Acquirers	Pros	Cons
Industry leaders and established players	Interested in acquiring technology to enhance their offerings. Can provide access to a large customer base. Can offer established infrastructure and resources.	May have less interest in acquiring startups if they already have similar technology or solutions. May not be willing to pay a premium for the startup.
Private equity firms	Can provide financial resources for growth and expansion. Often have expertise in specific industries and can provide guidance and support. Can acquire startups more quickly than other potential acquirers.	May not have the same level of expertise in the specific technology or industry as the startup. May be focused on short-term goals and not long-term innovation.
Strategic partners	Have a vested interest in acquiring the startup's technology or eliminating competition. Can provide access to a larger customer base. May already have established partnerships with the startup.	May not be willing to pay a premium for the startup. May have less interest in acquiring the startup if they already have similar technology or solutions.
Bigger competitors	Offer resources and expertise to develop and scale the technology. Access to larger customer bases, distribution networks, infrastructure, and established processes. Can provide financial resources, stability, and long-term innovation.	May have less interest in acquiring startups if they already have similar technology or solutions. May acquire the customer base only. May not be willing to pay a premium for the startup. May acquire and shut down the AI startup.
Customer	Have firsthand experience with the startup's technology and its value. They may be interested in integrating the technology into their own business. Can provide access to a large customer base.	May not have the financial resources to acquire the startup. May not have the same level of expertise in the specific technology or industry as the startup.

One effective way to find potential acquirers for your AI startup is through online platforms and marketplaces such as AngelList or Crunchbase. These platforms provide a wealth of information on companies in your industry or niche, including their funding, industry focus, and other relevant criteria. Using these platforms, you can identify potential acquirers interested in acquiring your AI technology to enhance their offerings or gain a competitive advantage.

Another effective way to find potential acquirers is attending industry conferences and events. These events offer an opportunity to network with potential acquirers and investors and learn more about your industry's latest trends and developments. By attending these events and networking with attendees, you can identify potential acquirers interested in your AI startup and its technology. Furthermore, these events often have industry leaders and established players as attendees, making it an ideal place to connect with potential acquirers with the resources and expertise to develop further and scale your technology. Advisory firms can also be a valuable resource for identifying potential acquirers for AI startups. Investment banks, law firms, and other advisory firms specializing in mergers and acquisitions can provide expert guidance and advice on identifying potential acquirers and negotiating the terms of an acquisition. These firms deeply understand the market and can provide valuable insights on potential acquirers based on their experience working with companies in your industry or niche. They can also help you prepare for the acquisition process and ensure you get the best possible deal. Additionally, advisory firms can provide introductions and networking opportunities to potential acquirers, increasing your chances of success.

Understanding Your Strategic Value

When looking for potential acquirers, AI startup founders should focus on identifying and emphasizing intangible assets that can drive up the value of their company. These can include unique products and services that potential acquirers cannot find elsewhere. Having a strong, relevant, culturally accepted brand is also essential, as this can attract potential acquirers with excellent products but lack a strong brand. Intellectual property such as copyrights, trademarks, patents, and trade secrets are valuable intangible assets that can protect unique aspects of the business and attract premium acquirers.

Another key asset is a powerful, unique, and proprietary distribution network. Many potential acquirers are trying to expand their customer base, and a distribution network that is both powerful and unique can be very attractive to them. Additionally, having a loyal customer base can be very valuable as potential acquirers will see the value in having enthusiastic customers about the product or service.

Data is also an essential asset for AI startups as the accuracy and reliability of AI models depend on the data fed into the learning algorithms. If an AI startup has unique and diverse data acquired overtime, it can be more attractive to potential acquirers. Institutional knowledge, which refers to the tacit knowledge of building and solving problems using particular AI methods, can also be valuable to potential acquirers.

Finally, partner exclusivity, which refers to exclusivity in contracts or agreements, can be valuable for potential acquirers. For example, having unique technology vendors or long-term distribution deals with large technology distributors can be very attractive. This type of exclusivity can be worth a tremendous amount, especially if it is secured with an exclusive agreement before everyone knows about it. AI startup founders need to identify and implement as many forms of these value drivers or intangible assets as possible to stack value in their business.

Searching and Assessing a Potential Acquirer

Several factors must be considered to facilitate a successful transaction when considering whether a prospective acquirer is a good fit for your AI startup. These factors include

- Understanding your startup's goals and top priorities and determining the characteristics and standards you seek in a prospective acquirer

- Identifying the reasons behind your decision to sell your business to narrow down the pool of potential acquirers who suit your objectives

- Identifying what kind of acquirer would be an excellent fit for your firm, whether it be an acquirer with strategic or financial interests

- Assessing whether or not a prospective acquirer is a good cultural match for your team's employment and a successful merger

- Ensuring that the possible acquirer has the financial resources necessary to purchase your business

- Determining which businesses are driven by a feeling of urgency and have the motivation necessary to move forward with the purchase process

- Ascertaining whether or not your prospective purchaser possesses the level of expertise required to successfully complete the transaction

- Evaluating whether the potential acquirer's values and commitments are aligned with your own

By carefully considering these factors, you can locate the ideal acquirer for your AI startup and pave the way for a successful acquisition.

To ensure a fruitful acquisition, thoroughly evaluating each potential acquirer is crucial for AI startups. One effective method of assessing acquirers is using a table that compares each candidate based on several key factors (Table 10-2). This assessment table includes evaluating the value and culture match, financial capability, strategic alignment, urgency, and technology capability of potential acquirers. By carefully considering these factors, AI startups can make well-informed decisions and increase the chances of a successful acquisition.

Table 10-2. Assessment Table: AI Startup vs. Potential Acquirer

Assessment Criteria	Potential Acquirer A	Potential Acquirer B
Value and culture match	8/10	9/10
Financial capability	10/10	7/10
Strategic match	9/10	8/10
Urgency	8/10	6/10
Technology capability	7/10	9/10

Here's an explanation of the preceding table:

- *Value and culture match*: This assessment criterion determines the compatibility of the potential acquirer's values and culture with those of the AI startup. A high score indicates a strong alignment of values and culture, while a low score indicates the opposite.

- *Financial capability*: This assessment criterion evaluates the financial strength and capability of the potential acquirer to purchase the AI startup. A high score indicates the potential acquirer has the required financial resources for acquisition, while a low score indicates the opposite.

- *Strategic match*: This assessment criterion measures the potential acquirer's strategic fit with the AI startup. A high score indicates that the potential acquirer's goals and objectives align with those of the AI startup, while a low score indicates the opposite.

- *Urgency*: This assessment criterion evaluates the potential acquirer's motivation and urgency to acquire the AI startup. A high score indicates a strong desire and willingness to move forward with the acquisition process, while a low score indicates the opposite.

- *Technology capability*: This assessment criterion assesses the potential acquirer's technology capabilities and expertise, specifically in the AI industry. A high score indicates a strong technology capability and expertise, while a low score indicates the opposite.

In the table (Table 10-2), two potential acquirers have been assessed based on the five criteria. The scores assigned to each criterion represent the level of compatibility between the AI startup and the potential acquirer. By comparing the scores, the AI startup can determine which potential acquirer is the best fit for acquisition.

Approaching Potential Acquirers and Initiating Conversations

To successfully sell your AI startup, it is crucial to approach potential acquirers and initiate a dialogue with them effectively.

The following are some techniques to help you do so:

- Creating a compelling pitch that highlights the unique value proposition of your AI product or service is vital. The presentation should be tailored to address the potential acquirer's strategic goals and concerns.

- Utilizing your network to communicate with prospective purchasers can be an effective method. Attending industry events and broadening your professional network can help you meet potential customers in person.

- Starting a targeted outreach method is important to reach out to potential customers. Researching the acquirer's company and industry can help personalize your outreach according to their specific challenges.

- Emphasizing your track record of success with case studies and testimonials can help establish credibility and build confidence with prospective acquirers.

- Persistence and respect for the potential acquirer's time and priorities are key factors in the process. When engaging with possible purchasers, you must follow up consistently while respecting their time and priorities.

Having different pitches for potential acquirers is important because it allows the startup to tailor their message and value proposition to each potential acquirer's specific needs and goals. For example, if a startup is building computer vision systems for retail object classification and planogramming (Figure 10-1), they may have different pitches for each potential acquirer:

- Suppose the potential acquirer is a retail analytics company. In that case, the startup could pitch that their computer vision system can complete the acquirer's product portfolio and offerings, making them more competitive in the market.

- Suppose the potential acquirer is an ecommerce company. In that case, the startup could pitch that their computer vision system will improve the acquirer's product search system, resulting in a better user experience and increased sales.

Figure 10-1. Retail object classification

By customizing their pitch to each potential acquirer, the startup can better communicate the benefits of their product and increase the likelihood of a successful acquisition.

Preparing the Company for Sale

Preparing a startup for sale requires careful consideration and strategic planning. It's important to position the startup for sale, demonstrate its strategic value to potential acquirers, and create a compelling sales pitch and presentation. By following these guidelines, startups can increase their chances of successful acquisition and achieve their desired outcomes.

Maximizing AI Startup Value

When preparing an AI startup for a potential sale, it is important to recognize that acquirers are typically not solely interested in revenue or cash flow. Instead, the intangible assets of the company often hold the most value. It is crucial to recognize that while revenue and cash flow are desirable qualities in an AI startup, they are not the primary driver of an acquirer's interest.

Building, operating, and selling AI products are intricate undertakings that pose significant financial challenges, making financial success unlikely to be the strongest suit of AI companies. Thus, AI startup founders need to identify intangible assets in their AI business, which can drive up the company's value. While AI products may be a sound bargaining chip, they must solve specific questions to be valuable.

According to our benchmark studies, 24 AI products have been shown to reduce costs for customers, nine increase revenue, nine minimize security risks, and eight save time in customer processes. To maximize the value of the company when preparing for a sale, several key steps must be taken, including identifying and showcasing intangible assets, simplifying operations, documenting institutional knowledge, building a strong management team, and improving financial reporting.

A compelling narrative must be created that highlights the company's value, positioning it as an attractive investment opportunity and maximizing its value in the eyes of potential acquirers.

First and foremost, you should focus on identifying and showcasing your intangible assets. These assets often make a company valuable, including product uniqueness, engineering and operationalization secret recipes, market share, customer loyalty, intellectual property, certifications gained, and more. Below are ways to determine the value of your intangible assets:

1. Show that your AI product results from years of real-world implementation and operationalization, with innovation and originality, proved in patents and scientific publications.

2. Conduct testimonials. By asking your customers how your product or service has benefited them in the past, you can identify specific metrics that demonstrate its value. For example, suppose your AI product has been testified quantitatively to reduce costs, increase revenue, reduce security risks, and save your customers' time. In that case, these factors can justify a higher price tag for your company.

Another important step to take when preparing for a sale is to streamline your operations and document your institutional knowledge systemically. This might involve simplifying your organizational structure, writing product documentation and standard operation procedure, adopting BPM (business process management) practice, and automating your development and operationalization of software and AI systems using DevOps, MLOps, and ModelOps. Doing so can increase your company's profitability and demonstrate to potential acquirers that you are a well-managed organization.

In addition to these steps, retaining a solid management and technical team is essential. Acquirers want to see your company's strong team that can drive growth, build innovative solutions, and manage operations effectively.

You should also improve your financial reporting and ensure your books are in order. This will help build confidence in potential acquirers and demonstrate that your company is a good investment opportunity. Ultimately, when preparing for a sale, the goal is to create a compelling narrative showcasing your company's value.

Therefore highlighting your intangible assets (IP, managed institutional knowledge), demonstrating your operational efficiency, structuring your technical and financial documentation, and showcasing your strong team will position your company as an attractive acquisition opportunity and maximize its value in the eyes of potential acquirers.

Valuation Methods for AI Startups

Valuation is essential for any startup seeking investment or sale. The value of a startup is not just limited to its monetary worth but also includes factors like intangible assets, uniqueness, and the quality of its team. Determining startup valuation can be approached through subjective and objective methods, such as researching valuations for comparable companies, constructing a revenue or EBITDA multiple, and assessing the industry's market size and situation.

Here are brief explanations of the ten common methods for determining startup valuation:

1. *Standard Earnings Multiple Method*: This method calculates a startup's value based on a multiple of its one to three years' average profit. Investors commonly use it to determine a company's free cash flow and potential for driving incremental value to a purchaser. In the case of AI startups, the multiple typically ranges between 5 and 8 × the past three years' average EBITDA (yearly), while in SaaS businesses, it may fall in the 8–12 range.

2. *Human Capital Plus Market Value Method*: This method assesses a startup's team's value and potential market size. The investor evaluates the team's expertise and calculates a mathematical valuation based on the obtainable market volume. It helps assess a startup's potential for future profits.

3. *5x Your Raise Method*: This method determines a startup's value based on the amount of money it has raised. It is commonly used in conversations between startups and venture capitalists, and the idea behind this method is that a startup's value should be five times the amount of money it has raised.

4. *Scorecard Method*: This method uses a weighted scoring system to assign a score to various factors such as the team, market, product, and traction. These scores are then used to determine the overall value of the startup.

5. *First Principles Method*: This method breaks down a startup's value into its individual components, such as its technology, market, and team, and values each component separately. It is based on the concept of reducing a complex problem to its basic elements and then building it back up.

6. *Pre-money Method*: This method calculates a startup's value before an investment is made based on its assets, liabilities, and potential future revenue.

7. *Post-money Method*: This method calculates a startup's value after an investment is made based on its assets, liabilities, and potential future revenue, taking into account the investment made.

8. *Real Options Method*: This method values a startup based on its potential future options and how they affect its value. It involves assessing a startup's potential future opportunities, such as the ability to enter new markets or develop new products.

9. *Market Approach Method*: This method determines a startup's value based on its potential market value. It involves assessing the market demand for a startup's product or service and the competition in the market.

10. *Cost Approach Method*: This method calculates a startup's value based on the cost of creating a similar business from scratch. It is based on the concept of a startup's potential future income.

The most common method to value AI startups is the Standard Earnings Multiple Method, which calculates the startup's valuation based on a multiple of its past three years' average EBITDA. The multiple for AI startups is typically between 5 and 8 × the past three years' average EBITDA, although for SAAS businesses, it can range from 8 to 12.

Many investors prefer this method as it provides insight into the company's free cash flow and how it will drive incremental value to a purchaser. The Standard Earnings Multiple Method is a popular valuation method as it is relatively simple to calculate and objectively measures the startup's financial performance.

It also allows investors to assess the potential return on investment for the purchaser, which is important when considering the purchase of an AI startup. Additionally, the method is useful for valuing AI startups with a proven track record of profitability, which can be difficult to value using other methods that focus on future potential.

AI startups have smaller multiples than SaaS because AI startups often require more significant investments in data acquisition, computing infrastructure, and research and development, resulting in lower profit margins and higher operating costs.

Additionally, AI startups may have a longer sales cycle as they may need to consult with potential customers to customize their solutions, which can further impact their revenue and profitability.

On the other hand, SaaS businesses generally have lower operational costs and higher margins due to their scalable and repeatable subscription-based business model. Moreover, AI startups are often still in the development stage, with uncertain revenue streams and higher levels of risk. While AI technology has the potential to be highly profitable and disruptive, it can take time for startups to generate consistent revenue and demonstrate their ability to scale. These factors can contribute to the differences in multiples between AI startups and SaaS businesses.

Valuating an AI startup can be complex, as many factors exist beyond revenue or profit. However, here is a simplified step-by-step approach to valuate an AI startup:

1. Identify the company's stage of development. Is the company in the seed stage or growth stage? This will help determine the type of valuation method to use.

2. Determine the company's current and future potential revenues. Estimate the company's current and future potential revenues based on the market size and competitive landscape. This can be done by looking at similar companies in the same industry and their revenue growth rates.

3. Assess the company's assets and liabilities. Consider the company's assets and liabilities, including intellectual property, patents, brand reputation, and outstanding debts or legal issues.

4. Choose a valuation method. As discussed earlier, several methods can be used to value an AI startup. One of the most common is the Standard Earnings Multiple Method. This involves taking the company's average EBITDA over the past three years and multiplying it by a factor of 5–8 for AI-first startups and AI toolkit startups or 8–12 for AI-powered SaaS startups. This will provide an estimated valuation range for the company.

5. Consider scenario analysis to account for the uncertainties in the startup's future revenue growth and market conditions. Conducting scenario analysis with pessimistic, conservative, and optimistic scenarios is useful. This involves estimating the company's valuation under each scenario to give a range of potential valuations.

For example, an AI startup has had an average EBITDA of $500,000 over the past three years, and the Standard Earnings Multiple Method suggests a valuation range of $2.5–4 million. A scenario analysis might produce the following valuations:

- *Pessimistic scenario*: Revenue growth slows, and the company only achieves a valuation of $2.5 million.

- *Baseline scenario*: The company continues its current growth rate, resulting in a valuation of $3.5 million.

- *Optimistic scenario*: The company experiences rapid growth and is valued at $4 million.

By considering multiple scenarios, you can better understand the potential range of valuations for the startup, which can help guide negotiations with potential investors or acquirers.

Creating a Compelling Story

When selling a company, creating a compelling sales pitch and story is crucial to attracting potential acquirers. It is not sufficient to talk about the company's historical performance. While a company's past performance is important, it is equally essential to communicate its future goals and potential growth and innovation. This approach enables potential acquirers to envision the company's potential growth and creates excitement about the possibility of acquiring the company.

In addition to discussing the company's future goals and growth potential, it is essential to present the company's strategic alignment and financial aspects from the acquirer's perspective. A more compelling story that demonstrates how the AI product can benefit the acquirer's business and innovation strategy can be used to illustrate the future possibilities of the acquisition. It is essential to picture the future for the acquirer company and highlight how the acquisition news in the media could boost the stock value and the investors' excitement.

Remembering that potential acquirers often have more resources than the company being sold is essential. They believe they can do better with those resources, so it is important to leverage the acquirer's perspective and math. For example, if a company has a small team and generates a revenue of US $1 million, a potential acquirer with a three-time team size can envision the three-time potential revenue they could generate with the products.

Let's learn from some hypothetical case studies. Niramai is an Indian healthcare AI startup focusing on early breast cancer detection through AI-powered thermography. To pitch their company to healthcare technology giants such as

Siemens Healthineers, GE Healthcare, or Medtronic, Niramai would need to emphasize its unique value proposition and future growth potential:

1. Niramai would need to present a compelling story about how their technology will benefit the acquirer's business and innovation strategy. They would need to highlight how their AI-powered thermography can complement existing imaging technologies used by these companies and provide a more accurate and cost-effective solution for early breast cancer detection. For example, they could emphasize the potential cost savings for the healthcare giants and how their technology can enhance patient care by detecting cancer at an earlier stage.

2. Niramai would need to present a clear and comprehensive vision for the company's future. This would involve showcasing their future goals and how they plan to achieve them. For example, they could discuss plans to expand into other markets, develop new AI-powered products, or partner with other healthcare organizations.

3. Niramai would need to use scenario analysis to demonstrate the company's potential value to the healthcare giants. This would involve presenting different scenarios with optimistic, conservative, and pessimistic projections of the company's future growth and revenue potential. For example, they could present a scenario where their technology is adopted globally, resulting in significant revenue growth and market domination. They could also present a scenario where the technology is slow to be adopted, resulting in slower revenue growth and market penetration.

4. Niramai must demonstrate their ability to execute their plans and deliver results. This would involve highlighting their team's expertise, experience, and track record of success. For example, they could showcase the credentials of their management team, the awards they have received, the patents granted, and the partnerships they have formed.

In conclusion, creating a compelling sales pitch and story highlighting the company's future growth and innovation, leveraging the acquirer's perspective and math, and picturing the future for the acquirer company is critical to successfully selling a company. A well-crafted sales pitch that illustrates the company's potential can attract potential acquirers and generate excitement about the possibility of acquiring the company.

Negotiating the Sale

Negotiating the sale of an AI startup can be a complex and daunting process. It involves a variety of considerations, including legal and financial matters, as well as technical and labor aspects. To successfully navigate this process, it is essential to have a clear understanding of the negotiation strategies and techniques, the key legal and financial considerations, and the due diligence process. Also, handling objections and counteroffers is critical to successful sales. In this context, technical and labor due diligence are important for assessing the technical and human resources of the AI startup. This introduction will provide an overview of the key considerations involved in negotiating the sale of an AI startup, including negotiating the terms of the sale, handling objections and counteroffers, key legal and financial considerations, and technical, labor, financial, and legal due diligence.

Negotiating the Terms of the Sale

You've done the prep work and presented and met with potential acquirers. Next, the interested acquirers will sign letters of intent (LOIs) plus Non-disclosure Agreements (NDAs). Selling an AI company involves a complex set of considerations that must be examined when reviewing an LOI. While an LOI is merely a tentative expression of interest, an LOI carries more weight and typically involves more serious discussions between the parties involved.

Before accepting an LOI, it is important to understand that it is a non-binding document outlining the proposed transaction's key terms and conditions. While it is not legally binding, it serves as a roadmap for negotiations between the parties and sets the framework for the deal's final agreement. It is also important to ensure that the LOI contains adequate protections for the seller, such as due diligence and confidentiality provisions.

It is worth noting that while an LOI is an essential step in the M&A process, it does not guarantee that a deal will ultimately be reached. Further negotiations and due diligence may be required before the parties can reach a final agreement. Sometimes we can have a more detailed document that outlines the basic terms of the potential deal, including the purchase price, the structure of the transaction, and any contingencies or conditions referred to as a term sheet. As such, having a qualified legal and financial team on board is important to guide you through the process and protect your interests.

First and foremost, the value of the technology, especially related to AI being sold, must be carefully evaluated. This may include the company's proprietary algorithms, datasets, MLOps/ModelOps platform, and machine learning models, which could significantly impact the deal's purchase price and payment structure.

Evaluating the acquirer's technical capabilities and experience in the AI industry is also crucial. The acquirer's expertise in the field could be crucial in ensuring the continued success of the company post-acquisition. The acquirer's plans for integrating the company's technology into their own operations and how they intend to leverage the technology to achieve their strategic goals should be examined.

Another critical consideration is the potential impact of the acquisition on employees, customers, and other stakeholders. The acquirer's plans for retaining key employees, maintaining customer relationships, and managing any potential reputational risks should be closely evaluated. In some cases, it may be necessary to negotiate specific protections for employees, such as retention bonuses or guarantees of job security.

The terms of the deal itself should also be carefully evaluated. The purchase price, payment structure, and any contingencies or conditions that must be satisfied before closing the deal should be reviewed in detail. This could include conditions related to the company's financial performance, intellectual property ownership, or regulatory compliance. It is essential to ensure that the LOI contains adequate protections for the seller, such as due diligence and confidentiality provisions.

In addition to these factors, it is important to be aware of any relevant regulations or legal requirements that may impact the sale. For example, if the company's technology involves the use of personal data, the sale may be subject to data protection laws and regulations. Compliance with privacy law, competition law, and other relevant laws should also be considered.

Overall, selling an AI company requires careful consideration of various factors, including the value of the technology, the acquirer's capabilities, the impact on stakeholders, and any legal or regulatory requirements. By engaging qualified legal and financial experts and carefully reviewing the terms proposed in an LOI, the seller can ensure that they make informed decisions and protect their interests throughout the process. With the right approach, a successful sale can result in a positive outcome for both the seller and the acquirer.

Handle Objections and Counteroffers

When it comes to handling objections and counteroffers in the context of M&A, it is important to remember that negotiations can be complex and multifaceted. It is about getting the best price for your company and ensuring that the deal terms are fair, reasonable, and aligned with your strategic objectives.

One important aspect of handling objections and counteroffers is maintaining a positive and constructive tone throughout the negotiation process. Even if you disagree with the acquirer's position, it is important to maintain a professional and courteous demeanor and to focus on finding common ground and working toward a mutually beneficial solution.

Another critical strategy for handling objections and counteroffers is to be proactive in anticipating and addressing potential issues before they become deal-breakers. This requires a deep understanding of your company's strengths, weaknesses, and value proposition and a thorough knowledge of the market and industry trends.

In some cases, it may be necessary to bring in outside experts or advisors to help you navigate complex issues or respond to objections from potential acquirers. This may include legal counsel, financial analysts, or industry consultants who can provide specialized expertise and guidance.

Ultimately, the key to successfully handling objections and counteroffers in M&A is to remain flexible, creative, and strategic in your approach. This may involve exploring alternative deal structures or financing options or rethinking certain aspects of the deal to address the acquirer's concerns. Focusing on your strategic objectives and staying open to new ideas and approaches can increase your chances of achieving a successful outcome and maximizing your company's value.

It is also worth noting that effective communication and transparency are critical to managing objections and counteroffers in M&A. Be honest and up front about your concerns and goals, and encourage the acquirer to do the same. This can help build trust and foster a productive negotiation process, ultimately leading to a successful deal.

In conclusion, handling objections and counteroffers is critical to the M&A process and requires careful planning, communication, and strategic thinking. By staying focused on your strategic objectives, remaining flexible and creative, and seeking expert guidance when needed, you can confidently navigate the negotiation process and achieve a successful outcome that maximizes your company's value.

In addition to the strategies mentioned earlier, it is important to understand the acquirer's perspective and motivations when handling objections and counteroffers. By understanding what the acquirer is looking for in the deal, you can tailor your responses and solutions to meet their needs and expectations better.

It is also crucial to clearly understand the market and industry trends, as this can help you anticipate potential objections and counteroffers from acquirers. This includes being aware of new competitors, market disruptors, and emerging technologies that may impact your company's value.

Another important consideration when handling objections and counteroffers is a strong understanding of your company's intellectual property (IP) portfolio. This includes patents, trademarks, copyrights, and trade secrets. Acquirers may be concerned about potential IP infringement or litigation, so addressing these concerns early in the negotiation process is important.

However, an acquirer may make a counteroffer that includes an *earn-out clause*, which means that a portion of the purchase price is contingent on the company achieving certain financial or operational targets after the sale. While this can be an attractive option for acquirers who want to mitigate risk, it can also be a source of contention for sellers who may feel their company's value is undervalued. In these cases, it is important to carefully evaluate the terms of the earn-out and negotiate for fair and reasonable terms.

Lastly, it is important to clearly understand the legal and regulatory landscape surrounding the sale of an AI company. This includes compliance with data privacy laws, intellectual property regulations, and antitrust laws. Ensuring compliance with these regulations is critical to avoid potential legal issues and delays in the sale process.

In essence, when handling objections and counteroffers in the context of selling an AI company, it is important to maintain a positive and constructive tone, be proactive in anticipating potential issues, seek expert guidance when needed, and understand the acquirer's perspective and motivations. By keeping these strategies in mind and staying focused on your strategic objectives, you can confidently navigate the negotiation process and achieve a successful outcome that maximizes your company's value.

Key Legal and Financial Considerations During the Negotiation Process

In addition to regulatory issues, several other legal and financial aspects should be considered during the negotiation process:

- *Terms of the deal/term sheet*: It is important to carefully evaluate the terms of the deal to ensure that they are fair and reasonable. It is also important to make sure that they are aligned with your strategic objectives. This includes considering the purchase price, payment structure, earn-out clauses, and any other terms that may impact the value of the deal.

- *Tax implication*: It is important to have a thorough understanding of the tax implications of the sale, both for your company and for the individual shareholders. This includes evaluating the tax implications of different deal structures, such as stock sales vs. asset sales, and considering strategies for minimizing tax liabilities.

- *Legal documentation*: It is important to ensure that all necessary legal documents are in order and that the transaction is properly documented. This includes drafting and negotiating the purchase agreement, conducting due diligence, and ensuring compliance with all applicable laws and regulations.

- *Communication strategy*: It is important to consider the impact of the sale on your employees, customers, and other stakeholders. This includes developing a communication strategy to ensure that employees are kept informed about the sale and its potential impact on their jobs and working with customers to ensure a smooth transition.

- *Post-transaction integration*: It is important to have a plan in place for post-transaction integration, to ensure that the company can continue to operate smoothly and effectively under new ownership. This includes identifying key personnel and ensuring that they are retained, developing a plan for integrating technology and systems, and establishing clear lines of communication between the new ownership and existing employees.

In short, there are several key legal and financial considerations to keep in mind during the negotiation process when selling an AI company. These include regulatory issues, purchase price and payment structure, tax implications, legal documentation, employee and stakeholder impact, and post-transaction integration. By carefully considering these factors and seeking expert guidance when needed, you can navigate the sale process with confidence and achieve a successful outcome that maximizes the value of your company.

Due Diligence

Due diligence is crucial for the acquisition of an AI startup as it verifies the company's information, operations, and financial performance to ensure that the acquisition is profitable. Technical, labor, financial, and legal due diligence are important aspects of the acquisition process for AI startup founders. Technical due diligence examines the startup's technology, while labor due diligence reviews the workforce. Financial due diligence analyzes the financial statements, and legal due diligence ensures compliance with regulations. Preparing for due diligence is crucial for AI startup founders, such as organizing financial and legal documents, establishing clear intellectual property ownership, and developing a strong technical team. Thorough due diligence can lead to a successful acquisition and a strong foundation for future growth and success.

In this section, we will describe a step-by-step process for conducting the four types of due diligence: technical, labor, financial, and legal. Every kind of due diligence requires a specific set of procedures to ensure a thorough investigation of the startup's operations, assets, and potential liabilities. By following these steps, acquirers can gain a clear understanding of the startup's technical capabilities, workforce, financial performance, and legal compliance and make informed decisions about the viability of the acquisition.

It's important to note that the results of the due diligence process can also impact the negotiation terms, particularly the purchase price. For example, suppose the due diligence reveals potential legal or financial risks. In that case, the acquirer may be more hesitant to proceed with the acquisition or may negotiate a lower purchase price to account for the additional risks. On the other hand, if the due diligence reveals strong technical capabilities or potential for future growth, the acquirer may be willing to offer a higher purchase price to secure the acquisition. Therefore, AI startup founders need to be aware of the due diligence process and ensure that their company is well-prepared to address any potential issues that may arise during the process. This can help maximize the value of the company and lead to a successful acquisition.

Technical Due Diligence

Technical due diligence is a crucial aspect of the acquisition process for AI startups. This involves an in-depth examination of the technical details related to the startup's products, systems, operations, and procedures to ensure that the acquirer fully understands the technology and potential risks involved. Here are the steps for technical due diligence:

1. *Product roadmap review*: Review the product roadmap of the AI startup. This will provide insight into the company's future product development plans and how they align with the acquirer's business goals.

2. *System architecture and infrastructure review*: Examine the system architecture and infrastructure of the AI startup. This includes a review of the hardware and software systems, network topology, and cloud services used by the startup.

3. *Code review*: Conduct a thorough review of the AI startup's code. This includes an assessment of the code quality, maintainability, and scalability. It should also examine the AI models used by the startup to ensure they are robust and accurate. Additionally, the acquirer should evaluate the AI platform used by the startup and determine its capabilities and limitations.

4. *Dataset review:* The acquirer should review the datasets the AI startup uses to train its models. This includes an examination of the quality, quantity, and diversity of the data. It should also verify that the data is ethically sourced and compliant with relevant regulations.

5. *Documentation review:* In this step, the acquirer should review the startup's documentation, including technical specifications, user manuals, and API documentation.

6. *Process review:* The acquirer should review the startup's process for developing and deploying its AI products. This includes an assessment of the team's skills and experience and how they collaborate to deliver quality products. The acquirer should also assess the startup's development process, including its use of continuous integration/continuous deployment (CI/CD) and MLOps. The acquirer should also evaluate the startup's service delivery process and determine if it aligns with its own processes.

In summary, conducting thorough technical due diligence is essential for AI startup acquisition. It helps the acquirer fully understand the technology, potential risks, and product potential, which can affect the negotiation terms such as price. By following the step-by-step process, acquirers can evaluate the startup's product roadmap, system architecture, code, datasets, documentation, and processes to ensure that they are making a sound investment decision.

Financial, Legal, and Commercial Due Diligence

Financial, legal, and commercial due diligence are crucial steps in the acquisition process of an AI startup. The goal of these due diligence processes is to evaluate the company's financial, legal, and commercial aspects to ensure that the acquisition is a profitable and viable investment for the acquirer.

Here are the steps involved in conducting due diligence:

1. *Business and revenue model review:* This step involves evaluating the company's overall business and revenue model to understand how it generates revenue and operates. The goal is to ensure the company's revenue streams are sustainable and profitable.

2. *Existing customer review:* This step involves reviewing the company's existing customer base, including contracts, demand profit pools, and testimonials. The objective is to determine the level of customer satisfaction and loyalty and identify potential risks associated with the customer base.

3. *Existing partner review*: This step involves reviewing the company's existing partner relationships, including contracts and testimonials. The goal is to understand the revenue generated from these partnerships and assess the potential for future growth.

4. *Growth strategy review*: This step involves evaluating the company's growth strategy, marketing, go-to-market (GTM) and sales strategy, market analysis, and positioning. The objective is to assess the company's potential for future growth and identify potential risks associated with its growth strategy.

5. *Competitive landscape analysis*: This step involves evaluating the competitive landscape of the company's industry. The goal is to understand the company's market position and identify potential risks associated with its competition.

6. *Intellectual property and patent review*: This step involves reviewing the company's intellectual property and patents to ensure that the company owns its technology and has secured the necessary patents to protect its technology.

7. *Regulatory compliance review*: This step involves evaluating the company's compliance with relevant regulations and laws. The goal is to ensure that the company complies with applicable regulations and identify potential risks associated with non-compliance.

8. *Financial analysis*: This step involves analyzing the company's financial statements, including revenue and growth projections, cost structure analysis, capital expenditure analysis, and financial performance metrics. The objective is to evaluate the company's financial performance and identify potential risks associated with its financials.

9. *Risk assessment and mitigation strategy*: This step involves identifying and assessing potential risks associated with the company's operations and developing a strategy to mitigate those risks.

10. *License and certification review*: A license and certification review for AI startups assesses the company's compliance with industry-specific standards and regulations, such as CMMI for software development, ISO for quality management systems, and NIST for technology and security. Additionally, the review may evaluate compliance with data privacy and security regulations like GDPR and HIPAA and ethical and transparent AI algorithms and data collection practices. Its purpose is to ensure compliance with relevant laws and regulations and that products and services meet quality standards.

To prepare for financial, legal, and commercial due diligence, AI startup founders should ensure that they have organized their financial and legal documents, established clear intellectual property ownership, and developed a strong understanding of their business model and growth potential. This includes having a clear understanding of the company's revenue streams, customer base, and marketing strategy.

The management team should also be prepared to answer detailed questions from the acquirer about their financial performance, legal status, and commercial potential. By being well-prepared for financial, legal, and commercial due diligence, AI startup founders can ensure that the acquisition process runs smoothly and that the company is well-positioned for future growth and success.

Labor Due Diligence

Labor due diligence is an important aspect of the acquisition process, as it helps the acquirer understand the workforce of the AI startup and ensure that they have the necessary skills and experience to support the company's growth. Labor due diligence aims to evaluate the startup's talent, culture, compensation, benefits, and any potential legal or compliance issues related to its workforce.

The following are the step-by-step processes of labor due diligence in AI startup acquisition:

1. *Review of employment agreements*: The acquirer will review the startup's employment agreements to ensure they comply with applicable laws and regulations. This may include reviewing employment contracts, offer letters, and other relevant agreements.

2. *Review of benefits and compensation*: The acquirer will review the startup's employee benefits and compensation packages to ensure they are competitive and in line with industry standards. This may include reviewing health insurance plans, retirement plans, and other benefits.

3. *The organizational chart and team structure*: The acquirer will review the startup's organizational chart to understand the reporting structure and identify any key employees or departments critical to the company's success. This will help the acquirer assess the startup's talent and determine if any changes need to be made after the acquisition.

4. *Employee review*: The acquirer will review the startup's employee performance records and interview key employees to assess their skills, experience, and cultural fit with the acquiring company.

5. *Compliance review*: The acquirer will review the startup's compliance with labor laws, including any potential legal issues related to its workforce. This may include reviewing any current or past legal disputes or investigations related to the company's employment practices.

To prepare for labor due diligence, AI startup founders should ensure that their employment agreements are up to date and comply with applicable laws and regulations. They should also ensure that their employee benefits and compensation packages are competitive and in line with industry standards. Furthermore, founders should maintain accurate and up-to-date employee records and be transparent with potential acquirers about any potential labor or compliance issues.

Closing the Deal

Closing the acquisition deal is a critical phase in acquiring an AI startup. It involves the final transfer of ownership and the transition from the seller to the acquirer. This phase also includes the development of a communication strategy to inform existing and future customers of the acquisition, as well as the preparation of press releases. Additionally, the transition from seller to acquirer must be planned carefully, including managing employees, customers, technology, and operations, including MLOps. This section will discuss the critical components of closing an acquisition deal for an AI startup.

Finalize the Sale and Transfer Ownership of the Company

Completing a merger or acquisition transaction can be complex and requires careful planning and coordination. The process involves several steps that must be followed to ensure a smooth and successful closure. Here are the key steps involved:

1. *Meeting closing conditions*: Before closing a deal, it's essential to ensure that all closing conditions have been met, such as obtaining regulatory approvals or shareholder approval.

2. *Signing final agreements and documentation*: Once closing conditions are met, the next step is to sign final agreements and documentation transferring ownership of the business. This includes documents such as title transfer documents, bills of sale, and other legal documents.

3. *Financial adjustments*: Financial adjustments are necessary to determine final purchase price modifications based on working capital and debt variables. All parties involved in the transaction must agree on these revisions before the closure can take place.

4. *Transfer of funds*: Once financial adjustments have been made, the transfer of funds can occur, including payments to shareholders, tax payments, and other financial activities associated with the purchase.

5. *Integration*: The acquired company must be integrated into the acquirer's existing operations, which may involve changes in management, employment, and other aspects of the business. The integration process must be carefully designed and implemented to minimize disruption and maximize the value of the deal.

6. *Post-closing concerns*: It's essential to anticipate and resolve any post-closing concerns, such as disagreements over purchase price revisions or regulatory compliance issues. Planning ahead of time and anticipating potential complications can help ensure a smooth and successful closing process.

To facilitate the closing process, working closely with your legal, financial, and management teams is essential.

Communication Strategy

Finalizing the acquisition process involves more than just completing the legal and financial paperwork. Communicating effectively with all stakeholders is essential to ensure a smooth transition and maintain positive relationships. Here are some steps to finalize the acquisition process with a robust communication strategy:

1. *Communicate with existing and future customers*: It is crucial to inform your existing and future customers of the acquisition and what it means for them. You should explain how the acquisition will impact the services, products, and support they receive. You may also want to highlight any benefits arising from the acquisition, such as access to new technologies or increased resources. Providing a clear and concise message to your customers can help maintain their loyalty and prevent any misunderstandings or concerns.

2. *Communicate with partners*: The acquisition may impact your vendors and suppliers (i.e., GPU provider, cloud provider), and keeping them informed of the changes is essential. You should explain how the acquisition will affect your relationship and any changes they may need to make to their processes, such as existing contracts. Open communication can help avoid any disruptions to the development and operational process and prevent any negative impacts on the quality or delivery of products or services.

3. *Press release strategy*: Issuing a press release is an effective way to announce the acquisition to the media and the broader public. The press release should provide an overview of the acquisition, including its rationale, the parties involved, and the expected benefits. It should also highlight notable achievements or milestones leading up to the acquisition, such as significant product releases or revenue growth. The press release should be clear, concise, and easy to understand, with quotes from key stakeholders to add credibility and context.

In short, a well-planned communication strategy is crucial to finalizing the acquisition process. Communicating effectively with customers, partners, and the public through press releases can help ensure a smooth transition and maintain positive relationships with all stakeholders.

The Transition from Seller to Acquirer

The transition from an AI startup to an acquirer can be complex, and several key aspects must be considered to ensure a smooth and successful transition. Here are some points to consider in each of the three primary areas of transition:

1. Employees

    - *Transfer of employees*: The process of transferring employees to the acquirer can involve legal and logistical considerations, including employment contracts and benefits. It is important to ensure that employees are treated fairly and receive clear communication regarding any changes to their employment status.

    - *Contracts and terms*: All employee contracts and terms must be reviewed and updated to reflect the acquisition. This includes any non-compete clauses, confidentiality agreements, and intellectual property agreements.

    - *Potential pitfalls and risk management*: Failure to properly transfer employees can result in legal disputes, morale issues, and loss of key talent. It is important to communicate clearly with employees and involve them in the transition process as much as possible.

2. Customers

    - *Transfer of customers*: Acquiring an AI startup means acquiring its customer base. It is essential to ensure that customers are aware of the acquisition and understand any changes that may occur in their relationship with the company.

    - *Novations of commercial and service contracts, including customer service*: It is necessary to transfer all contracts with customers and ensure they are aware of any changes to their terms of service or pricing.

    - *Potential pitfalls and risk management*: Failure to communicate effectively with customers can lead to lost business and damage to the acquirer's reputation. It is important to prioritize customer service during the transition period and to have a plan to address any concerns or issues that may arise.

3. Technology

- *Transfer of support software licenses*: All software licenses should be reviewed and transferred to the acquirer. This includes licenses for version control, task management, project management tools, and any other software critical to the AI startup's operations.

- *Transfer of code repository*: Code repositories must be transferred, and it is important to ensure that all code is up to date and in compliance with licensing agreements.

- *Cloud services*: If the AI startup uses cloud services, it is necessary to ensure that all accounts and services are transferred to the acquirer.

- *Transfer of MLOps*: Machine learning operations (MLOps) must be transferred, and it is important to ensure that all data and models are properly transferred and integrated.

- *Integration with acquirer systems*: All systems must be integrated with the acquirer's systems to ensure smooth operation and avoid any potential issues.

- *Potential pitfalls and risk management*: Failure to properly transfer technology can lead to operational disruptions and lost data. It is important to ensure that all technology is properly transferred and tested before full integration with the acquirer's systems. Additionally, it is important to have a plan to address any technology-related issues that may arise during the transition period.

CASE STUDY: IDENTIFAI ACQUISITION

Introduction

Identifai, an AI startup specializing in biometrics-based eKYC technology, was recently acquired by a confidential acquirer. In this case study, we will examine the key factors that led to the success of this acquisition, including Identifai's unique technology, competitive advantages, and strong business team. We will also look at the process of Identifai's acquisition, including the selection of potential acquirers, negotiations, due diligence, and post-acquisition integration.

Identifai's Unique Technology

Identifai had an advanced R&D team of world experts with PhD and master's in computer vision and deep learning. A top confidential investor invested in their AI technology. They had IP on advanced liveness detection computer vision models with explainable AI capability, the first in the world. Identifai also had a proprietary algorithm that enabled face matching with millions of facial data in under one second. They had already integrated with the Indonesian citizen ID database with 208 million IDs stored.

Identifai's Competitive Advantages

Despite having several competitors, Identifai was the eKYC market leader in Indonesia, and they had secured more than 40 brand names in banks and FinTech. Even though their EBITDA was still low, their growth potential was huge. Identifai founders had already set up an exit plan and were scouting potential acquirers.

The Acquisition Process

Identifai's team found three potential acquirer candidates: national digital banks (buyer 1), a FinTech company (buyer 2), and a market leader technology company specializing in digital signature (buyer 3). The Identifai team assessed the three candidates and decided that buyer 3, the market leader technology company specializing in digital signature, had an edge in strategy and culture match, was financially secure, was ready to buy, and had an advanced technology team. The Identifai team pitched the story that their eKYC technology would complete the portfolio of buyer 3 and enable them to become the market leader of digital verification platforms in Southeast Asia, even Asia.

The Identifai team showed testimonials from satisfied customers in national banks and FinTech and provided three scenarios of potential revenues for buyer 3: pessimistic, baseline, and optimistic. After negotiations, both parties, Identifai and buyer 3, agreed on a price. They signed an LOI and NDA, agreeing on the terms of the sale, including retaining key employees, maintaining key customers, and transferring IPs.

Due Diligence

Buyer 3 performed comprehensive technical, commercial, financial, and labor due diligence. Upon technical due diligence, it was found out that some dataset was proprietary and could not be transferred, so they renegotiated the price. The new price was agreed upon, and the Identifai team signed the final agreement and transferred ownership of the company.

Post-acquisition Integration

Identifai and buyer 3 then began communicating the acquisition to customers and partners. They worked together to create a clear and concise message about the acquisition, emphasizing customer benefits and the commitment to maintaining quality service. They also outlined any potential technical or operational impacts and worked to address any concerns or questions that arose from customers or partners.

Novation agreements had to be signed with all of Identifai's customers to finalize the acquisition. The vast majority of customers were happy to continue their relationship with buyer 3, but a few were unwilling to sign the novation agreement. Buyer 3 worked to understand their concerns and, in some cases, offered additional incentives or accommodations to try to keep the customer relationship intact. Ultimately, four customers decided to end their relationship with Identifai/buyer 3.

Once the acquisition was finalized and all necessary agreements were signed, Identifai's technology and systems needed to be migrated and integrated with buyer 3's existing infrastructure. This process required careful planning and coordination between the Identifai and buyer 3 technical teams, as they were using different cloud providers and had different system architectures. After several months of work, the migration was completed successfully.

With the systems fully integrated, the Identifai team began working as part of buyer 3 to serve customers and develop new products and services. The team was able to leverage its expertise in biometrics eKYC technology to enhance buyer 3's digital verification platform and further solidify its position as a market leader in Southeast Asia and beyond.

In conclusion, the acquisition of Identifai by buyer 3 was a complex but ultimately successful process. Identifai's strong position in the eKYC market and cutting-edge biometrics technology made it an attractive acquisition target for several potential buyers. By carefully assessing the different options and selecting the most suitable buyer based on culture fit, financial security, and technical capabilities, Identifai was able to secure a reasonable price for its technology and ensure a smooth transition for its employees and customers. Despite some challenges, the acquisition was completed successfully, and the combined expertise of Identifai and buyer 3 is now driving innovation and growth in the digital verification space.

Conclusion

Exiting a startup can be complex, particularly in the AI industry, where technology and market trends are rapidly evolving. However, having a well-planned exit strategy can help founders achieve their goals and maximize the value of their startup. There are several potential exit strategies, including acquisition, IPO, and merger, and each has advantages and disadvantages. It is essential to carefully consider the options and choose the strategy that aligns with the startup's and its stakeholders' goals. Additionally, founders must start thinking about their exit plan as early as possible to ensure they have enough time to prepare and execute the strategy properly. From our discussion, we have found that acquisition is often the best option for AI startups, particularly those in their early stages of development. However, it is crucial to carefully select the acquirer and ensure that they share the same strategic and cultural values as the startup to ensure a smooth transition and maximize the value of the acquisition.

In summary, having a clear and well-planned exit strategy is essential for the success of any AI startup. By carefully considering the options and selecting the right acquirer, founders can ensure a successful exit and maximize the value of their startup..

Key Takeaways

- It is important to have an exit strategy in place from the beginning of the startup journey.

- The most common exit strategies for AI startups are acquisition, IPO, and merger.

- The right exit strategy will depend on the goals of the startup and its stakeholders. But acquisition is the most suitable option for AI startups.

- Building a strong team and IP portfolio can increase the value of the startup and make it more attractive to potential acquirers or investors.

- The strategic match between the AI startup and the acquirer is the most important aspect, even compared with the financial.

- Communicating clearly with customers, partners, and employees throughout the exit process is crucial to ensure a smooth transition.

- Due diligence is a critical step in the acquisition process, and startups should be prepared to provide comprehensive technical, financial, and commercial information to potential acquirers.

- Negotiating key terms, such as retaining key employees and maintaining customer relationships, can help ensure a successful exit.

- The cultural fit between the startup and the acquirer is important to ensure a smooth transition and successful integration.

- Startups should carefully evaluate potential acquirers based on their strategic vision, financial stability, and technology capabilities.

- It is important for startups to have a realistic understanding of their value and potential for growth in order to negotiate favorable terms in the acquisition process.

- IP protection is crucial for startups to ensure that their proprietary technology and data are safeguarded adequately during acquisition.

- The acquisition process can be time-consuming and require significant resources, so startups should be prepared to invest the necessary time and effort to ensure a successful outcome.

- Post-acquisition, startups should be prepared to navigate potential changes in company culture and priorities and adapt to new roles and responsibilities within the acquirer organization.

- Ultimately, a successful exit can provide significant rewards for founders, employees, and investors and pave the way for future opportunities and growth in the AI industry.

Final Thoughts

The future of AI startups is indeed very promising, and we are currently witnessing the emergence of new and exciting AI technologies that are based on generative AI. In fact, when this book was written, OpenAI announced the release of GPT-4, marking the beginning of the era of artificial general intelligence (AGI), where machines can perform any intellectual task that a human being can. This new era, characterized by the incredible proficiency of large language models (LLMs) like GPT-4 in generating coherent and contextually relevant text, signals a breakthrough in our understanding and application of AI. However, it's essential to note that the road to AGI is not without its challenges.

Despite the leaps in innovation, LLM-based generative models still grapple with issues of unpredictability. Therefore, while LLMs like GPT-4 signal the dawn of the AGI era, more traditional AI methods based on artificial narrow intelligence (ANI) principles are far from obsolete.

ANI, characterized by its specialization in one narrowly defined task, offers a level of predictability and control that LLMs currently struggle to match. ANI-based models have been widely applied in enterprise settings, offering reliable solutions to specific problems – from spam filtering and recommendation systems to fraud detection and customer segmentation. Despite lacking the "general" intelligence of LLMs, these systems have been battle-tested and refined over years of enterprise use.

The strengths of ANI – its predictability, controllability, and proven effectiveness in enterprise settings – ensure its continued relevance in the AI landscape. Thus, as we stand on the brink of the AGI era, we find ourselves in a hybrid landscape where the broad capabilities of LLMs coexist with the targeted effectiveness of ANI-based solutions, one complementing the other's strengths and mitigating its weaknesses.

As AI technology advances and evolves, we can expect it to become even more integrated into every aspect of our lives. This means that businesses of all kinds must be prepared to leverage AI in some way in order to stay competitive. It is, therefore, essential for business executives, entrepreneurs, product managers, and software engineering professionals to understand how to effectively leverage this incredible technology to create innovative and successful AI startups. In the future, we anticipate AI startups to be better equipped in addressing critical global issues such as climate change, cancer, diabetes, hunger, waste management, energy, and clean water.

In conclusion, this book has provided a comprehensive guide to building successful AI startups, from validating the market to developing user interfaces, designing the architecture, and creating go-to-market and exit strategies. We hope the information presented in this book has helped you navigate the complexities of building AI startups and AI product development. For those seeking more information and resources, we encourage you to visit our website at www.aistartupstrategy.com.

You will find updated news, articles, templates, cheatsheets, and other resources to assist you in your AI startup journey there. We will also offer more advanced and personalized online courses on AI product management and startup strategy to help you achieve your goals. We are also collaborate with AI Business Institute (www.aibusinessinstitute.com). Together, we have developed an engaging certification online course on AI product management. This comprehensive course not only expands upon the topics covered in the book but also offers a wealth of practical case studies and valuable connections to AI-oriented Venture Capital firms. It serves as an invaluable resource for professionals looking to enhance their understanding and proficiency in the dynamic field of AI product management. Thank you for reading, and we wish you the best of luck in your AI startup endeavors.

Index

Printed in the USA
CPSIA information can be obtained
at www.ICGtesting.com
LVHW020516081123
763370LV00001B/11